הגדה של פסח

THE BRESLOV HAGGADAH

The Traditional Pesach Haggadah

with commentary based on the teachings of
Rebbe Nachman of Breslov

compiled and adapted by
Rabbi Yehoshua Starret

including the Story of the Exodus, related anecdotes
and additional commentary on Pesach, the Omer and Shavuot
compiled and translated by
Chaim Kramer

Edited by
Moshe Mykoff

Published by
BRESLOV RESEARCH INSTITUTE
JERUSALEM/NEW YORK

Copyright © 1989 BRESLOV RESEARCH INSTITUTE

ISBN NUMBER   0-930213-35-1 (hardcover)
ISBN NUMBER   0-930213-36-x (softcover)

No part of this publication may be translated,
reproduced, stored in any retrieval system or transmitted,
in any form or by any means,
electronic, mechanical, photocopying, recording or otherwise,
without prior permission in writing from the publishers

First Edition

for further information:
Rabbi Chaim Kramer
Breslov Research Institute
POB 5370
Jerusalem, Israel   91053

or:
Breslov Research Institute
New York, USA

Table of Contents

Section A:

Publisher's Preface 7

Foreward 9

Overview 11

The Haggadah 21

Searching for Chametz 22

Burning the Chametz 22

Eruv Tavshilin 24

Candle Lighting 24

The Seder Plate (preparing for the Seder) 24

Yom Tov Morning Kiddush 156

Sefirat Ha'Omer 158

Section B: (other end of book)

Appendix A: The Story of the Exodus 1

Appendix B: Pesach Anecdotes 39

Appendix C: Until Shavuot 69

Reflections *85*

In loving memory

of my dear parents

David and **Dora Steinbigle**

There were never more loving parents.

Seymour

Publisher's Preface

Moshe instituted the custom which calls on each Jew to study the laws of Pesach prior to Pesach, the laws of Shavuot prior to Shavuot, and the laws of Sukkot prior to Sukkot (Megillah 32a).

This particularly applies to Pesach, as its laws are many and very complex (Mishnah Berurah 429:1).

The most oft repeated declaration in Jewish history is: "Hear O Israel, God, Who is our Lord, is One God!" (Deuteronomy 6:4). Throughout the ages, this cry of faith has resounded in the hearts of Jews everywhere. We proclaim that God is *the One and the Only*. Implied by this, as the Baal Shem Tov explained, is that everything which exists in this world is, in actuality, a concept through which a person can attain knowledge of God. As a result, some of us achieve knowledge of God through religion. Others will come to see Him through nature. Still others attain this awareness through joy or tragedy, etc. It is, as it were, God presenting a distinctive face to each individual.

The same is true of the festivals. At their source, Pesach, Shavuot and Sukkot are one; yet here, on Earth, we experience and celebrate each festival differently. Each festival has its own character, its own feeling and face. And each has its own distinctive mitzvot — the directives which reveal Godliness to us and allow us to reach out to Him from wherever we are.

This distinctiveness is perhaps nowhere more evident than from the Festival of Pesach. No other event on the Jewish calendar evokes such a rich blend of feelings and emotions. The exhaustion from the preparations; the anticipation of the Seder; the *nachat* of family celebration; the fulfilled feeling of attained freedom; they all combine to give us that distinctive experience we call Pesach.

The mitzvot associated particularly with Pesach also play a vital part in giving this holiday its distinctive character and face. Its laws are very complex; its statutes, many. Pesach requires much study, much spiritual preparation as well. Yet, these are the things which give it meaning, which make *this* holiday special. And all these laws and statutes; all our study and preparations; all our varied emotions and great excitement — they do one other thing. Together with the reciting of the Haggadah, they actively bring us to the real goal of this festive night: the experiencing of True Freedom!

*

Although the Rebbe himself said, *"Gor mien zach is Rosh HaShonoh"* (My main thing is Rosh HaShanah), the connection between PeSaCh and [Rebbe] NaChMaN — both with a numerical value of 148 — has not, and could not go unnoticed.

The first Haggadah printed with a commentary based on Rebbe Nachman's teachings was compiled by Reb Alter Tepliker (d. 1919) and published at the turn of this century. Reb Alter called it *Haggadah Or Zoreiach — The Haggadah of Shining Light*. In 1985, the Breslov Research Institute, in conjunction with Reb Nachman Burstein and his son, Reb Avraham Shimon, expanded Reb Alter Tepliker's original work by including additional material from the teachings and oral traditions of Breslover Chassidut.

At about the same time, it became obvious that the time was right for Breslov Research to undertake the publishing of a English Breslover Haggadah as well. The demand for even more of Rebbe Nachman's teachings to be translated was quite clear. It was also clear that the commentary to this Haggadah had to be more than a surface translation of Rebbe Nachman's Pesach teachings. To fill that demand, this Haggadah had to bring out the inner depths of the Rebbe's lessons — it had to be a "living lesson" — so as to bring home the vibrancy of Judaism and Pesach, and their relevance to today.

Both the beginning research and basic outline of this English Haggadah were completed by mid 1986. But work on this project has proven more complex and time consuming than at first anticipated. The logistics of where to begin and then how to coordinate the Hebrew text and its English translation with the Commentary and the Midrashic Story of the Exodus required careful planning. This meant going back to the drawing board more than once. Next, it was decided to include an appendix on Breslov stories and anecdotes whose themes relate to the Haggadah's text and teachings. Many stories from Breslov lore had to be considered and reviewed. In the end, the work was well worth it, as this appendix adds a flavor and imparts lessons in ways which only "telling a story" can. And finally, to make this Haggadah a book to-come-back-to after the Seder night, another appendix was added; offering passages from *Likutey Halakhot* on various Pesach-related topics including: Sefirat HaOmer, Chol HaMoed, the Seventh Day of Pesach, Pesach Sheynee, Lag B'Omer and Shavuot. Again, this meant more time in production, as sifting through Reb Noson's eight volume work is in itself a full-time endeavor. Thus, 1986 quickly became Pesach 1989 before *Rebbe Nachman's English Haggadah* was ready to take its place at your Seder table.

The Breslov Research Institute extends its heartfelt thanks to its contributing staff, who collaborated in bringing this encyclopedic Haggadah to fruition. First and foremost to Reb Yehoshua Starret, who researched and compiled Rebbe Nachman's teachings for the commentary on the Haggadah. To Moshe Mykoff for yet another incredible editing gem. Reb Ozer Bergman for his invaluable assistance and suggestions. Avraham Greenbaum for his editing contributions and recommendations. Last, but not least, to our dear friends Gershon and Chana Ginsburg, whose interest and encouragement helped see this project through, from its embryonic stage until the finish.

May it be the will of the Almighty that we merit to see the Coming of Mashiach, the Rebuilding of the Holy Temple and the Ingathering of the Exiles; so that we may all celebrate Pesach, this year, and every year, in Jerusalem. Amen!

Chaim Kramer
Kislev, 5749

Foreward

This Haggadah is for the searching contemporary Jewish soul. The individuals searching for Meaning in Life. Searching for Da'at — for Jewish Awareness. For Higher Awareness of God. For deeper awareness of themselves. For Awareness that is not mere intellectual perception, but deep emotional experience. For Awareness that was lacking in Mitzrayim. For Awareness that is lacking today. And, for Awareness that can be had *only* by searching, by yearning.

The Original Redemption was brought about by Unevoked Benevolence. By an emanation of Da'at, of Awareness. Basically, the Jewish People were uninspired. Without initiative. Undeserving. But, *now*, the Ultimate Redemption will not be that way. We must *yearn* for Awareness, we must evoke it (*Likutey Moharan* II, 74; *Kokhavey Or* p.125).

The commentary on this Haggadah, based in theme and spirit on the bottomless wells of Breslov teachings, is an effort to bring to the english reader an extract of Rebbe Nachman's message in not only a language, but also a "language" that he can understand. It does not, by any means, present an entire picture of the wealth of Breslov thought on Pesach and the Haggadah. Nor does it show the breadth and profundity of Rebbe Nachman's lessons or the deep spiritual experience that learning them is. Such a work would be literally impossible. What it does attempt to do, is to convey certain pertinent messages to that searching Jewish soul and to provide him with a guide of how to evoke the Awareness we are searching for.

This commentary was originally written as individual pieces running through the Haggadah text. As such, it can be opened at any point and read — either during the Seder, before or after. It assumes of the reader a basic knowledge of the Pesach Story on the physical level. Some may therefore do well to first read through the Story of the Exodus (Appendix A).

Effort was made that each piece be as self-contained as possible. Nevertheless, the entire commentary can be seen as one interwoven book, revolving around the Haggadah. Each piece sheds light on others, and is better understood in the context of others. Some pieces may raise questions which could not be answered at that point, but can be resolved from some other point in the commentary. Allusions are sometimes made from one piece to another (and to Midrashic lore) in such a way as not to detract from the main message being conveyed. The entire commentary can be depicted by the jacket cover: pieces of Matzah. Each piece can be "eaten" by itself. But, pieced together, a more complete picture arises. And, with each reading, that picture will become clearer. The Overview is an integral part of this picture.

Due to style and technical reasons, a full source-noting was not feasible. Any questions on this matter, or regarding anything else in the commentary, including comments in general, can be addressed to me, care of the Breslov Research Institute, Jerusalem.

At this point, I express my deepest gratitude to Rabbi Chaim Kramer, director of the Breslov Research Institute, for giving me the great privilege of working on this Haggadah. His foresight and devotion have seen it through to the end. May God grant him the strength to continue his efforts. My deepest thanks to Moshe Mykoff for the superb job of editing the difficult text. Many thanks to all those who looked over the manuscript and offered very constructive critique. To my wife, of course, who devotedly read every new draft and encouraged me throughout. And, in expressing what is in my heart to God for bringing me in touch with Rebbe Nachman and for giving me the fortitude to finish this work, I am left speechless.

Working on this Haggadah has been deeply rewarding. If I have been instrumental in conveying Rebbe Nachman's message to inspire even a single Jew to "piece together" his life, helping him take leave of his "Mitzrayim" and come to some degree of Awareness, then it shall be all the more so. We will then be that much closer towards bringing together all the "pieces" of the Jewish People. May the Mashisach come soon, in our generation, and bind us all together, Amen.

Yehoshua Starret
Tevet, 5749

Overview

Pesach. What comes to mind? For some it is a story of ancient times. An epoch which shifted the direction of human history. The birth of the Jewish People as we know it. For others it is the hectic preparations which leave us drained for the duration of the Festival. And for some it is the sitting down to the Seder and rehashing the unanswerable paradoxes of Jewish thought. While for others it is the discussions of various theoretical Halakhic/Midrashic points.

But is there nothing more to it? Doesn't the Haggadah tell that we are obligated to see ourselves as if *we* left Mitzrayim? Is this obligation to be nothing more than having a vicarious fantasy into antiquity? Can we, in a free, democratic world, even be expected to experience the pain of Bondage? Or the joy of Redemption?

There must be more to it. After all, aren't we taught that the Exodus shows Creation to be more than a once-upon-a-time Event? (*Ramban,* Exodus 20:2). The Jewish Creation is something much more dynamic. Aren't we taught that the Egyptian Bondage is seen as a Rectification for Adam's "sin" — his Miscalculation? (*Sha'ar HaPesukim, Shemot*). And of the two million Jewish men, women and children, not including the millions of gentiles who came with, each of whom perceived something different.

There must be more to it.

In The Beginning... (Genesis 1:1)

Space. Time. Life. Three dimensions of Creation. Three realms of human experience. Man — each individual man — is a microcosm of each.

There is vast Space out there. We all know that. Our finite minds just cannot grasp the magnitude of the universe. We know that Time marches on. There was existence, the stuff of history, on Earth before us. It will continue to be there when we are gone. And there is Life. Hidden. Somewhere. The Secret of Life. The flash of the elusive experience. What is the meaning of it all?

And what *is* the relevance of Universe to us on speck-of-dust Earth? What implication *does* Human History, Jewish History, have to our mundanity? And what meaning can Life have if we are too busy with the drudgery of living it?

> *Creation. Then the Fall of Man. The Flood. Then Noach. Terach. Then Avraham, Yitzchak and Yaakov. The Exile, the Exodus, and the Torah Giving. Then the Golden Calf. The Tabernacle, the Land of Israel, the Judges, the Prophets, and the Holy Temple. Then the Destruction. Purim, the Second Temple, and Chanukah. Then the Second Destruction. The Diaspora. The Arab lands. Western Europe. The Crusades. The Inquisition. Then Central Europe. Pogroms. Russia. The Cossacks. Then the "Enlightenment." Out of the ghettos... Auschwitz. Treblinka. Bergen-Belsen. Then Reviving. Rebuilding. Re-Souling...*

Reading through Jewish History, we search to relate to it. To feel part of it. Not to be just "visionaries" into the past. We may even try to imagine how it must have been to live in those times, only to be carried away... "If only I had lived then! How exciting! How inspiring! *Then* I would have been a good Jew!"

In doing this, we will have already missed the point. We *don't* merely want to be "visionaries," escapists from life into a distant past. We want to draw from the past. To bring meaning and purpose into our everyday lives.

But how? How are we to relate to the teaching that every human being is himself an entire world? A microcosm of Universe; of History; of Life? What pertinent messages do the most esoteric secrets of Creation bear for our daily lives, then?

...Let Us Make Man (Genesis 1:26)

Adam, Man, was created with a profound and innate Knowledge of God's existence. That God-Consciousness was inherent in his every action. In his every thought. His soul was imprinted with that Truth just as every child's soul is imprinted with certain fundamental knowledge. Every child innately knows how to learn to speak. How to walk.

But is the child *aware* of that knowledge? Certainly not. He just "knows." Adam, too, just "knew." But, he didn't *know* that he knew. He did not yet have Da'at. Intimate Knowledge. Awareness. Experience of that Knowledge. He was God-Conscious, but without Da'at, without being aware of that great Knowledge within him.

And how could he have been? Da'at, Awareness, comes only when there is differentiation. Only when there is objective knowledge of something and its absence, its contrast. Could we be aware of day if not for night? Could we be aware of joy if not for pain? And would we even be aware of life if not for death? Adam, too, could not become truly aware of his Paradise without a taste of its absence.

And without that awareness, there can be no appreciation. No experience. Man cannot appreciate that Paradise without an awareness of what is "outside." And without that appreciation, God's Benevolence to Man — the manifest Goal of Creation — cannot be complete. And even if God *had* provided Adam with an awareness and appreciation, it would have been pure Grace. Unearned. And God's Plan is for Man to *earn* his Paradise. To make *himself*.

So God gave Man an opportunity. A chance to experience a taste of Godlessness. To become aware of the Paradise he was in. A chance to enter an even higher Gan Eden. He gave him Temptation (see *Zohar* II, 55a).

But the Serpent was Cunning... (Genesis 3:1)

But Man was brash. He was subtly conceited (see Haggadah p.35). Overanxious to experience God (*Likutey Halakhot, Gezeilah* 5:7). So he was lured into thinking it was God's Will for him to transgress. *Then* he would appreciate God! Or so he thought...

If only Man had endured the pain of temptation... If only he had perceived the experience of temptation as an opportunity to cling to God, to yearn and cry out to be saved from that temptation... If only he had seen God hiding in the pain of that temptation, seen the Tree of Life hidden inside the Tree of Knowledge... (*Chizkunee*, Genesis 2:16; *Hadar Zekenim, Tosafot*, Genesis 3:22; *Yalkut Reuveni*, Bereshit 33b). That itself would have been his awareness of the Dark, his experience of pain, his taste of Godlessness... If only he had clung to the Tree of Life until the Sabbath... He would have then legitimately partaken of it, and been also granted from the Tree of Knowledge — he would have become fully aware of God (*Chesed L'Avraham* 1:8).

But Man didn't see things that way. He saw only the "serpent." He heard only the voice of temptation. He "saw," he "knew," what *he* thought to be evil in Creation. A realm of existence beyond his personal, inner experience of the world. He became very curious. Curious to *know,* to experience God's "Non- Existence." "How can that be," he asked himself, "when I know God is everywhere?" (*Likutey Halakhot, Apotropus* 2:11).

But, God said no! Adam "knew" that. So he rationalized (*Likutey Halakhot, Ribit* 5:8). "Surely, I can better serve God once I have an intimate knowledge of this evil. Surely, once evil becomes an integral part of my inner experience, my controlling it will then be that much greater!" Man wanted to control things, as well... (see Haggadah p.27). And he rationalized again. "Surely, once I taste it, I will see for myself its bitterness. But, if I don't, I may be forever gnawed by the question, 'Maybe the serpent was right?'" (It is told that this is what Reb Elimelekh of Lizhensk answered his brother, Reb Zushia, when asked why they — who were also part of the First Man's composite soul — had allowed Adam to transgress. This was *their* "transgression.")

Perhaps *all* these thoughts and many more went through Man's mind. Don't *we* find ourselves with several motivations for a single act? Surely, Adam, the composite human being of all his billions of descendants, had all of *our* thoughts on his mind...

And Man Took From the Fruit... (Genesis 3:6)

And so Man — that Man whose God-Consciousness was innate — reached out to experience what he saw as evil. To become aware of the Darkness. To taste Godlessness. To experience transgression. But to have that experience, he had first to become "unaware" of God. By "closing his eyes." "Turning his head." "Pushing God from his mind." So Man enraptured himself in what he saw as evil, presuming that it would bring him to an even higher level.

Man got what he wanted. Godlessness. "Non-Existence." But, alas, Man had fallen into the Kelipot — the Mental Barriers. Now, Awareness was no longer dormant within him. That God-Consciousness which had been awaiting actualization was now actively constricted (*Likutey Halakhot, Edut* 4:5; cf. *Bereshit Rabbah* 19:7). Inherent Knowledge was gone. His thoughts, his actions, were no longer an expression of that Knowledge. He now felt as if *he* wanted evil. He could not erase that experience from his mind.

God gave Man another opportunity. A slap!

"And *now*...lest he eat from the Tree of Life...God banished him from Gan Eden..." (Genesis 3:22-3).

"Go!" God said. "Out of My Presence!" God sent Man into Exile. A *spiritual* exile. The physical was only "symbolic." The correlative manifestation of the spiritual.

And Man went.

How he regretted his misdeed! How he repented! (*Eruvin* 18b).

...If only he had cried out, "No! I shall not go! No! I *cannot* go! No! My life is meaningless without You! I have erred! I am not deserving! But You can forgive! You are Above human rationale!"

...If only he had "followed" in the footsteps of Moshe, Moshe who took God's cue. It was after the Golden Calf. Told by God, "And *now*, leave Me be and I will destroy them!" Moshe protested! (see Haggadah p.77). He stood his ground. He knew what God *really* wanted. (*Yalkut Shimoni* and *Shemot Rabbah* on Exodus 32:10).

Adam, Man, would have then seen the Cherubim and the Flaming Sword which bar entry to Gan Eden for what they really are: a Mental Barrier, an illusion (*Paneach Raza* and *Bachaya* on Genesis 3:24). He would have realized God's true intent; that when God says NOW, He means: *Forget the past!* (*Bereshit Rabbah* 21:6; cf. Ibn Gabirol, *Keter Malkhut* prayer; see also in Haggadah p.61).

...And when a father slaps his son, does he mean the slap?

But Man, feeling only the slap, went away from his Father. He went through life bearing the unbearable pain that only a father's slap can give. Rejection! The pain of Distance.

And who can measure the pain of the father who cries out for having driven away his own son?

And all because of a misunderstanding...

Yet the Father cries out to Man ever since: *"Ayekah —* Where are you?" But Man, once "slapped," has shut out that Voice. The Father too, is in "Exile." Exiled by Man (*Zohar* I, 53b).

And This is the Story of Man... (Genesis 5:1)

The Story of Man. The story of every man. We are born in pain. And first thing, we receive a "slap" (above the upper lip, as well; *Nidah* 30b). We are brought up in the pain of being helpless in an adult world. And then we bear the pain of bringing more children into the world. Universal pains. And then there are all our personal pains...

So we seek to escape from this pain. To bury it deeper and deeper. To deny it. And sometimes to deny its Source. "All right, if that's what You think of me, then I don't need You either!" We invert the pain into anger at its Conceiver.

But the pain remains. The gnawing emptiness doesn't go away. All the world's pleasures and riches cannot fill the void in the soul. All the veneration that humanity can afford will not raise the soul that seeks it to replace a lost sense of endowed worth. All the Torah Knowledge in Creation cannot give Meaning to Life, if that knowledge is a mere intellectual conception, and certainly not if it is a tool for self- aggrandizement.

It is the pain, the emptiness of "Non-Existence." An experiential void we feel at the deepest level of our soul. The knowing that we have strayed. That our lives have lost Meaning. That we are out of touch with God. If anything, it is an experience of Gehennom. In this world. (*Likutey Moharan* II, 119). For to live in the purely physical, is to live in Gehennom.

And the thirst of the soul can only be filled with Existence. With Awareness of God. With the Joy of Existence. With a Meaningful Jewishness. And if Adam had not yet experienced six millenia of human suffering to wonder what had gone awry with his life, *we* have. We know that pain. Have we not experienced it long enough? Is it not yet time to experience the Joy?...

And These are the Jewish People who Descended to Mitzrayim (Exodus 1:1)

But, because Man decided to bury his Pain, the Distance only grew greater and greater. Until, finally, Mankind's spiritual exile materialized into the physical: the Jewish People in Mitzrayim.

And there, in Egypt, the Jewish People descended deeper and deeper. Their Jewish Awareness, their awareness of God, of themselves, grew less and less. They became oblivious to their own situation. The reality of their spiritual descent. Are we aware of *our* situation? How can we be if, for whatever reason, we deny the possibility of Higher Reality? A higher plane of Life? (see Haggadah p.82). In so doing, we only deny *ourselves* the opportunity of becoming aware of our own situation. Awareness comes only with the knowledge of differentiation...

Finally, all that was left was a vestige of Jewishness. Traditional — perhaps even "rabbinical" — attire. Characteristic names and a unique language. A sort of clansmanship. A clinging to tradition. An unexplainable desire to retain some "Jewish self-identity." Not knowing why or what, "something" just told them to hold on. Almost like today....

Then Moshe came, bearing the promise of Redemption. At first, they believed. Moshe then gradually brought them to Awareness. But they could not yet put that Awareness into action. Two hundred and ten years in depraved Egypt had had its affect.

...Nearly a year since Moshe's arrival. Nine Plagues, and Pharaoh still unbudging. During the Plague of Darkness, millions of Jews died. Four fifths of the populace wiped out in one week — those who God saw weren't yet ready. How disheartening it was to bury all their brothers!

On the brink of despair. Thoughts of dashed hopes went through their minds. Feelings of the same through their hearts. Perhaps they weren't worthy. Rapidly, they were sinking into the 50th level of spiritual descent: the realm of Resignation and Despair. Had they entered that level, there would have been no hope. We can only change when we don't despair (see Haggadah p.56).

But Moshe reassured them that they were still God's People. Wanting to believe, they slaughtered the Pesach lamb. But, everything hung in the balance. Everything depended on the stroke of midnight. Would God appear?

And, there, in the depths, at the farthest point, at the nadir, the Jewish People were brought to realize that God *is* everywhere. That He can be reached not by hastily trying to be close, but by realizing the ultimate Distance. By experiencing the pain of that Distance, and knowing that there — *there* in the *Darkness* is God!

In showing them this, God also showed them there is no need to *ever* despair. There is no forlorn soul that cannot be retrieved. No situation that cannot be redeemed. There is no misdeed that cannot be corrected. There is HOPE! Even at the brink of despair.

Thus, Awareness does not come all at once. It is a Process. The rule of Gradual Progression (see Haggadah p. 82). Adam wanted it all at once. We all know what happened...

If Adam was hasty in approaching God, the Jewish ordeal in bondage had taught them patience. If they performed their Seder in haste, it was only because God had so commanded (*Megaleh Amukot, Shemot* p. 16a). If Adam was subtly conceited in trying to be "too" close, they were humbled by being aware of the Distance. And therein lay the Rectification of Man's "sin" — his Original Miscalculation.

And Pharaoh said: I Am Not Aware (Exodus 5:2)

A child's awareness is very limited. He is little aware of himself and his surroundings. During the formative years, our awareness grows. Then, unless we consciously seek its development, the Process comes to a sudden stop.

Set for life.

So some of us continue through life with certain illusions. As a child's reality — his role-playing and games — is illusion to us, our's is illusion to those with Higher Awareness. We "role-play." Take seriously our "games" of Prestige, Power and Money, of Intellectual advancement and Earthly pleasure.

For us, Reality proves too disturbing. Awareness provides no comfort. So we consciously decide to live in illusion, rather than endure the Awareness Process. The rule of Gradual Progression.

And for some of us, the Process gets ensnared in a different way. We get stuck for decades in the pain of a long-gone past. Constricted. We live today as if events, people and situations are the same as they were when our developing awareness halted at the time of our painful experience. As if time had stopped. All the way back then. We're still trying to avenge our pain, rather than experience and accept it.

For us, letting go of the pain proves too disturbing. Awareness provides no comfort. So we consciously hold onto our constriction, rather than endure the Awareness Process. The rule of Gradual Progression.

Illusion. Constriction. A halt in the Process. The Constrictor of Awareness, the Master of Illusion, is "Pharaoh" (see Haggadah p. 55). Each of us must go through his "Mitzrayim." We all have illusions, we all have our pains. And to ask "But why me?" is like asking "Why did the Jewish People suffer in Mitzrayim?" Each of us is a microcosm of Time, of Jewish History. But in the End, we will all leave Mitzrayim.

"Pharaoh" is also the "Serpent" (*Siftei Kohen, Bereshit* 6c) — the Primordial Constrictor of Awareness and Master of Illusion. He fooled Man out of Gan Eden. With illusion he enticed Man to curiosity, to reach out for an experience of Godlessness; and then with constriction convinced him that he'd already been banished, that it was "too late" to protest. And, as the Evil One, "Pharaoh" even now enslaves us in this world in Gehennom (Rambam, *Igeret HaMussar; Sefer HaLikutim, Shemot; Chesed L'Avraham* 5:10). But in the End, we will all return to Gan Eden.

And, being Jewish does not begin only once we're free of "Pharaoh's" illusions and constrictions, for illusions and constrictions exist at every level. Being Jewish begins with the Process itself. With the Gradual Progression of overcoming *our* "Pharaoh," and with our ongoing efforts to raise ourselves to ever - higher levels of Awareness.

Yet, it sometimes takes time to overcome illusion. How long was the world supposed terracentric? And, now we are saying it is heliocentric, when really we think it is egocentric...

So "Pharaoh" needs not to be taken too seriously. He's just here to tempt us, to make us aware. If in the past we decided to listen to "Pharaoh," who tells us "I am not aware" — now we can tell him "I know who you are, but *yes, I want* to be aware!"

And, if we have lived our lives until now in ignorance, we must now do what we can. If in the past God withheld from us knowledge, it is not for us to ask to understand. With the knowledge we had, we did our best. More than that, God does not demand.

Pesach, Matzah and Maror — In Our Generation (Haggadah)

Adam, Man, ate from the Etz HaDa'at, the Tree of Knowledge. Its fruit, in fact, was ordinary grain (*Sanhedrin* 70b). But, the simple fact that God forbade it, made it the "forbidden tree." The numerical value of CHaMeTZ — leavened bread, together with Se'OR — leavening, is 639. ETZ HaDA'aT is also 639. When Man ate from it, he "ate leavened bread." He had his taste of Godlessness. Experienced what he saw as evil. Impaired his Awareness.

This, then, is the Matzah, the unleavened bread. Symbolizing Perfection of Da'at. Of Intimate Knowledge. Of Awareness. And of Experience. And of knowing that it is all Divine Grace. Knowing that all experiences are One — it is all God Himself (*Likutey Moharan* I, 4). This is beyond human intellect; but then again, God is Above reason. We can reach Him only with Intimate Knowledge. With Experience. With Heart. With Emotion (*Likutey Moharan* I, 33:4).

On Pesach we eat Matzah. But, we must make sure to "eat" the Matzah of Perfected Da'at. In so doing, we rectify Adam's Misconception — his "leavened bread" (*Bnai Yissaschar, Nisan* 8:4,7).

And this is the Story of Pesach. The Story of Creation. Of the continual and continuous Process of Creation. Adam, Man, knew of Creation. But he fell. He could not raise himself up again. He could not forget his past deed. He was overburdened with guilt. Adam was unaware of Creation as being NOW! So, when God appeared in Mitzrayim, His message to the Jewish People was: NOW is another Creation! And, in changing the "laws of nature," He showed: I have changed Nature — you can change *yours!*

For every man, in every generation, is a microcosm. Of Space. Of Time. Of Life. Jewishness is not something which took place only in some distant, or even recent

18

past. It is not something which takes place only in some pristine corner of the world. Nor is it the franchise of those of us who have an unbroken tradition. In fact, true Jewishness is not to be found in the laurels of those of us whose "Jewishness" begins and ends with an unspoken flaunting of that tradition. Neither can it be found in the stale Jewishness of yesterday. No matter how enthused we were then — *today,* yesterday is gone, and we must start again. Creation is a Process. So is Jewishness.

Jewishness is HERE! Jewishness is NOW! And Jewishness is with YOU! And *within* you! Every Jewish soul in some way relives the entire Story of Creation. Creation. The Fall of Man. The Flood... (*Likutey Halakhot, Ona'ah* 3:1; *Ibid., Shiluach Haken* 4:61). But *this* time, each time, with *our* lives, the story is *ours* to rewrite. It is time to transcend the illusory constrictions of the mind. To cease living out the script of limited human awareness. To forget the past and begin Jewishness. And NOW! is the time to begin.

God Himself created previous worlds that did not satisfy His Plan. So He destroyed them and forgot them. Improved upon them. Used those intentional "mistakes" as lessons. Lessons for *us.* If the "world" we have created for ourselves is not according to Plan, scrap it! Start afresh. Create *new ones.* And turn those experiences — even failures! — into lessons.

And this, then, is the Telling of the Story. The Story of Man. The story of every man. Experiencing the Exile, the Distance. Eating the Maror, tasting the pain, the bitterness of adversity. Every human being is himself an entire world. And it is into *that* world which God wants to bring Joy. To instill Awareness of the Divine, to bestow the Joy of Creation. But that Joy, that Awareness, can only be found in the appreciation of our individual Maror.

Each Jew who left Egypt, each Jew who leaves Mitzrayim, has a different experience. And proportionate to the experience of Pain, is the experience of Redemption. Redemption from the internalized desire to know what we see as evil (*Likutey Halakhot, ibid; Ma'alot HaTorah* p. 22b Jerusalem ed.). Redemption in knowing the Sweetness of the Pain. Redemption in knowing that God does not mean the "slap." And Redemption in knowing that the story of our lives, of *our* Bondage and Redemption, is Meaning. Esoteric Meaning. And with this Meaning we will see ourselves out of Mitzrayim (see Haggadah p.61).

Destitute. The young man was without an extra penny to buy a present for his bride-to-be.

Bemoaning his plight to Reb Nosson, hoping to hear some words of encouraging advice, those words were not long in coming.

"So what is your problem?" queried Reb Nosson. "Our forefather Yaakov also didn't have a penny. When escaping from Esau, he was divested of everything he owned. He had nothing to give his bride-to-be, Rachel, and could only bemoan his plight with acceptance" (Rashi, Genesis 29:11).

The young man didn't get the message.

*"How can you compare me with our forefather Yaakov?" he argued.
"His every life-occurrence was laden with esoteric meaning."*

*"In your life, too, there is esoteric meaning in every occurrence," Reb
Noson explained* (Siach Sarfei Kodesh Breslov, #710).

We may not know what that meaning is. At least let us be aware that there
is that Meaning.

So, sitting down to the Seder does not mean the recital of a history book.
Nor is it meant to be the intellectual resolution of any Jewish paradox. And it is
even much more than an Halakhic or Midrashic discussion.

Sitting down to the Seder is nothing less than the Intimate Experience of
Jewishness itself. Meaningful Jewishness. The Seder is a cry of anguish to God
for those of us who are still in "Mitzrayim." The Seder is encouragement for
us to become more aware of that "Mitzrayim." And the Seder is praise to God
for whatever extent we have already left that "Mitzrayim."

We need not have "lived then" to be Jewish. We can be Jewish — right NOW!

These are the Festivals, They Call Out Holiness (Leviticus 23:4)

Voices in the air. Spiritual Voices. Our ears cannot hear them, but our minds pick
them up. Or the voice of "Pharaoh." Of temptation. Of illusion. Of constriction.
The thoughts that go through our minds that we *know* we don't really want.

...A voice of curiosity. Adam was curious. And so are we all. It is the nature
of the child to be curious. There's nothing wrong with that. But what are we
curious about?

...And the Voice, the Call of the Festival. Whenever it comes. Wherever we are.
The gnawing which gets us to feel something very basic is missing. The searching
for something and not knowing what, which shows us our lives have gone awry.
It is the Voice, the Call of the Festival which tell us that: Yes, it is time to return
to God...

We have been curious long enough chasing after "Pharaoh." Wondering what
it's like to live Godlessly. The time has now come to give up the chase, to change
the direction of our curiosity.

The air also carries the Voice of the Tzaddik (*Likutey Moharan* I, 17:5). What
is it like to experience the world through *his* eyes? To hear the Voice of God
resounding in the mind, and see oneself as standing before Him? What is it like to
be above the illusory honor of this world? To be unmoved by financial or physical
pleasure? To be in touch with the Spark of Divine within, and to *know*, to *do* what
we should? And, what is it like to bring Joy into the Space of every step we
take on speck-of-dust Earth? To bring Awareness into the limited Time we spend
upon it? To find Meaning in Life, the Secret of Life; and to bring God into our
lives, into mundanity — and to make them meaningful?

And there is a great deal more...

The distance between Gehennom and Gan Eden is exceedingly small (*Kohelet
Rabbah* 14:3), in fact, they both exist in this world simultaneously. It's all a matter
of where *we* want to live: under "Pharaoh" in Gehennom, or free of him in Gan

Eden (see *Likutey Moharan* I, 191). And the greater our awareness of the contrast, the greater our appreciation.

The choice is ours, it will always be. The Tree of Knowledge will exist even when we return to Gan Eden. But then we will *know* — we will be so *aware* — that we will see in that Tree only good (*Likutey Halakhot, Birkhot HaPeirot* 5:17, *Ta'arovet* 1:8).

We will see beyond the momentary Darkness an Eternal Light. A Light which dispels "Pharaoh's" Illusion. Listen for the Voice of the Tzaddik, he will guide us. He will teach us to see Gan Eden existing right before our very eyes.

THE HAGGADAH
הגדה של פסח

סדר בדיקת חמץ

קודם שיתחיל לבדוק, יטול ידיו ויברך ברכת הבדיקה בשמחה, ויאמר:

הֲרֵינִי מוּכָן וּמְזֻמָּן לְקַיֵּם מִצְוַת עֲשֵׂה וְלֹא תַעֲשֶׂה שֶׁל בְּדִיקַת חָמֵץ לְשֵׁם יְחוּד קוּדְשָׁא בְּרִיךְ הוּא וּשְׁכִינְתֵּהּ עַל יְדֵי הַהוּא טָמִיר וְנֶעֱלָם בְּשֵׁם כָּל יִשְׂרָאֵל:

וִיהִי נֹעַם יְיָ אֱלֹהֵינוּ עָלֵינוּ וּמַעֲשֵׂה יָדֵינוּ כּוֹנְנָה עָלֵינוּ וּמַעֲשֵׂה יָדֵינוּ כּוֹנְנֵהוּ.

בָּרוּךְ אַתָּה יְהוָה אֱלֹהֵינוּ מֶלֶךְ הָעוֹלָם אֲשֶׁר קִדְּשָׁנוּ בְּמִצְוֹתָיו וְצִוָּנוּ עַל בִּעוּר־חָמֵץ:

ומיד אחר הבדיקה יבטלנו ויאמר:

כָּל חֲמִירָא וַחֲמִיעָא דְּאִיכָּא בִרְשׁוּתִי דְּלָא חֲמִיתֵּהּ וּדְלָא בִעַרְתֵּהּ וּדְלָא יְדַעְנָא לֵיהּ לִבָּטֵל וְלֶהֱוֵי הֶפְקֵר כְּעַפְרָא דְאַרְעָא:

וטוב לומר בלילה וביום ג' פעמים לשון כל חמירא דכן מדות חכמים:

יְהִי רָצוֹן מִלְּפָנֶיךָ ה' אֱלֹהֵינוּ וֵאלֹהֵי אֲבוֹתֵינוּ שֶׁתְּזַכֵּנוּ לְפַשְׁפֵּשׁ בְּנִגְעֵי בָתֵּי הַנֶּפֶשׁ אֲשֶׁר נוֹאַלְנוּ בְּעֵצַת יֵצֶר הָרָע וּתְזַכֵּנוּ לָשׁוּב בִּתְשׁוּבָה שְׁלֵמָה, וְאַתָּה בְּרַחֲמֶיךָ תְּסַיְּעֵנוּ וְתַעְזְרֵנוּ עַל דְּבַר כְּבוֹד שְׁמֶךָ וְתַצִּילֵנוּ מֵאִסּוּר חָמֵץ אֲפִילוּ מִכָּל שֶׁהוּא, בְּשָׁנָה זוֹ וּבְכָל שָׁנָה וְשָׁנָה, כָּל יְמֵי חַיֵּינוּ, אָמֵן, כֵּן יְהִי רָצוֹן:

סדר שריפת חמץ

ביום י"ד בניסן בשעה חמישית יעשה לחמץ מדורה בפני עצמו וישרפנו, ותיכף יבטלנו, ויאמר:

הִנְנִי מוּכָן וּמְזֻמָּן לְקַיֵּם מִצְוַת עֲשֵׂה וְלֹא תַעֲשֶׂה שֶׁל שְׂרֵפַת חָמֵץ לְשֵׁם יְחוּד קוּדְשָׁא בְּרִיךְ הוּא וּשְׁכִינְתֵּהּ עַל יְדֵי הַהוּא טָמִיר וְנֶעֱלָם בְּשֵׁם כָּל יִשְׂרָאֵל:

וִיהִי נֹעַם יְיָ אֱלֹהֵינוּ עָלֵינוּ וּמַעֲשֵׂה יָדֵינוּ כּוֹנְנָה עָלֵינוּ וּמַעֲשֵׂה יָדֵינוּ כּוֹנְנֵהוּ.

כָּל חֲמִירָא וַחֲמִיעָא דְּאִיכָּא בִרְשׁוּתִי דְּחַזְתֵּיהּ וּדְלָא חֲזִתֵּיהּ, דַּחֲמִתֵּהּ וּדְלָא חֲמִתֵּיהּ, דְּבִעַרְתֵּהּ וּדְלָא בִעַרְתֵּהּ לִבָּטֵל וְלֶהֱוֵי הֶפְקֵר כְּעַפְרָא דְאַרְעָא:

יְהִי רָצוֹן מִלְּפָנֶיךָ ה' אֱלֹהֵינוּ וֵאלֹהֵי אֲבוֹתֵינוּ כְּשֵׁם שֶׁאֲנִי מְבַעֵר חָמֵץ מִבֵּיתִי וּמֵרְשׁוּתִי כָּךְ תְּבַעֵר אֶת כָּל הַחִיצוֹנִים וְאֶת רוּחַ הַטֻּמְאָה תְּבַעֵר מִן הָאָרֶץ וְאֶת יִצְרֵנוּ הָרָע תְּבַעֲרֵיהוּ מֵאִתָּנוּ וְתִתֶּן לָנוּ לֵב בָּשָׂר וְכָל הַסִּטְרָא אַחֲרָא וְכָל הָרִשְׁעָה כֶּעָשָׁן תִּכְלֶה וְתַעֲבִיר מֶמְשֶׁלֶת זָדוֹן מִן הָאָרֶץ וְכָל הַמְּעִיקִים לַשְּׁכִינָה תְּבַעֲרֵם בְּרוּחַ בָּעֵר וּבְרוּחַ מִשְׁפָּט כְּשֵׁם שֶׁבִּעַרְתָּ אֶת מִצְרַיִם וְאֶת אֱלֹהֵיהֶם בַּיָּמִים הָהֵם וּבַזְּמַן הַזֶּה:

Searching for Chametz

On the evening before Pesach, one must search for chametz throughout the house. It is customary to place ten pieces of carefully wrapped bread in various places, which are collected while searching the house for chametz. Before beginning the search for chametz one should wash his hands and recite the following blessing with joy:

I am ready and prepared to perform the mitzvah of searching for Chametz. Blessed are You, God, King of the universe, Who has made us holy with His mitzvot, and commanded us to remove Chametz.

One then searches the entire house, collecting all chametz that he sees. Upon completion, the chametz is set aside (to be burned the next morning) and the following declaration is then said:

Any chametz in my possession which I did not see, remove, or know about, shall be nullified and become ownerless as the dust of the earth.

May it be Your will, God, that we merit to search our souls for the blemishes that we foolishly placed in it by following the evil inclination's advice, and that we merit true repentance. Please, God, in Your mercy and for Your honor, help us to be protected from the prohibition of chametz, even from a crumb; this year and every year, for as long as we live. Amen, may it be Your will.

Burning the Chametz

On the morning of the 14th day of Nissan, the eve of Pesach, one must dispose of all chametz (that was not already sold) in his possession. The following is said:

I am ready and prepared to perform the mitzvah of disposing of all Chametz.

One then burns the Chametz.

The following declaration is to be made after burning the chametz:

Any Chametz in my possession which I did or did not see, which I did or did not destroy, shall be nullified and become ownerless as the dust of the earth.

May it be Your will, God, that just as I have removed the chametz from my house and properties, so too, should You remove all the forces of evil, and the spirit of evil shall be removed from the earth. May our evil inclination be removed from us and may You grant us a pure heart. May all the forces of the "Other Side" and wickedness vanish like smoke and the kingdom of the wicked be eradicated. May You destroy all those that challenge the Divine Presence with vengeance and judgment, just as you destroyed the Egyptians and their idols in those days at this season, Amen.

סדר עירוב תבשילין

יקח דבר אפוי ומבושל כגון מצה וביצה ויזכה על ידי בני משפחתו ויאמר:

בָּרוּךְ אַתָּה יְהוָה אֱלֹהֵינוּ מֶלֶךְ הָעוֹלָם אֲשֶׁר קִדְּשָׁנוּ בְּמִצְוֹתָיו וְצִוָּנוּ עַל מִצְוַת עֵרוּב:

ויאמר:

בַּהֲדֵין עֵרוּבָא יְהֵא שָׁרֵא לָנָא לַאֲפוּיֵי, וּלְבַשּׁוּלֵי, וּלְאַצְלוּיֵי, וּלְאַטְמוּנֵי, וּלְאַדְלוּקֵי שְׁרָגָא, וּלְתַקָּנָא, וּלְמֶעְבַּד כָּל צָרְכָנָא, מִיּוֹמָא טָבָא לְשַׁבַּתָּא, לָנוּ וּלְכָל יִשְׂרָאֵל הַדָּרִים בָּעִיר הַזֹּאת.

סדר הדלקת נרות

בָּרוּךְ אַתָּה יְהוָה אֱלֹהֵינוּ מֶלֶךְ הָעוֹלָם אֲשֶׁר קִדְּשָׁנוּ בְּמִצְוֹתָיו וְצִוָּנוּ לְהַדְלִיק נֵר שֶׁל (שַׁבָּת וְשֶׁל) יוֹם טוֹב: בָּרוּךְ אַתָּה יְהוָה אֱלֹהֵינוּ מֶלֶךְ הָעוֹלָם שֶׁהֶחֱיָנוּ וְקִיְּמָנוּ וְהִגִּיעָנוּ לַזְּמַן הַזֶּה:

סדר הקערה לפי מנהג האריז״ל

תקח ג׳ מצות שמורות ויניח הכהן למעלה סוד (חכמה), ואחריו לוי (בינה), ולמטה הימנו ישראל (דעת). ועליהן תניח: לימינך, הזרוע (חסד), וכנגדו לשמאל, ביצה (גבורה), ותחתיהם באמצע מרור (תפארת); וחרוסת תחת הזרוע (נצח), וכנגדו תחת הביצה כרפס (הוד), והחזרת שעושין עמו כורך תחת המרור (יסוד); והקערה (מלכות) הכוללת כל עשרה ספירות דאבא. (באה״ט סי׳ תע״ג).

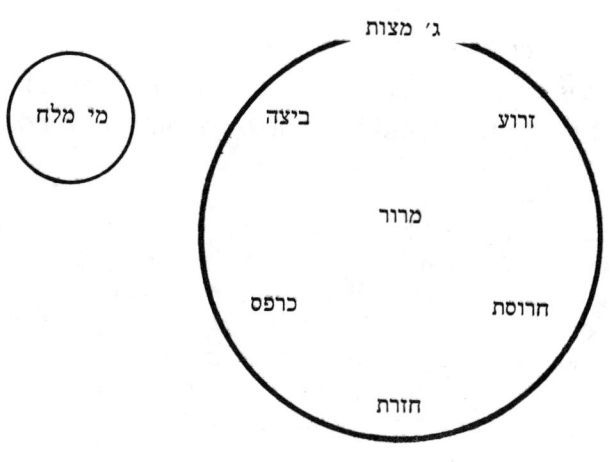

Eruv Tavshilin

When a festival falls on Friday (or Thursday and Friday), it is forbidden to begin cooking then for Shabbat. Therefore, on the eve of the festival, one takes a baked and a cooked item, such as a matzah and an egg, sets them aside for eating only on Shabbat (as if he has already started to prepare for Shabbat), and recites the following:

Blessed are You, God, King of the universe, Who has made us holy with His mitzvot, and commanded us to keep the mitzvah of Eruv.

With this Eruv, we shall be permitted to bake, cook, roast, keep food warm, kindle a flame, and do all the necessary preparations for Shabbat on the festival; we and all Jews who live in this city.

Candle Lighting

The candles are lit and the blessings are recited. When the Festival falls on Shabbat, the words in parentheses are added.

Blessed are You, God, King of the universe, Who has made us holy with His mitzvot, and commanded us to light candles for (Shabbat and) the Festivals.

Blessed are You, God, King of the universe, Who has kept us alive, sustained us, and brought us to this season.

The Seder Plate

The Seder Plate is arranged according to the ARI z'l, as in the diagram below. One should bear in mind throughout the evening that when eating Matzah or drinking wine, one must recline on the left side. When eating Karpas or Maror, one should not recline at all.

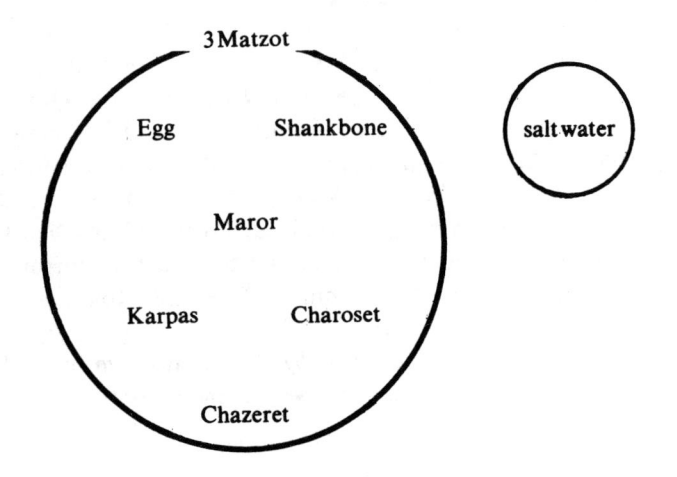

קוֹדֶם הַסֵּדֶר אוֹמֵר:

אַתְקִינוּ סְעוּדָתָא דְמַלְכָּא עִילָּאָה, דָּא אִיהוּ סְעוּדָתָא דְקוּדְשָׁא בְּרִיךְ
הוּא וּשְׁכִינְתֵּיה.

רִבּוֹנוֹ שֶׁל עוֹלָם, אַתָּה יוֹדֵעַ כִּי בָשָׂר אֲנַחְנוּ וְלֹא בִינַת אָדָם לָנוּ, וְאֵין אִתָּנוּ
יוֹדֵעַ עַד מָה. לָכֵן יְהִי רָצוֹן מִלְּפָנֶיךָ ה' אֱלֹהֵינוּ וֵאלֹהֵי אֲבוֹתֵינוּ, שֶׁיַּעֲלֶה
וְיָבֹא וְיֵרָאֶה וְיֵרָצֶה לְנַחַת רוּחַ לְפָנֶיךָ, כָּל הַמִּצְוֹת הַנַּעֲשִׂים בַּלַּיְלָה הַזֹּאת
עַל יָדֵינוּ, לְתַקֵּן כָּל אֲשֶׁר פָּגַמְנוּ בָּעוֹלָמוֹת הָעֶלְיוֹנִים (עַל יְדֵי חַטֹּאתֵינוּ
וַעֲוֹנוֹתֵינוּ וּפְשָׁעֵינוּ) וּלְתַקֵּן כָּל הַנִּצוֹצוֹת שֶׁנָּפְלוּ תּוֹךְ הַקְּלִיפוֹת, וְלִגְרוֹם
שֶׁפַע וּבְרָכָה רַבָּה בְּכָל הָעוֹלָמוֹת, וְאַל יְעַכֵּב שׁוּם חֵטְא וְעָוֹן וְהִרְהוּר רָע אֶת
מַעֲשֵׂה הַמִּצְוֹת הָאֵלֶּה. וִיהִי רָצוֹן מִלְּפָנֶיךָ ה' אֱלֹהֵינוּ וֵאלֹהֵי אֲבוֹתֵינוּ
שֶׁתְּצָרֵף מַחְשְׁבוֹתֵינוּ זֹאת הַפְּשׁוּטָה, עִם כַּוָּנַת בָּנֶיךָ יְדִידֶיךָ הַיּוֹדְעִים
וּמְכַוְּנִים כָּל שְׁמוֹתֶיךָ הַקְּדוֹשִׁים וְהַנּוֹרָאִים, וְכָל כַּוָּנוֹת וְזִיווּגֵי מִדּוֹת
הָעֶלְיוֹנוֹת הַנַּעֲשִׂים עַל יְדֵי מִצְוֹת הָאֵלֶּה:

וִיהִי נֹעַם יְיָ אֱלֹהֵינוּ עָלֵינוּ וּמַעֲשֵׂה יָדֵינוּ כּוֹנְנָה עָלֵינוּ וּמַעֲשֵׂה יָדֵינוּ כּוֹנְנֵהוּ:

In this way, a legacy of futile efforts is passed on from generation to generation. It really is a pity. Everything gets "out of Order."

How wonderful it would be if we would only accept the Hand of Providence, recognizing life's flow as outside our volition. Then we would see. Then we would know. We would see that all things *are* under Control; view that which happens in the context of *our* mission. We would know that life is beyond our control; understand that life can only be lived. Experience the Order and learn from it. "What message is God sending me now? How do I apply it to *my* mission, *my* purpose?" And with this acceptance, with this recognition, we would not be thrown off by what others do. We would see and know that in the context of *our* lives, their actions are pre-ordained. (When Shim'i ben Geirah cursed King David, was King David upset by an act beyond his control? No! He recognized the Hand of Providence. "Leave him be!" he said, "for it was God Who ordained that he curse David!" Samuel II 16:10.)

Yehi Ratzon (May it be Your Will): As we sit down to the Seder, to the order, the Divine Order, may we see our lives as under control — Your Control! (*Likutey Halakhot, Pidyon Bekhor* 3).

Prior to beginning the Seder, the following is said:

I prepare the meal of the Exalted King; this is the meal of the Holy One and the Divine Presence.

Master of the universe! You know that we are of flesh and that we have no understanding. Let it be Your will, God, that our mitzvot, those that we perform this evening, ascend and be accepted before You; to undo the blemishes caused by our sins and to rectify all the "sparks" that fell into the kelipot. Let us merit to cause abundance and blessings to fill all the worlds and let not our sins obstruct these mitzvot that we will perform. May it be Your will, God, that You add and attach our simple intentions in performing these acts to those of Your children who do understand the secrets of these mitzvot and the unifications of Your Holy Names, Amen.

סדר — UNDER CONTROL

"In the beginning, Elohim created...." Elohim, the Divine Name of Power and Control, created. There was Disorder: Void, Emptiness, Exile. Then there was Order: A Beginning, Night and Day, Redemption. One Day. A Second, Third... Sixth Day. Shabbat — a day of rest and harmony. Elohim created His Creation with Divine Seder. Everything was in Order. Creation was under His Control. Elohim created Adam, the first man. He gave Man a mission, a purpose, an order to his life. But Creation, the flow of life — that was not meant to be under his control.

...*God* controls all events.

But that Control is hidden. "Hidden" because *we* don't see it. We must open our eyes to reveal it. To see Providence in our personal lives. To the degree that we are able to feel that Guiding Hand, we experience our lives as under Control. In Order. To the degree that we seek to control, we feel out of control. And, Order in our lives will elude us. For the only thing we can control is our own free will: namely, the decision to accept Control.

Adam sought to control. He complied with the voice that claimed "you shall be as Elohim" (Genesis 3:5). Adam sought to control his life and his world. We, his descendants, cannot claim to be any better. Accomplices to his misdeed, we are ensnared in *our* drive for power and control.

As children we wanted to control our parents; and later, our friends and teachers. We grew into adulthood seeking to control our children and the world around us.

סימנים לסדר של ליל פסח

קַדֵּשׁ. וּרְחַץ. כַּרְפַּס. יַחַץ. מַגִּיד. רָחְצָה. מוֹצִיא. מַצָּה. מָרוֹר. כּוֹרֵךְ. שֻׁלְחָן עוֹרֵךְ. צָפוּן. בָּרֵךְ. הַלֵּל. נִרְצָה:

על מצה וגפן צריך הסבה על צד שמאל. מרור וכרפס אין צריך הסבה.

(*Likutey Moharan* I, 37; *Likutey Halakhot, Ribit* 5:16). But don't we all know of God already?

Moshe, the Tzaddik, the pinnacle of mankind, spoke "face to face" with God. He had access to the most profound secrets of the Torah, he knew the mysteries of existence. Moshe *knew* that despite his life-long struggles for spiritual elevation, all his attainments were nothing but Divine Gifts. He perceived of himself as nothing more than a spokesman of the Almighty. In transmitting the Torah, he experienced God.

Our talents, our attainments are also nothing but Divine Manifestation. To elevate Torah learning above a mere ego experience of our intellectual capacities, in coming to know that it is all God, Moshe is our guide.

The Exodus, too, was a manifestation of the Divine. But without Moshe, we could never see it. The Egyptians didn't see it. The Jews who didn't want to believe in Moshe, who refused to accept that a human being could attain such heights, also didn't see it. We need a human example of how to internalize that awareness. Moshe, the Tzaddik, accomplished so much, yet attributed nothing to himself. It was all God. Our talents are also nothing but a Divine Manifestation. Moshe is our guide.

Moshe was preeminent throughout the Redemption. From start to finish, he performed many miracles.

Moshe was hidden throughout the Redemption. He *knew* it was all God.

Moshe is hidden throughout the Haggadah. But we *know* he is there to guide us.

KaDeSh and DaT, each has the numerical equivalent of 404. NiRTZaH is MoSheH, they both equal 345. Pervading the Haggadah from start to finish, from Kadesh to Nirtzah, is the *Dat Moshe* — the complete and guiding faith of the Tzaddik (*Oneg Shabbat* p. 169; Vilna Gaon on Haggadah, "And God took us out").

The Order of the Seder

The Seder comprises fifteen observances, which have been summarized in the familiar rhyme: Kadesh, U'rchatz, Karpas, etc. No day in the Jewish calender affords a person such a broad selection of mitzvot compacted into a few hours as the Seder evening. Many people therefore recite the entire order before the Seder and then repeat each word when reaching that mitzvah to which it applies, i.e., Kadesh, before Kiddush, U'rchatz, before washing the hands, etc.

KADESH - recite Kiddush over wine

U'RCHATZ - wash hands without a blessing

KARPAS - eat a vegetable dipped in salt water

YACHATZ - break middle matzah, put away larger part for Afikoman

MAGID - tell the story of the Exodus from Egypt

RACHTZAH - wash the hands with a blessing before the meal

MOTZI - recite blessing on matzah

MATZAH - recite special blessing on the matzah, then eat it

MAROR - eat the bitter herb

KOREKH - eat a sandwich of matzah and bitter herbs

SHULCHAN OREKH - eat the meal

TZAFUN - eat the Afikoman

BAREKH - recite the Birkhat HaMazon

HALLEL - recite the Hallel

NIRTZAH - if one performs the above, God accepts our observance

קדש...נרצה — HIDDEN GUIDANCE

Throughout the Haggadah, the mention of Moshe's role is conspicuously absent. In fact, the Haggadah emphasizes that God alone delivered the Jewish People without intermediaries.

Yet, we find God saying to Moshe, "If you do not go to redeem them, there is no one else capable of doing so" (*Shemot Rabbah* 3:4-5). The pivotal role of Moshe, the Tzaddik, is indeed glaring throughout the Torah narrative. Why *did* God have to send Moshe at all? Couldn't He have implemented the Exodus without any human involvement?

"God created the world so that man should ultimately come to *know* Him"

קַדֵּשׁ

מוזגין לו כוס ראשון ומקדש עליו. מוזג אחר דרך חירות. בשבת מתחילין מיום הששי. כשחל במוצאי
שבת אומרים כסדר יקנה"ז, היינו: יין, קידוש, נר, הבדלה, זמן. וקודם הקידוש יאמר זה בלחש:

הִנְנִי מוּכָן וּמְזֻמָּן לְקַיֵּם מִצְוַת כּוֹס רִאשׁוֹן מֵאַרְבַּע כּוֹסוֹת. לְשֵׁם יִחוּד קוּדְשָׁא בְּרִיךְ
הוּא וּשְׁכִינְתֵּיהּ עַל יְדֵי הַהוּא טָמִיר וְנֶעְלָם בְּשֵׁם כָּל יִשְׂרָאֵל:

וִיהִי נֹעַם יְיָ אֱלֹהֵינוּ עָלֵינוּ וּמַעֲשֵׂה יָדֵינוּ כּוֹנְנָה עָלֵינוּ וּמַעֲשֵׂה יָדֵינוּ כּוֹנְנֵהוּ:

לשבת:

וַיְהִי עֶרֶב וַיְהִי בֹקֶר:

יוֹם הַשִּׁשִּׁי. וַיְכֻלּוּ הַשָּׁמַיִם וְהָאָרֶץ וְכָל צְבָאָם: וַיְכַל אֱלֹהִים בַּיּוֹם הַשְּׁבִיעִי
מְלַאכְתּוֹ אֲשֶׁר עָשָׂה וַיִּשְׁבֹּת בַּיּוֹם הַשְּׁבִיעִי מִכָּל מְלַאכְתּוֹ אֲשֶׁר עָשָׂה: וַיְבָרֶךְ
אֱלֹהִים אֶת יוֹם הַשְּׁבִיעִי וַיְקַדֵּשׁ אֹתוֹ כִּי בוֹ שָׁבַת מִכָּל מְלַאכְתּוֹ אֲשֶׁר בָּרָא אֱלֹהִים
לַעֲשׂוֹת:

סַבְרִי מָרָנָן וְרַבָּנָן וְרַבּוֹתַי:

בָּרוּךְ אַתָּה יְהֹוָה אֱלֹהֵינוּ מֶלֶךְ הָעוֹלָם בּוֹרֵא פְּרִי הַגָּפֶן:
בָּרוּךְ אַתָּה יְהֹוָה אֱלֹהֵינוּ מֶלֶךְ הָעוֹלָם אֲשֶׁר בָּחַר בָּנוּ מִכָּל
עָם וְרוֹמְמָנוּ מִכָּל לָשׁוֹן וְקִדְּשָׁנוּ בְּמִצְוֹתָיו. וַתִּתֶּן לָנוּ יְהֹוָה
אֱלֹהֵינוּ בְּאַהֲבָה (לשבת שַׁבָּתוֹת לִמְנוּחָה וּ) מוֹעֲדִים לְשִׂמְחָה
חַגִּים וּזְמַנִּים לְשָׂשׂוֹן (לשבת אֶת יוֹם הַשַּׁבָּת הַזֶּה וְ) אֶת יוֹם חַג
הַמַּצּוֹת הַזֶּה זְמַן חֵרוּתֵנוּ (לשבת בְּאַהֲבָה) מִקְרָא קֹדֶשׁ זֵכֶר
לִיצִיאַת מִצְרָיִם. כִּי בָנוּ בָחַרְתָּ וְאוֹתָנוּ קִדַּשְׁתָּ מִכָּל הָעַמִּים.
(לשבת וְשַׁבָּת) וּמוֹעֲדֵי קָדְשֶׁךָ (לשבת בְּאַהֲבָה וּבְרָצוֹן) בְּשִׂמְחָה
וּבְשָׂשׂוֹן הִנְחַלְתָּנוּ. בָּרוּךְ אַתָּה יְהֹוָה מְקַדֵּשׁ (לשבת הַשַּׁבָּת וְ)
יִשְׂרָאֵל וְהַזְּמַנִּים:

But we must express our yearnings (*Likutey Moharan* I, 31:7). We must channel them
into the beauty of Kiddush over a cup of wine.

Wine will fuel our yearnings. And it will dissolve the inhibitions which keep us
from expressing them (*Likutey Halakhot, Netilat Yadaim* 6:19).

KADESH

I am ready and prepared to perform the mitzvah of drinking the first of the four cups of wine.

On Friday evening begin here:
And it was evening and it was morning,
The Sixth Day. The heavens and the earth were finished, and all that was in them. On the Seventh Day God completed His work, that which He had done, and He abstained on the Seventh Day from all His work which He had done. God blessed the Seventh Day and sanctified it, because on it He abstained from all His work which God created to make (Genesis 1:31-2:3).

On all other nights begin here:

Attention my masters:
Blessed are You, God, King of the universe, Who creates the fruit of the vine.

Blessed are You, God, King of the universe, Who has chosen us from all the nations, exalted us above all languages, and made us holy with His mitzvot. You, our God, have given us, with love, (Sabbaths for rest,) special times for gladness, festivals and seasons for joy, (this Sabbath and) this Festival of Matzot, the season of our freedom, (in love,) a holy convocation, recalling the Exodus from Egypt. For You have chosen and sanctified us above all peoples, (and the Sabbath) and Your holy festivals (in love and favor), in gladness and joy You have granted us. Blessed are You, God, Who sanctifies (the Sabbath,) Israel and the Festivals.

קידוש — A CALL OF YEARNING

The bustling Erev Pesach is coming to a close. We see it on the clock, we feel it in the air. We *know* that our time is up. We can already hear the Calling of the Festival.

"Oh God! I'm not ready yet!"

"The preparations aren't finished! I'm not in the proper frame of mind."

"Oh God! Help me be ready to accept my Jewishness!"

Allow this gnawing in our hearts to pour forth. Then let it become a great yearning for God. From our distance we desire closeness, from the depths we aspire to the heights. Yearning elevates the soul. This is our Neshamah Yeteirah — the extra, the Higher Soul (*Likutey Moharan* I, 31:9; See *Kedushat Levi* pp. 62d-63a that there is an aspect of the Neshamah Yeteirah on the Festivals as well as on Shabbat).

למוצאי שבת:

בָּרוּךְ אַתָּה יְהֹוָה אֱלֹהֵינוּ מֶלֶךְ הָעוֹלָם בּוֹרֵא מְאוֹרֵי הָאֵשׁ:
בָּרוּךְ אַתָּה יְהֹוָה אֱלֹהֵינוּ מֶלֶךְ הָעוֹלָם הַמַּבְדִּיל בֵּין קֹדֶשׁ לְחוֹל בֵּין אוֹר לְחֹשֶׁךְ
בֵּין יִשְׂרָאֵל לָעַמִּים בֵּין יוֹם הַשְּׁבִיעִי לְשֵׁשֶׁת יְמֵי הַמַּעֲשֶׂה בֵּין קְדֻשַּׁת שַׁבָּת
לִקְדֻשַּׁת יוֹם טוֹב הִבְדַּלְתָּ וְאֶת יוֹם הַשְּׁבִיעִי מִשֵּׁשֶׁת יְמֵי הַמַּעֲשֶׂה קִדַּשְׁתָּ. הִבְדַּלְתָּ
וְקִדַּשְׁתָּ אֶת עַמְּךָ יִשְׂרָאֵל בִּקְדֻשָּׁתֶךָ: בָּרוּךְ אַתָּה יְהֹוָה הַמַּבְדִּיל בֵּין קֹדֶשׁ לְקֹדֶשׁ:

בָּרוּךְ אַתָּה יְהֹוָה אֱלֹהֵינוּ מֶלֶךְ הָעוֹלָם שֶׁהֶחֱיָנוּ וְקִיְּמָנוּ
וְהִגִּיעָנוּ לַזְּמַן הַזֶּה:

וְשׁוֹתִין הַכּוֹס בַּהֲסִבַּת שְׂמֹאל: וְאֵינוֹ מְבָרֵךְ בְּרָכָה אַחֲרוֹנָה

וּרְחַץ

נוֹטֵל יָדָיו לְצוֹרֶךְ טִיבוּל רִאשׁוֹן כְּדִין נט"י לִסְעוּדָה. וְלֹא יְבָרֵךְ עַל הַנְּטִילָה:

כַּרְפַּס

יִקַּח מֵהַכַּרְפַּס פָּחוֹת מִכַּזַּית וְטוֹבְלוֹ בְּמֵי מֶלַח וִיכַוֵּן בְּבִרְכַּת בּוֹרֵא פְּרִי הָאֲדָמָה
לִפְטוֹר בָּהּ הַמָּרוֹר וְהַכּוֹרֵךְ. וְיֹאכַל בְּלֹא הֲסִבָּה. וּמְבָרֵךְ בְּרָכָה זוֹ:

בָּרוּךְ אַתָּה יְהֹוָה אֱלֹהֵינוּ מֶלֶךְ הָעוֹלָם בּוֹרֵא פְּרִי הָאֲדָמָה:

ורחץ — A MEETING OF HANDS

Preparing to eat the Karpas, an appetizer of commonplace vegetable, we wash our hands. *U'rechatz* (Hebrew), washing and cleansing. *U'rechatz* (Aramaic), trusting.

Our meal may be nothing more than a bit of commonplace vegetable. We should not take it for granted. It is nothing less than Divinely granted.

Trust God! There is no reason to be dejected. We are all sustained by the same Benevolent Hand which apportions with Divine Discretion.

Let us then raise our hands in yearning to God. Ask Him to provide us from *His* Hand in times of want and in times of plenty (*Likutey Halakhot, Netilat Yadaim* 6:26).

כרפס — GRATIS BREAD

God sustains all life. Gratis. Its perpetuation, per se, is necessary for the Divine Plan of Creation.

On Saturday night, add the following two blessings:

Blessed are You, God, King of the universe, Who creates the lights of fire.

Blessed are You, God, King of the universe, Who distinguishes between holy and mundane, between light and darkness, between Israel and the nations, between the Seventh Day and the six days of work; between the holiness of Shabbat and the holiness of a Festival You have distinguished, and have sanctified Shabbat above the six days of work. You distinguished and sanctified Your nation, Israel, with Your holiness. Blessed are You, God, Who distinguishes between [one] holiness and [another] holiness.

On all nights conclude here

Blessed are You, God, King of the universe, Who has kept us alive, sustained us, and brought us to this season.

One drinks the wine while reclining to his left side. More than half the cup should be drunk.

U'RCHATZ

All wash their hands as if washing for bread, but do not recite a blessing.

KARPAS

Everyone takes a small piece of a vegetable (cucumber, parsley, potato, etc.) other than maror, dips it into salt water, and recites the following blessing (one should bear in mind that the blessing also applies to the Maror and to the Korekh):

Blessed are You, God, King of the universe, Who creates the fruit of the earth.

One then eats the Karpas without reclining.

שהחיינו — MEANING

As we recite the Kiddush, we bring to mind the miracles of Redemption. We proclaim *to ourselves* God's Ultimate Will and Providence. We become aware of the Divine Guidance permeating our lives.

Inherent in the security of that knowledge is an uplifting serenity. We rise above time, above the ephemeral experiences we call life. Every moment is infused with eternal meaning.

We now usher in the Festival. Its lesson imbues meaning into every aspect of life. It is for that meaning in our lives that we now express our gratitude to God for giving us life at *this* moment (*Likutey Halakhot, Birkhat Hoda'ah* 6:62; *Birkhat Re'iyah* 3).

יחץ

יקח האמצעית מהג' מצות ויבצענה לשתים: חלק הגדול כורכו במפה נקיה
וישמרנו לאפיקומן, וחלק הקטנה משאיר בין שתי המצות השלמות.

Kisufa (Aramaic), shame and humiliation. *Kisuf* (Hebrew), longing and yearning.

We must become aware of our humiliating situation. Then we will long for God. Even in the moment of our shame, He has not forsaken us.

Let us cry out for human sustenance, for Matzah, the bread of great yearning — the Nahama de'Kisufa (*Likutey Halakhot, Netilat Yadaim* 6:22,32,35).

"Oh God! Is there no more meaning to my eating beyond self-perpetuation?!"

And God will reply, "With *yearning* you can attain human sustenance." And we will be appeased.

יחץ — BREAD OF UNAWARENESS

Matzah symbolizes great awareness of God. The Jewish People ate it on the night of Redemption. They also brought the Matzah forth with them from Egypt. In it, they experienced the taste of manna, Bread from Heaven. It epitomized the clear perception that man's sustenance is directly from God.

Mankind, though, is not yet ready for this overwhelming experience of God. Preparation is required. We must bring the deepest fibers of our souls into harmony and be *willing* to accept this eminent Truth.

First, we must put aside all notions of "knowing" God. We must realize that to know God is to realize that we can never really know Him.

We must therefore break the Matzah; separate this great awareness into fathomable sections. The larger portion is set aside for the "end." In the End of Days, Man *will* rise again to his destined level of Awareness. Until then, we can utilize only the smaller part, the Lechem Oni, which is symbolic of the lack of that great knowledge.

Upon this Lechem Oni, upon this knowledge of our Unawareness, we recite the Haggadah. These are our prayers and words of faith that ultimately God *will* redeem us from the Darkness of Unawareness (*Likutey Halakhot, Giluach* 3:13-14).

YACHATZ

The middle Matzah is broken into two unequal parts. The smaller part is replaced between the two whole Matzot, and the larger part is put away for later use as the Afikoman. There is a custom that children try to 'steal' the Afikomen, who then try to ransom it when the time comes for it to be eaten. (The host should be aware that should the ransom be high, one is permitted to use another piece of Matzah, just as in the case if the Afikomen was lost.)

Man is the one exception in Creation. He is created to be different, unique. God wants him to *earn* his sustenance. How? By praying! Man must become *aware* of the Hand that feeds him. His prayers must be the sincere and enthusiastic expression of that awareness, not the means of manipulation. Awareness! Prayer! This is Man's true essence. (The Talmud teaches: Mav'eh, the beseecher, this is Man; *Bava Kama* 3b). *This* man, his prayer, is the purpose of Creation. If he would but pray, God would sustain him; no other act or physical effort on his part would be required.

Man once had the opportunity for true humanness. This was in Gan Eden. He had only to pray. His yearning, his prayers, would have "created" his sustenance. God would have made his prayers a reality.

But Adam was not satisfied. He wanted to be *like* God. To *create* worlds (*Likutey Halakhot, Orlah* 5:3). He became aware of *himself* — that he "could." Conceit at its most subtle level. When he prayed, it was not simple yearning. He used his prayer. The "fruit" of his prayer became his goal; his prayer only a means (*Likutey Halakhot, Minchah* 7:29; *Tefillin* 6:4). Sometimes, we, too, use "prayer" for hidden motives....

God said to man: "You have abused your prayer; distorted your purpose; corrupted your essence. You have lost your true humanness, the source of your sustenance. Your existence is now only a means towards your ultimate re-elevation. Together with your animals, I shall continue to sustain you. Gratis. You shall eat the greens of the field. Your bread will be bread of humiliation — Nahama de'Kisufa" (it is humiliating to receive gratis) (*Likutey Halakhot, Mekach U'Memkar* 4:2).

"Oh God!" Adam cried out. *"Shall I share a plate with my donkey?"*

God replied, "With toil you can attain human sustenance." And Man was appeased.

Before the Seder we eat simple greens. We look at ourselves honestly, astonished by how far *we* have fallen into a less than human existence.

מַגִּיד

יְכַוֵּן לְקַיֵּם מִצְוַת עֲשֵׂה דְאוֹרַיְיתָא לְסַפֵּר בְּלֵיל פֶּסַח סִפּוּר יְצִיאַת מִצְרַיִם. וְיֵשֵׁב
בְּאֵימָה וּבְיִרְאָה בְּלֹא הֲסִיבָה.

וְרָאוּי לְכָל אֶחָד לוֹמַר מֵאֹמֶר הַזֹהַר שֶׁמַּלְהִיב לְבָבוֹת עַל נַחַת הַשְּׁכִינָה בְּשָׁעָה זוֹ.

פְּקוּדָא בָּתַר דָּא לְסַפֵּר בְּשַׁבְחָא דִּיצִיאַת מִצְרַיִם דְּאִיהוּ חִיּוּבָא דְּבַר נַשׁ לְאִשְׁתָּעָאֵי
בְּהַהוּא שְׁבָחָא לְעָלְמִין. הָכֵי אוּקִימְנָא, כָּל בַּר נַשׁ דְּאִשְׁתָּעָאֵי בִּיצִיאַת מִצְרַיִם וּבְהַהוּא
סִפּוּר חָדֵי בְּחֶדְוָה, זַמִּין אִיהוּ לְמֶחֱדֵי בִּשְׁכִינְתָּא לְעָלְמָא דְּאָתֵי וּלְמֶעֱבַד לֵיהּ חָדוּ
מִכֹּלָּא, דְּהַאי אִיהוּ בַּר נַשׁ דְּחָדֵי בְּמָארֵיהּ. וְקוּדְשָׁא בְּרִיךְ הוּא חָדֵי בְּהַהוּא סִיפּוּר. בֵּיהּ
שַׁעֲתָא כָּנֵישׁ קוּדְשָׁא בְּרִיךְ הוּא לְכָל פַּמַלְיָא דִּילֵיהּ וְאָמַר לוֹן: זִילוּ וְשִׁמְעוּ סִיפּוּר
דְּשַׁבְחָא דִּילִי דְּקָא מִשְׁתָּעוּ בָּנַי וְחָדָאן בְּפוּרְקָנִי. כְּדֵין כּוּלְּהוּ מִתְכַּנְּשִׁין וְאַתְיִין
וּמִתְחַבְּרִין בַּהֲדַיְיהוּ דְּיִשְׂרָאֵל וְשָׁמְעוּ סִיפּוּרָא דְּשַׁבְחָא דְּקָא חָדָאן בְּחֶדְוָה דְּפוּרְקָנָא
דְּמָארֵיהוֹן. כְּדֵין אַתְיִין וְאוֹדָן לֵיהּ לְקוּדְשָׁא בְּרִיךְ הוּא עַל כָּל אִינוּן נִיסִּין וּגְבוּרָאן
וְאוֹדָן לֵיהּ עַל עַמָּא קַדִּישָׁא דְּאִית לֵיהּ בְּאַרְעָא דְּחָדָאן בְּחֶדְוָה דְּפוּרְקָנָא דְּמָארֵיהוֹן
כְּדֵין אִיתּוֹסַף לֵיהּ חֵילָא וּגְבוּרְתָּא לְעֵילָּא. וְיִשְׂרָאֵל בְּהַהוּא סִיפּוּרָא יָהֲבֵי חֵילָא
לְמָארֵיהוֹן כְּמַלְכָּא דְּאִיתּוֹסַף חֵילָא וּגְבוּרְתָּא כַּד מְשַׁבְּחִין גְּבוּרְתֵּיהּ וְאוֹדָן לֵיהּ וְכוּלְּהוּ
דַּחֲלִין מִקַּמֵּיהּ וְאִסְתַּלַּק יְקָרֵיהּ עַל כּוּלְּהוּ. וּבְגִין כָּךְ אִית לְשַׁבְחָא וּלְאִשְׁתָּעֵי בְּסִיפּוּר
דָּא כְּמָה דְּאִתְּמַר. כְּגַוְונָא דָּא חוֹבָה אִיהוּ עַל בַּר נַשׁ לְאִשְׁתָּעֵי קַמֵּי קוּדְשָׁא בְּרִיךְ
הוּא וּלְפַרְסוּמֵי נִיסָּא בְּכָל אִינוּן דְּעָבִיד. וְאִי תֵּימָא: אֲמַאי אִיהוּ חוֹבָתָא? וְהָא וְקוּדְשָׁא
בְּרִיךְ הוּא יָדַע כֹּלָּא, כָּל מַה דְּהֲוָה, וְיֶהֱוֵי, לְבָתַר דְּנָא! אֲמַאי פַּרְסוּמָא דָּא קַמֵּיהּ עַל
מַה דְּאִיהוּ עֲבַד וְאִיהוּ יָדַע? אֶלָּא וַדַּאי אִיצְטְרִיךְ בַּר נַשׁ לְפַרְסוּמֵי נִיסָּא וּלְאִשְׁתָּעָאֵי
קַמֵּיהּ בְּכָל מַה דְּאִיהוּ עֲבַד. בְּגִין דְּאִינוּן מִילִּין סַלְּקִין וְכָל פַּמַלְיָא דִּלְעֵילָּא מִתְכַּנְּשִׁין
וְחָמָאן לוֹן וְאוֹדָן כּוּלְּהוּ לְקוּדְשָׁא בְּרִיךְ הוּא וְאִסְתַּלַּק יְקָרָא עֲלוֹהִי עֵילָא וְתַתָּא.
בָּרוּךְ ה' לְעוֹלָם, אָמֵן וְאָמֵן.

Through the Telling, we bring to life *their* stories. In turn, may God bring to life
the story of *our* Redemption (*Likutey Halakhot, Nedarim 5:6-8*).

> *And when the Mashiach will come, he will also tell stories. Of what
> we all have been through every day of our lives. The meaning of our past
> suffering, the redeeming affect of our past tribulations* (Rabbi Nachman's
> Stories #10, The Burger and the Pauper p.229).

Yehi Ratzon: *May we merit to appreciate that meaning, experience
that redemption — in our lives!*

MAGID

One should recite the Haggadah in a loud voice with reverence for God and the miracles He wrought us. Some recite the following passage from the Zohar prior to beginning Magid, as it extolls those who participate whole-heartedly in the Seder.

It is a mitzvah to recite the story of the Exodus, for it is an eternal praise. Everyone who joyously participates in telling the story of the Exodus will rejoice with God in the World to Come, for he is one who rejoices with his Master. And God rejoices with this recital.

At the time when one is recalling the Exodus, God gathers His heavenly entourage and says to them: "Go, hear the praises with which My children praise Me and how they rejoice in My redemption." All the heavenly hosts descend to join with the Jews and listen to the story of the Exodus and praises of God. Then they ascend and praise God for all the miracles He performed for the Jews, as well as praising the Jews who rejoice in His redemption. The forces of holiness gain strength and God's Name is elevated. Each additional recital strengthens holiness and elevates God's glory still further. Therefore it is imperative that we recall the Exodus and even all the other miracles that God performed for us.

Should you ask, "Why is this recital necessary? Doesn't God know everything that has happened, that is happening and that will happen?" The answer is that it is the *talking* about the miracles, the praises which ascend, that causes the heavenly hosts to gather; and this in turn causes the elevation of God's glory, above and below, throughout all Creation (*Zohar* II, 40b).

מגיד — TELLING THE STORY

Man is incapable of a sudden confrontation with his Creator. The overwhelming experience of such awareness is just too awesome. Truth, the stark Truth, must be camouflaged. Only then, can the soul gradually absorb it.

God, so to speak, camouflaged Himself in stories. These are the stories of Creation and of Adam and Eve. The stories of the Flood and of the Patriarchs. The stories of Jewish exile and redemption. God is hidden in all the stories of human history. And, in the as yet untold stories of each and every human being. His trials. His tribulations. And his salvation.

At the Pesach Seder we tell stories — Magid. We recount the stories of the Exile in, and the Redemption from Egypt. These represent the collective stories of mankind. They typify the individual stories of each and every one of us. As we relate the details *of* these stories, we must relate *to* them. Be aroused *by* them. See the Hand of God in the stories of our own lives.

כשאומר ההגדה יהא המצות מגולין לקיים לחם עוני שעונין עליו דברים הרבה. וכל פעם שנוטל הכוס בידו יכסה המצות.

וקודם שיתחיל הא לחמא יאמר זה:

הֲרֵינִי מוּכָן וּמְזֻמָּן לְקַיֵּם מִצְוַת עֲשֵׂה לְסַפֵּר בִּיצִיאַת מִצְרָיִם. לְשֵׁם יִחוּד קוּדְשָׁא בְּרִיךְ הוּא וּשְׁכִינְתֵּיהּ עַל יְדֵי הַהוּא טָמִיר וְנֶעְלָם בְּשֵׁם כָּל יִשְׂרָאֵל:

וִיהִי נֹעַם יְיָ אֱלֹהֵינוּ עָלֵינוּ וּמַעֲשֵׂה יָדֵינוּ כּוֹנְנָה עָלֵינוּ וּמַעֲשֵׂה יָדֵינוּ כּוֹנְנֵהוּ.

הָא לַחְמָא עַנְיָא דִּי אֲכָלוּ אַבְהָתָנָא בְּאַרְעָא דְמִצְרָיִם. כָּל דִּכְפִין יֵיתֵי וְיֵיכוֹל. כָּל דִּצְרִיךְ יֵיתֵי וְיִפְסַח. הַשַּׁתָּא הָכָא לְשָׁנָה הַבָּאָה בְּאַרְעָא דְיִשְׂרָאֵל. הָשַׁתָּא עַבְדֵי לְשָׁנָה הַבָּאָה בְּנֵי חוֹרִין:

our thoughts. What we eat and *how* we eat it influences our mental processes. Eating just for pleasure or the alleviation of hunger is beneath the level of man. Our thought processes sink below human level. We become prey to undesirable fantasy.

We must therefore *break* those spontaneous thoughts the moment we become aware of them. We must not allow them to *rise* to our human consciousness. Year-round, we recite a blessing first, and only then partake of our food. Through the blessing we become aware of the higher meaning of human consumption. Then we can "break bread" — break off those unwanted thoughts.

On Pesach we eat Matzah. Unfermented bread, unfermented thoughts. It is symbolic of true human consumption. We break it even before a blessing is recited. We show that with "Matzah," we can abruptly break off undesired thoughts and keep our minds pure.

"This is the Bread of Declaration!" — our food for thought.

Through the Lechem Oni, the broken bread, we come to its second aspect: The Bread of Declaration. By harnessing our eating habits — by harnessing our thought processes — we can express ourselves in prayer before God. We are free of disturbing thoughts. Now we can sit down to the Seder to recount, experience, and declare the wonders of the Redemption (*Likutey Halakhot, Betziat HaPat* 3:2-3).

כל דכפין — EMULATING GOD

God took us out of bondage as an unevoked act of Kindness. We were not ready. We were undeserving.

We must emulate God; performing acts of unevoked kindness. We must make ourselves deserving of the Divine Grace. Before Pesach, give much Tzedakah. Call out to the needy to come join us. Through this, we will merit to eat the Matzah, the symbol of Divine Grace (*Likutey Halakhot, Kibud Av V'Aim* 2:4,6,16).

השתא הכא — A JEWISH DESIRE

Nearly a century old, the weak and amnesic R' Shmuel Meir Anshin lay in bed entertaining an audience with the important things he did remember.

Throughout the evening, when reciting the Haggadah, the matzot should be uncovered. However, whenever the cup of wine is lifted or held, the matzot should be covered.

I am ready and prepared to perform the mitzvah of reciting the Haggadah.

This is the bread of affliction that our fathers ate in the land of Egypt. All who are hungry, come and eat! All in need, come and join in celebrating Pesach! This year we are here, next year we will be in the land of Israel! This year we are slaves, next year we will be free men!

הא לחמא אנא — A MATTER OF TASTE

This is the Bread of Poverty! Of material poverty and affliction. Of spiritual poverty and cynicism. It is the bread our ancestors ate in bondage.

This bread, the *very same* bread, is the Bread of Redemption! We brought it forth from Egypt, it tasted like Bread from Heaven. The bread did not change. Our awareness of its Source did!

> *The morning after the Seder. The long prayer service had just ended. Everyone was still dizzy from the wine, exhausted from the long night. But it was great.* Another Seder! Another Pesach! *Everyone was elated.*
> *Everyone except one.*
> "I'm glad that's over with," *he grumbled.* "I just can't take all that wine, and the Matzah gives me constipation. And what's the need to say all that Haggadah? Can't the rabbis take us into consideration? Oh well, it'll be over in a week. Before you know it, we'll be back to routine."
> *Stunned by the outburst, the others looked on in consternation. No one wanted to embarrass him, but no one knew how to approach him. Looking at him in silence, they all sighed.*
> *What a pity. For him it was just another Seder... just another Pesach....*

Two people can externally experience the same event. The one who is spiritually impoverished will perceive affliction and suffering. Internally he will taste the dryness of a Godless experience. The one who is aware of the Source of all events will perceive Benevolent Providence. He will gain insight into God's Infinite Unity. He will see how it is expressed through the multitude of human events and worldly phenomena.

This is the "Bread of Experience." It's a matter of taste.

We call out to those who are still grappling in the exile of spiritual poverty: Come! Let us partake of the Bread of Experience. Let us together learn how to "eat", how to taste life, to experience God throughout. It may still be painful, but *next year* in the Land of Israel! It is only a matter of time. Next year we will experience true freedom.

הא לחמא אנא — FOOD FOR THOUGHT

Throughout the year, the physical reality of our bread is Chametz, leavened, fermented bread. It is indicative of, indeed, it is the cause of the fermentation of

מוזגין כוס שני וכאן הבן שואל מה נשתנה:

מַה נִּשְׁתַּנָּה הַלַּיְלָה הַזֶּה מִכָּל הַלֵּילוֹת?

שֶׁבְּכָל הַלֵּילוֹת אָנוּ אוֹכְלִין חָמֵץ וּמַצָּה.
הַלַּיְלָה הַזֶּה כֻּלּוֹ מַצָּה:

שֶׁבְּכָל הַלֵּילוֹת אָנוּ אוֹכְלִין שְׁאָר יְרָקוֹת.
הַלַּיְלָה הַזֶּה מָרוֹר:

שֶׁבְּכָל הַלֵּילוֹת אֵין אָנוּ מַטְבִּילִין אֲפִילוּ פַּעַם אֶחָת.
הַלַּיְלָה הַזֶּה שְׁתֵּי פְעָמִים:

שֶׁבְּכָל הַלֵּילוֹת אָנוּ אוֹכְלִין בֵּין יוֹשְׁבִין וּבֵין מְסֻבִּין.
הַלַּיְלָה הַזֶּה כֻּלָּנוּ מְסֻבִּין:

עֲבָדִים הָיִינוּ לְפַרְעֹה בְּמִצְרָיִם וַיּוֹצִיאֵנוּ יְהֹוָה אֱלֹהֵינוּ מִשָּׁם בְּיָד חֲזָקָה וּבִזְרֹעַ נְטוּיָה וְאִלּוּ לֹא הוֹצִיא הַקָּדוֹשׁ בָּרוּךְ הוּא

God Himself, so to speak, appeared in Egypt. The Jewish People experienced a most profound Inspiration. God revealed that each moment is a new creation. He Wills the "laws of nature." He can also change them. Each moment of our lives is also a new creation. Let us apply this Knowledge to the "laws" of our misguided second nature and change them.

Yet, in order for this to happen, this Knowledge must be broken into simple lessons so that even a child can understand. So that the immaturity in each one of us will be willing to accept it. It is therefore the *child* that asks the Questions. And if none are present, we ask ourselves. In perceiving God, we are all like children, curious to understand the inconceivable.

Through Question and Discussion we can even overcome the Kelipot, the mental barriers, which block our perception of this great Lesson (*Nachat HaShulchan*).

עבדים היינו — FAITH IS THE ANSWER
Nowhere in the Haggadah do we find explicit answers to the Mah Nishtanah Questions. What *is* said, does not suffice to explain the numerous laws and customs associated with the Seder and the Festival.

The second cup of wine is poured and the children ask the Four Questions.

Why is this night different from all other nights?

[Why is it] that on all other nights we may eat either Chametz or Matzah, and on this night we may eat only Matzah?

[Why is it] that on all other nights we may eat any kind of vegetables, and on this night we must eat Maror?

[Why is it] that on all other nights we are not required to dip our foods even once, and on this night we are required to do so twice?

[Why is it] that on all other nights we may eat either sitting or reclining, and on this night we must recline?

We were slaves to Pharaoh in Egypt, but God brought us out from there with a strong hand and an outstretched arm. If God had not brought out

> *"If you want to be a real Jew,"* he declared, *"you must avail yourself of Eretz Israel!"* (cf. Advice, Land of Israel, *3*).
>
> *"Eretz,"* R' Shmuel Meir asserted, *"means* I want!*"* *(RaTZon, desire, and eReTZ have the same root.)*
>
> *"Israel means A Jew!"* he concluded. *"So, if you want to* be *a real Jew, you must always* want *to be a Jew!"*
>
> Kabbalistically, *eretz,* the earth, signifies Malkhut, the lowest level of holiness. Malkhut rectified is Eretz Israel. Through it we can come to the highest level, Keter, which signifies God's desire for us.

"This year we are here, but next year..."

We now express our desire: "Next year may we be in *Ar'ah d'Yisrael."* The Aramaic *Ar'ah* has two meanings: It is Eretz, land — Next year may we be in the Land of Israel. It is also Ratzon, desire — Next year may we achieve Jewish Desire.

Every year, on this night, there is a Divine Arousal and Desire for God to redeem His People. We, in turn, desire just that.

May *our* desire unite with *God's...*

Next year in Yerushalayim!

מה נשתנה — OVERCOMING BARRIERS TO PERCEPTION

Man's knowledge and awareness develop gradually from childhood and throughout adulthood. But in this world, how is man *ever* to perceive God, to experience the Divine, when his physical eyes blind him and his bodily senses deny? In Egypt, the Jewish People were trapped physically, spiritually and emotionally in an all encompassing bondage. What great Knowledge would it take for them to realize that they *could* overcome the barriers and rise above their mental constrictions?

אֶת אֲבוֹתֵינוּ מִמִּצְרַיִם הֲרֵי אָנוּ וּבָנֵינוּ וּבְנֵי בָנֵינוּ מְשֻׁעְבָּדִים
הָיִינוּ לְפַרְעֹה בְּמִצְרָיִם. וַאֲפִילוּ כֻּלָּנוּ חֲכָמִים כֻּלָּנוּ נְבוֹנִים
כֻּלָּנוּ זְקֵנִים כֻּלָּנוּ יוֹדְעִים אֶת הַתּוֹרָה מִצְוָה עָלֵינוּ לְסַפֵּר
בִּיצִיאַת מִצְרָיִם. וְכָל הַמַּרְבֶּה לְסַפֵּר בִּיצִיאַת מִצְרַיִם הֲרֵי זֶה
מְשֻׁבָּח:

מַעֲשֶׂה בְּרַבִּי אֱלִיעֶזֶר וְרַבִּי יְהוֹשֻׁעַ וְרַבִּי אֶלְעָזָר בֶּן עֲזַרְיָה
וְרַבִּי עֲקִיבָא וְרַבִּי טַרְפוֹן שֶׁהָיוּ מְסֻבִּין בִּבְנֵי בְּרַק וְהָיוּ
מְסַפְּרִים בִּיצִיאַת מִצְרַיִם כָּל אוֹתוֹ הַלַּיְלָה עַד שֶׁבָּאוּ
תַלְמִידֵיהֶם וְאָמְרוּ לָהֶם רַבּוֹתֵינוּ הִגִּיעַ זְמַן קְרִיאַת שְׁמַע שֶׁל
שַׁחֲרִית:

ואפילו כולנו — TELLING AWAY THE DARKNESS

By discussing the Redemption, we evoke the same Light of Inspiration which emanated on the original night in Egypt.

Through this Light, many Jews around the world are aroused to God. Even alienated Jews. Sometimes even gentiles.

Even "wise men and scholars" — those who "know the Torah" — are sometimes asleep in the Darkness of Godlessness (*Likutey Moharan* I 60:6). They, too, need to be aroused by the stories we tell.

And the more Telling we do, the more Light is revealed (*Nachat HaShulchan*).

מעשה ברבי אליעזר — GOD IS EVERYWHERE

The multitude of worldly phenomena; the chronicles of human history; the episodes of our daily lives. All have one thing in common. They are there to give us a perception of God's Unity and Oneness. Tools for God to implement His Ultimate Will. The hidden thread woven throughout is that God is everywhere!

These great Sages spent the entire night Telling; discussing the phenomena, chronicles and episodes of the Exodus. When morning came, all present had experienced the singular lesson of the entire story: God is everywhere!

It was then time to recite the morning Shema. With the experience of the previous night, they could now attest to God's Presence over all corners of existence. And, in declaring His Oneness, they bore witness: God can be found, even in the abyss of spiritual void! (*Likutey Halakhot, Nesiat Kapayim* 2:2).

our fathers from Egypt, then we, our children and our children's children would have remained enslaved to Pharaoh in Egypt. Therefore, even if all of us are wise, all of us are clever, all Elders [of our people], all fully versed in the Torah, we would still be obligated to recall the Exodus. Whoever tells about it at length is praiseworthy.

Rabbi Eliezer, Rabbi Yehoshua, Rabbi Elazar son of Azaryah, Rabbi Akiva and Rabbi Tarfon were celebrating the Seder in Bnei Brak. They were discussing the Exodus the entire night, until their students came and said to them: Rabbis, the time has arrived for reading the morning Sh'ma.

The Answer remains hidden. But it is implicit.

In Egypt we experienced great miracles. We *saw* God's Benevolent Guiding Force behind the veil of nature.

Today, we see it not. But we *know* it is there.

Our Knowing comes from Faith. This is the Answer.

In not seeing, we must fulfill His Will, the Mitzvot, with simple faith. They are simple, physical acts. But behind their veil, we *know* He is there (*Likutey Halakhot, Pesach* 9:7-8).

עבדים היינו לפרעה — INVERTED SELF-IMAGE

"Pharaoh" indicates Imagination (*Likutey Moharan* I 54:6). PHaRaOH is a permutation of HaORePH, the back or nape of the neck. He is symbolic of the "back" of human rational intellect — Imagination.

We've all had illusions about ourselves. At times, we may have fallen into the "exile" of self-delusion. Our self-image became inverted. And though we all possess noble souls — we are *all* the King's son — even so, we perceived ourselves as vassals, held in bondage by the forces which worked upon us. We imagined ourselves as powerless to control the outside influences or the inside emotions. We saw ourselves as inevitable sinners (see *Rabbi Nachman's Stories*, The Exchanged Children, p. 231ff).

It may have been many years before we became more aware of the true nature of our *selves*. Decades before we learned to appreciate the nobility of our Jewish souls. But now, we will take leave of our "exile." But now, we will be set free from being slaves to Imagination.

And now, we will look back on the events which led up to our "redemption." We will clearly see that "...it was God Who took us forth..."

אָמַר רַבִּי אֶלְעָזָר בֶּן עֲזַרְיָה הֲרֵי אֲנִי כְּבֶן שִׁבְעִים שָׁנָה וְלֹא זָכִיתִי שֶׁתֵּאָמֵר יְצִיאַת מִצְרַיִם בַּלֵּילוֹת עַד שֶׁדְּרָשָׁהּ בֶּן זוֹמָא, שֶׁנֶּאֱמַר: "לְמַעַן תִּזְכֹּר אֶת יוֹם צֵאתְךָ מֵאֶרֶץ מִצְרַיִם כֹּל יְמֵי חַיֶּיךָ". יְמֵי חַיֶּיךָ הַיָּמִים. כֹּל יְמֵי חַיֶּיךָ הַלֵּילוֹת. וַחֲכָמִים אוֹמְרִים יְמֵי חַיֶּיךָ הָעוֹלָם הַזֶּה. כֹּל יְמֵי חַיֶּיךָ לְהָבִיא לִימוֹת הַמָּשִׁיחַ:

בָּרוּךְ הַמָּקוֹם בָּרוּךְ הוּא בָּרוּךְ שֶׁנָּתַן תּוֹרָה לְעַמּוֹ יִשְׂרָאֵל. בָּרוּךְ הוּא. כְּנֶגֶד אַרְבָּעָה בָנִים דִּבְּרָה תוֹרָה. אֶחָד חָכָם. וְאֶחָד רָשָׁע. וְאֶחָד תָּם. וְאֶחָד שֶׁאֵינוֹ יוֹדֵעַ לִשְׁאֹל:

Divine Will, irrevocable Desire for the Jewish People, is numerically 346. Between them stands MoSheH, numerically 345. Moshe, the Tzaddik — the central point of the Jewish People, the archetypal point of all Jewish souls — will help us become conscious of the Shmad we are facing, become aware of our *unawareness* of God. He will then help us traverse the chasm between Shmad and Ratzon, and see us through the paradox of irrevocable Desire. The Tzaddik will also kindle the desire for God which lies buried in our hearts, enabling us to then experience *God's* irrevocable Desire for us (*Likutey Moharan* I, 215; *Likutey Halakhot, Birkhot Hashachar* 5:22,61-2).

No matter how low we may fall, no matter how removed we may be, we can always return to God, the Ever-Present.

For *this* point we praise God; for making us His People, for giving us the Torah.

כנגד ארבעה בנים — FOUR VOICES TOGETHER

Every letter in the Torah refers to and is the root of a Jewish soul. Each one of us is somehow linked to a specific letter.

Thus, the Torah encompasses the entire stratum of Jewishness. From the greatest Tzaddik to the greatest sinner — together. The Torah is relevant to all and addresses a unique message to each individual. Let each one of us search for his letter, his message, with sincere honesty — through the eyes of his personal life-experiences (*Nachat HaShulchan*).

*

Rabbi Elazar son of Azaryah said: I am like a man of seventy years, yet I was never able to prove that one is obliged to mention the Exodus at night, until Ben Zoma explained it. It is written in the Torah: 'That you may remember the day when you came out of the land of Egypt, all the days of your life' (Deuteronomy 16:3). 'The days of your life' refers to the days; 'all the days of your life' includes the nights. The Sages taught: 'The days of your life' refers to this world; 'all the days of your life' refers to the time of Mashiach.

Blessed is the Ever-Present, blessed is He. Blessed is the One Who has given the Torah to His people Israel, blessed is He. The Torah speaks of four sons: a wise one, a wicked one, a simple one, and one who does not know how to ask.

אמר רבי אלעזר בן עזריה — THE LIGHT OF NIGHT

There are *days* we feel enlightened. We are in touch with ourselves. Feel close to God. In tune with our personal missions.

On these days we remind ourselves that the Redemption was premature. We were not ready, we did not earn it with merit. The account is still open. The debt has yet to be covered in full. We pay it with *our* "exile." Tomorrow we may be in the Dark. Let us not be complacent in the Light of this *day*.

There are days we feel pessimistic and dejected. Detached from ourselves. Alienated from God. Strayed from our missions.

Rabbi Elazar ben Azaryah said: Recall the Redemption, *all* the days — even when it is *night!*

On these days, the *nights* of our lives, we must also recall the Redemption. We *know* the Redeemer will deliver us from "exile," just as He delivered the Jewish People from Exile. God will redeem our suffering. He will give meaning to our torment, transform our affliction to joy. He has bound Himself to do this. And it is this which enlightens our Darkness.

From the Sages we learn: Recall the Redemption, *all* the days — even in the days of the Mashiach. Even in the Eternal Light of that Day, we will recall the first Redemption, the original source of our courage (*Nachat HaShulchan*).

ברוך שנתן תורה — THE POINT OF JEWISHNESS

Why *did* God choose the Jewish People from all the nations? Why *did* He "take out a nation from among a nation," when there was no basic difference in their behavior? Why *did* He bind Himself to redeem a People no matter what they do?

The answer is beyond our comprehension. Divine Wisdom. A point we cannot fathom. It is the very *point* of Jewishness in every Jewish heart.

ShMaD, annihilation, whether physical or spiritual, is numerically 344. RaTZON,

חָכָם מָה הוּא אוֹמֵר? "מָה הָעֵדוֹת וְהַחֻקִּים וְהַמִּשְׁפָּטִים אֲשֶׁר צִוָּה יְהוָה אֱלֹהֵינוּ אֶתְכֶם". וְאַף אַתָּה אֱמֹר לוֹ כְּהִלְכוֹת הַפֶּסַח, אֵין מַפְטִירִין אַחַר הַפֶּסַח אֲפִיקוֹמָן:

hears. He listens to hear the underlying messages being conveyed so that he can help those in need, assist those who are lacking. We must also learn to hear ourselves, to hear our own true inner voice. Listen to the silent speech, the incessant thoughts of the mind. *"Mah hu o'mer?"* — What is it really trying to tell me?

Speech also has very great power. That which we talk about will have a self-fulfilling effect upon our lives. There are times we may feel distant from God or insincere in our speech and devotions. We feel Unwise. Despite these feelings, indeed, because of them, we need muster our enthusiasm and talk about closeness to God or emulate sincere prayer. This is Wisdom. And, if we are aware of what we are doing and open our hearts to the experience, our feelings and emotions will follow (*Likutey Moharan* II, 44; *Rabbi Nachman's Wisdom* #174).

"Chakham mah hu" — How do we identify the wise one? *"O'mer"* — listen to him speak.

"Chakham mah hu" — how can we become the wise one? *"O'mer"* — through speaking.

חכם — THE WISE SELF: WISDOM WITH MEASURE

When the wise one inquires about the Divine Laws, we tell him everything; down to the very last Halakhah of the Pesach: the Law of Afikoman.

But when he is wise and omniscient in his own eyes, when the Wise Self seeks to delve beyond human comprehension, we tell him: After the *Peh-sach,* we do not partake of the *Afiku-man!*

Peh is the mouth; Sach is the power of speech (*Pri Etz Chaim,* 21:7). Afiku-man (Aramaic): literally, bring on different kinds of desserts.

After the *Peh-sach* — after discussing the Revealed Torah about which it is permissible for the mouth to speak — we do not partake of the *Afikoman* — we do not discuss "the desserts," the Hidden Mysteries which cannot be spoken about openly in this world (*Likutey Halakhot, Pesach* 9:7-8).

After the meal, the taste of the Pesach must remain in our mouths (*Pesachim* 119b; *Orach Chaim* 478). After all the intricacies and deep explanations we have spoken about and understood, we must still retain Pure Faith. God's ways can never really be understood. The Pesach denotes that faith. In Egypt, the Jewish People slaughtered the Paschal Lamb with Pure Faith. They didn't understand at all.

Sometimes, the question of the Wise Self indicates his overriding expectation to experience God, to partake of the Divine. Then we tell him: Yes, a Jew must always yearn to experience God, to see and feel himself standing before Him. But we must not let this become the sole criterion and reason for our devotion. The

The wise son, what does he say? 'What are the statements, regulations and laws that God has commanded you?' (Deuteronomy 6:20). Instruct him in the laws of Pesach, that after eating the Pesach sacrifice, we do not eat anything!

Four Children: the wise, the wayward, the simple, the sleeping.

Four Worlds: Atzilut, Beriyah, Yetzirah, Asiyah.

All are essential to the Divine Plan of Creation. Each manifests a different aspect of the Divine.

All the children, all the Jewish souls, are integral to the Jewish People. Symbolic of the four levels of Jewish Awareness. All are intrinsic to God's Plan for humanity. Each is imbued with a unique way of perceiving the Divine. Only *together,* is the unity of the Jewish People complete (cf. *VaYikra Rabbah* 30:12; *Pri Etz Chaim* 21:7; *Sha'ar HaMitzvot, Shmini*).

The wise one. His wisdom makes him beloved. Yet, sometimes, he is enchanted with his own sagacity. Teach him to use his abilities with measure.

The wayward one. His mistake is that he perceives of *himself* as evil. Show him that this wickedness is not his birthright. It is an acquired trait, a trait from which he can be set free. It must, however, be made clear to him that his current behavior will not earn him redemption.

The simple one. Do not be fooled by his simplicity. He may be well aware of his genius, but he does not flaunt it. He knows the evil tendency within him, but maintains his innocence.

The sleeping one. He is the child who is unable to ask. He is unaware of his unique capabilities, uninspired by what he sees in others. His soul is like tinder. It waits to be ignited by the spark of God within him, by someone who will tell him *just that...* with the right words and in the right way.

Rather than search in others, we must delve into our*selves.* We all, to varying degrees, have aspects of the Four Children — the Four Selves — within us. We must integrate the positive elements and rechannel the negative.

As we hear the voices of the children, as we learn how to handle them, let us also learn how to deal with the voices of the different selves inside us. Only together, is *our* Jewishness complete.

חכם מה הוא אומר — LEARN TO LISTEN, LEARN TO SPEAK

Speech is the essence of man. That which a person talks about and the way he speaks — his words and phrases, his intonations of enthusiasm or indifference, sincerity or cynicism — reveals what he really has in his heart (*Likutey Moharan* I, 43, 56, 173).

"*Mah hu o'mer?*" — What is he really saying? Learn to listen. Learn to hear. Learn to feel and relate. When others talk, the wise man doesn't apply preconceived notions. He listens. When others speak, the wise man doesn't classify and judge. He

רָשָׁע מָה הוּא אוֹמֵר ? "מָה הָעֲבוֹדָה הַזֹּאת לָכֶם". לָכֶם וְלֹא
לוֹ. וּלְפִי שֶׁהוֹצִיא אֶת עַצְמוֹ מִן הַכְּלָל כָּפַר בָּעִקָּר. וְאַף אַתָּה
הַקְהֵה אֶת שִׁנָּיו וֶאֱמָר לוֹ. "בַּעֲבוּר זֶה עָשָׂה יְהוָה לִי בְּצֵאתִי
מִמִּצְרָיִם". לִי וְלֹא לוֹ. אִלּוּ הָיָה שָׁם לֹא הָיָה נִגְאָל:

say." We shall tell ourselves: "God passed over the houses of those Jews who lived amongst the Egyptians" — of those who had all but entirely assimilated. So, too, will God redeem those who are still lost in the modern-day Mitzrayim (*Oneg Shabbat,* p. 183).

To illuminate his soul, to kindle his heart, the wicked one must come in contact with a Tzaddik. The more distant one is from God, the greater the Light needed to elevate him (*Likutey Moharan* I, 30:1-2). For this reason, the wise one — Atzilut, the highest World — is juxtaposed to the wayward one — Asiyah, the lowest World (*Pri Etz Chaim,* 21:7; *Likutey Halakhot, Netilat Yadaim* 6:16). The Tzaddik will *know* through to his heart. He will be able to reach him.

And sometimes, the mockery is only a facade for inner confusion, a defense for his own lack of surety. Deep down, he craves guidance. The Tzaddik, because he knows how to listen, can tell that the wayward one's scoffing is actually a cry for help. He perceives of *himself* as wicked. He cannot see himself as worthy in God's eyes.

The Tzaddik will tell him: "With Pure Faith, I accepted upon myself to carry out the Divine Will. I did not question how can *I,* in the shackles of my physical existence, take responsibility for such an awesome task? And, 'For *this,* did God perform miracles when I went forth from Egypt. But as for you, had you been *there,* you would not have been redeemed.' "

Explicit is rebuke! When we are confronted with the stark contrast between where we could and should be and where we really are, we are devastated. We look within ourselves for some merit, some redeeming feature. We cannot accept such total rejection (*Tzaddik* #569).

Implicit is profound guidance and encouragement! *No one* was really worthy of the Redemption, yet God took us out. God, then, will extricate *anyone* from his personal bondage, provided he turns to Him in Pure Faith.

Ultimately, God will redeem every Jewish soul. Only there, in the partial and temporary redemption from Egypt, were some souls not worthy. But in the Redemption to Come, we will *all* go out. Even those who were unworthy and died in Egypt will participate in the Ultimate Future (*Asarah Ma'amarot, Chikur HaDin* 3:21; *Yisrael Kedoshim,* p. 61d; They were not yet "ripe," *Shir HaShirim Rabbah* 2:13).

49

The wicked son, what does he say? 'What does this service mean to you' (Exodus 12:26). 'To you' [he says] but not about himself. Because he has excluded himself from the community, he has denied [the Exodus and] God. Therefore, you must answer bluntly, 'Because of this God did for me when *I* went out from Egypt' (Exodus 13:8). 'For me,' not for him. Had he been there, he would not have been redeemed.

essential service of God is the Halakhot: the simple, physical acts of the Mitzvot. Indeed, devotion to God is greatest when it involves self-sacrifice, when we are not motivated by inspiration. On the other hand, we dare not be presumptuous and self-wise. If God does provide us with "Pesach," with Higher Awareness, we should see it as Divine Grace and not as our due (*Nachat HaShulchan*).

רשע — THE WAYWARD SELF: A REASSURING REBUKE

From the way he speaks, we know that the wayward one — the Wayward Self — is not searching for answers. His words are similar to those of the Wise Self, but his intonation is one of mockery. He is just airing his "questions," getting them out into the open (*Oneg Shabbat,* p. 182).

To argue his case, the Wayward Self uses what he sees as clear logic. He "shows" the Halakhah to affirm his views. What he is really showing is how he feels about God. His so called openness may be no more than a means for venting hidden frustrations. A sign of his spiritual bankruptcy.

The Tzaddik will expose the emptiness of his argument; unmask the concealed emotions. Perhaps the Wayward Self is angry with God. Perhaps he is rationalizing, seeking to explain away his lack of devotion. As long as we hide from and keep hidden how we *really feel* about God, we remain with inner peace unattainable and world peace beyond us. Mankind will continue to blunder. The Tzaddik teaches us how to bring these buried thoughts and emotions to the surface. Then he lets us know how we *should* feel about God.

The Tzaddik also makes it clear that when we hear the Wayward Self raising these "questions" within us, it does not mean that we are evil. Rather, let us hear in them a message, a call to strengthen our faith.

The "questions" of the wayward one, the Wayward Self, are asked. They are answered. And, once answered, others — including the "others" inside ourselves — are silenced (*Likutey Halakhot, Gittin* 4:8).

The wayward one has been vindicated. He, too, serves a purpose in God's Plan. He is rightfully one of the Four Holy Sons (*Sha'ar Hamitzvot, Shmini; Pri Etz Chaim* 21:7).

He himself, though? Ultimately, even the wayward one will be rectified. In response to his "question" the Torah prescribes (Exodus 12:26-27), "And you shall

תָּם מַה הוּא אוֹמֵר? "מַה זֹּאת"? "וְאָמַרְתָּ אֵלָיו בְּחֹזֶק יָד
הוֹצִיאָנוּ יְהֹוָה מִמִּצְרַיִם מִבֵּית עֲבָדִים":

וְשֶׁאֵינוֹ יוֹדֵעַ לִשְׁאֹל אַתְּ פְּתַח לוֹ. שֶׁנֶּאֱמַר: "וְהִגַּדְתָּ לְבִנְךָ
בַּיּוֹם הַהוּא לֵאמֹר בַּעֲבוּר זֶה עָשָׂה יְהֹוָה לִי בְּצֵאתִי
מִמִּצְרָיִם":

יָכוֹל מֵראשׁ חֹדֶשׁ? תַּלְמוּד לוֹמַר בַּיּוֹם הַהוּא: אִי בַּיּוֹם
הַהוּא, יָכוֹל מִבְּעוֹד יוֹם? תַּלְמוּד לוֹמַר בַּעֲבוּר זֶה:
בַּעֲבוּר זֶה לֹא אָמַרְתִּי אֶלָּא בְּשָׁעָה שֶׁיֵּשׁ: מַצָּה, וּמָרוֹר,
מֻנָּחִים לְפָנֶיךָ:

מִתְּחִלָּה עוֹבְדֵי עֲבוֹדָה זָרָה הָיוּ אֲבוֹתֵינוּ. וְעַכְשָׁיו קֵרְבָנוּ
הַמָּקוֹם לַעֲבוֹדָתוֹ, שֶׁנֶּאֱמַר, "וַיֹּאמֶר יְהוֹשֻׁעַ אֶל כָּל הָעָם, כֹּה
אָמַר יְהֹוָה אֱלֹהֵי יִשְׂרָאֵל בְּעֵבֶר הַנָּהָר יָשְׁבוּ אֲבוֹתֵיכֶם מֵעוֹלָם

month come to a close, when the moon immediately begins a new cycle. As soon
as we become aware of the Darkness, we, too, become enlightened by even the
slightest indication of Light.

One might presume therefore that the *"Light* of the New Moon" is sufficient by
which to recite the Haggadah. Perhaps this Inspiration, the Lesson of relentless
and spontaneous *starting anew,* is sufficient to experience the Redemption? No!
We must still have Matzah and Maror. These are the tangible things which enable
us to internalize the Redemption (*Nachat HaShulchan*).

מתחילה — UNHOLY BEGINNINGS

How is it that we find Jewish souls grappling with impulses that are typically
non-Jewish? How is it that we find holy souls struggling with the urge to commit an
unholy deed? "Perhaps my soul isn't purely Jewish?" The self-doubt is tormenting.

The Haggadah tells us: Experiencing such impulses is nothing out of the ordinary.
In fact, it is inherent in the very nature of the Jewish People. Was not Avraham,
our forefather, a product of pagan civilization? Did not his father, Terach, submit
him to execution for smashing the heathen images?

The simple son, what does he say? 'What does [all] this mean?'' To him you shall say, 'With a strong hand God brought us out from Egypt, from slavery' (Exodus 13:14).

As as for the son who does not know how to ask, you must begin for him, as is written: 'You shall tell your son on that day "Because of this, God did for me when I went out from Egypt" ' (Exodus 13:8).

One might think that the obligation [to recite the story of the Exodus] applies from the first day of Nissan. Therefore the Torah says: 'On that day.' 'That day' might be understood [that the Seder is to begin] during the day. Therefore, the Torah adds, 'Because of *this*' — only at a time when Matzah and Maror are before you.

Initially our ancestors were idol worshipers, but now God has brought us to serve Him. As is written: 'And Yehoshua spoke to the people: God, Lord of Israel, said, "Your fathers dwelt beyond the [Euphrates] River,

תם — THE SIMPLE SELF: A SIMPLE ANSWER

The simple one? The Simple Self asks a "simple" question. *Mah zot? —* What is this?" Mah denotes Torah; Zot implies Divine Manifestation (*Zohar* III:297b). Thus, Divine Manifestation is only via the Torah.

The Simple Self asks the obvious: "The Exodus from Egypt came about through Divine Manifestation, did it not? And it occurred prior to the Giving of the Torah. If so, how was this possible?"

Simple is the answer we give to the Simple Self: For this reason God had to take us out with a Strong Hand (*Nachat HaShulchan*).

The simple one is satisfied. He seeks no further explanation; no sophisticated, intellectual exposition. His *soul* understands (*Tzaddik* #271, 388).

ושאינו יודע לשאול — THE SLEEPING SELF: AN AWAKENING OF LIGHT

Finally, there is the one who is unable to ask, the Sleeping Self. When we come in contact with one who is incapable or even ashamed to ask about God — when we experience a spiritual vacuum, a sleep, inside ourselves — it is *we* who must take the initiative. With the great Light which enters the world on the Seder night, we must illuminate all places. The "father" is aware and awake. He must rouse his "son" to ask. In others and in *ourselves,* we must awaken the Sleeping Self (*Nachat HaShulchan*).

יכול מראש חדש — INSUFFICIENT LIGHT

The one unable to ask corresponds to the Divine Manifestation at its lowest level. This is symbolized by the moon at wane. Yet, no sooner does the lunar

תֶּרַח אֲבִי אַבְרָהָם וַאֲבִי נָחוֹר וַיַּעַבְדוּ אֱלֹהִים אֲחֵרִים: וָאֶקַּח
אֶת אֲבִיכֶם אֶת אַבְרָהָם מֵעֵבֶר הַנָּהָר וָאוֹלֵךְ אוֹתוֹ בְּכָל אֶרֶץ
כְּנַעַן וָאַרְבֶּה אֶת זַרְעוֹ וָאֶתֶּן לוֹ אֶת יִצְחָק. וָאֶתֵּן לְיִצְחָק אֶת
יַעֲקֹב וְאֶת עֵשָׂו, וָאֶתֵּן לְעֵשָׂו אֶת הַר שֵׂעִיר לָרֶשֶׁת אוֹתוֹ,
וְיַעֲקֹב וּבָנָיו יָרְדוּ מִצְרָיִם״:

בָּרוּךְ שׁוֹמֵר הַבְטָחָתוֹ לְיִשְׂרָאֵל. בָּרוּךְ הוּא. שֶׁהַקָּדוֹשׁ בָּרוּךְ
הוּא חִשַּׁב אֶת הַקֵּץ לַעֲשׂוֹת. כְּמָה שֶׁאָמַר לְאַבְרָהָם אָבִינוּ
בִּבְרִית בֵּין הַבְּתָרִים. שֶׁנֶּאֱמַר: ״וַיֹּאמֶר לְאַבְרָם יָדוֹעַ תֵּדַע כִּי-
גֵר יִהְיֶה זַרְעֲךָ בְּאֶרֶץ לֹא לָהֶם וַעֲבָדוּם וְעִנּוּ אֹתָם אַרְבַּע
מֵאוֹת שָׁנָה: וְגַם אֶת הַגּוֹי אֲשֶׁר יַעֲבֹדוּ דָּן אָנֹכִי וְאַחֲרֵי כֵן
יֵצְאוּ בִּרְכֻשׁ גָּדוֹל״:

יכסה המצות ויקח הכוס בידו: ויאחזהו עד מצלינו מידם
וְהִיא שֶׁעָמְדָה לַאֲבוֹתֵינוּ וְלָנוּ. שֶׁלֹּא אֶחָד בִּלְבָד עָמַד
עָלֵינוּ לְכַלּוֹתֵנוּ אֶלָּא שֶׁבְּכָל דּוֹר וָדוֹר עוֹמְדִים עָלֵינוּ
לְכַלּוֹתֵנוּ. וְהַקָּדוֹשׁ בָּרוּךְ הוּא מַצִּילֵנוּ מִיָּדָם:

Contraposing the Land of Israel is Mitzrayim (Egypt). In this land there are no
miracles, no prayer, no faith. When we utter our prayers without faith in their
power, we have been spiritually exiled into "Mitzrayim." No matter where we are.

God promised the Land to Avraham. But Avraham lacked a point of faith.
"How can I really know?" he asked, fearing that God's Plan could be altered by
human misdeeds. He could not understand how it is not. (The *Ramban* on Genesis
15:7 teaches that Man has free choice. Even so, God has His Plan: the future of the Jewish People.
In the end, God will have *His* way. See also *Likutey Halakhot, Shutfim B'karka* 5:10). The moment
Avraham requested this knowledge, God informed him: "You wish to know which
can only be *known* through faith? Then know that you and your descendants are
already in exile" (*Likutey Moharan* I, 7:1, 9:5).

If so, then the Jewish People were indeed exiled in "Mitzrayim" for 400 years!

והיא שעמדה — UPLIFTING
KOS is numerically 86.

The Divine Name Elohim alludes to Malkhut, the Divine Manifestation indicating
faith, the source of the Jewish People. ELoHIM is also 86.

[including] Terach, the father of Avraham and the father of Nachor, and they served other gods. And I took your father Avraham from beyond the River and led him throughout the land of Canaan, and I multiplied his seed and gave him Yitzchak. And I gave to Yitzchak [two sons], Yaakov and Esav; to Esav I gave Mount Seir, to possess it, but Yaakov and his sons went down to Egypt" ' (Joshua 24:3,4).

Blessed is He who keeps His promise to Israel, blessed is He! For the Holy One, blessed is He, planned the end [of their bondage], in order to fulfill what He had said to our father Avraham at the Covenant of the Halves. As is written: 'And He said to Avram: "You should know for certain that your descendants shall be strangers in a land that is not their own; and they will enslave them, and shall treat them harshly, for four hundred years. But I will also judge the nation that they shall serve, and afterwards they shall leave with great wealth" ' (Genesis 15:13-14).

The Matzot are covered, and the cups of wine are lifted.

It is this that has stood by our fathers and us; for not only one [enemy] has risen up against us to destroy us, but in all generations they rise up against us to destroy us. But the Holy One, Blessed is He, saves us from their hands.

From the time of Avraham until the Final Redemption, the Jewish People must go through a purification process; cleansing itself of the gentile tendencies in its nature. And specifically those souls which *can* do it, have been entrusted with the task.

On this night of the Jewish People's continuous rebirth we recall these Unholy Beginnings. But then we call out: "And NOW! God has brought us to His service." At this precise moment we can commence to tread upon the path of our forefathers. It matters not *what* we have done until now.

Thus we repeat Joshua's words, directed at the entire nation. *Anyone* who desires to come closer to God needs to be aware of this (*Nachat HaShulchan*). Let *no one* shy away for fear of failure. Even Terach was purified through Avraham's selfless struggles. Eventually, even *he* was brought to Jewishness and was reincarnated as Nachum Ish Gamzu, Rabbi Akiva's mentor (*Likutey Torah*, Job; *Bava Batra* 15b; *Sha'ar Hagilgulim* 36).

ברוך שומר — THE PROMISED LAND OF FAITH

The Land of Israel is very holy. It is beyond nature. It is a Land of Miracles, a Land of Prayer, a Land of Faith. When we truly have faith in the power of prayer, in the power of our personal prayer, we can perform miracles. Then, we live in "the Land." No matter where we are.

יַעֲמִיד הַכּוֹס וִיגַלֶּה הַמִּצְווֹת:

צֵא וּלְמַד מַה בִּקֵּשׁ לָבָן הָאֲרַמִּי לַעֲשׂוֹת לְיַעֲקֹב אָבִינוּ. שֶׁפַּרְעֹה לֹא גָזַר אֶלָּא עַל הַזְּכָרִים וְלָבָן בִּקֵּשׁ לַעֲקֹר אֶת הַכֹּל

restrain and repress human awareness of the Divine. When the Jewish People fell from their lofty level of awareness, when their Da'at went into "exile," they entered a physical exile. They became enslaved to the human Pharaoh in Egypt (*Pri Etz Chaim* 21:1; *Likutey Moharan* I, 62).

However, the control which "Pharaoh" commands is limited. He is not empowered to eradicate Godliness from the world. He can only decree on the "males." This is the Masculine, the dynamic experience of serving God with heightened perception and enthusiastic desire. (In the *Pri Etz Chaim* 21:7 we find that Pharaoh's decree: "HaBeN HaYiLOD HaYe'ORaH" [throw every newborn male into the Nile,] is numerically MayTZaR [with its three letters] — the constricted consciousness of the mind.) "Pharaoh" will prevent the Jewish People from coming to a Masculine Maturity, but he will allow the females to live. He will allow us to practice a Feminine, passive version of Jewishness. This serves his purpose. A decree against Awareness. When our mitzvot are performed with apathy, we cannot rise above our personal difficulties in serving God. And, we certainly cannot elevate the rest of the world towards the Ultimate Rectification.

To this aim, the king of Egypt kept us perpetually busy, our minds incessantly preoccupied with worldly illusions (see Exodus 5:4-9). Even today, "Pharaoh" allows us to toil assiduously in the intricacies of Torah study (cf. *Zohar* I:27a) and zealously exert ourselves in rigid stringencies of the Halakhah. He also keeps our minds troubled with the unanswerable paradoxes in Judaism.... Anything we ask for, he will grant us. With one exception. "Pharaoh" denies us the thing we need most: the time and composure to yearn for greater awareness of God, so that we might become aware of what our Jewishness is all about (*Likutey Halakhot, Petter Chamor* 3).

As our Da'at, our awareness of God, descends into "exile," we also become unaware of ourselves, of our alienation from God. We aren't even aware that we aren't aware (*Sefer Baal Shem Tov, Shemot* #16-18; *Panim Yafot,* Exodus 3:7). We don't know what there is to be aware of. Our Jewishness becomes a role we play. We act it out as if we mean it for real. Our mitzvot become emotionless motions, our prayers heartless words (cf. *Rabbi Nachman's Wisdom* #111). Our main motivation may be nothing more than social conformance, or adherence to tradition. Or perhaps, the egoistic gratification of being "good Jews." And so — in our "exile," our Unawareness — the Voice of God's Will becomes no more than the internal voice of our natural tendencies; and God Himself, merely the symbol of our self-righteousness.

If only we would become aware of our predicament, this in itself would be great in the eyes of God.

55

The cups are returned to the table and the Matzot uncovered.

Go and learn what Lavan the Aramean planned to do to our father Yaakov! Pharaoh decreed that only the male children [should be put to

We lift up the cup of wine, the KOS. We lift up the fallen Shekhinah, the Divine Manifestation of Malkhut. We lift up our faith. We uplift ourselves and declare:

Many are the counterforces which obstruct the Jewish People from elevating humanity to its ultimate goal. Many are the hindering forces which manifest themselves in the physical and spiritual/emotional world of every individual Jew who seeks to come close to God.

Even more myriad, though, are the Wonders of Guidance, the encouragement and support which God provides for all who *truly* seek to come close to Him.

It is the strength of faith we derive from those Wonders which enables us to overcome all the adverse experiences we encounter in our path (*Likutey Halakhot, Basar Bechalav* 4:13-14).

צא ולמד — GUIDELINES TO SELF-REDEMPTION

Throughout the Torah narratives, we hear of individuals and nations who were enemies of the Jewish People. These were real people. The events took place in this world.

On a deeper level, they symbolize and represent the counterforces which oppose the forces of holiness. Each of these individuals or nations is the embodiment, so to speak, of a particular force (*Likutey Halakhot, Basar Bechalav* 4:13). Fittingly, the names of the real people were identical with or indicative of those of the counterforces they embodied (cf. *Zohar* II:17a).

These forces have manifested themselves throughout history and on a world scale. The repeated physical persecution of the Jewish People will attest to that. The counterforces also manifest themselves on a very personal level, presenting opposition to each and every Jewish soul. We may experience them as internal dialogue or as external persuasion. Any negative thought or emotion interfering with our Jewishness tells us that these forces are real.

To master these opponents, we must first become aware of them and their methods and arguments. We must identify them as forces within our internal, spiritual world, yet as external and foreign to our real Jewish selves. Only by being "redeemed" from our erroneous self-identification with them, can we learn to fight them. If, however, we identify with these forces, we remain hopelessly blind to their control over us.

We need Guidelines to self-redemption.

The Torah narratives are our guidelines; teaching us to deal with the "Pharaohs" and "Lavans" of our lives. Let us follow the Torah's advice.

פרעה לא גזר — A DECREE AGAINST AWARENESS

"Pharaoh" is king of "MiTZRayIM." He rules over the MayTZaRIM — the constrictions of the Mind, the limitations of Awareness. It is his function to

שֶׁנֶּאֱמַר: "אֲרַמִּי אֹבֵד אָבִי וַיֵּרֶד מִצְרַיְמָה וַיָּגָר שָׁם בִּמְתֵי
מְעָט וַיְהִי שָׁם לְגוֹי גָּדוֹל עָצוּם וָרָב":

God Himself." His argument can be very convincing. ("Lavan" and "Bilaam" are one concept, one force. Some sources even state that Lavan and Bilaam were one and the same person, or a reincarnation. Thus, Lavan's penchant for pride, though not immediately apparent in the Torah's depiction of him, does clearly manifest itself in Bilaam, an individual well known for his haughty arrogance.) (*Avot* 5:19; *Likutey Moharan* I, 12:1)

Standing at the 50th, the most advanced Level of Holiness, desiring nothing but the performance of God's Will, we must overcome an equally advanced Level of Unholiness — the counterforce of "Lavan" and his attack against Jewishness. When we lose awareness that our attainments are a gift of God, when we seek credit for ourselves, we stand over an abyss which descends to the lowest levels. We become bound to an arrogance which has no bounds; ready to do anything to save our pride (*Likutey Halakhot, Netilat Yadaim Shacharit* 3:5).

"Lavan" also functions below "Pharaoh." The Jewish People in Egypt had nearly slipped below the 49th level, into the bottomless void of "Lavan" — Despair! Their entire lives they had been slaves to Pharaoh. Their existence was a continuous string of transgressions. Had the Redemption not happened when it did, "Lavan" would have entered their minds and convinced them there was no hope of ever changing (*Likutey Halakhot, Tefillin* 6:35).

"Lavan" continues to use this approach even today. When he cannot inflate us with "Awareness" so that we become haughty and replace Jewishness with *Self*ishness, he deflates us with "despair" so that we lose our hope in Jewishness altogether. Here as well, "Lavan" speaks to us in a voice which each person perceives as his own: "Certainly someone who has sinned as much as you have, who has ignored God's Will and followed his own whims, can never hope to improve. Who are you trying to fool?" His argument can be very convincing.

Even so, we must not listen to "Lavan." We cannot afford to let him stifle our arousal and uproot our Jewishness. Pay him no mind when he reproves us that just yesterday we committed such and such a transgression... (*Likutey Halakhot, Basar Bechalav* 4:12).

"Pharaoh" we can "work with"; we can talk to him. God ordered Moshe to speak to Pharaoh. Ultimately even the ruler of Egypt was himself brought to an awareness of God (*Pirkey d'Rabbi Eliezer* #43; *Yalkut Shimoni, Yonah* 3). We must likewise talk to the "Pharaoh" within us. We must talk to God honestly, so that "Pharaoh" will hear. We must also listen for what "Pharaoh" is saying, so that we can know how to respond. With time and effort, we will eventually hear our own "Pharaoh" telling us: "You know better than that. Don't allow yourself to be fooled by my illusions."

death], but Lavan wanted to uproot the whole [Jewish nation], as is written: 'The Aramean sought to destroy my forefather. He [Yaakov] went down to Egypt and lived there, few in number; and there he became a nation, great, mighty and numerous' (Deuteronomy 26:5).

> *The predictions for the year were ominous. A strange grain-disease was spreading, and whoever ate from the infected wheat, went insane. The disease was coming this way.*
>
> *The king of the land conferred with his trusted prime minister. "What shall we do? We haven't enough grain stored to supply for the entire population."*
>
> *"As rulers of this country," suggested the prime minister, "it is imperative that we put aside sufficient grain, so that we won't have to eat from this year's harvest."*
>
> *"But wait," retorted the king. "If we do that, we will be the only sane ones. Everyone else will be insane. They will therefore think that they are sane, and it is we who are the insane." The king thought for a moment and then said, "We must also eat from this grain. But we will put a mark on our foreheads, so that at least we will know that we are insane!* (Rabbi Nachman's Stories #26, p. 481).

We don't always *have the courage* to rise above social norms. Sometimes we also "eat the grain" and follow the crowd. But we must not succumb to "Pharaoh's" decree. Let us at least be aware that there is more to be aware of, more to Jewishness....

לבן בקש — ATTACKING JEWISHNESS THROUGH PRIDE AND DESPAIR

Yet, "Pharaoh's" power has its limits. He can counter only the limited 49 Levels of Holiness. Not so "Lavan." His power is virtually limitless. He can even counter the 50th, the all encompassing Level of Holiness. (This highest Level of Holiness is symbolized by a dazzling white, a color that comprises all colors. Fittingly, its counterforce of evil is "Lavan" — the *white one*.) This 50th level indicates a deep desire for nothing but the performance of God's Will. It is the source of the Jewish People, of our Jewishness. "Lavan" aims to uproot it entirely. (The physical exile under Pharaoh was also limited. There was a time limit of 400 years. The exile under Lavan — the source of Esav-Edom, our present diaspora — has no specific limits.) (*Likutey Halakhot, Behemah V'Chayah T'horah 4:17, Kaddish 1:4*)

A person may have surmounted "Pharaoh" and his illusions, he may have come to Higher Awareness of God. Now he is confronted by an even greater delusion — that of the *self*. "Lavan" enters a person's mind in the guise of holiness (*Likutey Moharan*, I, 1; *Likutey Halakhot, Matanah 5:13*). He is a master at this deception. In a voice which the person perceives as his own, "Lavan" tells him: "Certainly someone as 'holy' and as scholarly as you deserves great honor. To deny it, to humble yourself and refrain from demanding your due would be nothing less than a demeaning and belittling, not of your person, but of the very glory of the Torah and even

‏"וַיֵּרֶד מִצְרַיְמָה". אָנוּס עַל פִּי הַדִּבּוּר:

‏"וַיָּגָר שָׁם". מְלַמֵּד שֶׁלֹּא יָרַד יַעֲקֹב אָבִינוּ לְהִשְׁתַּקֵּעַ בְּמִצְרַיִם אֶלָּא לָגוּר שָׁם. שֶׁנֶּאֱמַר: "וַיֹּאמְרוּ אֶל פַּרְעֹה לָגוּר בָּאָרֶץ

We need therefore speak about God and converse with Him. In our own native tongues — our own Aramaic — we need verbalize, declare and confess in spontaneous prayer. And through this, we will become aware of the contrast between "Lavan the Aramean" and the Holy Tongue. We will then recognize "Lavan's" deviousness; realize how incongruous our actions are with what we *know* to be God's Will.

Prayer in one's native tongue is the elevation, the sanctification of the nobler elements of the "Aramaic tongue." We perfect our personal "Holy Tongue" and incorporate it into the Holy Language. Then "Lavan" has no influence upon us (*Likutey Moharan* I, 19).

Like our forefather Yaakov, we have fled from Lavan and uncovered his tactics (*Likutey Halakhot, Tefillin* 6:35).

אנוס על פי הדבור — IMPELLED PRAYER

It may have been beyond our control. Sometimes we feel almost compelled to transgress God's Will, we feel *drawn* into Mitzrayim (*Likutey Moharan* II, 48; *Tzidkat HaTzaddik* #43, 156).

God, though, *never* suspends our free will. We may actually feel we are being coerced, but this is only "by Divine Decree." It's a test. God's test. He wants us to realize our potential. Only by our overcoming these obstacles to fulfilling His Will can our latent capabilities be actualized.

To overcome our difficulties, to realize our potential, there must be Prayer — the expression of our inner desires. As we pray to God to transcend these obstacles, God helps us see ourselves doing so and it then becomes reality.

But sometimes, our voices are trapped. No words. No calling out. Everything caught in MayTZaR hagaron, the straits of our throat. The voice of holiness is suppressed. We feel hampered in expressing ourselves before God. Stuck! It may be social norms or personal inhibitions. Either way, it is MiTZRayim. We are in "exile" (*Pri Etz Chaim* 21:7).

God then intentionally provides us with obstacles, with difficulties, even with suffering. It is His way of motivating us, of impelling us, of nudging us along. We must make use of these "incentives" and turn to Him to help us transcend our limitations. Where do we start? With Prayer.

An'nus? — feeling compelled?

Al Pi HaDibur — your voice is in "exile."

Pray! Do what you can to speak out your heart before God (*Likutey Moharan* I, 66:4).

'He went down to Egypt' — impelled, by [God's] word.

'And he lived there' — this teaches that our father Yaakov did not go to Egypt to settle there permanently, just temporarily, as is written: 'And the sons of Yaakov said to Pharaoh: "We have come to live in this land

But from "Lavan" we must flee. Just as our forefather Yaakov did. We cannot deal with him, he is too beguiling. We cannot talk to him, he speaks a language of deceit. He is an impostor. His aim is to destroy us. He wants to extinguish the flame of holiness which burns deep in our hearts, to confound the very foundations of our Jewishness (*Likutey Halakhot, Tefillin* 6:35).

ארמי — DECEIT UNCOVERED

The story of the Exile and Redemption is now unfolded in the form of a commentary on the Viduy Bikurim, the First Fruits Confession (Deuteronomy 26:5-10). The season for bringing the first-fruits to the Temple commenced on the 50th day of the Omer Counting. This coincides with the Shavuot Festival — the day of the Giving of the Torah. Only with the Divine Guidance we derive from the Torah can we escape from "Lavan," the counterforce of the 50th level (*Likutey Halakhot, Behemah V'Chayah Tehorah* 4:22). The radiant truth of the Torah, the eternal Truth of God, will disperse the deceitful enlightenment of "Lavan." (Our forefather Yaakov embodied the Torah. His every action was an expression of it. He was therefore able to withstand Lavan even before the actual Giving of the Torah.)

The lesson of the First Fruits Confession is an important one. In presenting the Bikurim — the *new* fruit — we focus on the yearly, on the daily, and on the unremitting renewal and regenesis of each aspect of God's Creation. From this we can draw an inexhaustible faith in the power of our own renewal and self-resurgence. Unfailing belief in this God-given strength is what enables us to overcome the defeatist thoughts of "Lavan the Deceiver" who would have us believe that we are old and hardened, and cannot change (*Likutey Halakhot, Basar Bechalav* 4:13).

The required declaration over the first-fruits is called the Bikurim Confession (*Yad, Bikurim* 3:10). In order to draw from these wellsprings of renewal, there must be a process of Viduy: verbalization, declaration, confession.

"Lavan" wants to extinguish the flame of holiness — the spark of Jewishness — which burns deep in our hearts. But he knows we will not commit an obvious transgression of God's Will.

So he approaches us as the "Aramean." Aramaic is a sister language to the Holy Tongue. "Lavan" makes cunning use of this likeness. He enters our minds disguised as a holy obligation, a mitzvah! (*Likutey Halakhot, Matanah* 5:13). How blind we are to his true intentions! He will have us perpetrate grave and demoralizing acts, convincing us that we are fulfilling great and holy deeds. Sometimes, it is all but impossible to distinguish between his evil voice and the voice of holiness (*Likutey Halakhot, Cheylev V'Dam* 1:5-6).

בָּאנוּ כִּי אֵין מִרְעֶה לַצֹּאן אֲשֶׁר לַעֲבָדֶיךָ כִּי כָבֵד הָרָעָב בְּאֶרֶץ
כְּנַעַן וְעַתָּה יֵשְׁבוּ נָא עֲבָדֶיךָ בְּאֶרֶץ גֹּשֶׁן:

"בִּמְתֵי מְעָט" כְּמָה שֶׁנֶּאֱמַר: "בְּשִׁבְעִים נֶפֶשׁ יָרְדוּ אֲבֹתֶיךָ
מִצְרָיְמָה וְעַתָּה שָׂמְךָ יְהוָֹה אֱלֹהֶיךָ כְּכוֹכְבֵי הַשָּׁמַיִם לָרֹב":
וַיְהִי שָׁם לְגוֹי". מְלַמֵּד שֶׁהָיוּ יִשְׂרָאֵל מְצֻיָּנִים שָׁם:

בשבעים נפש — PROPHETIC SOULS

The seventy souls that went down into exile were the progenitors of the Jewish People. They embodied the Seventy Souls, the source of all Jewish souls, analogous to the seventy facets of Torah (*Likutey Moharan* I, 36:1). They comprised the full tapestry of Jewishness, the entire spectrum of Jew; from the holiest to the most remote (*Likutey Halakhot, Sukkah* 6:12).

"*B'shivim Nefesh* — with seventy souls — *Yordu Avosekha.*"

The Seventy Souls are also the source of prophecy; the seventy facets of the Torah being analogous to the spirit of prophecy. (See *Likutey Moharan* II, 8:7 that the Torah was transmitted via prophecy, and prophecy, in turn, reached its zenith with the giving of the Torah. Also see *Likutey Halakhot, Orlah* 4:10.) Thus, the seventy members of Yaakov's family who entered Egypt personified the prophetic spirit. The acronym for the above verse which tells of the "Jewish People's" descent into exile is NABiY, a prophet. Their very essence was prophecy.

Prayer is a function of prophecy. Prophecy is proportional to prayer. The prophet speaks the Word of God, his prayer *is* the Word of God. God makes his prayer a reality (*Likutey Moharan* II, 1:11; cf. *Bereishit Rabbah* 52:5; *Tikkuney Zohar* 21, p. 45a).

When any Jew, from whatever segment of the Seventy-Soul-tapestry of Jewishness, is confronted with personal exile in the constrictions of Mitzrayim — let him remember! Latent within himself is the wherewithal to overcome those limitations. The spirit of prophecy, the experience of prayer; they are within his reach. His birthright. The essence of his Jewish soul. He *can* uplift himself — to a more vivid perception of reality.

And, as we pray, as we yearn, God helps us see ourselves achieving that which we pray for. God makes our prayers reality.

מצויינים — JEWISH REGALIA: FOR NO REASON AT ALL!

Sometimes our spirits are low, our hearts heavy, our minds constricted. We lack the desire to serve God with enthusiasm. We are experiencing personal exile. Especially at these times, we must keep sight of our guideposts; persevere in the direction of our mission.

temporarily, for there is no pasture for the flocks that belong to your servants, for the hunger is harsh in the land of Canaan; now, please let your servants dwell in the land of Goshen" ' (Genesis 47:4)

'Few in number' — as is written: 'With seventy souls your fathers went down to Egypt, and now God has made you as numerous as the stars of heaven' (Deuteronomy 10:22).

'And there he became a nation' — which teaches that the Jews were distinctive there.

> *There are those of us who just can't seem to find happiness in life. There are those times in our normally happy lives when we just can't seem to find happiness. Whether chronic dejection or momentary discontent, our state of mind seems beyond control, our state of emotion compelled. If only we would know that there is meaning in our moods, we would then be able to overcome depression.*
>
> *There are souls which are meant to serve God from constrictions, destined to live all or part of life without satisfaction. Some of these souls are actually very sublime, but Divine Wisdom has predetermined their condition. If only they would know this and accept it as such, they would hasten the end to their suffering.*
>
> *And, in the end, the Benevolent One will make an accounting of all this pain and replace it with eternal rejoicing* (Sha'ar HaGilgulim 27).

ועתה ישבו בארץ גושן — TO DWELL IN THE JOY OF THE NOW

Sometimes we are in a situation, a state of mind or emotion from which we cannot presently escape. We may have even, God forbid, succumbed to the temptations of "Pharaoh"... become trapped in Mitzrayim.

Do not settle in the past. Do not permanently dwell in your predicament. The past — even from our "this-world" perspective — is already under the realm of God's Providence and beyond our jurisdiction. In the present, we need see the past as foreseen. Divinely given.

> *Free choice — life — is only now. By living right, now, the past is forgiven. We cannot choose now what to do or what we should have done in the past. We must view our past through the eyes of someone entrusted to correct another's errors. Living properly in the present — in the now — we correct the errors of the past.*

GoSheN is numerically SiMChaH, joy (353).

Let us dwell in Joy. Take courage. Reinforce virtues. Let us anticipate the time when we *will* leave Mitzraim, when the torment of "Pharaoh" will be all but forgotten (*Oneg Shabbat* p. 130).

"גָּדוֹל עָצוּם" כְּמָה שֶׁנֶּאֱמַר: "וּבְנֵי יִשְׂרָאֵל פָּרוּ וַיִּשְׁרְצוּ
וַיִּרְבּוּ וַיַּעַצְמוּ בִּמְאֹד מְאֹד וַתִּמָּלֵא הָאָרֶץ אֹתָם":

וָרָב כְּמָה שֶׁנֶּאֱמַר: "רְבָבָה כְּצֶמַח הַשָּׂדֶה נְתַתִּיךְ וַתִּרְבִּי
וַתִּגְדְּלִי וַתָּבֹאִי בַּעֲדִי עֲדָיִים שָׁדַיִם נָכוֹנוּ וּשְׂעָרֵךְ צִמֵּחַ וְאַתְּ
עֵרֹם וְעֶרְיָה: וָאֶעֱבֹר עָלַיִךְ וָאֶרְאֵךְ מִתְבּוֹסֶסֶת בְּדָמָיִךְ וָאֹמַר
לָךְ בְּדָמַיִךְ חֲיִי וָאֹמַר לָךְ בְּדָמַיִךְ חֲיִי":

Yet God *wants* to give, to share. To the infinitesimal degree that we are capable of receiving such knowledge, He *wants* us to experience His knowledge of Himself. So He attenuated His Infinity and divided the Indivisible. We can neither know how this was done nor even what it means. Nevertheless, God has allowed us to speak in such fashion so that we might have some inkling of the Divine.

And the divisions are 600,000.

They are the 600,000 souls. The roots of the Jewish People, the transmitters of the Divine. (In excess of this number are only branches and sub-divisions of the 600,000.) Analogous are the 600,000 letters of the Torah, the Word of the Divine.

(In actuality, our Torah scrolls have fewer than 305,000 letters. Among the explanations given are: 1) The Primordial Torah before the concealment of the original Light contained the 600,000 letters (*Sefer Halikutim*, Psalms 141). 2) The entire Oral Law was cryptically engraved on the first Tablets. These extra letters brought the total to 600,000 (*Ma'amar Hanefesh* 3:6). 3) The 600,000 includes the letters of the Targum, the Aramaic translation of the Torah, which was also given at Sinai (*Pnei Yehoshua, Kiddushin* 30a). 4)Adding silent letters to various vowels produces 600,000 (*Likutey Torah [Chabad], Behar* 43).)

God, in His Infinite Wisdom, saw the necessity of 600,000 "letters" — Jewish souls — for the transmittance of the Torah. The Jewish People, despite very trying conditions, were fruitful and multiplied. They increased miraculously, in order to produce this necessary quota (*Likutey Halakhot, Nizkei Shekheinim* 2:3).

ואת ערום ועריה... בדמיך חיי — RAISING THE "CHILDREN"

God knew the pitiful state of His People in Egypt. He saw them covered in the squalor of their blood: their foolishness and physical desires. They were caught in Mochin de'Katnut, an immature mentality. Spiritually, they resembled children.

> *Children are not active givers, they either take or receive. To see the world through the eyes of a child, to experience it with Mochin de'Katnut, is to say, "What is there for me to get out of it?" Be it pleasure or undue veneration...*

'Great, mighty' — as is written: 'And the children of Israel were fruitful and increased abundantly and multiplied. And they became very, very mighty; and the land was filled with them' (Exodus 1:7).

'And numerous' — as is written: 'I caused you to increase like the plants of the field; you increased and grew tall, and you matured. Your form was full, your hair was grown, but you were naked and bare. I passed over you and saw you covered with your blood, and I said to you: "Through your blood you shall live"; and I said to you: "Through your blood you shall live" ' (Ezekiel 16:6-7).

We may *feel* like submitting in despair. . . But we *want* to serve God sincerely, without ulterior motives. . .

Do not give up. We must do what we can in adhering to God's Will, in complying with His Commandments. The Mitzvot are our Tziyunim, our insignia of distinction. The regalia of our Jewish identity.

When we cling to God, even though we know not why we do so, or why we must endure what we do — when we serve God for *no reason at all* — God will help us for *no reason at all!* He will extricate us from our personal exile. He will endow us with insight into His mitzvot. He will allow us great joy: to array in His regalia (*Likutey Halakhot, Ta'arovet* 1:4).

> *Existence is joy. Just to be aware that we exist — be it here or even in the grave — and will continue to do so, at God's Will, is an exhilirating experience. God desires Existence. He rejoices in Existence. To serve Him with this joy is to share in His Existence.*
>
> *One time, the Baal Shem Tov became dejected. He lost touch with the inner experience of this great joy. He just could not reattain Awareness. He was sure he had lost his Future Reward — his Eternity.*
>
> *Despite it all. The Baal Shem Tov persisted. Out of touch with God... facing loss of Eternity... Meaning in life gone. Despite it all. The Baal Shem Tov persisted. He found Meaning in life. He served God... For no reason at all!*
>
> And God helped him. He brought the Baal Shem Tov back in touch with the Joy of Existence (Rabbi Nachman's Wisdom #48).

פרו וישרצו — INFINITY DIVIDED

There is the infinite. There is also the Infinite.

The first is an infinity of the universe. Of numbers, of divisions, of forms and shapes. It is infinite in its plurality, interminable in its finite entities. We know the part, but we cannot calculate the whole.

The Infinite is altogether different. It is the Infinite of His Unity. An Indivisible One. Incomprehensible, inconceivable, beyond what the mind can fathom.

"וַיָּרֵעוּ אֹתָנוּ הַמִּצְרִים וַיְעַנּוּנוּ וַיִּתְּנוּ עָלֵינוּ עֲבוֹדָה קָשָׁה":

"וַיָּרֵעוּ אֹתָנוּ הַמִּצְרִים" כְּמָה שֶׁנֶּאֱמַר: "הָבָה נִתְחַכְּמָה לוֹ פֶּן יִרְבֶּה וְהָיָה כִּי תִקְרֶאנָה מִלְחָמָה וְנוֹסַף גַּם הוּא עַל שֹׂנְאֵינוּ וְנִלְחַם בָּנוּ וְעָלָה מִן הָאָרֶץ":

"וַיְעַנּוּנוּ" כְּמָה שֶׁנֶּאֱמַר: וַיָּשִׂימוּ עָלָיו שָׂרֵי מִסִּים לְמַעַן עַנֹּתוֹ בְּסִבְלֹתָם, וַיִּבֶן עָרֵי מִסְכְּנוֹת לְפַרְעֹה אֶת פִּתֹם וְאֶת רַעַמְסֵס":

When any Jew lacks or loses Da'at, his awareness of God and his own self-awareness, he falls into spiritual exile under "Pharaoh's" domain. Once this happens, his actions are no longer governed by spiritual reality. Instead, he becomes enslaved by his imagination and illusions. Driven to act upon his misperceptions of reality and compulsively live his self-delusions, the labors of his life are spiritually meaningless. Oppressed by his desires, he seeks the mirage of prestige, money or physical pleasures (*Likutey Halakhot, Avodah Zarah* 3:4).

Even with our Torah and Mitzvot, if they are but an expression of the compelling force of a good upbringing — lacking personal enthusiasm and uniqueness — we are also building these sinking edifices for "Pharaoh." These deeds of ours cannot rise to their Source, for *we* have not risen above ours — our upbringing.

בסבלותם — SEEDS OF REDEMPTION
Perhaps as early as 60 years before the actual Exodus, the seeds of the Redemption were already sown.

"...And Moshe went out unto his brethren and he saw their burdens" (Exodus 2:11). He empathized with them. (This happened before Moshe was 20, perhaps as young as 12. *See Shemot Rabbah* 1:27, 30 and 5:2; *Ramban,* Exodus 2:23. He was 80 when he returned to Egypt; Exodus 7:7.)

Moshe, from his objective vantage point, from his higher awareness, *saw* the predicament of his brethren. They, despite their limited outlook, despite their narrowed awareness, came to Moshe. They related their problems to him. They sought counsel and consolation for their suffering (*Me'am Loez,* Exodus 2:11). Moshe, the Tzaddik, the archetypal Jew, confronted the enslaved mentality, the hard-life reality of the People. Two, very different perspectives. Both were edified and uplifted by the encounter.

When *our* awareness of God and of ourselves has waned, we enter into an accelerating "exile." By coming in contact with a Tzaddik, a source of great awareness, the process is reversed. The seeds of *our* redemption have been sown (*Likutey Moharan* I, 7:3).

'The Egyptians did evil to us. They oppressed us and laid heavy labors upon us' (Deuteronomy 26:6).

'The Egyptians did evil to us' — as is written: 'Let us deal cunningly with them, lest they multiply. If we should happen to be beset by war, they will join our enemies, fight against us, and leave the land' (Exodus 1:10).

'They oppressed us' — as is written: 'They placed taskmasters over them, to oppress them with their burdens, and they built storage cities for Pharaoh, [the cities of] Pisom and Ramses' (Exodus 1:11).

Their blood was burning with the desires of this world. The Jewish People were not worthy of Redemption. And even worse, they saw themselves as such (*Likutey Halakhot, Hoda'ah* 6:5).

God looked aside. He brought into play the few virtues the Jewish People still had. He embellished these "good points", in His eyes and in theirs. God then saw the Jewish People as being worthy of Redemption. They came to see themselves as being worthy of Redemption.

Then God redeemed His Children. He brought them up from Egypt. Raised them out of their immaturity.

"B'damayikh Chayee!" — from the midst of your blood, your struggles with the flesh, find life! Find virtue in the fact that deep in your heart, you really *do want* to serve God (*Likutey Halakhot, Hashkamat Haboker* 1:12).

ויֵרעו אותנו — IN THE EYE OF THE BEHOLDER
What evil did they do to us? *Va'yarei'u otanu* — they made us evil — in our own eyes (*Nachat HaShulchan*).

Pharaoh understood human nature. He knew that if he would treat the Jews with suspicion, as immoral people, they would tend to become just that. So Pharaoh in Egypt accused them of disloyalty and sought to seduce their daughters (*Sotah* 11b). He made us evil (*Siddur Otzar HaTefilot* p. 496d; *Mekhilta, Bo* 5; cf. *Midbar Kedemot, Gimel* 22).

Today, to overcome "Pharaoh," we need to outsmart him. *We* must use human nature. Let us treat others with Jewish dignity. Let us treat ourselves with Jewish esteem. The Jewish soul is very noble. We must eye it with regard and nurture it with respect (*Likutey Moharan* I, 37:7). Great power lies in the "eye" of the beholder. We must *see* only virtue, in all and in ourselves. It is this which will bring our true potentials to fruition (*Likutey Moharan* I, 282; *Rabbi Nachman's Azamra*, passim).

ויענונו — SINKING EDIFICES
The Jewish People in Egypt were compelled to engage in meaningless, unproductive labor. The building sites of Pitom and Ramses were swamps and these cities which the Jews were forced to erect would continually sink into the ground (*Shemot Rabbah* 1:10).

"וַיִּתְּנוּ עָלֵינוּ עֲבוֹדָה קָשָׁה" כְּמָה שֶׁנֶּאֱמַר: "וַיַּעֲבִידוּ מִצְרַיִם
אֶת בְּנֵי יִשְׂרָאֵל בְּפָרֶךְ":

"וַנִּצְעַק אֶל יְהֹוָה אֱלֹהֵי אֲבוֹתֵינוּ וַיִּשְׁמַע יְהֹוָה אֶת קוֹלֵנוּ
וַיַּרְא אֶת עָנְיֵנוּ וְאֶת עֲמָלֵנוּ וְאֶת לַחֲצֵנוּ":

"וַנִּצְעַק אֶל יְהֹוָה אֱלֹהֵי אֲבוֹתֵינוּ" כְּמָה שֶׁנֶּאֱמַר: "וַיְהִי
בַיָּמִים הָרַבִּים הָהֵם וַיָּמָת מֶלֶךְ מִצְרַיִם וַיֵּאָנְחוּ בְנֵי יִשְׂרָאֵל מִן

of the moment; cannot hear the ensuing voice of compunction (*Likutey Halakhot, Milah* 4:2).

This is "PhaRAoH," numerically he is ShaNaH (355) (*Regel Yesharah*). He enslaves us under time, he constricts us in our personal Mitzrayim. He tells us there is time, that we will live for generations. Lulled into Mochin de'Katnut, immature consciousness, we are like children who think of life as continuing forever. Many of us do not wake up until we can only look back and say "it was all like a dream."

It was.

These are the Yamim ha'Rabim, the "many days" — the time illusion of "Pharaoh." And his death denotes our awareness, in retrospect, of this delusion.

Cry out to God while there is still time. We dare not wait until the last minute. But even if we have, there is always hope. How long we live is not important. Eternity is earned by possessing true faith, even if only for a moment.

ויאנחו — LIFE-SIGHS

When the Jewish People were in bondage in Egypt, when *we* become enslaved to the "Pharaoh" of today, dominant was and is an absence of Da'at — a lack of conscious awareness of God. Speech, the manifestation and expression of our Da'at, also becomes suppressed. From within and from without. It was so in Pharaoh's police state. It is so today under "Pharaoh's" current edicts, which we commonly refer to as social convention. It is these rules which leave us embarrassed, "prohibited" from expressing even the repressed and limited awareness of God that we *do* possess.

How, though, can we ever come to a higher consciousness when we see Awareness as beyond human perception? How could the Jewish People in Egypt rise above their situation when they had come to accept their status quo as "the way things are"? As "that's life," and "such is human nature"? (*Zikaron Zot*, Exodus 2:23).

God changed the status quo. Pharaoh became deathly ill. His court physicians advised that he slaughter Jewish children and bathe in their blood. The Jewish People were horrified, dumbfounded. Shaken from complacency, yet helpless. Or were they? They began to sigh.

'They laid heavy labors upon us' — as is written: 'The Egyptians forced the children of Israel to do slave labor' (Exodus 1:13).

'And we cried out to God, the God of our fathers. And He heard our voice, and He saw our suffering, our burden and our oppression' (Deuteronomy 26:7).

'And we cried out to God, the God of our fathers' — as is written: 'And it came to pass during that long period, that the king of Egypt died. The children of Israel moaned because of the hard labor, and they cried out.

בפרך — SMOOTH TALK, MIRROR IMAGE

b'PHaReKH — b'PheH RaKH, with a smooth tongue.

Pharaoh said, "Come work for me just today" (*Yalkut Shimoni, Shemot* 1:13).

"Pharaoh" says: "Listen to me just this once. I will not bother you again. Just one more time. It is for everyone's benefit."

And, aside from the internal dialogue he implants in our minds, "Pharaoh" employs another method.

In Egypt, Pharaoh himself took a pail and shovel and began to work. Whoever *saw* this, did likewise (*Yalkut Shimoni, Ibid.*).

"Pharaoh" is Impaired Imagination (*Likutey Moharan* I, 54:6). Together with his smooth talk, he gives us a mental picture — an internal image — of ourselves carrying out his edicts. Once we see ourselves in "Pharaoh's mirror," we are virtually compelled to become a part of the illusion.

We must use Imagination to our benefit and enoble it. How? By seeing ourselves independent of Impaired Imagination. As clearly as possible, we need visualize ourselves unbound. Free to do God's Will.

Redemption begins when a Jew *sees* himself free of "Pharaoh's" constrictions and *hears* himself deaf to "Pharaoh's" temptations.

בימים הרבים — TIME ILLUSION

Time is a dimension of our life experiences (*Likutey Halakhot, Gittin* 3:12, 4:7). We cannot imagine a different existence, nor envision an alternate reality.

Yet, beyond our imagination there is a level of life above time, a plane of transcendent time.

At that level, SHaNah, a year, is SHiNuy, a change. CHoDeSH, a month, is CHaDaSH, a renewal (*Maggid Devarav L'Yaakov,* #116). Renewal is the essence of Creation. Awareness of this ongoing process is what enables us to take part in it. Acting, and not just acted upon. We can renew ourselves; change the direction of our lives. We can become partners with God in the act of Creation. Then we will have transcended time. Brought transcendent time into our lives.

Paradoxically, when we are trapped in earthly time, we stagnate. It progresses and moves ahead. We don't. It changes, but we don't change with it. Feeling that we cannot break out of its constrictive power, that we cannot transcend our limitations, we become servants to our desires. We cannot see beyond the pleasure

הָעֲבֹדָה וַיִּזְעָקוּ וַתַּעַל שַׁוְעָתָם אֶל הָאֱלֹהִים מִן הָעֲבֹדָה":

"וַיִּשְׁמַע יְהוָה אֶת קֹלֵנוּ" כְּמָה שֶׁנֶּאֱמַר: "וַיִּשְׁמַע אֱלֹהִים
אֶת נַאֲקָתָם וַיִּזְכֹּר אֱלֹהִים אֶת בְּרִיתוֹ אֶת אַבְרָהָם אֶת יִצְחָק
וְאֶת יַעֲקֹב":

There are people born into or brought up in "servitude." Their circumstances lead them to become enslaved to "Pharaoh." From within and without, they encounter obstacles in serving God. Jewishness for them is very difficult and entails deep inner sacrifices. When they turn to God from their "bondage," God takes great concern.

God sent Moshe, born a Levite but raised an Egyptian prince, to redeem his brothers from their spiritual bondage. Moshe refined what was his own very coarse nature. He overcame it. He worked on himself until he understood his brothers' hardships. Until he felt for them. Until their pain was his. Then Moshe was able to elevate his brethren from their "bondage," to take them out of slavery.

We pray to God, asking that He once again send Moshe, the ultimate redeemer, to extricate us from our bondage (cf. *Likutey Moharan* II, 7:4).

ותעל שועתם — SEARCHING FOR THE REDEEMER

From the depths of their spiritual bondage, the Jewish People were stirring, searching for God. Consequently, Moshe, the Tzaddik, the comprehensive soul of the Jewish People was *also* searching.

Moshe knew he was the destined redeemer (*Arba Meot Shekel Kesef*, p. 68c; *Likutey Halakhot, Hoda'ah* 6:59). But he didn't *know* that he knew. He couldn't see himself as being worthy of such an awesome task. He couldn't see the Jewish People as being worthy of Redemption (Exodus 3-4; *Likutey Halakhot, Sheluchin* 5:19). He hadn't been afforded the vision to see through to the Ultimate Redemption (*Ibid.*).

Moshe went out into the wilderness to seek. He was searching for God, for *himself,* for the redeemer of the Jewish People (*Shemen HaTov* p. 23b). And despite all that Moshe could not see, God saw! He saw that Moshe, despite all his self doubts and conflicts, had entered the Wilderness, had ventured out in search...

God then said to Moshe: "It is this seeking against all odds and searching against all logic which is necessary to bring about the Redemption. Now, go!" (*Likutey Halakhot, Sheluchin, Ibid.*).

We all know that within ourselves we have the resources to bring about our personal redemption, our own share in the Universal Redemption. But we must come to *know* that we know. If we would only search hard enough, we, too, would find Moshe, the Tzaddik, the redeemer — in *our* generation and in *our*selves.

וישמע קולנו ...נאקתם — A GROAN IN THE VOID

God knew that certain of the Jewish children were not worthy of being redeemed. They were just not ready. So when the enslaved Jews failed to produce their quota

And from the bondage their prayers rose up to God' (Exodus 2:23).

'And God heard our voice' — as is written: 'God heard their groaning and God recalled His covenant with Avraham, Yitzchak, and Yaakov' (Exodus 2:24).

The sigh of a Jewish heart is very dear to God, even if it be muffled and inaudible. Through it we "breathe life" into the world. We bring to life the things which we are lacking (*Likutey Moharan* I, 8:1). If nothing else, the sigh expresses that deep in our heart we know what we lack. And, as long as we know this, to whatever degree — there is hope. We hope. We yearn. And, in time, our yearnings turn to reality.

As they sighed, thoughts of the inexpressible desires buried deep in their hearts came to mind. They began to reflect upon their predicament. They cried out, wordlessly, to God (and when our speech is in "exile," we must utilize our voice to cry out simply to God) (*Likutey Halakhot, Birchat Hare'ach* 1:3).

They cried. Became in touch with themselves. And the more they cried, the more in touch they became. More *aware* of God. Of how far they had strayed from Him!

As they cried out in MiTZRayim, from the MayTZaR, from the awareness of their constrictions, those constrictions were transformed into TZeMeR, the Supernal "hairs" which transmit Divine Benevolence (*Likutey Halakhot, Reishit HaGez* 4:2).

God appeared to Moshe. "Tell them that I've heard how they cry out. Tell them that I'm aware of their pain. Tell them that they shall be redeemed." God sent Moshe into Mitzrayim, to extricate the Jewish People from their constrictions.

Through Moshe, the Tzaddik, we discover that we must cry out — even when there are no words. Through Moshe, the Tzaddik, we become aware of our pain — our spiritual pain. Through Moshe, the Tzaddik, we draw the breath of new life into the world, into ourselves — and are redeemed.

And when *any* Jew is motivated by an awareness of his constrictions to turn to God — from Maytzar to Tzemer — even if his turning is no more than a "hairsbreadth," God reciprocally opens those Divine Channels of Influence and extricates him from his personal Mitzrayim.

מן העבודה — BORN INTO BONDAGE

There are angels who are endowed with a profound perception of the Divine. They serve God with awesome holiness and unbridled devotion. God's desire for their service is limited, qualified.

There are people born into and brought up in "freedom." They have negligible "living problems": physical, emotional or spiritual. Jewishness for them can become facile and often beneficial. The Tribe of Levi was exempt from the bondage in Egypt (*Shemot Rabbah* 5:16). They were also free of the spiritual servitude, the "spiritual living problems" which afflicted their brothers. As such, they did not, they could not, understand their brothers' suffering. They prayed. God did not respond to their prayer.

"וַיַּרְא אֶת עָנְיֵנוּ" זוֹ פְּרִישׁוּת דֶּרֶךְ אֶרֶץ כְּמָה שֶׁנֶּאֱמַר: "וַיַּרְא אֱלֹהִים אֶת בְּנֵי יִשְׂרָאֵל וַיֵּדַע אֱלֹהִים":

their bondage. No one knew, though, the workings of the other's heart (*Shemot Rabbah* 1:36). Speech, the expression of Da'at, was also in "exile" — restricted and inhibited (*Likutey Moharan* I, 62). They were ashamed to talk about God, to speak of His Existence. Deep down, they *knew* how far they were from Him.

Yet, God did know the workings of their hearts. There was an emanation, a manifestation of the Divine Da'at. Moshe, the Tzaddik, the embodiment of Da'at, was sent to uplift the Jewish People. A trusted messenger, Moshe instilled them with this Da'at. He brought them in touch with themselves and with each other — with the intimate workings of their hearts.

Moshe brought them in touch with God.

וירא... וידע — EYES OF EXPERIENCE

We see with our eyes and we see with our minds. But we only *see* with our hearts.

All human eyes see the same world, yet no two people have ever seen the same. Our individual experiences, personalities and prejudices color the world we see. Many of us block out the things we don't want to see — most of all, ourselves. The world we do see is very limited.

We will also not see that of which we have no internal image. Yosef's brothers didn't see him, they had never before seen him with a beard (*Rashi*, Genesis 42:8). How will *we* recognize the Mashiach if we have never seen him before, if we have never tasted the beauty of his teachings?... (See *Tzaddik* #260).

But then, there are things we do see, that our minds do grasp. Even so, we still don't seem able to *experience* that knowledge. Our actions are not the spontaneous expression of that understanding. Our hearts, our emotions, are "uncircumcised" (*Likutey Moharan* I, 141). They are enveloped, surrounded by an imaginary Wall-of-Limitations (*Rabbi Nachman's Wisdom*, #232). We may believe in God, but we don't believe that *we* can experience Him.

> *...If only we would open our hearts to experience the joy of serving the Creator with pure innocence, without intellectual sophistication... Let us experience Now, and leave understanding for Later....*
>
> *The joy of Creation, of Existence, would be ours. Our hearts would express themselves in word and in action. We would live as we know we should. We would see the Future even in this world.*

God *saw* the Jewish People. They had entered the Divine Heart. God *knew* what to do...(*Aderet Eliyahu, Zot Habrachah* 33:9; *Likutey Halakhot, Arvit* 4:27; *Sefer HaLikutim, Bereishit* 3:1).

'And He saw our suffering' — this refers to the separation of husband and wife, as is written: 'God saw the children of Israel and God knew' (Exodus 2:25).

of bricks, *these* children were thrown into the walls (*Sanhedrin* 101b, 103b; *Aderet Eliyahu, Nitzavim* 29:17).

As they lay dying, near-corpses, crushed under the pressure of the wall above, their groans ascended to Heaven. Though these children did not merit Redemption, their groans certainly hastened it (*Yalkut Shimoni; Pirkei d'Rabbi Eliezer* #48).

Scripture uses the term groan in reference to Chalal, a corpse (*Shemot Rabbah* 1:34; Ezekiel 30:24). Chalal has another meaning: namely, void — the Vacated Space. God created a level of existence where He appears not to exist. A paradox. God must exist everywhere. Nothing can exist without His permeating Existence. Yet these voids do exist, and they are not just esoteric concepts (*Likutey Halakhot, Minchah* 7:22). They can be a dire reality in our lives. They are the spiritual/emotional "black holes" of life.

These are the situations in which we feel estranged from God; filled with questions and contradictions about ourselves, about Him, about Providence. Why did God do this to me? Why do I suffer like this? Why did He allow me to do what I did? Is there still any hope for me? Looking into the depths of our souls, we see only a vacuum. Who am I?

We have fallen into the Vacated Space. Found ourselves in a void. Ask no questions in this non-place, in this seemingly Godforsaken place. God's existence here, as everywhere, is imperative — but a paradox nonetheless (*Likutey Moharan* I, 64).

There is only one way out. We must search for God despite His "absence." We must cry out to Him, and groan from the pressure of our suffering. Where God has concealed Himself, we must reveal Him (*Likutey Moharan* II, 12). Believe God is right here. With you. Wherever you are.

Those Jewish children in Egypt had fallen into the Vacated Space. There are Jewish "children" today who still suffer in those very same spiritual voids.

Yehi Ratzon: May the groans of their search make the "children" of today worthy of a redemption. May they show us the yearning for God hidden beyond the void. And may God, in their merit, hasten the Final Redemption.

וירא את ענינו — GETTING INTIMATELY IN TOUCH WITH GOD

In Mitzrayim, Da'at — the intimate Knowledge and conscious Awareness — is in "exile." It is absent. Our knowledge of God degenerates from a dynamic experience to an intellectual conception.

In Egypt, the Jewish People were denied marital relations, the intimate knowledge of another human being. They were also denied the intimate knowledge of one another. Deep in their hearts, they were returning to God to deliver them from

"וְאֶת עֲמָלֵנוּ" אֵלּוּ הַבָּנִים כְּמָה שֶׁנֶּאֱמַר: "כָּל הַבֵּן הַיִּלּוֹד
הַיְאֹרָה תַּשְׁלִיכוּהוּ וְכָל הַבַּת תְּחַיּוּן":

"וְאֶת לַחֲצֵנוּ" זוֹ הַדְּחַק כְּמָה שֶׁנֶּאֱמַר: "וְגַם רָאִיתִי אֶת
הַלַּחַץ אֲשֶׁר מִצְרַיִם לוֹחֲצִים אוֹתָם":

"וַיּוֹצִיאֵנוּ יְהוָה מִמִּצְרַיִם בְּיָד חֲזָקָה וּבִזְרֹעַ נְטוּיָה וּבְמוֹרָא
גָּדוֹל וּבְאֹתוֹת וּבְמֹפְתִים":

People entered into bondage to refine this inherited trait (*Likutey Halakhot, Gezeilah* 5:7; *Megaleh Amukot, Shemot*, p. 16a).

There will come a time in our lives when we will open our eyes and see that with all of "Pharaoh's" compulsive haste, we have accomplished nothing. Sinking edifices....

In realizing this, we will have learned patience and acquired perseverance.

ויוציאנו — A BETTER FUTURE

The cry of the Jewish People came before God. Appearing to Moshe from the burning bush, God revealed Himself with the Divine Name EHYEH — *I Will Be* — indicating the Future (*Likutey Moharan* I, 6:2; *Likutey Halakhot, Keriat Ha'Torah* 6:19-20; *Kedushat Levi*, p. 32a).

> *Breslov. There he was, rummaging through the rubble and cinder, salvaging whatever hadn't been ravaged by the fire which had destroyed his home. Incessant tears rolled down his drawn cheeks and onto the incinerated remnants of his house, as he — broken but undaunted — persisted in his search through the debris. Maybe, with God's help, he might just find some scraps, some pieces of wood which could be useful for starting life anew. All else had gone up in flames.*
>
> *Just then, Reb Noson passed by with some followers. Reb Noson never missed an opportunity to observe God's ways, and this time there was indeed an important lesson.*
>
> *"Do you see?!" he exclaimed.*
>
> *"The man's life is in ruins. His home, his assets, his life as he knew it; they are no more. He has no place on earth to call his own.*
>
> *"But do you see him giving up in despair? No! He is too busy thinking of the future, gathering together whatever he can from the past.*
>
> *"The same is true with us. In our journey through this world, we may at some point see our lives going up in flames. We have transgressed God's Will, the fires of this world have engulfed us. The suffering we have caused ourselves seems unbearable.*

'Our burden' — these are the children, as is written: 'Every newborn son you shall throw into the Nile river, but every daughter you shall let live' (Exodus 1:22).

'And our oppression' — this was the pressure [placed upon the Jews] as is written: 'I have also seen the oppression with which the Egyptians oppress them' (Exodus 3:9).

'God brought us out of Egypt with a mighty hand, with an outstretched arm, with great fear, with signs and with wonders' (Deuteronomy 26:8).

כל הבן הילוד — SPARKING DYNAMIC JEWISHNESS

Pharaoh decreed death to the newborn males of the Jewish People. This symbolized his method of breaking the Jewish spirit. (Kabbalistically, the Masculine, dynamic force connects to joy and contentment, the Feminine, receptive force to sorrow and discontentment. Pharaoh, therefore, allowed the newborn females to live.)

When we are despondent and pessimistic, we are hard put to muster the strength of character to stand up to "Pharaoh's" temptations. "Pharaoh" creates for us all kinds of situations to dampen our spirits. We are then prey to his underlying objectives.

We need to do what we can to keep our spirits high, full of cheer and optimism. As long as we are enthusiastic and happy with our lot, we can see through "Pharaoh's" illusion.

It was the Jewish midwives in Egypt who endeavored to keep the male born alive. It is they, the contemporary Tzaddikim of every generation, who toil to rouse and kindle the invincible Jewish spirit. With their words of elevating encouragement, they add fire to the Godly flame which burns in our hearts. Sparking dynamic Jewishness. Instilling in every Jewish "child" the awareness that God is with him. No matter what we have been through or are going through, ultimately God *will* redeem us. God *will* extricate us from the "Pharaoh" of our lives (*Likutey Halakhot, Hoda'ah* 6:58).

לחצנו זו הדחק — COMPULSIVE HASTE

"Pharaoh" is constantly exerting pressure upon us. We always feel in a rush to get somewhere, in a hurry to achieve, yet we don't know why.

Sometimes, even when we are aroused to God, we also feel pressured. We want to become good Jews, now. Instantly! We want to be rid of past temptations, today. This moment! We haven't the patience for the slow edification process we must endure.

Adam, the first human, also succumbed to this trait of impatience. The Jewish

"וַיּוֹצִיאֵנוּ יְהוָֹה מִמִּצְרַיִם". לֹא עַל יְדֵי מַלְאָךְ וְלֹא עַל יְדֵי
שָׂרָף וְלֹא עַל יְדֵי שָׁלִיחַ. אֶלָּא הַקָּדוֹשׁ בָּרוּךְ הוּא בִּכְבוֹדוֹ
וּבְעַצְמוֹ. שֶׁנֶּאֱמַר: "וְעָבַרְתִּי בְאֶרֶץ מִצְרַיִם בַּלַּיְלָה הַזֶּה
וְהִכֵּיתִי כָל בְּכוֹר בְּאֶרֶץ מִצְרַיִם מֵאָדָם וְעַד בְּהֵמָה וּבְכָל
אֱלֹהֵי מִצְרַיִם אֶעֱשֶׂה שְׁפָטִים אֲנִי יְהוָֹה":

"וְעָבַרְתִּי בְאֶרֶץ מִצְרַיִם בַּלַּיְלָה הַזֶּה" אֲנִי וְלֹא מַלְאָךְ.

"וְהִכֵּיתִי כָל בְּכוֹר בְּאֶרֶץ מִצְרַיִם" אֲנִי וְלֹא שָׂרָף.

"וּבְכָל אֱלֹהֵי מִצְרַיִם אֶעֱשֶׂה שְׁפָטִים" אֲנִי יְהוָֹה אֲנִי וְלֹא
הַשָּׁלִיחַ. "אֲנִי יְהוָֹה" אֲנִי הוּא וְלֹא אַחֵר:

בְּיָד חֲזָקָה זוֹ הַדֶּבֶר כְּמָה שֶׁנֶּאֱמַר: "הִנֵּה יַד יְהוָֹה הוֹיָה
בְּמִקְנְךָ אֲשֶׁר בַּשָּׂדֶה בַּסּוּסִים בַּחֲמוֹרִים בַּגְּמַלִּים בַּבָּקָר וּבַצֹּאן
דֶּבֶר כָּבֵד מְאֹד":

In reward, God temporarily "cleared" their vision. He opened the doors of their perception (*Shemot Rabbah* 5:9). Now they saw it! They knew it! It was God Himself, not an angel, who passed through Egypt that night. It was God Himself, not a seraph, who brought the plagues upon the Egyptians. It was God Himself, not a messenger, who brought the Jewish People to Awareness. They experienced a most serene joy. They experienced knowing that God was with them and that they were His People.

God then closed the doors. He took away that which He had bestowed. The Jewish People began to yearn. Forty-nine consecutive days. Day after day. Finally, at Mount Sinai — this time in the merit of what they had achieved through their yearning — the doors opened again.

And it is for the reopening of those doors that we now await... and yearn.

ביד חזקה — A MESSAGE FROM ABOVE
In Egypt, the Jewish People were steeped in their physical existence. They could not transcend their baser drives. Eating was for no other purpose but self-gratification (cf. *Likutey Moharan* I, 62:5; *Likutey Halakhot*, *Treifot* 2:4). They just weren't *aware* that there is anything holy in physical pleasures.

> *There is no inherent "evil" to permissible pleasures, only in our remaining enslaved to them. When rather than experience the Divine,*

'God brought us out of Egypt' — not through an angel, not through a seraph and not through a messenger. It was the Holy One, Blessed is He, alone and in His glory. As is written: 'On that night I will pass through the land of Egypt and I will slay every first-born in the land of Egypt, from man to beast, and all the gods of Egypt I will judge, [for] I am God' (Exodus 12:12).

'On that night I will pass through the land of Egypt' — I, and not an angel;
'And I will slay every first-born in the land of Egypt' — I, and not a seraph;
'And all the gods of Egypt I will judge' — I, and not a messenger;
'[for] I am God' — I, and no other.

'With a mighty hand' — this is [the plague of] pestilence, as is written: 'Behold! God's Hand will be upon your livestock in the field, upon the horses, mules and camels, the cattle and the sheep, a very severe pestilence' (Exodus 9:3).

> *"We must not give up! We must always remember the actions of this man! Let's salvage the good traits we can still find within us; rebuild upon our virtues. Let's look to the future and build a new life, an even better life than the one we now live."*

The Jewish People in Egypt had no past to fall back on. They had no present to draw from. God brought them out. His message to them, and to us, is one of hope: *"I Will Be* with you!" — You do have a future!

ועברתי — OPENING THE DOORS OF PERCEPTION

The human psyche, constricted in earthly existence, cannot normally sustain a direct confrontation with the Creator. The experience is just too overwhelming. The soul is engulfed by its Source, by awareness of God's Reality.

For nearly a year, the Jewish People in Egypt had been undergoing a slow process of purification, of elevation. They witnessed — they "experienced" — the Ten Plagues. How would *we* be effected by such events?...

Meanwhile, the Egyptians were steeped in black magic. They could not *see* the Hand of God. To them it was just another force used for controlling nature, albeit superior to their own. The more they saw, the more obstinate and oppressive they became.

The Jewish People were commanded to slaughter the Pesach lamb — symbol of the Egyptian deity — at the very zenith of the Egyptians' zodiacal powers. But the Jewish People were still entrenched in Egyptian ways. These ways had become deeply rooted in their souls (*Shemot Rabbah* 16:2). Yet there was a difference: In carrying out God's command, the Jews exhibited simple faith. In carrying out God's Will, they exhibited contempt for the Egyptians and their powers.

"וּבִזְרֹעַ נְטוּיָה" זוֹ הַחֶרֶב כְּמָה שֶׁנֶּאֱמַר: "וְחַרְבּוֹ שְׁלוּפָה בְּיָדוֹ נְטוּיָה עַל יְרוּשָׁלָיִם":

"וּבְמוֹרָא גָּדֹל" זוֹ גִּלּוּי שְׁכִינָה כְּמָה שֶׁנֶּאֱמַר: "אוֹ הֲנִסָּה אֱלֹהִים לָבוֹא לָקַחַת לוֹ גוֹי מִקֶּרֶב גּוֹי בְּמַסּוֹת בְּאֹתוֹת וּבְמוֹפְתִים וּבְמִלְחָמָה וּבְיָד חֲזָקָה וּבִזְרוֹעַ נְטוּיָה וּבְמוֹרָאִים גְּדֹלִים כְּכֹל אֲשֶׁר עָשָׂה לָכֶם יְהוָה אֱלֹהֵיכֶם בְּמִצְרַיִם לְעֵינֶיךָ":

Moshe, the Tzaddik, is the collective consciousness of the Jewish People. He knows the awareness of each individual. His own awareness transcends and encompasses that of all other created beings. When Moshe "took God to task" in prayer, he did so as the spokesman of the Jewish People.

It was these prayers which brought about the plagues — the Lessons — and the Miracles of the Redemption (*Likutey Halakhot, Devarim Hayotzim min Hachai* 2:4). And when Moshe stretched out his arms in such prayer to God, this was his "sword of conquest" (*Likutey Halakhot, Matnot Kehunah* 2:2; cf. *Likutey Moharan* I, 2:1; *Shebolei Haleket, Orach Chayim* #218, p. 97a).

זו גילוי שכינה — BELIEVING IS SEEING

> *"And I, Daniel, alone saw the vision; and the people who were with me did not see the vision"* (Daniel 10:7).

The objective reality of Divine Manifestation is a very subjective experience. No two people have the same experience. Neither can they convey their perception of it to one another. We tend to see only that which we *really want* to see (*Rabbi Nachman's Wisdom* #1).

God revealed Himself in Egypt. Those who *wanted* to believe — Jew or gentile — pursued Him into the wilderness. They saw. Those who refused to believe — gentile or Jew — did not live to leave record of *their* experience. They did not see. God, indeed, took out "a nation from amidst a nation" (This refers to Jew from among Jews and gentile from among gentiles.) (*Sha'ar HaPesukim, Shemot*).

The Torah lessons of the Tzaddik are *his* experience of the Divine. We can believe it, accept it, follow his teachings, and attain therewith *our* experience of the Divine. We, too, can see. Or we can deny it and say: "God has not appeared to you!" (Exodus 4:12).

We can decide to believe, if we choose.

And we can choose, if we only want to.

'With an outstretched arm' — this is the sword, as is written: 'His sword was drawn in his hand, stretched out over Jerusalem' (1 Chronicles 21:16).

'With great fear' — this is the revelation of the Divine Presence, as is written: 'Or has God ever attempted to take unto Himself one nation from amidst another nation, with trials, signs and wonders; with war, a mighty hand, and an outstretched arm and with great fear, as God did for you in Egypt before your eyes?' (Deuteronomy 4:34).

Man is compelled to experience the physical — this is "evil." The solution: Strive to remain aware of God, to yearn for the Source of all Pleasure, even in the very midst of physical pleasure.

God sent forth a Hand of Strength. He instilled within them a higher soul, a soul which would predominate and refine their animal nature. (The instilling of a higher soul is an aspect of birth. The birth process, which entails contractions and passage through the narrow birth canal, indicates constrictions. It is God's Hand of Strength which implements all constrictions.)

God smote the animals of the Egyptians. He simultaneously smote the "animals" of the Jewish People (*Yalkut Reuveni, Shemot*, p. 216).

When we endeavor to enoble our hunger and palatal drives, to experience them as a message from Above to yearn for God — the Source of our life, our sustenance — God will also send forth His Hand of Strength to instill in us an even nobler soul (*Likutey Moharan* I, 67).

ובזרוע נטויה זו החרב — THE GOD-CONQUERING PRAYER-SWORD

Becoming more aware of our distance from God, of our limitations, we realize our inability to transcend our humanness without Divine Help. The time has come for us to "take God to task" (*Likutey Moharan* II, 8:2-3; *Parparaot LeChokhmah; Yerushalmi, Berakhot* 4).

Let us "argue" with God, let us "Sing to the One who rejoices when conquered" (*Pesachim* 119a). We must not think it inappropriate, or improper. God is waiting for us to ask, to plead — yes, even to protest! He wants us to overcome Him! (*Rabbi Nachman's Wisdom*, #69, 70; *Likutey Halakhot, Keriat Shma* 5:10).

"No matter what! I still want to be a Jew! I really do *want to serve You properly. It's just that I'm human, and all of life's distractions get in my way.*

"Haven't we suffered enough in our lifetime? Hasn't mankind suffered enough for its humanness?

"Isn't it time for us to rise above our human follies? How long? How long? How long will You withhold Your Divine Help. The time has surely come for You to help us forget about the past and bring about the future!"

"וּבְאֹתוֹת" זֶה הַמַּטֶּה כְּמָה שֶׁנֶּאֱמַר: וְאֶת הַמַּטֶּה הַזֶּה תִּקַּח בְּיָדֶךָ אֲשֶׁר תַּעֲשֶׂה בּוֹ אֶת הָאֹתוֹת":

"וּבְמֹפְתִים" זֶה הַדָּם כְּמָה שֶׁנֶּאֱמַר: "וְנָתַתִּי מוֹפְתִים בַּשָּׁמַיִם וּבָאָרֶץ":

כשיאמר "דם ואש ותמרות עשן" ישפוך ג' שפיכות ולא על ידי האצבע אלא מהכוס עצמו לתוך כלי. וכן יעשה בשפיכת היין בעשר מכות בכל מכה שפיכה אחת וכן בסימניהן.

דָּם. וָאֵשׁ. וְתִמְרוֹת עָשָׁן:

דָּבָר אַחֵר: "בְּיָד חֲזָקָה" שְׁתַּיִם. "וּבִזְרֹעַ נְטוּיָה" שְׁתַּיִם. "וּבְמֹרָא גָּדוֹל" שְׁתַּיִם. "וּבְאֹתוֹת" שְׁתַּיִם. "וּבְמֹפְתִים" שְׁתַּיִם: אֵלּוּ עֶשֶׂר מַכּוֹת שֶׁהֵבִיא הַקָּדוֹשׁ בָּרוּךְ הוּא עַל הַמִּצְרִים בְּמִצְרַיִם וְאֵלּוּ הֵן:

דָּם. צְפַרְדֵּעַ. כִּנִּים. עָרוֹב. דֶּבֶר. שְׁחִין. בָּרָד. אַרְבֶּה. חֹשֶׁךְ. מַכַּת בְּכוֹרוֹת:

עשר מכות — PLAGUE-LESSONS

The very same phenomenon, the singular act of God which the Egyptians experienced as a plague, the Jewish People experienced as an uplifting revelation (*Sefer Baal Shem Tov, Va'era,* 6-7). Let us search for lessons *we* can take in order to "inflict a plague" with which to overcome the "Egyptian" within us.

דם — WAIT!

One of the things we must know when we are first aroused to return to God is that we cannot expect to rid ourselves of our baser nature and unwanted desires overnight. We cannot enter the Gates of Holiness with our first knock. God tells us to wait! We must first refine ourselves. We must confess — admit to *ourselves* the stark reality of our past and present life — before we can continue higher into the future.

In our returning to God, this deep *humiliation* together with the social *embarrassment* we may have to endure is the spilling of our own blood. We must acquiesce to this, and thereby gain entry through the Gates.

The Egyptians tasted the waters — the Divine Knowledge — as blood. We, the Jewish People, tasted the "blood" as water — as Divine Benevolence (*Likutey Moharan* I, 6:2).

'With signs' — this refers to the staff, as is written: 'Take this staff in your hand, with which you shall perform the signs' (Exodus 4:17).

'And with wonders' — this is blood, as is written: 'I will show wonders in heaven and on earth:

When reciting each of these punishments and again when reciting the plagues one should pour some wine from the cup (with his finger or a spoon).

'Blood, and fire, and pillars of smoke' (Joel 3:3).

Another explanation [of the verse]:
'With a mighty hand' — indicates two plagues;
'With an outstretched arm' — another two;
'With great fear' — another two;
'With signs' — another two;
'And wonders' — another two.

These are the Ten Plagues which the Holy One, Blessed is He, brought upon the Egyptians in Egypt, namely:

Blood; Frogs; Lice; Wild Animals; Pestilence; Boils; Hail; Locusts; Darkness; Slaying of the Firstborn.

זה המטה — STAFF OF FREE WILL

Sometimes we really *want to change.* We sincerely desire to better our ways and draw ourselves closer to God. But we feel entrenched in our habits and ways. We cannot *see* ourselves changing.

God then says to us: "Take the Mateh, the staff, in your hand."

The Mateh is that which can be swayed at will — your free will! Take it in your hand. Realize that you are endowed with complete freedom of action. No force binds you to predetermined behavior. Become *aware* that you are empowered to take charge of your life. Come to *see* yourself as possessing this awesome gift... for with it, you will perform "the signs," the miracles (*Tzaddik* #162; *Likutey Moharan* II, 110).

מופתים זה הדם — MIRACULOUS TRANSFORMATION

One's blood is the vehicle of his soul. Speech is its instrument, its essence.

To extricate a free-will-being who is languishing in the baser elements and desires of the "blood"; to raise him to an awareness of God and the nobler elements of the blood; to refine his blood, his DaM, into ADaM, into true humanity, so that his soul's voice resounds forth, so that his speech — his speaking about God — is fire, his prayers pillars of smoke...

This is indeed "a wonder," a miracle! (*Tzaddik* #94; *Likutey Halakhot, Chelev V'Dam* 4:9).

דבר — SPONTANEOUS CHANGE

Pestilence is generally spread by contagion. But *this* pestilence was different. It was contracted spontaneously! *All* the Egyptian cattle died at the same moment. (This is evident from Exodus 9:5-7. God set a specific time for the plague. After that moment there was no time or need for Pharaoh to request a respite. It was all over. The verb used in v. 3 is present tense. The plague had no duration in the past or future). It was the DeVeR; the DeVaR Hashem, the Word of God. (A "contagious" disease can sometimes be contracted in a spontaneous fashion directly from Heaven, *Tzaddik* #459)

"Pharaoh" would have us believe that even this obvious Manifestation is accidental. *We* know that even the seemingly accidental is Manifestation. Nature is but a "glove" on God's Hand. In truth, there is no nature at all (*Likutey Moharan* I, 250; *Ibid.,* 13).

And the same can be said of our personal "nature," our character and personality, as unmalleable and incorrigible as it may seem to be. If we could truly accept it as *G-d's* Hand, we could change it quite quickly. Sometimes spontaneously!

שחין — DIGGING FOR THE JEWISH HEART

Contrary to the norm, these boils were dry on the inside and moist on the outside (*Bava Kama* 80b).

Sometimes that is exactly how we feel. Dry. Barren. Unenthused. Disinterested. Any "moisture" we do have in the service of God is only on the *outside*. A pretense. A show.

Even so, we dare not give up. We must persist. Dig deeper. Underneath that inner shell of dryness is a boundless fountain of energy and spirit. It is the Jewish Heart. Sometimes it is necessary to dig, and keep on digging, in order to find it.

ברד — GEHENNOM IN THIS WORLD

With this plague, the sentence of Gehennom was exacted upon the Egyptians. Sitting down, they were burnt by hail. Standing up, they were burnt by fire (*Shemot Rabbah* 12:4).

There is a Gehennom of fire. There is a Gehennom of snow (*Yerushalmi, Sanhedrin* 10:3; *Tanchuma, Re'eh* 13; *Zohar* I:238b).

When we are burning with earthly passions, enflamed by emotions out of control — when we "stand up" and act out our desires — we experience the fire, the turbulence of Gehennom. Even in this world.

When we are aroused to return to God but become depressed over our past, embarrassed to approach Him with our burden of misdeeds — when we "sit down" and obey those disheartening voices — we experience the ice, the inertia of Gehennom. Even in this world (*Likutey Halakhot, Basar Bechalav* 5:28).

Yehi Ratzon: God! Embarrass us so that we control our burning emotions! Enflame our hearts to return to You, despite our past!

צפרדע — HEARING THE VOICE OF GOD

In any sincere attempt to bring ourselves closer to God, we must simultaneously seek to exclude all negative influences upon our lives. But the outside world is so full of these adverse voices that we must endeavor to silence them and curtail their influence within our minds by sounding our own voice of holiness.

This is the TZePhaRDEAH: TZiPoR, the bird, the incessant voice of DEAH — Da'at of holiness.

The Egyptians were invaded by frogs — the Tzephardeah — which entered into every hidden corner and aspect of their lives. We, the Jewish People, must bring the unremitting Voice of God — the Tzipor Deah — into every aspect of our lives (*Likutey Moharan* I, 3).

כנים — HUMBLE ESTEEM

Pharaoh's magicians were unable to bring about lice. The forces of evil have no power over such a minute and insignificant creature (Rashi, Exodus 8:14).

> *True humility is the greatest of virtues. It is not found with self-deprecation, nor can it coexist with low self-esteem. It is the awareness of Divinely endowed value, the essence of high self-esteem. It is the desire to share our talents with others, rather than seek veneration. The realization that, on our own, we are* nothing — *that is what humility demands* (Rabbi Nachman's Wisdom #140).

And, proportionate to our humility, the forces of "Pharaoh" have no power over us. We endure the suffering brought on by "Pharaoh's" illusions with humility, yet are too aware of our endowed value to obey him. It does not befit us! (*Likutey Moharan* I, 4:9 and 52).

ערוב — CUTTING THE TIES

In the assemblage of wild animals which overran Egypt was a curious species. Attached to the land by an umbilical cord, it attacked whatever came within its perimeter. Some say that this beast was actually primitive man "tied to the land" psychologically (*Aruch, aden*). Only by severing the creature's cord could it be overcome. At the time of the plague, many of them were transported to Egypt *with the land* to which they were attached (*Kilayim* 8:4; *Kol Eliyahu, Va'era*).

There is an element in man that can witness miracles, see the Divine *on earth* (Exodus 8:18), yet remain attached to the land. Unmoved. Bound to earthly desires. Unable to give them up. This element in a person will "attack" both ideas and people who would have him be free.

When we become aware of those ties and want to sever them, let us have the courage to make the painful "cut." Let us make a change in our behavior, even if only a small one, for God will help us to continue. The Tzaddik will guide us (cf. *Likutey Moharan* I, 11:1,3,5).

רַבִּי יְהוּדָה הָיָה נוֹתֵן בָּהֶם סִמָּנִים:
דְּצַ"ךְ עֲדַ"שׁ בְּאַחַ"ב:

וימלא הכוס יין.

The "first-born" symbolizes Wisdom — perspectives and ideas, positive or otherwise (*Likutey Moharan* I, 1). These can be dynamic perspectives, constantly changing to incorporate every deeper insight into the Divine. Or they can be the stagnant bigoted ideas of the convicts in Egypt. When God smote the first-born of these convicts (Exodus 12:29; *Shemot Rabbah* 18:10), He also smote their "first-born."

All of us identify with our ideas and preconceived notions of life. They are our individual way of viewing the world. The products of our nature and previous life experiences, they *are* our world. We cling to them as we cling to life itself; unaware of any alternative realities. As we go through this world, we seek to fit everything into these fixed pictures we have of "the way things are" or how they "ought to be." How much more we would grow if we would *have the courage* to experience the insecurity of reorientation.

Until the Mashiach, there is yet time for subtle, gradual, relatively painless transformation. Once he arrives, that option will come to a sudden end.

The Mashiach will more than likely be very different than most of us expect. His ideas may even clash radically with our own. Ideas about ourselves. About Jewishness. About God. For some of us, accepting his ideas may mean forgoing personal prestige. For others, it may mean leaving a dungeon of suffering at the price of changing our cherished beliefs. For those of us who will not be ready, it will certainly be very traumatic (*Rabbi Nachman's Wisdom* #228).

Yehi Ratzon: God! May You give us the courage to change and be ready for the Mashiach!

דצך עדש באחב — GRADUAL PROGRESSION APPLIED

Trying to advance in Jewishness too far, too fast, can be disastrous. We take on modes of behavior far beyond our inner nature. Then, we either delude ourselves and lose contact with our inner selves, or we break down when our souls rebel. Either way, we lose control of our minds. And sometimes, our sanity (*Likutey Halakhot, Hoda'ah* 6:5).

> *The royal prince had inexplicably lost his sanity. Thinking he was a turkey, he sat crouched and naked under the table, pecking at bones and crumbs. The royal physicians gave up all hope of curing him of this madness, and the king suffered tremendous grief. Then a sage came and offered to cure the prince.*
>
> *The sage undressed and sat under the table. The prince now had company. "Who are you?" asked the prince. "What are you doing here?"*
>
> *"And you?" replied the sage. "What are you doing here?"*

Rabbi Yehudah grouped them by their initials:

DeTZaKH, ADaSH, B'ACHaB

Refill the cup.

ארבה — A CHANGE OF DIRECTION

Following the plague, God changed the direction of the wind and all the locusts were carried out of Egypt. Including those which the Egyptians had preserved in salt (Exodus 10:19; *Shemot Rabbah* 13:7).

Sometimes we feel "salted." "Preserved." "Fossilized" in our ways. We can't bring ourselves to listen to the voice of change. We just can't hear it.

God sent a new wind, a new spirit, into the mummified of His People. The message was loud and clear.

Let us breathe in this spirit. Let us hear the message: There is no change we can't accomplish if we only *want* to leave our personal Mitzrayim (cf. *Siftei Kohen, Shemot* 10:19).

חשך — ELUSIVE DESIRES

How thick was the darkness in Egypt? It was like the gold coin, the Dinar (*Shemot Rabbah* 14:1).

What's the connection?

We *all* know that darkness is not tactile. Yet the Egyptians felt they could touch it.

The same is true of money. People whose lives are darkened with avarice really feel they can get their hands on whatever they desire. But like the darkness, it only eludes them (*Parparaot LeChokhmah, Shemot Rabbah* 14).

מכת בכורות — SLAYING OUR PRECONCEIVED NOTIONS

The last of the Ten Plagues. The essential lesson for bringing about a redemption. *The* Redemption.

The Egyptians must have known they would succumb in the end. Though they certainly didn't want to know. Who could be found to replace their slave populace? To whom could they "offer the position"?

Eventually they hit upon a plan. They would approach the convicted criminals, men who had been given life-sentences, with an offer.

"We'll pardon your life-sentences and make you our slaves," the Egyptians told them. "Then we can send away the Jews."

The convicts refused.

"We'd rather stay locked in the dungeon forever than see the Jews go free," they answered unanimously.

The convicts preferred to spend their lives in misery rather than change their ideas about the Jews.

רַבִּי יוֹסֵי הַגְּלִילִי אוֹמֵר: מִנַּיִן אַתָּה אוֹמֵר שֶׁלָּקוּ הַמִּצְרִים בְּמִצְרַיִם עֶשֶׂר מַכּוֹת וְעַל הַיָּם לָקוּ חֲמִשִׁים מַכּוֹת. בְּמִצְרַיִם מַה הוּא אוֹמֵר? "וַיֹּאמְרוּ הַחַרְטֻמִּים אֶל פַּרְעֹה אֶצְבַּע אֱלֹהִים הִיא". וְעַל הַיָּם מַה הוּא אוֹמֵר "וַיַּרְא יִשְׂרָאֵל אֶת הַיָּד הַגְּדֹלָה אֲשֶׁר עָשָׂה יְהֹוָה בְּמִצְרַיִם וַיִּירְאוּ הָעָם אֶת יְיָ וַיַּאֲמִינוּ בַּייָ וּבְמֹשֶׁה עַבְדּוֹ": כַּמָּה לָקוּ בְאֶצְבַּע עֶשֶׂר מַכּוֹת. אֱמֹר מֵעַתָּה בְּמִצְרַיִם לָקוּ עֶשֶׂר מַכּוֹת וְעַל הַיָּם לָקוּ חֲמִשִׁים מַכּוֹת:

And it shouldn't have been.

After each plague there was a respite (Rashi, Exodus 7:25). A chance for Pharaoh to reconsider. A chance for the Jewish People to internalize the lesson. After all, it is the "Egyptian" *within* that the Jew needs to elevate (*Sefer Baal Shem Tov, Va'era,* 4). Each plague, each lesson, is a preliminary for the next. Each requires knowledge of the preceding. If the Egyptian would have been subdued otherwise, the Jew would not have learned his lesson.

This, then, is Rabbi Yehudah's message. He is not merely telling us the obvious acronym for the plagues, grouping them according to their actual order of appearance (their order in Psalms 78 and 105 being different). No, Rabbi Yehudah wants to draw our attention to something more. Note the sequence of the lessons — their preciseness and progressiveness (*Shiboley HaLeket, Orach Chaim* #218). This is the rule of Gradual Progression — applied.

ויאמינו — FAITH: IN YOURSELF

Faith. It's when we don't understand. When we aren't aware. When we don't know why or how. Why did God do this to me? How can I start serving God without knowing what it will entail? When we ask ourselves, "How can God expect this of me? After all, I am only human!" it is then that we need faith. Faith in God. In His Benevolence. In His Wisdom. And faith in ourselves. Faith that we *can* rise above humanness.

Throughout the duration of the plagues, all through that entire year, Moshe strove to gradually bring the Jewish People to greater and greater awareness of God. It was he who showed them how to see — how to understand — the Ten Plagues, each with its important Lesson. They experienced these Lessons. They slaughtered the Pesach lamb in Faith and merited a Divine Revelation. In the morning, when they left Egypt, they thought they knew God. Little did they realize that they were still in "Mitzrayim."

On the sixth day in the wilderness, Pharaoh overtook them. They were trapped!

Rabbi Yosi the Galilean said: From where do we know that the Egyptians were struck by ten plagues in Egypt, but by fifty plagues at the Sea? About Egypt it is written: 'And the magicians said to Pharaoh, It is the *Finger* of God' (Exodus 8:15). About the Red Sea it is written: 'When Israel saw the great *Hand* which God directed against the Egyptians, the people feared God, and believed in God and in His servant Moshe' (Exodus 14:31). How many plagues did they receive with the finger [of God]? Ten! It follows that since there were Ten Plagues in Egypt, there were fifty at the Red Sea [where they were struck with a Hand].

"I'm a turkey," stated the prince.

"So am I!" the sage declared.

They sat together for quite some time, until they became good friends. Certain that he had won the prince's confidence, the sage signalled the king's servants to throw him two shirts. He said to the prince, "What makes you think that a turkey can't wear a shirt? You can wear a shirt and still be a turkey." So they put on shirts, still sitting under the table pecking at bones and crumbs.

After a while, the sage again signalled and two pairs of pants were thrown under the table. Just as before, he said, "What makes you think that a turkey must go without pants?"

The sage continued in this manner until they were both completely dressed. Then he signalled one more time, and they were given regular food from the table. Again the sage said, "What makes you think that a turkey is doomed to eat only crumbs and bones? You can eat whatever you want and still be a turkey!" They both ate the food.

Finally, the sage said, "What makes you think a turkey must sit under the table? Even a turkey can sit at the table."

...And we all know *that if you can sit at a table, you're* not *a turkey.*

The sage continued in this manner until the prince was completely cured (Rabbi Nachman's Stories #25).

We were overanxious. In search of instant Jewishness. Perhaps too proud to work on ourselves gradually, unable to *accept* our present difficulty. We did not know the rule of Gradual Progression.

We must listen to the sage who advises us to change slowly, but surely. The self image which we create in the process will then have the time to penetrate deeper and become our inner nature.

Perhaps the events in Egypt should have been different. God surely could have brought all the plagues at once. Or, He could have immediately subdued the Egyptians by smiting them with the final plague right at the outset. But the actual scenario was neither of these.

רַבִּי אֱלִיעֶזֶר אוֹמֵר: מִנַּיִן שֶׁכָּל מַכָּה וּמַכָּה שֶׁהֵבִיא הַקָּדוֹשׁ
בָּרוּךְ הוּא עַל הַמִּצְרִים בְּמִצְרַיִם הָיְתָה שֶׁל אַרְבַּע מַכּוֹת
שֶׁנֶּאֱמַר: "יְשַׁלַּח בָּם חֲרוֹן אַפּוֹ עֶבְרָה וָזַעַם וְצָרָה מִשְׁלַחַת
מַלְאֲכֵי רָעִים". עֶבְרָה אַחַת. וָזַעַם שְׁתַּיִם. וְצָרָה שָׁלֹשׁ.
מִשְׁלַחַת מַלְאֲכֵי רָעִים אַרְבַּע. אֱמֹר מֵעַתָּה בְּמִצְרַיִם לָקוּ
אַרְבָּעִים מַכּוֹת וְעַל הַיָּם לָקוּ מָאתַיִם מַכּוֹת:

רַבִּי עֲקִיבָא אוֹמֵר: מִנַּיִן שֶׁכָּל מַכָּה וּמַכָּה שֶׁהֵבִיא הַקָּדוֹשׁ
בָּרוּךְ הוּא עַל הַמִּצְרִים בְּמִצְרַיִם הָיְתָה שֶׁל חָמֵשׁ מַכּוֹת
שֶׁנֶּאֱמַר: "יְשַׁלַּח בָּם חֲרוֹן אַפּוֹ עֶבְרָה וָזַעַם וְצָרָה מִשְׁלַחַת
מַלְאֲכֵי רָעִים". חֲרוֹן אַפּוֹ אַחַת. עֶבְרָה שְׁתַּיִם. וָזַעַם שָׁלֹשׁ.
וְצָרָה אַרְבַּע. מִשְׁלַחַת מַלְאֲכֵי רָעִים חָמֵשׁ. אֱמֹר מֵעַתָּה
בְּמִצְרַיִם לָקוּ חֲמִשִּׁים מַכּוֹת וְעַל הַיָּם לָקוּ חֲמִשִּׁים וּמָאתַיִם
מַכּוֹת:

כַּמָּה מַעֲלוֹת טוֹבוֹת לַמָּקוֹם עָלֵינוּ:
דַּיֵּנוּ: אִלּוּ הוֹצִיאָנוּ מִמִּצְרַיִם וְלֹא עָשָׂה בָהֶם שְׁפָטִים
דַּיֵּנוּ: אִלּוּ עָשָׂה בָהֶם שְׁפָטִים וְלֹא עָשָׂה בֵאלֹהֵיהֶם

כמה מעלות — **FAINT ECHOES FROM THE SYMPHONY OF FUTURE ASCENT**

Fifteen Divine Favors, fifteen Levels of Ascent from the Exodus to the building of the Holy Temple.

There were also fifteen steps leading up to the inner courtyard of the Holy Temple. During the celebration of the Water Libation Ceremony on Sukkot, the Levites stood on these fifteen steps and sang praise to God. It was the most joyous event of the year (*Sukkah* 51b). (Year round, the Levi'im stood on a special podium inside the Temple courtyard and sang while the daily wine libations were offered.)

"If He had... but not... *Dayeinu!*" The time has come for us to sing, to ascend the fifteen Levels, the fifteen Steps of celebration. Time to praise God for His fifteen Divine Favors.

Rabbi Eliezer said: From where do we know that each plague that the Holy One, Blessed is He, visited upon the Egyptians in Egypt, consisted of four plagues? It is written: 'He sent forth upon them His burning anger: fury, rage, trouble, and messengers of evil' (Psalms 78:49). *Fury*, is one. *Rage*, two. *Trouble*, three and *Messengers of evil*, four. Thus, they were struck by forty plagues in Egypt, and two hundred at the sea.

Rabbi Akiva said: From where do we know that each plague that the Holy One, Blessed is He, visited upon the Egyptians in Egypt, consisted of five plagues? It is written: 'He sent forth upon them His burning anger, fury, rage, trouble, and messengers of evil' (*Ibid.*). *Burning anger*, is one. *Fury*, two. *Rage*, three. *Trouble*, four and *Messengers of evil*, five. Thus, they were struck by fifty plagues in Egypt, and two hundred and fifty at the sea.

The Ever-Present has bestowed so many favors upon us!

If He had brought us out of Egypt, but had not judged the Egyptians — *Dayeinu*, it would have been enough!
If He had judged them, but not their idols — *Dayeinu!*

Not knowing why this was happening or how to proceed. Again it was Moshe who showed them the way — taught them to understand. He lifted up his arms in prayer. When the sea split, they entered on dry land. But they were too concerned with escaping to realize what had just happened.

On the other side, with Egypt behind them, with the Egyptians drowning below them, they looked back to see how far they'd come. *Now* they realized what Moshe had done.

But again they did not understand! A *human* so aware of God? A man whose prayers are so far above those of others? A man whose prayers split the sea, whose prayers humbled the superpower of antiquity? (*Likutey Halakhot, Birkhot HaShachar* 5:76). Moshe's knowledge of God was beyond them, beyond *their* ability to understand. So they put aside their "knowledge" and served God with something higher. They served Him with Pure Faith (*Likutey Halakhot, Giluach* 3:18). And, in overcoming their illusion that they could know God through reason, they came to understand that they had — first now! — left Mitzrayim.

And, having seen all that Moshe had done for them, having witnessed all that he had achieved, they believed in Moshe. And when Moshe told them, "Know! it is not that I am special; *you* can achieve the same!" then they also believed in the "spark of Moshe" — the spark of the Tzaddik that can be found within each and every one of us (*Rabbi Nachman's Wisdom* p.29; *Tzidkat HaTzaddik* #154).

אִלוּ עָשָׂה בֵאלֹהֵיהֶם וְלֹא הָרַג אֶת בְּכוֹרֵיהֶם ‏ דַּיֵּנוּ:

אִלוּ הָרַג אֶת בְּכוֹרֵיהֶם וְלֹא נָתַן לָנוּ אֶת מָמוֹנָם ‏ דַּיֵּנוּ:

אִלוּ נָתַן לָנוּ אֶת מָמוֹנָם וְלֹא קָרַע לָנוּ אֶת הַיָּם ‏ דַּיֵּנוּ:

אִלוּ קָרַע לָנוּ אֶת הַיָּם וְלֹא הֶעֱבִירָנוּ בְתוֹכוֹ בֶּחָרָבָה ‏ דַּיֵּנוּ:

אִלוּ הֶעֱבִירָנוּ בְתוֹכוֹ בֶּחָרָבָה וְלֹא שִׁקַּע צָרֵינוּ בְּתוֹכוֹ ‏ דַּיֵּנוּ:

אִלוּ שִׁקַּע צָרֵינוּ בְּתוֹכוֹ

וְלֹא סִפֵּק צָרְכֵּנוּ בַּמִּדְבָּר אַרְבָּעִים שָׁנָה ‏ דַּיֵּנוּ:

אִלוּ סִפֵּק צָרְכֵּנוּ בַּמִּדְבָּר אַרְבָּעִים שָׁנָה

וְלֹא הֶאֱכִילָנוּ אֶת הַמָּן ‏ דַּיֵּנוּ:

אִלוּ הֶאֱכִילָנוּ אֶת הַמָּן וְלֹא נָתַן לָנוּ אֶת הַשַּׁבָּת ‏ דַּיֵּנוּ:

אִלוּ נָתַן לָנוּ אֶת הַשַּׁבָּת וְלֹא קֵרְבָנוּ לִפְנֵי הַר סִינַי ‏ דַּיֵּנוּ:

אִלוּ קֵרְבָנוּ לִפְנֵי הַר סִינַי וְלֹא נָתַן לָנוּ אֶת הַתּוֹרָה ‏ דַּיֵּנוּ:

אִלוּ נָתַן לָנוּ אֶת הַתּוֹרָה וְלֹא הִכְנִיסָנוּ לְאֶרֶץ יִשְׂרָאֵל ‏ דַּיֵּנוּ:

אִלוּ הִכְנִיסָנוּ לְאֶרֶץ יִשְׂרָאֵל

וְלֹא בָנָה לָנוּ אֶת בֵּית הַבְּחִירָה ‏ דַּיֵּנוּ:

עַל אַחַת כַּמָּה וְכַמָּה טוֹבָה כְפוּלָה וּמְכֻפֶּלֶת לַמָּקוֹם עָלֵינוּ.
שֶׁהוֹצִיאָנוּ מִמִּצְרַיִם. וְעָשָׂה בָהֶם שְׁפָטִים. וְעָשָׂה בֵאלֹהֵיהֶם.

Symphony. The good points we see in ourselves, upon which we can build a more spiritual life — each one is yet another stone in the Holy Temple of the Future (*Likutey Halakhot, Hashkamat HaBoker* 4).

...When the libations were poured and as they drained into the caverns which opened to the bowels of the earth, the Levi'im stood... on the 15 steps which led to the Holy Temple, singing the songs of God... to raise up those souls which had fallen into the netherworlds... to show them that even in the depths of their existence there is hope, there is God; and by building on their virtues, they will come to see Him (*Likutey Halakhot, Arev* 37).

As we sing the traditional melody of *Dayeinu* with its fifteen Levels, let us listen carefully for that faint echo....

If He had judged their idols, but not slain their first-born — *Dayeinu!*
If He had slain their first-born, but not given us their wealth — *Dayeinu!*
If He had given us their wealth, but not split the Red Sea before us — *Dayeinu!*
If He had split the sea, but not taken us through it on dry land — *Dayeinu!*
If He had led us through the sea on dry land, but not drowned our oppressors in it — *Dayeinu!*
If He had drowned our oppressors in it, but had not provided for our needs in the wilderness for forty years — *Dayeinu!*
If He had provided for our needs in the wilderness for forty years, but not fed us Manna — *Dayeinu!*
If He had fed us Manna, but not given us the Shabbat — *Dayeinu!*
If He had given us Shabbat, but not led us to Mount Sinai — *Dayeinu!*
If He had led us to Mount Sinai, but not given us the Torah — *Dayeinu!*
If He had given us the Torah, but not brought us into the Land of Israel — *Dayeinu!*
If He had brought us into the Land of Israel, but not built a Holy Temple for us — *Dayeinu!*

Therefore, how much more so do we owe thanks to the Ever-Present for all His many, many, favors!

1) He brought us out of Egypt
2) judged the Egyptians
3) judged their idols

There are souls that have fallen into the depths. They are submerged in the abyss of Godlessness and spiritual unawareness. They are drowning in pursuit of the illusory pleasures of this world.

When we sing holy tunes, when the serene beauty of spiritual music reaches our ears, we are powerfully drawn to God. We can actually *see* ourselves transcending our human limitations, giving up the roles, the external baggage we've acquired. We reach out for any virtue we can find in ourselves and want nothing else but to serve God wholeheartedly... And when we then listen closely, we can hear the faint echo of the most sublime music in Creation — the Symphony of the Future. The harmony of Man with God, of Man with Creation. The harmony of Man with himself. It is *this* symphony which will permanently elevate us to the selfless service of God. And even now, we can draw strength and encouragement from its distant echo.

It is *we* who compose this awesome melody. The virtues we find from amongst our own shortcomings and misdeeds — each one is yet another note in this great

וְהָרַג אֶת בְּכוֹרֵיהֶם. וְנָתַן לָנוּ אֶת מָמוֹנָם. וְקָרַע לָנוּ אֶת הַיָּם. וְהֶעֱבִירָנוּ בְּתוֹכוֹ בֶּחָרָבָה. וְשִׁקַּע צָרֵינוּ בְּתוֹכוֹ. וְסִפֵּק צָרְכֵּנוּ בַּמִּדְבָּר אַרְבָּעִים שָׁנָה. וְהֶאֱכִילָנוּ אֶת הַמָּן. וְנָתַן לָנוּ אֶת הַשַּׁבָּת. וְקֵרְבָנוּ לִפְנֵי הַר סִינַי. וְנָתַן לָנוּ אֶת הַתּוֹרָה. וְהִכְנִיסָנוּ לְאֶרֶץ יִשְׂרָאֵל. וּבָנָה לָנוּ אֶת בֵּית הַבְּחִירָה לְכַפֵּר עַל כָּל עֲוֹנוֹתֵינוּ:

עד כאן אומרים בשבת הגדול

רַבָּן גַּמְלִיאֵל הָיָה אוֹמֵר כָּל שֶׁלֹּא אָמַר שְׁלֹשָׁה דְבָרִים אֵלּוּ בַּפֶּסַח לֹא יָצָא יְדֵי חוֹבָתוֹ וְאֵלּוּ הֵן: פֶּסַח. מַצָּה. וּמָרוֹר:

אין להגביה התבשיל כי אם להביט בו שלא יהיה כמגביה קדשים בחוץ

פֶּסַח שֶׁהָיוּ אֲבוֹתֵינוּ אוֹכְלִים בִּזְמַן שֶׁבֵּית הַמִּקְדָּשׁ הָיָה קַיָּם עַל שׁוּם מָה? עַל שׁוּם שֶׁפָּסַח הַקָּדוֹשׁ בָּרוּךְ הוּא עַל בָּתֵּי

Though the most important thing in our lives is to be free of these distractions, and yet, if we still serve Him *with* them, then...

God will see our undaunted determination to serve Him, and then...

...and then the "sea" will split. It will disappear! (*Likutey Halakhot, Shiluach Haken* 4:7).

פסח על שום מה — EQUI-DISTANT/EQUI-CLOSE

There are Upper Worlds. There are Lower Worlds.

On Earth itself, there are the more spiritually refined worlds — the "higher worlds." There are also the less spiritual, more material worlds — the "lower worlds."

There are those of us who were born into Jewishness or entered it at an early age. We were fortunate. We should be grateful. Thank God. But sometimes we forget. We fall into a habitual performance of our Jewishness, thinking that to know the Torah intellectually is, per se, to know God. That to perform His mitzvot with cold, rational meticulousness is, per se, to be close to Him. Even so, we continue to see ourselves as living in the "higher worlds."

Some of us were less fortunate. We were born at a time when, or in a place where, True Jewishness was unheard of. We didn't stand a chance. Or, there

4) slew their first-born
5) gave us their wealth
6) split the Sea for us
7) led us through it on dry land
8) drowned our oppressors in it
9) supplied our needs in the wilderness for forty years
10) fed us Manna
11) gave us the Shabbat
12) brought us to Mount Sinai
13) gave us the Torah
14) brought us to the Land of Israel
15) and built us a Holy Temple to atone for all our sins.

Some congregations recite the Haggadah on the Great Shabbat (the Shabbat preceding Pesach) from after 'Ma Nishtanah' i.e., 'We were slaves...' until here.

Rabbi Gamliel used to say: Whoever does not make clear [the reasons for] the following three things at the Pesach Seder, has not fulfilled his obligation [of Magid]: the Paschal Lamb, the Matzah, and the Maror.

One should look at the bone on the Seder plate (but not point at it or lift it), and then say the following:

The Paschal Lamb that our fathers ate when the Holy Temple was still standing — what was the reason for it? It was because the Holy One, Blessed is He, passed over the houses of our fathers in Egypt, as is

קרע לנו את הים — INTO THE SEA OF TURBULENT DISTRACTIONS

Up ahead, the sea. From behind, Pharaoh's army. To the sides, beasts of the wilderness... The Jewish People were trapped (*Rashi*, Song of Songs 2:14).

And then... they cried out to God.

The Almighty indicated that they go forth into the sea.

We are sometimes overtaken by "Pharaoh's" forces. Surrounded by disturbing thoughts. No matter where we turn, we cannot rid ourselves of them (cf. *Likutey Moharan* I, 72).

Let us venture into the turbulent sea of painful distractions. Let us cross the impasse of perturbing thoughts. We must serve God no matter what. Remain deaf to those voices which attack.

"And the Jewish People *went into the sea...*" up to their noses (*Shemot Rabbah* 21:9). And then... the sea split.

When *we* experience the "sea" as up to our noses, finding ourselves inundated by those distractions, then...

אֲבוֹתֵינוּ בְּמִצְרַיִם. שֶׁנֶּאֱמַר: "וַאֲמַרְתֶּם זֶבַח פֶּסַח הוּא לַיהוָה
אֲשֶׁר פָּסַח עַל בָּתֵּי בְנֵי יִשְׂרָאֵל בְּמִצְרַיִם בְּנָגְפּוֹ אֶת מִצְרַיִם
וְאֶת בָּתֵּינוּ הִצִּיל וַיִּקֹּד הָעָם וַיִּשְׁתַּחֲווּ":

אוחז המצה בידו ומראה אותה להמסובין:

מַצָּה זוֹ שֶׁאָנוּ אוֹכְלִים עַל שׁוּם מָה? עַל שׁוּם שֶׁלֹּא הִסְפִּיק
בְּצֵקָם שֶׁל אֲבוֹתֵינוּ לְהַחֲמִיץ עַד שֶׁנִּגְלָה עֲלֵיהֶם מֶלֶךְ מַלְכֵי
הַמְּלָכִים הַקָּדוֹשׁ בָּרוּךְ הוּא וּגְאָלָם, שֶׁנֶּאֱמַר: "וַיֹּאפוּ אֶת
הַבָּצֵק אֲשֶׁר הוֹצִיאוּ מִמִּצְרַיִם, עֻגֹת מַצּוֹת כִּי לֹא חָמֵץ, כִּי

(Rashi, Exodus 12:30,33; Shemot Rabbah 18:10). The blood on the doorposts was to
serve as a sign of protection, yet the Egyptians taking refuge inside the Jewish
homes were also struck down (Shemot Rabbah 18:2).

Inside the Jewish heart, though, there was total peace and serenity. The Jews
knew that beneath the total chaos was Divine Order. Shining through the great
turmoil was Divine Providence. And they knew that it was actually their recognition
of the Source of that chaos — their knowledge of that "Disorder" — which had
saved them (Likutey Halakhot, Pidyon Bechor 3).

ולא יכלו להתמהמה — BEYOND THE POINT OF NO RETURN

When our forefather Yaakov alluded to the far limits of the forthcoming exile, he
did so with a very specific word: He said, "r'du." Numerically, R'DU is 210 — the
actual amount of years the Jewish People were physically in Egypt (Genesis 42:2;
Rashi, Ibid.). Yaakov told his sons, "r'du — go down!" To experience Redemption,
God has us go down. We must first experience a spiritual descent, a plunge which
may bring us to the nadir of Godlessness.

But God is everywhere! The "closer" we are, the more He conceals His Presence.
But the "farther" we are, the more He must reveal Himself.

And just beyond that "farthest" point, when we feel we have reached the end
of the road of a Godless life, when we know that we can go no further without
destroying ourselves — there, albeit concealed, is God Himself! We are standing at
the very threshold of holiness... but we need someone to tell us this.

Moshe, the Tzaddik, knew the souls of his brethren. He was aware of the extent
of their decline. When they had reached the point of "no return," when there was
"no more time to wait," he let them know... that God is with them (Likutey Halakhot,
Rosh Chodesh 3:1).

written: 'You shall say, it is a Pesach sacrifice to God, because He passed over the houses of the Children of Israel in Egypt. He struck the Egyptians, but He saved our households; and the people kneeled and bowed down' (Exodus 12:27).

The Matzah is held up for all to see and the following is recited:

This Matzah that we eat — what is the reason for it? It is because the dough of our fathers did not have time to become Chametz before God revealed Himself to them and redeemed them, as is written: 'And they baked Matzah from the dough which they had taken with them from Egypt; it did not become chametz, because they were driven out of Egypt

are those of us who were born into Jewishness. But something happened along the way. We fell. And now, we see ourselves as "lower" than those of the "higher worlds." We feel ourselves to be farther from God than those whom *we* presume to be "closer."

The Jewish People in Egypt were becoming more and more aware of their *distance* from God. Of how they had fallen into a physical existence, of how they had strayed from God's Will. And then Moshe told them that they would soon be leaving. They were hardly able to believe Moshe when he first returned to Egypt with word of the Redemption. It seemed even more implausible now. How unworthy they saw themselves! (*Pesikta* p. 47b). But Moshe met with the People. He spoke with them. He gave them to *understand* the secret of the Pesach lamb.

And when they slaughtered the lamb — the animal symbolic of their own physical existence — the fragrance of that sacrifice rose up High. God, as it were, descended into the depths of depraved Mitzrayim. He let it be known that before Him, the "low" and the "high" are one and the same, they can all be equally close. Yet all remain infinitely far. For to know God, is to *know* the magnitude of one's distance.

And the Jewish People *experienced* the secret of the Pesach lamb. They experienced Redemption (*Likutey Halakhot, Netilat Yadaim* 6:16).

פסח אשר — KNOWING THE DISORDER

When God created the world, He instilled in it an inherent harmony. There is a supreme order, Divine Order, in Providence.

Pharaoh sought to undermine that Divine Control and Order. He claimed divine powers for himself (*Rashi,* Exodus 7:15). He wanted to control.

God threw Egypt into total chaos, He created great mayhem. They had been warned that the first-born would be smitten, but now, many who were not known to be first-born lay dead. It seemed to them as if they were *all* going to die.

גֵּרְשׁוּ מִמִּצְרַיִם וְלֹא יָכְלוּ לְהִתְמַהְמֵהַּ, וְגַם צֵדָה לֹא עָשׂוּ לָהֶם":

אוחז המרור בידו ומראה אותו להמסובין:

מָרוֹר זֶה שֶׁאָנוּ אוֹכְלִים עַל שׁוּם מָה? עַל שׁוּם שֶׁמֵּרְרוּ הַמִּצְרִים אֶת חַיֵּי אֲבוֹתֵינוּ בְּמִצְרַיִם שֶׁנֶּאֱמַר: "וַיְמָרְרוּ אֶת חַיֵּיהֶם בַּעֲבֹדָה קָשָׁה, בְּחֹמֶר, וּבִלְבֵנִים, וּבְכָל עֲבֹדָה בַּשָּׂדֶה, אֵת כָּל עֲבֹדָתָם אֲשֶׁר עָבְדוּ בָהֶם בְּפָרֶךְ":

בְּכָל דּוֹר וָדוֹר חַיָּב אָדָם לִרְאוֹת אֶת עַצְמוֹ כְּאִלּוּ הוּא יָצָא מִמִּצְרַיִם שֶׁנֶּאֱמַר: "וְהִגַּדְתָּ לְבִנְךָ בַּיּוֹם הַהוּא לֵאמֹר בַּעֲבוּר זֶה עָשָׂה יְהֹוָה לִי בְּצֵאתִי מִמִּצְרָיִם": שֶׁלֹּא אֶת אֲבוֹתֵינוּ

Even this, then, is but Divine Mercy.

God enjoins us to eat the Maror, the bitter herb; the Chasa, the romaine lettuce.

In the depths of our MaROR, which is numerically MaVeT (446), spiritual lifelessness, God gives us an awareness of our situation. He gives us a taste of that bitterness. He gives us the CHaSA (69), which is numerically CHaYYiM (68) — Life (with 1 being added for the word itself. The method of adding 1 in constructing a *gematria* [numerological value] is used extensively in Kabbalistic writings. It usually denotes the necessity to apply an extra "One," a more profound level of Divine Knowledge, in order to appreciate the meaning of the numerical connection. Cf. *Shomer Emunim [Hakadmon]* 1:21).

And through this, we come to yearn and cry out for Redemption (*Nachat HaShulchan*).

בכל דור ודור — A NONRECURRENT OPPORTUNITY

God is constantly improving His World, rectifying the intended flaws which were inherent in the act of Creation. In *every generation*, the world is spiritually enriched in some way. Progress is made toward the Ultimate Goal.

In *every generation*, there are souls that are extracted from their spiritual bondage. Others are made aware that they are *still* in bondage.

Every day, God is refining His Works, elevating man to a greater awareness of the Divine. *Every day* is like a new generation (*Kohelet Rabbah* 1:4). A period in history that has never been and will never again be. *Today* is a nonrecurrent opportunity to return to God... *Tomorrow* will be something entirely different.

The Exodus symbolizes this ongoing process (*Likutey Halakhot, Pesach* 7:11). Let us see ourselves taking part (*Likutey Halakhot, Shechitah* 4:3).

and could not wait. Neither had they prepared any provisions for themselves for the way' (Exodus 12:39).

The Maror is held up for all to see and the following is recited:

This Maror that we eat — what is the reason for it? It is because the Egyptians made the lives of our fathers bitter in Egypt, as is written: 'They embittered their lives with hard work; [working with] mortar and bricks, and through all kinds of field work; all their hard labor at which they made them slave' (Exodus 1:14).

In every generation one must regard himself as though he personally had gone out from Egypt, as is written: 'You shall tell your son on that day, "Because of this, God did for *me* when *I* went out from Egypt" ' (Exodus 13:8). It was not only our fathers that God redeemed, but He also

וגם צדה לא עשו — BYPASSING REASON

The Jewish People had become very accustomed to their restricted life in Egypt. All their curtailed needs were provided for by the Egyptians (cf. *Ramban* and *Rabbenu Bachye*, Numbers 11:5). They could not even imagine life otherwise, let alone give up their "security" for what seemed to them a dubious promise of a higher level of existence. They just couldn't be *reasoned* with.

God bypassed their reason. He brought them to Higher Awareness. He let them experience a great arousal. They followed God out into the desert, into the Wilderness. They asked no questions, they had no more doubts, they needed no "reason." They knew!

Yehi Ratzon: Oh God! In our own lives, when You beckon us, may we be worthy of doing the same (*Likutey Halakhot, Giluach* 3:12).

מרור על שום מה — BITTERSWEET DARKNESS

The knowledge that God is always with us, the awareness that He will never forsake us — this is true peace and harmony. It is the tranquility and harmony we experience when we *know* that our life has meaning and purpose. It is the sweet serenity and at-oneness with God that we feel when we realize that we are fulfilling His Will.

But we would never know it, we could never become aware of it, unless we first experience bitterness, the absence of serenity and peace; just as we cannot appreciate light without prior knowledge of darkness (*Likutey Moharan* I, 27:7; *Likutey Halakhot, Netilat Yadaim* 6:16).

But how are we to *see* the darkness, when we've never "seen the light?" How are we to know that we *are* in spiritual exile, when we cannot perceive beyond the physical?

בִּלְבַד גָּאַל הַקָּדוֹשׁ בָּרוּךְ הוּא אֶלָּא אַף אוֹתָנוּ גָּאַל עִמָּהֶם
שֶׁנֶּאֱמַר: "וְאוֹתָנוּ הוֹצִיא מִשָּׁם לְמַעַן הָבִיא אֹתָנוּ לָתֶת לָנוּ
אֶת הָאָרֶץ אֲשֶׁר נִשְׁבַּע לַאֲבֹתֵינוּ":

יקח הכוס ויכסה המצות ויאמר:

לְפִיכָךְ אֲנַחְנוּ חַיָּבִים לְהוֹדוֹת לְהַלֵּל לְשַׁבֵּחַ לְפָאֵר
לְרוֹמֵם לְהַדֵּר לְבָרֵךְ לְעַלֵּה וּלְקַלֵּס לְמִי שֶׁעָשָׂה
לַאֲבוֹתֵינוּ וְלָנוּ אֶת כָּל הַנִּסִּים הָאֵלּוּ: הוֹצִיאָנוּ מֵעַבְדוּת
לְחֵרוּת; מִיָּגוֹן לְשִׂמְחָה; וּמֵאֵבֶל לְיוֹם טוֹב; וּמֵאֲפֵלָה
לְאוֹר גָּדוֹל; וּמִשִּׁעְבּוּד לִגְאֻלָּה. וְנֹאמַר לְפָנָיו שִׁירָה
חֲדָשָׁה הַלְלוּיָהּ:

means *path*.) When we can praise and thank God for these difficulties, we have uncovered these paths, these Halakhot (see *Likutey Moharan* II, 2:1-2; *Likutey Moharan* I, 56:3-4). Strewn along these paths are the conceptions that only we can have of Divine Benevolence. Only *we* have lived our lives. Only *we* can perceive the Divine Message enclothed in the story of our lives (cf. *Rabbi Nachman's Wisdom* #1; *Tzaddik* #98).

> *Rabbi Akiva had a very holy soul. But it had an unholy beginning. It was brought into this world in a very ignoble fashion. He descended from the union of Sisera, the Kanaanite general, with Yael, the wife of Chever the Qenite* (Judges 4:18; Sha'ar HaGilgulim 34; Sefer HaGilgulim 57). *For the first 40 years of his life, Rabbi Akiva was a product of circumstances, trapped by the forces of evil.*
>
> *After many years of inner struggle, God helped him to rise above the compelling factors of his origin and background. Rabbi Akiva then praised God and was grateful for all his hardships. He deduced many, many Halakhot, many paths to God, from all the "thorns" he had experienced during his life* (Menachot 29b; Ohr LaShamayim, Chukat). *(The letters of the Torah scroll, representing the Jewish souls, are only complete with these "thorns," the Tagim, the hairlines of ink which crown various letters).*

If from the depths of our hearts we can praise God for His *benevolence* of the past, if we can perceive Him *throughout* our past adversity, if we can taste in that bitterness a *sweetness* of the Divine — *then* we shall know that we have indeed left our "exile." It is something of the past.

97

redeemed *us* with them, as is written: 'And He brought us out from there, so that He might lead us and give us the Land which He had promised to our fathers' (Deuteronomy 6:23).

The Matzot are covered and the cup is held.

Therefore it is our duty to thank, to praise, to esteem, to glorify, to exalt, to honor, to beautify, to extol and pay tribute to the One Who has performed all these miracles for our fathers and for us. He led us from slavery to freedom; from sorrow to joy; from mourning to festivity; from darkness to bright light; and from bondage to redemption! Let us therefore sing before Him a new song, Hallelu-Yah!

לפיכך — PERSONAL PSALMS

We now introduce the Hallel, the joyous song to God; and we introduce it with a pertinent lesson. There are ten Levels of Praise, ten Expressions of Song. With them, King David composed Tehillim (Psalms, six chapters of which form the Hallel prayer). King David, the "Sweet Singer of Israel," knew many misfortunes in his life. But he never saw them as reason for sorrow. He knew the Source of his pain to be the Benevolent God, so he continued to praise Him. Amidst all his suffering, amidst all his pain, King David kept composing his Tehillim.

"Therefore, it is *our* duty to thank... He led *us*..."

The Haggadah makes mention of five antithetical pairs. They comprise the ten Levels of Tehillim. When in *enslavement* we know we are are really *free* — free to *rejoice* amidst *sorrow*, to be *festive* in *mourning*, to *enlighten* our *darkness* until God *redeems* us from *bondage* — then we are ready to recite Hallel (*Likutey Halakhot, Piryah Verivyah 3:9,29*).

"*Let us sing before Him a new song, Hallelu-Yah!*"

> *...And in the Future, when the fires of Gehennom abate, when six millenia of human suffering are out of the way, there — there in the purified Gehennom — around God we will dance, singing Him praise for all that past suffering (Ibid.; Asarah Ma'amarot, Chikur Hadin 5:5).*

הלל המצרי — SOMETHING OF THE PAST

Unique to this night of the Seder, is the divided Hallel Prayer. The portion we recite after the meal is more in the context of a prayer for the Future Redemption. It is unrelated to the past.

What we say now is called *Hallel Hamitzri*, the "Egyptian" Hallel. It is a thanksgiving for the *present* in context of the past.

But even more, it is a thanksgiving *for* the past! We are grateful to God for bringing us into exile, for giving us the experience of bitterness in our lives.

The personal difficulties we all go through, these are the Halakhot of our lives. They are the "laws," the individual *paths* which lead us to God. (Halakhah also

יניח הכוס מידו ויגלה המצות:

הַלְלוּיָהּ הַלְלוּ עַבְדֵי יְהוָה הַלְלוּ אֶת שֵׁם יְהוָה: יְהִי שֵׁם יְהוָה
מְבֹרָךְ מֵעַתָּה וְעַד עוֹלָם: מִמִּזְרַח שֶׁמֶשׁ עַד מְבוֹאוֹ מְהֻלָּל
שֵׁם יְהוָה: רָם עַל כָּל גּוֹיִם יְהוָה עַל הַשָּׁמַיִם כְּבוֹדוֹ: מִי
כַּיהוָה אֱלֹהֵינוּ הַמַּגְבִּיהִי לָשָׁבֶת: הַמַּשְׁפִּילִי לִרְאוֹת בַּשָּׁמַיִם
וּבָאָרֶץ: מְקִימִי מֵעָפָר דָּל מֵאַשְׁפֹּת יָרִים אֶבְיוֹן: לְהוֹשִׁיבִי
עִם נְדִיבִים עִם נְדִיבֵי עַמּוֹ: מוֹשִׁיבִי עֲקֶרֶת הַבַּיִת אֵם הַבָּנִים
שְׂמֵחָה הַלְלוּיָהּ:

בְּצֵאת יִשְׂרָאֵל מִמִּצְרָיִם בֵּית יַעֲקֹב מֵעַם לֹעֵז: הָיְתָה יְהוּדָה
לְקָדְשׁוֹ יִשְׂרָאֵל מַמְשְׁלוֹתָיו: הַיָּם רָאָה וַיָּנֹס הַיַּרְדֵּן יִסֹּב
לְאָחוֹר: הֶהָרִים רָקְדוּ כְאֵילִים גְּבָעוֹת כִּבְנֵי צֹאן: מַה-לְּךָ
הַיָּם כִּי תָנוּס הַיַּרְדֵּן תִּסֹּב לְאָחוֹר: הֶהָרִים תִּרְקְדוּ כְאֵילִים
גְּבָעוֹת כִּבְנֵי צֹאן: מִלִּפְנֵי אָדוֹן חוּלִי אָרֶץ מִלִּפְנֵי אֱלוֹהַּ
יַעֲקֹב: הַהֹפְכִי הַצּוּר אֲגַם מָיִם חַלָּמִישׁ לְמַעְיְנוֹ מָיִם:

and sometimes curtailed in order to comply with *His* Will? If so, and if we are consistent in this path, it is surely meritorious. We become His servants and praise Him as our Master.

As such, though, we know no inner peace. We face constant turmoil between His Will and ours. To a greater or lesser degree, we inevitably come to see God as a restrictive authority upon our lives.

If only we would see ourselves as God's *children,* experiencing Him as the Loving Father we are all searching for... If we would accept His Will as our own, knowing it is for our best... We would have *no* desires of our own. Desiring only a closeness with Him... We would perceive of "our" aspirations as the expression of the Divine Spark within.

We open this chapter of Hallel as servants and conclude it as children.

If we persist in praising God as Master, while knowing that there *is* a higher experience to yearn for — namely, God as Loving Father — then someday we will taste that inner peace, that inner joy (*Likutey Halakhot, Birkhot HaShachar* 3:18,43).

The cup is replaced and the Matzot uncovered.

Hallelu-Yah! Praise, you servants of God, praise the Name of God! Blessed is the Name of God, from now and forever. From the rising of the sun until its setting, let God's Name be praised. High above all nations is God, His glory is above the heavens. Who is like God, our God, Whose throne is on high, yet He looks down so low to see the heavens and the earth! He raises up the poor out of the dust, lifts up the needy from the dunghill; in order to seat him with princes, with the princes of His people. He turns a barren housewife into a joyful mother of children, Hallelu-Yah! (Psalm 113).

When Israel went out of Egypt, the house of Yaakov from a people of a foreign tongue; Yehudah became His holy one, Israel His kingdom. The [Red] Sea saw and fled, the Jordan [River] turned back. The mountains danced like rams, the hills like lambs. What ails you, Sea, that you flee? the Jordan, that you turn back? [the] mountains, that you dance like rams; you hills like lambs? Tremble, earth, before the Master, before the God of Yaakov. He Who turns the rock into a pool of water, the bedrock into a flowing spring (Psalm 114).

הללויה — PARADOXICAL PRAISE

The worlds were brought into existence with ten Divine Utterances. Corresponding to these ten are the ten Expressions of Praise found in the Psalms (*Pesachim* 117a; *MaHarsha, Ibid.*). Indeed, man's Awareness and his expressed praise of God is the goal, the purpose of Creation. The ten *Divine* Utterances find their culmination in the ten *human* expressions.

The pinnacle of these expressions is *Hallelu-Yah,* a single word, a single utterance. In it are merged the praise of God (Hallel) and the Divine Name (Yah). As long as man perceives of his praise as "independent" of God, as arising from his *own* initiative, the praise is not complete.

But then, what *is* man's role? If it is God who inspires His own praise, of what value is human Awareness, of what worth is human expression of praise?

Let us cease trying to comprehend the fusion of Divine Arousal and human initiative. For us, this will always remain a paradox. Rather, we must endeavor to *experience* it: praising God for allowing us the opportunity to praise Him, cognizant of God's union with the Jewish soul (*Likutey Halakhot, Keriat Shma* 5:16).

הללו עבדי... — TRANSCENDING GOD'S AUTHORITY

How do we experience our relationship with God? Do we perceive of ourselves as individuals having *our own* desires and aspirations which have to be channeled

יכסה המצות יקח הכוס בידו ויאמר:

בָּרוּךְ אַתָּה יְהֹוָה אֱלֹהֵינוּ מֶלֶךְ הָעוֹלָם אֲשֶׁר גְּאָלָנוּ וְגָאַל אֶת אֲבוֹתֵינוּ מִמִּצְרַיִם וְהִגִּיעָנוּ הַלַּיְלָה הַזֶּה לֶאֱכָל בּוֹ מַצָּה וּמָרוֹר. כֵּן יְהֹוָה אֱלֹהֵינוּ וֵאלֹהֵי אֲבוֹתֵינוּ יַגִּיעֵנוּ לְמוֹעֲדִים וְלִרְגָלִים אֲחֵרִים הַבָּאִים לִקְרָאתֵנוּ לְשָׁלוֹם שְׂמֵחִים בְּבִנְיַן עִירֶךָ וְשָׂשִׂים בַּעֲבוֹדָתֶךָ וְנֹאכַל שָׁם מִן הַזְּבָחִים וּמִן הַפְּסָחִים (למוצאי שבת: מִן הַפְּסָחִים וּמִן הַזְּבָחִים) אֲשֶׁר יַגִּיעַ דָּמָם עַל קִיר מִזְבַּחֲךָ לְרָצוֹן וְנוֹדֶה לְךָ שִׁיר חָדָשׁ עַל גְּאֻלָּתֵנוּ וְעַל פְּדוּת נַפְשֵׁנוּ: בָּרוּךְ אַתָּה יְהֹוָה גָּאַל יִשְׂרָאֵל:

הִנְנִי מוּכָן וּמְזֻמָּן לְקַיֵּם מִצְוַת כּוֹס שֵׁנִי מֵאַרְבַּע כּוֹסוֹת לְשֵׁם יִחוּד קוּדְשָׁא בְּרִיךְ הוּא וּשְׁכִינְתֵּיהּ עַל יְדֵי הַהוּא טָמִיר וְנֶעְלָם בְּשֵׁם כָּל יִשְׂרָאֵל: וִיהִי נֹעַם יְיָ אֱלֹהֵינוּ עָלֵינוּ וּמַעֲשֵׂה יָדֵינוּ כּוֹנְנָה עָלֵינוּ וּמַעֲשֵׂה יָדֵינוּ כּוֹנְנֵהוּ.

בָּרוּךְ אַתָּה יְהֹוָה אֱלֹהֵינוּ מֶלֶךְ הָעוֹלָם בּוֹרֵא פְּרִי הַגָּפֶן:

ושותה בהסבת שמאל ואינו מברך ברכה אחרונה:

רחצה

נוטל ידיו ומברך:

בָּרוּךְ אַתָּה יְהֹוָה אֱלֹהֵינוּ מֶלֶךְ הָעוֹלָם אֲשֶׁר קִדְּשָׁנוּ בְּמִצְוֹתָיו וְצִוָּנוּ עַל נְטִילַת יָדָיִם:

ואסור לדבר עד אחרי אכילת המצה ואם אפשר עד אחרי כורך מה טוב

The Matzot are covered and the cup is held.

Blessed are You, God, King of the universe, Who redeemed us and redeemed our fathers from Egypt and brought us to this night, on which we eat Matzah and Maror. God, God of our fathers: bring us to celebrate future festivals and holidays may they come to us in peace. Let us be happy in the rebuilding of Your city and joyful in Your service; and there we shall eat the sacrifices and Pesach offerings (on Saturday nights say: the Pesach offerings and sacrifices) whose blood will be sprinkled upon the sides of Your altar for acceptance. We shall then thank You with a New Song for our redemption and for the deliverance of our souls. Blessed are You, God, Who has redeemed Israel!

The blessing over the second cup of wine is recited:

I am ready and prepared to perform the mitzvah of drinking the second cup of wine.

Blessed are You, God, King of the universe, Who creates the fruit of the vine.

The second cup of wine is then drunk while leaning on the left side.

RACHTZAH

Wash the hands and recite the blessing.

Blessed are You, God, King of the universe, Who has made us holy with His mitzvot, and commanded us to wash the hands.

One should not talk until after eating the Matzah (preferably that of the Korekh).

רחצה — GETTING READY

We wash a second time to strengthen our Rechitzah, our (faith and) trust in God. This, so that when the Divine Voice beckons to us a second time, we will be ready... (*Likutey Halakhot, Netilat Yadaim* 6:26; above, *U'rechatz*.)

מוֹצִיא

יקח המצות ויאחז בידיו כל שלשתן ויאמר:

הִנְנִי מוּכָן וּמְזֻמָּן לְקַיֵּם מִצְוַת אֲכִילַת מַצָּה לְשֵׁם יִחוּד קוּדְשָׁא בְּרִיךְ הוּא וּשְׁכִינְתֵּיהּ עַל יְדֵי הַהוּא טָמִיר וְנֶעְלָם בְּשֵׁם כָּל יִשְׂרָאֵל: וִיהִי נֹעַם יְיָ אֱלֹהֵינוּ עָלֵינוּ וּמַעֲשֵׂה יָדֵינוּ כּוֹנְנָה עָלֵינוּ וּמַעֲשֵׂה יָדֵינוּ כּוֹנְנֵהוּ.

בָּרוּךְ אַתָּה יְהוָֹה אֱלֹהֵינוּ מֶלֶךְ הָעוֹלָם הַמּוֹצִיא לֶחֶם מִן הָאָרֶץ:

מַצָּה

יניח מצה התחתונה ותופס העליונה והפרוסה ויברך, ויכוין לפטור בברכת אכילת מצה, מצה של כורך, ואכילת האפיקומן:

בָּרוּךְ אַתָּה יְהוָֹה אֱלֹהֵינוּ מֶלֶךְ הָעוֹלָם אֲשֶׁר קִדְּשָׁנוּ בְּמִצְוֹתָיו וְצִוָּנוּ עַל אֲכִילַת מַצָּה:

ויאכלם בהסבת שמאל בלי מלח:

מָרוֹר

יקח כזית מרור ויטבול בחרוסת ויאמר:

הִנְנִי מוּכָן וּמְזֻמָּן לְקַיֵּם מִצְוַת אֲכִילַת מָרוֹר לְשֵׁם יִחוּד קוּדְשָׁא בְּרִיךְ הוּא וּשְׁכִינְתֵּיהּ עַל יְדֵי הַהוּא טָמִיר וְנֶעְלָם בְּשֵׁם כָּל יִשְׂרָאֵל: וִיהִי נֹעַם יְיָ אֱלֹהֵינוּ עָלֵינוּ וּמַעֲשֵׂה יָדֵינוּ כּוֹנְנָה עָלֵינוּ וּמַעֲשֵׂה יָדֵינוּ כּוֹנְנֵהוּ.

בָּרוּךְ אַתָּה יְהוָֹה אֱלֹהֵינוּ מֶלֶךְ הָעוֹלָם אֲשֶׁר קִדְּשָׁנוּ בְּמִצְוֹתָיו וְצִוָּנוּ עַל אֲכִילַת מָרוֹר:

ויאכלנו בלא הסיבה:

Pesach sacrifice, the Passover Seder. We may be eating the Matzah, the bread of Awareness. Specifically *now* we must chew the Maror. Only now can we properly experience the bitterness.

We *all* experience bitterness in our lives. The most painful bitterness is that of confusion. We know we are on the wrong path. We really want to return to God. We just don't know how (*Likutey Halakhot, Hoda'ah* 6:57).

MOTZI

Hold all three Matzot, and recite:
I am ready and prepared to perform the mitzvah of eating the Matzah.

Blessed are You, God, King of the universe, Who brings forth bread from the earth.

MATZAH

After returning the bottom Matzah to the Seder plate, raise the top and middle Matzot (bearing in mind that the blessing shall also apply to the matzah of the Korekh and Afikomen) and recite:

Blessed are You, God, King of the universe, Who has made us holy with His mitzvot, and commanded us to eat Matzah.

One then eats the matzah while leaning on the left side.

MAROR

Dip the Maror in the Charoset and recite the following:
I am ready and prepared to perform the mitzvah of eating the Maror.

Blessed are You, God, King of the universe, Who has made us holy with His mitzvot, and commanded us to eat Maror.

One then eats the Maror without reclining.

מוציא — SUSTAINED BY WISDOM

Unique among blessings is the one for bread. In it we specify that God brings it forth from the earth. Enclothed in this bread, the principal sustenance of man, is Divine Wisdom — the spark of God that gives us life. Of the entire universe, including even the Supernal Worlds, it is on this speck of dust, planet Earth, that Divine Wisdom is manifested to the greatest degree. "The *Earth* is full of His Glory" (Isaiah 6:3).

More than anything else, it is the knowledge, the awareness, that God is everywhere — that we can reach Him even from the depths of our earthly existence — which instills us with *life*.

This is the wisdom, the Divine Wisdom, which God implants in the bread we eat, which He "brings forth from the earth" (*Likutey Halakhot, Netilat Yadaim Le'Seudah* 6:54).

מרור — THE SWEET HERB OF ADVERSITY

We may already be experiencing a "redemption." We may be "partaking" of the

כּוֹרֵךְ

יקח כזית מהמצה השלישית וחזרת עמה וקודם האכילה יאמר:

זֵכֶר לְמִקְדָּשׁ כְּהִלֵּל. כֵּן עָשָׂה הִלֵּל. בִּזְמַן שֶׁבֵּית הַמִּקְדָּשׁ הָיָה קַיָּם הָיָה כּוֹרֵךְ (פֶּסַח) מַצָּה וּמָרוֹר וְאוֹכֵל בְּיַחַד לְקַיֵּם מַה שֶׁנֶּאֱמַר עַל מַצּוֹת וּמְרוֹרִים יֹאכְלֻהוּ:

ואוכל שתיהן ביחד בהסבת שמאל

It is this element of multiplicity in Creation which allows for the existence of evil, for the forces within and without man which seek to conceal the Creator. It is the dissension within man's heart, the dissidence between men's minds, which give rise to the actualization of that potential evil (*Likutey Moharan* I, 51 and 62:2; *Likutey Halakhot, Ribit* 5:1).

Matzah symbolizes Divine Manifestation; Maror, Divine Concealment. Together, they symbolize the plurality in Creation.

A commemoration of the Holy Temple, according to Hillel...

It is Hillel who symbolizes the transcending of contention between men. It is Hillel who realizes that all things *are* One. (The schools of Hillel and Shammai disagreed upon a vast range of Halakhic matters and had very divergent approaches to Jewish life. Even so, there was great accord and mutual respect between them; see *Shabbat* 14b and *Yevamot* 13b,14b. MoSheH is an acronym for Machloket [the dispute between] Shammai and Hillel, indicating that at their source, both opinions are one; see *Likutey Moharan* I, 56:8.)

It is the Holy Temple which symbolizes the great harmony in Creation (*Likutey Halakhot, Betziat HaPat* 5:16), the elevation of all things to their Source (*Likutey Halakhot, Pikadon* 4:19).

There, with the Holy Temple, we transcend plurality: we eat the Matzah and Maror as one. There, we experience the unity of mankind, the oneness of adversity and contentment (*Likutey Halakhot, Rosh Chodesh* 3:5).

שלחן עורך — ...AND FINALLY THE MEAL!

Once, a Jew and a German gentile were traveling together as beggars. The Jew told the gentile to make believe that he was Jewish (his native language being very similar to Yiddish), and the Jews would have pity on him. Since Pesach was approaching, the Jewish beggar taught his comrade how to behave at the Seder. He told him about Kiddush,

KOREKH

Take the bottom Matzah, put Maror on it, and recite the following passage:

A commemoration of the Holy Temple, according to Hillel's custom. This is what Hillel did at the time when the Holy Temple stood: he would combine [the Paschal Lamb,] Matzah and Maror, and eat them together. This, in order to fulfill what is written: 'They shall eat it [the Paschal Lamb] with Matzah and bitter herbs' (Exodus 12:8).

One then eats the Matzah-Maror sandwich while reclining to the left.

Let us partake of the Maror — let us *accept* the painful experiences of our past. We must realize that our personal Maror was necessary to implement our "redemption." We need to recognize that the depth of feeling we have for God, the depth of understanding we have of life, of ourselves, is only *because* of our past adversity (*Nachat HaShulchan*).

We can now dip our bitterness in CHaRoSeTH, in CHaS RuTH, the awareness of God's guiding mercy which pervades our affliction. (*Chas* means to have mercy. Ruth was the progenitor of King David who sang to God about his adversity.) Let us then praise God for *affording* us this experience (*Likutey Halakhot, Netilat Yadaim* 6:17; *Pri Etz Chaim* 21:7).

As we chew the Maror, we sweeten its bitterness. We mitigate its severity. We experience in it a taste of the Divine, our portion from Heaven (*Likutey Halakhot, Ibid.* See *Pri Etz Chaim* 21:3 that the chewing of the Maror is seen as the "grinding" of the manna in preparation for the Future).

> *The Maror, the bitter herb, is almost inedible. Indeed, year round we would not recite a blessing over it* (Orach Chayim #475, Magen Avraham 10). *But on this night, we are* aware *that even this bitterness is Sweet. Therefore, we would recite a blessing before eating it. (It is known that the ARI recited the appropriate blessing over wild, inedible fruits. He* knew *that they too came from God!* Yalkut Reuveni I, 42a-b.)
>
> *...And the year we eat — we experience — nothing other than the bitterness of the Maror, that year is still a time of "exile." Come Tish'ah B'Av, which that year will fall on the very same day of the week as the Seder, we will still re-experience the Destruction* (Siach Sarfey Kodesh Breslov II, 108).

כורך — A TRANSCENDING-PLURALITY SANDWICH

In this world we experience plurality. The oneness of all things, the Unity of God as it is manifested in Creation, is hidden. We find it difficult to comprehend how from the One comes the many.

שלחן עורך

וְאַחַר כָּךְ אוֹכְלִין סְעוּדָתָן וְשׁוֹתִין כָּל צָרְכָן.

צפון

יֹאכַל כְּזַיִת אֲפִיקוֹמָן וִיכַוֵּין שֶׁהוּא זֵכֶר לְקָרְבַּן פֶּסַח:

וּמִקֹּדֶם יֹאמַר זֶה

לְשֵׁם יִחוּד קוּדְשָׁא בְּרִיךְ הוּא וּשְׁכִינְתֵּיה, בִּדְחִילוּ וּרְחִימוּ, בִּרְחִימוּ וּדְחִילוּ,
לְיַחֲדָא שֵׁם י"ה ב־ו"ה, בְּיִחוּדָא שְׁלִים, בְּשֵׁם כָּל יִשְׂרָאֵל. הִנֵּה אָנֹכִי בָּא לְקַיֵּים
מִצְוַת אֲכִילַת הָאֲפִיקוֹמָן, זֵכֶר לְקָרְבַּן פֶּסַח הַנֶּאֱכַל עַל הַשׂוֹבַע קוֹדֶם חֲצוֹת
לַיְלָה. וּתְהֵא חֲשׁוּבָה אֲכִילָה זוֹ לִפְנֵי הַקָּדוֹשׁ בָּרוּךְ הוּא כְּאִילּוּ הִקְרַבְנוּ קָרְבָּן
פֶּסַח וַאֲכַלְנוּהוּ בִּמְקוֹם קָדוֹשׁ, לְתַקֵּן שָׁרְשׁוֹ בִּמְקוֹר עֶלְיוֹן. וִיהִי רָצוֹן מִלְּפָנֶיךָ ה'
אֱלֹהֵינוּ וֵאלֹהֵי אֲבוֹתֵינוּ, שֶׁתִּבָּנֶה בֵּית הַמִּקְדָּשׁ בִּמְהֵרָה בְיָמֵינוּ, וּתְזַכֵּינוּ לְהַקְרִיב

*"How was your Seder?" he asked. The disgruntled German then told
him what had happened.*

*"Fool!" replied the Jew. "If you had waited just a little longer, you
would have had a fine meal, as I had."*

The same is true when we want to come close to God. After all
the effort to begin, we are given a little bitterness. This bitterness is
needed to purify the body. But we might think that this bitterness
is all there is to serving God, so we run away from it. This is a
mistake. If we would only wait just a short while — if we would
allow ourselves to be purified — then we would experience every joy
and delight in the world in our closeness to God (*Rabbi Nachman's Stories*
#23).

צפון — HIDDEN!

Lost! Perhaps many years ago we took a wrong step. Heeded ill advice. We
weren't aware then of where it would lead us. Yet every step led us further and
further away. And with every step, with every act that distanced us from God, we
lost — we "shed" — a part of our soul (*Likutey Moharan* II, 88). And now... we are
lost! Unable to find our way back... (*Likutey Moharan* I, 206).

The Tzaddik! He towers far above the meandering paths of this world (*Mesilat
Yesharim* 3). He knows to where we have strayed. He can see those lost parts of our
soul strewn along these paths. To find ourselves, to find the lost parts, we must go

SHULCHAN OREKH

The meal should be conducted with great joy and happiness. A person should see to prepare many delicacies for the Seder meal and use the most expensive dishes and silverware that one owns. One should be careful, however, not to over-eat, as one still has to partake of the Afikomen and drink two more cups of wine after the meal.

Many eat a hard-boiled egg in remembrance of the Festival Sacrifice and also in remembrance of the Holy Temple, since the night of the week that Pesach falls is always the same night that Tisha b'Av will fall.

During the meal, many sing various songs, all with great joy over the miracles God has wrought for us. Others recount many additional stories and ideas that are presented in the Haggadah and expound upon them at this point, rather than earlier during the recital.

TZAFUN

One takes the Matzah that was set aside for the Afikomen and eats it, while reclining on the left side. It is forbidden to eat anything after the Afikomen so that the taste of Matzah remains in one's mouth. It is preferable to eat the Afikomen before midnight (the hours from nightfall to sunrise are divided in half, that point is midnight).

The following is said prior to eating the Afikomen:

I am fulfilling the mitzvah of eating the Afikomen in remembrance of the Paschal Lamb, which was eaten at the end of the meal, before midnight. Let it be considered before You, God, as if we have sacrificed the Paschal Lamb and eaten it in a holy place to rectify it at its Upper source. Let it be Your will, God, that the Holy Temple be rebuilt, speedily in our time, and let us merit to bring

washing the hands, eating the Matzah, and so on. The one thing he forgot to mention was the Maror.

Sure enough, when Pesach came, the German was invited to celebrate the Seder with a Jewish family. Being famished, he looked forward to enjoying all the fine foods which the Jew had told him about. However, the first thing he was given to eat was a small piece of celery dipped in salt water. Then he was obliged to sit patiently as the Haggadah was recited and some songs were sung. He hungered for the meal, but could say nothing. Finally, the Matzah was distributed. This made the German very happy, for the Jew had told him that after the Matzah, a meal fit for a king would be served.

Much to his surprise, the next thing the German was given was a piece of horseradish — the Maror! Thinking this to be the entire meal, he ran from the house, bitter and hungry. "Jews!" he muttered. "After all that ceremony, that's all they serve to eat!" He made his way back to his lodgings where he soon fell asleep.

A while later, the Jew arrived, happy and full from a good meal.

לְפָנֶיךָ חוֹבוֹתֵינוּ, וְלֶאֱכוֹל קָרְבַּן פֶּסַח בְּחַיִּים חִיּוּתֵינוּ, שֶׂה תָמִים, זָכָר בֶּן שָׁנָה, צְלִי אֵשׁ, מַצּוֹת וּמְרוֹרִים, בְּעִיר קָדְשֵׁינוּ וְתִפְאַרְתֵּינוּ, בִּמְהֵרָה בְּיָמֵינוּ, אָמֵן. וִיהִי נֹעַם יְיָ אֱלֹהֵינוּ עָלֵינוּ וּמַעֲשֵׂה יָדֵינוּ כּוֹנְנָה עָלֵינוּ וּמַעֲשֵׂה יָדֵינוּ כּוֹנְנֵהוּ. יִהְיוּ לְרָצוֹן אִמְרֵי פִי וְהֶגְיוֹן לִבִּי לְפָנֶיךָ ה' צוּרִי וְגוֹאֲלִי.

הִנְנִי מוּכָן וּמְזוּמָן לְקַיֵּם מִצְוַת אֲכִילַת אֲפִיקוֹמָן לְשֵׁם יִחוּד קוּדְשָׁא בְּרִיךְ הוּא וּשְׁכִינְתֵּיהּ עַל יְדֵי הַהוּא טָמִיר וְנֶעְלָם בְּשֵׁם כָּל יִשְׂרָאֵל: וִיהִי נֹעַם יְיָ אֱלֹהֵינוּ עָלֵינוּ וּמַעֲשֵׂה יָדֵינוּ כּוֹנְנָה עָלֵינוּ וּמַעֲשֵׂה יָדֵינוּ כּוֹנְנֵהוּ.

ברך

ימזוג כוס שלישי ויברך ברכת המזון

שִׁיר הַמַּעֲלוֹת בְּשׁוּב יְיָ אֶת־שִׁיבַת צִיּוֹן הָיִינוּ כְּחֹלְמִים: אָז יִמָּלֵא שְׂחוֹק פִּינוּ וּלְשׁוֹנֵנוּ רִנָּה אָז יֹאמְרוּ בַגּוֹיִם הִגְדִּיל יְיָ לַעֲשׂוֹת עִם־אֵלֶּה: הִגְדִּיל יְיָ לַעֲשׂוֹת עִמָּנוּ הָיִינוּ שְׂמֵחִים: שׁוּבָה יְיָ אֶת־שְׁבִיתֵנוּ כַּאֲפִיקִים בַּנֶּגֶב: הַזֹּרְעִים בְּדִמְעָה בְּרִנָּה יִקְצֹרוּ: הָלוֹךְ יֵלֵךְ וּבָכֹה נֹשֵׂא מֶשֶׁךְ־הַזָּרַע בֹּא־יָבֹא בְרִנָּה נֹשֵׂא אֲלֻמֹּתָיו:

Then the meal is over. And now, deep inside, we sense ourselves a bit embarrassed about how we engaged in purely physical pleasure. Empty pleasure. Our innards may be full, but our souls still crave.

We must appease the soul. Provide it with spiritual nourishment. This is the Grace after Meals. We give the soul a chance to express its yearnings, its cravings for God. We try to connect our hearts, our emotions, to the words we are reciting. We allow ourselves to become aroused. If those emotions were drowned out *while* we ate, *now* they can surface. With this verbal expression, we appease, we nourish the soul. And, in so doing, we have filled an empty pleasure with Meaning. We have transmuted our embarrassment into yearning.

But, what do we do when our spiritual arteries are clogged with deposits of a physical existence? When we just cannot open our hearts to allow the flow of emotion? When the words we recite are as empty as the meal we just finished?

We can at least want! We can *want* to recite the Grace with emotion! We can *want* to yearn for God! We can *want* to nourish our souls! And we can always *want* to *want*....

This is the Invitation to Grace:

Gentlemen! We now *want* to recite Grace! (*Likutey Halakhot, Birkhat HaMazon* 3:1,2,6).

the sacrifices before You. Let us merit to eat of the Paschal Lamb in our lifetime [as the law states]: a yearling, male lamb, roasted over an open fire, with Matzah and Maror, in our Holy City, the beautiful city of Jerusalem, speedily, in our time, Amen!

I am ready and prepared to perform the mitzvah of eating the Afikomen.

One then eats the Afikomen while leaning.

BAREKH

One fills the third cup with wine and recites the Birkhat HaMazon.

A Song of Ascents. When God returns the captives of Zion, we will be like dreamers. Then our mouth will be filled with laughter and our tongue with song. Then they will say among the nations: 'Great things has God done for them!' Great things God has done for us, for which we are very happy! Bring back, God, our prisoners, like flowing streams in dry land. They that sow in tears, shall harvest with rejoicing. He who cried while carrying the seed, will return with joy, bearing his bundles of sheaves.

to him. Study his teachings. Put them into practice (*Likutey Moharan* I, 188).

The Afikoman! Lost! It's gone!... No! The children have taken it. They're just hiding it. And now they're demanding a ransom....

What do they want for it?... Never mind. We must have that Afikoman! Where is it? It's not lost! Just hidden! It is *we* who don't know where it is. But the *children*... they know!

The soul! Lost? Gone?... No! Nothing is ever lost. Someone knows where it is. The "Children!" — the child within — has taken it. Our immaturity has misled us (*Likutey Halakhot, Sheluchin* 5:3). The soul? — it's just hidden. But how are we to get it back? The emotional price seems so taxing!

Never mind! I *must* find my soul! I will go to the Tzaddik. He will teach me how to be honest with myself. He will show me how to deal with the "children" (*Likutey Moharan*, I, 4; *Ibid.*, 188).

...And in the End, we will find the Afikoman. We will find the Hidden Matzah... the Hidden Awareness... the Hidden Parts of the Soul (*Likutey Halakhot, Birkhat HaPeirot* 5:7-9).

ברך — WE CAN ALWAYS WANT

When we are hungry, in essence it is the soul that craves. But, we aren't aware of it. We are too busy alleviating our physical discomfort or satisfying our palates.

הִנְנִי מוּכָן וּמְזֻמָּן לְקַיֵּם מִצְוַת עֲשֵׂה שֶׁל בִּרְכַּת הַמָּזוֹן שֶׁנֶּאֱמַר: "וְאָכַלְתָּ וְשָׂבָעְתָּ וּבֵרַכְתָּ
אֶת יְהוָה אֱלֹהֶיךָ עַל הָאָרֶץ הַטֹּבָה אֲשֶׁר נָתַן לָךְ:" לְשֵׁם יִחוּד קוּדְשָׁא בְּרִיךְ הוּא
וּשְׁכִינְתֵּיהּ עַל יְדֵי הַהוּא טָמִיר וְנֶעְלָם בְּשֵׁם כָּל יִשְׂרָאֵל: וִיהִי נֹעַם יְיָ אֱלֹהֵינוּ עָלֵינוּ
וּמַעֲשֵׂה יָדֵינוּ כּוֹנְנָה עָלֵינוּ וּמַעֲשֵׂה יָדֵינוּ כּוֹנְנֵהוּ.

נוטל ידיו במים אחרונים. ונוטל הכוס בידו:

המברך אומר:

רַבּוֹתַי נְבָרֵךְ (מיר ווילין בֶּענְטְשִׁין):

ועונין המסובין וחוזר המברך:

יְהִי שֵׁם יְיָ מְבֹרָךְ מֵעַתָּה וְעַד עוֹלָם:

המברך אומר:

בִּרְשׁוּת מָרָנָן וְרַבָּנָן וְרַבּוֹתַי נְבָרֵךְ (בעשרה אֱלֹהֵינוּ) שֶׁאָכַלְנוּ מִשֶּׁלּוֹ:

המסובין והמברך:

בָּרוּךְ (בעשרה אֱלֹהֵינוּ) שֶׁאָכַלְנוּ מִשֶּׁלּוֹ וּבְטוּבוֹ חָיִּינוּ:

בָּרוּךְ אַתָּה יְהוָה אֱלֹהֵינוּ מֶלֶךְ הָעוֹלָם הַזָּן אֶת הָעוֹלָם כֻּלּוֹ
בְּטוּבוֹ בְּחֵן בְּחֶסֶד וּבְרַחֲמִים הוּא נוֹתֵן לֶחֶם לְכָל בָּשָׂר כִּי
לְעוֹלָם חַסְדּוֹ. וּבְטוּבוֹ הַגָּדוֹל תָּמִיד לֹא חָסַר לָנוּ וְאַל יֶחְסַר
לָנוּ מָזוֹן לְעוֹלָם וָעֶד. בַּעֲבוּר שְׁמוֹ הַגָּדוֹל כִּי הוּא אֵל זָן
וּמְפַרְנֵס לַכֹּל וּמֵטִיב לַכֹּל וּמֵכִין מָזוֹן לְכָל בְּרִיּוֹתָיו אֲשֶׁר
בָּרָא. כָּאָמוּר פּוֹתֵחַ אֶת יָדֶךָ וּמַשְׂבִּיעַ לְכָל חַי רָצוֹן: בָּרוּךְ
אַתָּה יְהוָה הַזָּן בְּרַחֲמָיו אֶת הַכֹּל:

נוֹדֶה לְךָ יְהוָה אֱלֹהֵינוּ עַל שֶׁהִנְחַלְתָּ לַאֲבוֹתֵינוּ אֶרֶץ חֶמְדָּה
טוֹבָה וּרְחָבָה וְעַל שֶׁהוֹצֵאתָנוּ יְהוָה אֱלֹהֵינוּ מֵאֶרֶץ מִצְרַיִם
וּפְדִיתָנוּ מִבֵּית עֲבָדִים וְעַל בְּרִיתְךָ שֶׁחָתַמְתָּ בִּבְשָׂרֵנוּ וְעַל
תּוֹרָתְךָ שֶׁלִּמַּדְתָּנוּ וְעַל חֻקֶּיךָ שֶׁהוֹדַעְתָּנוּ וְעַל חַיִּים חֵן וָחֶסֶד
שֶׁחוֹנַנְתָּנוּ וְעַל אֲכִילַת מָזוֹן שָׁאַתָּה זָן וּמְפַרְנֵס אוֹתָנוּ תָּמִיד
בְּכָל יוֹם וּבְכָל עֵת וּבְכָל שָׁעָה:

וְעַל הַכֹּל יְהוָה אֱלֹהֵינוּ אֲנַחְנוּ מוֹדִים לָךְ וּמְבָרְכִים אוֹתָךְ
יִתְבָּרַךְ שִׁמְךָ בְּפִי כָּל חַי תָּמִיד לְעוֹלָם וָעֶד. כַּכָּתוּב וְאָכַלְתָּ

I am ready and prepared to perform the mitzvah of the Grace after meals.

The hands are then washed. When there are at least three males, thirteen years or older, begin here (for ten or more males add the words, our God):

Host:
Gentlemen, we want to say Grace!
Guests:
Blessed is the Name of God, from this time and forever.
Host:
Blessed is the Name of God, from this time and forever. With your permission, let us bless (our God), Whose food we have eaten!
Guests:
Blessed be (our God) Whose food we have eaten and through Whose goodness we live.
Host:
Blessed be (our God) Whose food we have eaten and through Whose goodness we live.
All:
Blessed is He!

If three adult males are not present, then begin here:

Blessed are You, God, King of the universe, Who feeds the whole world with His goodness, with grace, lovingkindness and mercy. He gives food to all flesh, for His love is endless. In His great goodness, we have never lacked, and never will lack sustenance, forever, for the sake of His great Name; for He is God Who feeds and sustains all, Who does good to all, and prepares food for all His creatures which He created. As it is written: 'Your hand is open, satisfying the desire of all life.' Blessed are You, God, Who compassionately gives food to all.

We thank You, God, that You gave our fathers a desirable, good and ample land; that You brought us out from Egypt and delivered us from slavery; that You sealed Your covenant in our flesh; that You taught us Your Torah; and that You made Your laws known to us; and for the life, grace and lovingkindness which You have favored us, and for the food with which You constantly provide and sustain us, every day, at all times and at every hour.

For all this, God, we give thanks to You and bless You; praised be Your Name in the mouths of all life, always and forever. As is written: 'You

וְשָׂבַעְתָּ וּבֵרַכְתָּ אֶת יְהֹוָה אֱלֹהֶיךָ עַל הָאָרֶץ הַטּוֹבָה אֲשֶׁר נָתַן
לָךְ: בָּרוּךְ אַתָּה יְהֹוָה עַל הָאָרֶץ וְעַל הַמָּזוֹן:

רַחֵם נָא יְהֹוָה אֱלֹהֵינוּ עַל יִשְׂרָאֵל עַמֶּךָ וְעַל יְרוּשָׁלַיִם עִירֶךָ
וְעַל צִיּוֹן מִשְׁכַּן כְּבוֹדֶךָ וְעַל מַלְכוּת בֵּית דָּוִד מְשִׁיחֶךָ וְעַל
הַבַּיִת הַגָּדוֹל וְהַקָּדוֹשׁ שֶׁנִּקְרָא שִׁמְךָ עָלָיו. אֱלֹהֵינוּ אָבִינוּ
רְעֵנוּ זוּנֵנוּ פַּרְנְסֵנוּ וְכַלְכְּלֵנוּ וְהַרְוִיחֵנוּ וְהַרְוַח לָנוּ יְהֹוָה
אֱלֹהֵינוּ מְהֵרָה מִכָּל צָרוֹתֵינוּ. וְנָא אַל תַּצְרִיכֵנוּ יְהֹוָה אֱלֹהֵינוּ
לֹא לִידֵי מַתְּנַת בָּשָׂר וָדָם וְלֹא לִידֵי הַלְוָאָתָם כִּי אִם לְיָדְךָ
הַמְּלֵאָה הַפְּתוּחָה הַקְּדוֹשָׁה וְהָרְחָבָה שֶׁלֹּא נֵבוֹשׁ וְלֹא נִכָּלֵם
לְעוֹלָם וָעֶד:

Instead, we chase after the closed Hand of Illusion; dreaming of the treasures we will enjoy once it's been opened. Happiness will be ours once we've obtained its contents. But ultimately the truth is known. Alas! *This* hand is empty! Our lives have passed in delusion (*Rabbi Nachman's Wisdom #6*).

> *The hapless and famishing beggar knocked feebly on the miser's door.*
>
> *"Sure you can have a meal," sneered the miser. "But first, do you see that pile of lumber out there? I want you to chop it into small pieces for me."*
>
> *Presuming that if he wanted a meal he had no choice but to comply, the beggar began the laborious task. He toiled for many long hours, comforted only by the thought of the delicious meal awaiting him once the work was done. After he'd finished, he returned to the miser for his "remuneration."*
>
> *"Just go right next door," the miser laughed, "there you'll get your meal."*
>
> *So off ran the beggar.*
>
> *Opening the door of his free-kitchen, the wealthy proprietor warmly received the beggar, and served him whatever was being given to the other beggars.*
>
> *Later, overhearing the beggar grumbling about the meager meal he'd received, especially after such hard labor, the proprietor asked him his story. After relating what had transpired, the beggar concluded, "And, as payment for my work, he sent me over here..."*
>
> *"You have it all wrong, my friend" counseled the proprietor. "The*

should eat, be satiated and you shall bless God for the good land that He gave you' (Deuteronomy 8:10). **Blessed are You, God, for the Land and for the food.**

Have mercy, God, on Your people Israel; on Your city Jerusalem; on Zion home of Your glory; on the royal house of David, Your chosen; and on the great and holy Temple which is called by Your Name. Our God, our Father, tend us, feed us, nourish and sustain us. Grant us relief quickly, God, from all our troubles. Let us, God, never be dependent upon the gifts of men, nor upon their loans, but we should depend only on Your full, open Hand that is holy and generous, so that we may neither be shamed nor disgraced for ever.

ונא אל תצרכינו — GIVE AND TAKE

Most of us have some means of earning a livelihood. We work, we toil, to provide items or services others are willing to pay for.

Yet some people don't seem to contribute anything to society. The communal funds that provide for them would appear to be better spent on human advancement. Its seems that they just take, giving nothing in return.

But, perhaps, God has intentionally denied them livelihood in order to provide *us* with the greatest reward of all: The experience, the fulfillment, of giving. To share with God in the joy of bestowing. To emulate Him in providing for His Creation, for our fellow human beings. To enrich our *own* lives with Meaning by imparting of ourselves. By parting with our own, to give to another. To endow our lives with that which only *giving* can do.

"Let us never be dependent upon the gifts of men..."

We all recite these words. Those of us who see ourselves as providers beseech God that we should always be able to do just that. We should never have to experience what we see as the shame of receiving.

Those of us who receive also beseech God. We beseech him that we not experience shame in our receiving (*Tzaddik #502; Rabbeinu Yonah, Mishlei* 18:23). That we be aware of our *giving*. Of our imparting Meaning to the lives of others. Of our bestowing them fulfillment by accepting their endowments. And of our having enriched *their* lives — spiritually, more than they can ever enrich ours — materialistically (*Rabbi Nachman's Wisdom #150; Ruth Rabbah* 5:9).

And we, the providers, again beseech God. To provide us with Awareness, with the true experience of Giving. Of Giving that is Receiving!

כי אם לידך — A TALE OF TWO HANDS

God's Hand is always open. Giving. Providing. Sustaining. But *we* are not always aware, not always appreciative of it.

לשבת:

רְצֵה וְהַחֲלִיצֵנוּ יְהוָֹה אֱלֹהֵינוּ בְּמִצְוֹתֶיךָ וּבְמִצְוַת יוֹם הַשְּׁבִיעִי הַשַּׁבָּת הַגָּדוֹל
וְהַקָּדוֹשׁ הַזֶּה כִּי יוֹם זֶה גָּדוֹל וְקָדוֹשׁ הוּא לְפָנֶיךָ לִשְׁבָּת בּוֹ וְלָנוּחַ בּוֹ
בְּאַהֲבָה כְּמִצְוַת רְצוֹנֶךָ וּבִרְצוֹנְךָ הָנִיחַ לָנוּ יְהוָֹה אֱלֹהֵינוּ שֶׁלֹּא תְהֵא צָרָה
וְיָגוֹן וַאֲנָחָה בְּיוֹם מְנוּחָתֵנוּ וְהַרְאֵנוּ יְהוָֹה אֱלֹהֵינוּ בְּנֶחָמַת צִיּוֹן עִירֶךָ וּבְבִנְיַן
יְרוּשָׁלַיִם עִיר קָדְשֶׁךָ כִּי אַתָּה הוּא בַּעַל הַיְשׁוּעוֹת וּבַעַל הַנֶּחָמוֹת:

אֱלֹהֵינוּ וֵאלֹהֵי אֲבוֹתֵינוּ יַעֲלֶה וְיָבֹא וְיַגִּיעַ וְיֵרָאֶה וְיֵרָצֶה
וְיִשָּׁמַע וְיִפָּקֵד וְיִזָּכֵר זִכְרוֹנֵנוּ וּפִקְדוֹנֵנוּ וְזִכְרוֹן אֲבוֹתֵינוּ
וְזִכְרוֹן מָשִׁיחַ בֶּן דָּוִד עַבְדֶּךָ וְזִכְרוֹן יְרוּשָׁלַיִם עִיר קָדְשֶׁךָ
וְזִכְרוֹן כָּל עַמְּךָ בֵּית יִשְׂרָאֵל לְפָנֶיךָ לִפְלֵיטָה לְטוֹבָה לְחֵן
וּלְחֶסֶד וּלְרַחֲמִים לְחַיִּים טוֹבִים וּלְשָׁלוֹם בְּיוֹם חַג הַמַּצּוֹת
הַזֶּה: זָכְרֵנוּ יְהוָֹה אֱלֹהֵינוּ בּוֹ לְטוֹבָה, וּפָקְדֵנוּ בוֹ לִבְרָכָה,
וְהוֹשִׁיעֵנוּ בוֹ לְחַיִּים טוֹבִים. וּבִדְבַר יְשׁוּעָה וְרַחֲמִים חוּס
וְחָנֵּנוּ וְרַחֵם עָלֵינוּ וְהוֹשִׁיעֵנוּ כִּי אֵלֶיךָ עֵינֵינוּ כִּי אֵל מֶלֶךְ
חַנּוּן וְרַחוּם אָתָּה:

וּבְנֵה יְרוּשָׁלַיִם עִיר הַקֹּדֶשׁ בִּמְהֵרָה בְיָמֵינוּ: בָּרוּךְ אַתָּה יְיָ
בּוֹנֵה בְרַחֲמָיו יְרוּשָׁלָיִם אָמֵן:

בָּרוּךְ אַתָּה יְהוָֹה אֱלֹהֵינוּ מֶלֶךְ הָעוֹלָם הָאֵל אָבִינוּ מַלְכֵּנוּ
אַדִּירֵנוּ בּוֹרְאֵנוּ גּוֹאֲלֵנוּ יוֹצְרֵנוּ קְדוֹשֵׁנוּ קְדוֹשׁ יַעֲקֹב רוֹעֵנוּ
רוֹעֵה יִשְׂרָאֵל הַמֶּלֶךְ הַטּוֹב וְהַמֵּטִיב לַכֹּל שֶׁבְּכָל יוֹם וָיוֹם
הוּא הֵטִיב. הוּא מֵטִיב. הוּא יֵטִיב לָנוּ. הוּא גְמָלָנוּ. הוּא
גוֹמְלֵנוּ. הוּא יִגְמְלֵנוּ לָעַד לְחֵן וּלְחֶסֶד וּלְרַחֲמִים וּלְרֶוַח
הַצָּלָה וְהַצְלָחָה בְּרָכָה וִישׁוּעָה נֶחָמָה פַּרְנָסָה טוֹבָה וְכַלְכָּלָה
וְרַחֲמִים וְחַיִּים וְשָׁלוֹם וְכָל טוֹב וּמִכָּל טוּב לְעוֹלָם אַל
יְחַסְּרֵנוּ: אָמֵן

On Shabbat add:

Be pleased, God, and strengthen us, through Your commandments and through the commandment of the Seventh Day, this great and holy Shabbat. For this day is great and holy before You, that we may rest and relax on it from all work, in love, as You desire. May it be Your will, God, to grant us that we have no trouble, sorrow or grief on our day of rest. Let us, God, merit to see the consolation of Zion, Your city, and the rebuilding of Jerusalem, Your city of holiness, for You are the Master of salvation and comfort.

God, God of our fathers, may there rise, come, reach, be seen, find favor, be understood, be recalled and remembered before You — our remembrance, and the remembrance of our fathers; the remembrance of Mashiach, the son of David, Your servant; the remembrance of Jerusalem, Your holy city; and the remembrance of Your people, Israel — for deliverance, for good, for grace, for lovingkindness and for mercy, for good life and for peace, on this Festival of Matzot. Remember us on it, God, for goodness, recall us on it for blessing, and save us on it for a good life. With the promise of salvation and mercy, favor and be gracious to us, have mercy upon us and help us. For to You alone our eyes are turned, for You, God, are a gracious and merciful King.

Rebuild Jerusalem, the Holy City, soon in our days. Blessed are You, God, Who rebuilds Jerusalem in His mercy. Amen.

Blessed are You, God, King of the universe, Almighty, our Father, our King, our Ruler, our Creator, our Redeemer, our Maker, our Holy One, the Holy One of Yaakov, our Shepherd, the Shepherd of Israel, the good King, the benevolent King — Who each and every day, did good, does good and will do good to us. It is He who has granted us, does grant us, and will forever grant us with grace, lovingkindness, mercy, relief, salvation, success, blessing, help, comfort, food and sustenance, mercy, life, peace and all good; and with all manner of good things — may He never deprive us.

---

work you did was for free and you're getting your meal for free!" (Siach Sarfey Kodesh Breslov *II, 273).*

Beware — *be aware* — of the "miser's" promises. He sustains no one. His hand is the Hand of Illusion. It is empty.

God sustains us all. He gives us our meal "free of charge." If we work for a living, we do so of our own choice — because of a situation, a servitude, which is actually of our own making; the remuneration for both our lack of deeds and our misdeeds (*Ibid.* 274).

הָרַחֲמָן הוּא יִמְלוֹךְ עָלֵינוּ לְעוֹלָם וָעֶד:

הָרַחֲמָן הוּא יִתְבָּרַךְ בַּשָּׁמַיִם וּבָאָרֶץ:

הָרַחֲמָן הוּא יִשְׁתַּבַּח לְדוֹר דּוֹרִים וְיִתְפָּאַר בָּנוּ לָעַד וּלְנֵצַח נְצָחִים וְיִתְהַדַּר בָּנוּ לָעַד וּלְעוֹלְמֵי עוֹלָמִים:

הָרַחֲמָן הוּא יְפַרְנְסֵנוּ בְּכָבוֹד:

הָרַחֲמָן הוּא יִשְׁבֹּר עֻלֵּנוּ מֵעַל צַוָּארֵנוּ וְהוּא יוֹלִיכֵנוּ קוֹמְמִיּוּת לְאַרְצֵנוּ:

הָרַחֲמָן הוּא יִשְׁלַח לָנוּ בְּרָכָה מְרֻבָּה בַּבַּיִת הַזֶּה וְעַל שֻׁלְחָן זֶה שֶׁאָכַלְנוּ עָלָיו:

הָרַחֲמָן הוּא יִשְׁלַח לָנוּ אֶת אֵלִיָּהוּ הַנָּבִיא זָכוּר לַטּוֹב וִיבַשֶּׂר לָנוּ בְּשׂוֹרוֹת טוֹבוֹת יְשׁוּעוֹת וְנֶחָמוֹת:

הָרַחֲמָן הוּא יְבָרֵךְ (אֶת אָבִי מוֹרִי בַּעַל הַבַּיִת הַזֶּה וְאֶת אִמִּי מוֹרָתִי בַּעֲלַת הַבַּיִת הַזֶּה אוֹתָם וְאֶת בֵּיתָם וְאֶת זַרְעָם וְאֶת כָּל אֲשֶׁר לָהֶם) (אוֹתִי וְאֶת אִשְׁתִּי וְאֶת זַרְעִי וְאֶת כָּל אֲשֶׁר לִי, אוֹתָנוּ וְאֶת כָּל אֲשֶׁר לָנוּ) (אֶת כָּל הַמְסֻבִּין כָּאן אוֹתָם וְאֶת בֵּיתָם וְאֶת זַרְעָם וְאֶת כָּל אֲשֶׁר לָהֶם) כְּמוֹ שֶׁנִּתְבָּרְכוּ אֲבוֹתֵינוּ אַבְרָהָם יִצְחָק וְיַעֲקֹב בַּכֹּל מִכֹּל כֹּל כֵּן יְבָרֵךְ אוֹתָנוּ כֻּלָּנוּ יַחַד בִּבְרָכָה שְׁלֵמָה וְנֹאמַר אָמֵן:

בַּמָּרוֹם יְלַמְּדוּ עֲלֵיהֶם וְעָלֵינוּ זְכוּת שֶׁתְּהֵא לְמִשְׁמֶרֶת שָׁלוֹם וְנִשָּׂא בְרָכָה מֵאֵת יְיָ וּצְדָקָה מֵאֱלֹהֵי יִשְׁעֵנוּ וְנִמְצָא חֵן וְשֵׂכֶל טוֹב בְּעֵינֵי אֱלֹהִים וְאָדָם:

לשבת:

הָרַחֲמָן הוּא יַנְחִילֵנוּ יוֹם שֶׁכֻּלּוֹ שַׁבָּת וּמְנוּחָה לְחַיֵּי הָעוֹלָמִים:

הָרַחֲמָן הוּא יַנְחִילֵנוּ לְיוֹם שֶׁכֻּלּוֹ טוֹב: (לליל הסדר מוסיפין) לְיוֹם שֶׁכֻּלּוֹ אָרֵךְ לְיוֹם שֶׁצַּדִּיקִים יוֹשְׁבִין וְעַטְרוֹתֵיהֶם בְּרָאשֵׁיהֶם וְנֶהֱנִין מִזִּיו הַשְּׁכִינָה וִיהִי חֶלְקֵנוּ עִמָּהֶם:

הָרַחֲמָן הוּא יְזַכֵּנוּ לִימוֹת הַמָּשִׁיחַ וּלְחַיֵּי הָעוֹלָם הַבָּא:

מִגְדּוֹל יְשׁוּעוֹת מַלְכּוֹ וְעֹשֶׂה חֶסֶד לִמְשִׁיחוֹ לְדָוִד וּלְזַרְעוֹ עַד עוֹלָם: עֹשֶׂה שָׁלוֹם בִּמְרוֹמָיו הוּא יַעֲשֶׂה שָׁלוֹם עָלֵינוּ וְעַל כָּל יִשְׂרָאֵל וְאִמְרוּ אָמֵן:

May the Merciful reign over us for ever and ever!

May the Merciful be praised in heaven and on earth!

May the Merciful be praised for all generations, may He be glorified through us forever and ever, and may He be honored through us for all eternity!

May the Merciful grant us our needs with honor!

May the Merciful break the yoke from our necks and lead us upright to our land!

May the Merciful send abundant blessings to this house and upon this table from which we have eaten!

May the Merciful send us the prophet Eliyahu, of blessed memory, and that he bring to us good tidings, salvations and consolations!

Recite whichever portion applies (any combination is permitted):

May the Merciful, bless:

   my father, master of this house, and my mother, mistress of this house,

   me, my wife (husband) and family and all that is mine,

   all that sit here,

   them and their house and family, together with all that is theirs; us, and all that is ours,

just as our fathers Avraham, Yitzchak and Yaakov were blessed in all, through all, and with all. May He bless us, all, with a complete blessing! To that we say: Amen!

On High, may merit be accepted about them and about us, so as to assure peace. May we receive a blessing from God and charity from the God Who saves us; and let us find favor and understanding in the eyes of God and man.

On Shabbat: May the Merciful bequeath to us the day that will be all Shabbat and rest in eternal life!

May the Merciful bequeath to us the day which is all good.
(at the Seder add) to the eternal day [the World to Come], to the day when the Tzaddikim will sit with crowns on their heads, enjoying the light of the Divine Presence — may our lot be with them!

May the Merciful make us worthy to merit reaching the days of Mashiach and to the life of the World to Come!

He is the tower of salvation to his [chosen] king, and does kindness to His anointed, David, and to his seed forever. He Who makes peace in His place on High; may He also bring peace upon all of us and for all Israel, and say: Amen!

יְראוּ אֶת יְיָ קְדֹשָׁיו כִּי אֵין מַחְסוֹר לִירֵאָיו: כְּפִירִים רָשׁוּ וְרָעֵבוּ וְדוֹרְשֵׁי יְיָ לֹא יַחְסְרוּ כָל טוֹב: הוֹדוּ לַיהֹוָה כִּי טוֹב כִּי לְעוֹלָם חַסְדּוֹ: פּוֹתֵחַ אֶת יָדֶךָ וּמַשְׂבִּיעַ לְכָל חַי רָצוֹן: בָּרוּךְ הַגֶּבֶר אֲשֶׁר יִבְטַח בַּיהֹוָה וְהָיָה יְהֹוָה מִבְטַחוֹ: נַעַר הָיִיתִי גַּם זָקַנְתִּי וְלֹא רָאִיתִי צַדִּיק נֶעֱזָב וְזַרְעוֹ מְבַקֶּשׁ לָחֶם: יְיָ עֹז לְעַמּוֹ יִתֵּן יְהֹוָה יְבָרֵךְ אֶת עַמּוֹ בַשָּׁלוֹם:

ואחרי ברכת המזון יאמר זה:

הִנְנִי מוּכָן וּמְזֻמָּן לְקַיֵּם מִצְוַת כּוֹס שְׁלִישִׁי מֵאַרְבַּע כּוֹסוֹת לְשֵׁם יִחוּד קוּדְשָׁא בְּרִיךְ הוּא וּשְׁכִינְתֵּיהּ עַל יְדֵי הַהוּא טָמִיר וְנֶעְלָם בְּשֵׁם כָּל יִשְׂרָאֵל: וִיהִי נֹעַם יְיָ אֱלֹהֵינוּ עָלֵינוּ וּמַעֲשֵׂה יָדֵינוּ כּוֹנְנָה עָלֵינוּ וּמַעֲשֵׂה יָדֵינוּ כּוֹנְנֵהוּ.

בָּרוּךְ אַתָּה יְהֹוָה אֱלֹהֵינוּ מֶלֶךְ הָעוֹלָם בּוֹרֵא פְּרִי הַגָּפֶן:

ושותה בהסבת שמאל ואינו מברך ברכה אחרונה:

Or, we can fear for ourselves. Fear Future retribution. Fear earthly authorities. Fear what people will say....

"Fear God, His holy ones; for they will not lack anything — those who fear Him."

We can fear for a vague tomorrow, a tomorrow that may never come. For a rainy day that may never arrive. For an old age we may never live to see. But we fear. We fear that the Infinite Creator who sustains the vast universe: the stars, the sun, the moon, the planets and all earthly life, may somehow "forget" about *us*. So we fear for ourselves. We fear for future sustenance. But in truth, we lack Fear.

"Fear *God*..." Be awe-inspired by the Infinite Creator who sustains the infinite universe. The stars, the sun, the moon, the planets. All earthly life. Be awe-struck in being that infinitesimal creature which God has made the pinnacle of His Creation. Be aghast with the awareness that the Infinite Creator takes great concern in providing for each and every one of the infinitesimal creatures that we are. And, quake from our fleeting doubts in... "for they will not lack anything — those who fear Him" (*Likutey Halakhot, Bekhor Behemah Tehorah* 4:22).

119

Fear God, His holy ones, for they will not lack anything — those who fear Him. Young lions suffer and are hungry, but they that seek God will not be in want of any good (Psalms 34:10,11). Give thanks to God, for He is good, His lovingkindness endures forever (Psalms 118:1). Open Your hand and satisfy the need of all that lives (Psalms 145:16). Blessed is the man that puts his trust in God, and to whom God becomes his trust (Jeremiah 17:7). I was young and have now grown old, yet I have never seen a righteous man abandoned, nor his children begging for bread (Psalms 37:25). God will give strength to His people, God will bless His people with peace (Psalms 29:11).

The blessing over the third cup is made after reciting the following:
I am ready and prepared to perform the mitzvah of drinking the third cup of wine.

Blessed are You, God, King of the universe, Who creates the fruit of the vine.

The cup is then drunk while leaning on the left side.

יראו — A FEARING LACK, LACKING FEAR

Emotions can be directed outward, or inverted inward back to ourselves.

Love! We can love God. Love His Creation. Love his creatures — our fellow man. We can contemplate all the things He grants us which we tend to take for granted. Our health... our family... our friends... our home... our very lives. Even the simple joy of breathing. Of being aware that we exist. And for all this, we can want to reciprocate. To give back. To do *something,* and not merely receive. To do His Will although we don't understand. To give of ourselves to Creation. To do our share in God's plan.

Or, we can love ourselves. Ignore all the gifts we already possess. Focus only on what we are lacking. We can give only when we anticipate in return.

Fear! We can fear God. We can be awe-inspired by the Infinite Creator who sustains the infinite universe. Be awe-struck in being an infinitesimal creature crawling on speck of dust Earth. Be aghast with the awareness that only this infinitesimal creature — Man — in all Creation, possesses free will. And, we can quake from the fleeting thoughts of misusing that free will.

הלל

מוזגין כוס לאליהו זכור לטוב ומוזגין כוס הרביעי ואומרים עליו הלל. פותחין
הדלת, לזכור כי ליל שמורים הוא, וכדאי הוא האמונה, שיבוא גואלנו הצדק ברנה,
ויבנה המקדש כבראשונה.

הָרַחֲמָן הוּא יִשְׁלַח לָנוּ בִּמְהֵרָה אֶת אֵלִיָּהוּ הַנָּבִיא זָכוּר לַטּוֹב, וִיבַשֶּׂר לָנוּ בְּשׂוֹרוֹת
טוֹבוֹת, יְשׁוּעוֹת וְנֶחָמוֹת. כָּאָמוּר: "הִנֵּה אָנֹכִי שֹׁלֵחַ לָכֶם אֵת אֵלִיָּהוּ הַנָּבִיא לִפְנֵי בּוֹא
יוֹם ה' הַגָּדוֹל וְהַנּוֹרָא: וְהֵשִׁיב לֵב־אָבוֹת עַל־בָּנִים וְלֵב בָּנִים עַל אֲבוֹתָם פֶּן אָבוֹא
וְהִכֵּיתִי אֶת הָאָרֶץ חֵרֶם": וְנֶאֱמַר: "הִנְנִי שֹׁלֵחַ מַלְאָכִי וּפִנָּה דֶרֶךְ לְפָנָי וּפִתְאֹם יָבוֹא
אֶל הֵיכָלוֹ הָאָדוֹן אֲשֶׁר אַתֶּם מְבַקְשִׁים וּמַלְאַךְ הַבְּרִית אֲשֶׁר אַתֶּם חֲפֵצִים הִנֵּה בָא אָמַר
ה' צְבָאוֹת":

so much to do. So much to correct.

Jealousy. Anger. Pride. They're destroying us! But how do we get rid of them?
Where do we start?

Unbridled physical desires. They're so compelling! How do we control them?
And how do we sublimate the ones we must engage in?

Gossip. Slander. Denegration. Bickering. The tongue seems to have a mind of
its own. But its ruining our friendships. Embittering our lives.

And sometimes, we just want to become better people. Better Jews. To become
more aware of God. More aware of ourselves. Help others do the same. But we
can't find the words to tell them. We can't even find the words to tell ourselves.

It's too much to deal with at one time. Perhaps, too much for an entire
lifetime. We must find one all-encompassing, prepotent attribute which will rectify
everything. Put everything in its proper place. Give us the proper perspective on
life. Something that will reach even the far recesses of our soul. Places we aren't
aware of.

Praise of God is just such an attribute! (*Likutey Moharan* I, 29:2,4,10).

As we verbalize our praise of God, we become more in touch with Reality.
We hear the words we recite. We listen for their meaning. We relate them to our
personal lives. We overcome illusion (*Likutey Moharan* I, 25:4).

The Infinite Creator reigns over this vast universe. He moves the galaxies, the
stars and the planets. He sustains life on earth. He directs human history. He guides
our personal lives. He listens to our prayers. He dries our tears. He comforts us
when we suffer. He lifts us when we fall. He is with us when we are born. He
is with us when we die. And, He fills with Meaning the life in between. No
human words can ever fully express the emotions which fill our heart.

But we praise. We do our best.

Jealousy? Anger? Pride? Unbridled physical desires?... There is no room in
Creation for such petty and meaningless emotion. We have filled even those far
recesses of our soul with Meaning. With Awareness of God.

We now recite the Hallel. Our effort to praise God (*Likutey Halakhot, Sukkah* 2:1).

HALLEL

The fourth cup is poured. One also pours a special cup of wine, called the Cup of Eliyahu (the Prophet Elijah; some place this cup on the table at the beginning of the Seder). The front door is then opened to show that this is the "Night of Protection" and there is no need to fear anyone or anything.

May the Merciful send us the prophet Eliyahu, of blessed memory, to bring us good tidings, salvations and consolations! As is written: 'Behold! I am sending to you Eliyahu the Prophet, before the awesome day of God arrives. He shall turn the hearts of fathers to their children and the hearts of children to their fathers; lest I come and smite the land with a curse' (Malakhi 3:24). And it is written: 'Behold! I will send My messenger and he will clear the way before Me; suddenly the Lord Who you seek will come to His Temple. And the angel of the covenant [Eliyahu] whose coming you desire will appear! says God, the Lord of Hosts' (Malakhi 3:1).

כוס אליהו הנביא — FILL THE CUP OF PEACE

The Future will be a time of great peace. There will be harmony in the animal kingdom, there will be rapport between men (Isaiah 2:4). There will be amity between man and animal, there will be a "domestication of the animal" in men (Isaiah 1:6-9). There will be a reconciliation between God and man. We will cease our attempts to understand His Ways. We will accept our humanness. We will realize we are not God, but men.

Moshe, the Tzaddik, came to bring peace to the Jewish People — inner peace from their spiritual struggles, freedom from their human bondage. Moshe, though, needed Aharon to help implement this. It was Aharon who was at peace with the preeminence of his younger brother Moshe, it was Aharon who brought peace between every Jew and *his* brother (*Likutey Halakhot, Prikah U'te'inah* 4:9). (In proportion to the peace which reigns between men, so are we able to talk to one another about the purpose of life and thus bring each one of us to his individual, inner peace, cf. *Likutey Moharan* I, 27:1.)

In the future, Moshe, the Tzaddik, will come to bring us the Ultimate Peace (*Tikkuney Zohar* 69). But it will be the prophet Eliyahu, Elijah, a descendant of Aharon, who brings peace among men. It is he who will reconcile the parents who didn't understand their children, with the children who misunderstood them (Malachi 3:24; *Likutey Halakhot, Netilat Yadaim* 6:15).

Let us now pour a cup of wine for Eliyahu, for although we see him not, his spirit walks among us. We can feel his presence when we are attentive, we can hear his message when we listen. Let us open our doors to the harbinger of peace with the faith that no harm can come us.

And preceding the Hallel — the prayer for Future Peace — we beseech God to help us overcome the external and *internal* obstacles to that peace.

הלל — THERE'S NO ROOM

Sometimes we feel overwhelmed. Where to turn? Where to begin? There's just

"שְׁפֹךְ חֲמָתְךָ אֶל הַגּוֹיִם אֲשֶׁר לֹא יְדָעוּךָ וְעַל מַמְלָכוֹת
אֲשֶׁר בְּשִׁמְךָ לֹא קָרָאוּ: כִּי אָכַל אֶת יַעֲקֹב וְאֶת נָוֵהוּ
הֵשַׁמּוּ": שְׁפָךְ עֲלֵיהֶם זַעְמֶךָ וַחֲרוֹן אַפְּךָ יַשִּׂיגֵם: תִּרְדֹּף
בְּאַף וְתַשְׁמִידֵם מִתַּחַת שְׁמֵי יְהוָה: סוֹגְרִין הַדֶּלֶת

לֹא לָנוּ יְיָ, לֹא לָנוּ, כִּי לְשִׁמְךָ תֵּן כָּבוֹד, עַל חַסְדְּךָ עַל
אֲמִתֶּךָ: לָמָּה יֹאמְרוּ הַגּוֹיִם, אַיֵּה נָא אֱלֹהֵיהֶם: וֵאלֹהֵינוּ
בַשָּׁמַיִם, כֹּל אֲשֶׁר חָפֵץ עָשָׂה: עֲצַבֵּיהֶם כֶּסֶף וְזָהָב, מַעֲשֵׂה
יְדֵי אָדָם: פֶּה לָהֶם וְלֹא יְדַבֵּרוּ, עֵינַיִם לָהֶם וְלֹא יִרְאוּ: אָזְנַיִם
לָהֶם וְלֹא יִשְׁמָעוּ, אַף לָהֶם וְלֹא יְרִיחוּן: יְדֵיהֶם וְלֹא יְמִישׁוּן,
רַגְלֵיהֶם וְלֹא יְהַלֵּכוּ, לֹא יֶהְגּוּ בִּגְרוֹנָם: כְּמוֹהֶם יִהְיוּ עֹשֵׂיהֶם,
כֹּל אֲשֶׁר בֹּטֵחַ בָּהֶם: יִשְׂרָאֵל בְּטַח בַּיְיָ, עֶזְרָם וּמָגִנָּם הוּא:
בֵּית אַהֲרֹן בִּטְחוּ בַיְיָ, עֶזְרָם וּמָגִנָּם הוּא: יִרְאֵי יְיָ בִּטְחוּ בַיְיָ,
עֶזְרָם וּמָגִנָּם הוּא:

יְיָ זְכָרָנוּ יְבָרֵךְ, יְבָרֵךְ אֶת בֵּית יִשְׂרָאֵל, יְבָרֵךְ אֶת בֵּית אַהֲרֹן:
יְבָרֵךְ יִרְאֵי יְיָ, הַקְּטַנִּים עִם הַגְּדֹלִים: יֹסֵף יְיָ עֲלֵיכֶם, עֲלֵיכֶם
וְעַל בְּנֵיכֶם: בְּרוּכִים אַתֶּם לַיהוָה, עֹשֵׂה שָׁמַיִם וָאָרֶץ:
הַשָּׁמַיִם, שָׁמַיִם לַיהוָה, וְהָאָרֶץ נָתַן לִבְנֵי אָדָם: לֹא הַמֵּתִים
יְהַלְלוּ־יָהּ, וְלֹא כָּל יֹרְדֵי דוּמָה: וַאֲנַחְנוּ נְבָרֵךְ יָהּ, מֵעַתָּה
וְעַד עוֹלָם, הַלְלוּיָהּ:

אָהַבְתִּי, כִּי יִשְׁמַע יְיָ אֶת קוֹלִי תַּחֲנוּנָי: כִּי הִטָּה אָזְנוֹ לִי,
וּבְיָמַי אֶקְרָא: אֲפָפוּנִי חֶבְלֵי מָוֶת וּמְצָרֵי שְׁאוֹל מְצָאוּנִי, צָרָה
וְיָגוֹן אֶמְצָא: וּבְשֵׁם יְיָ אֶקְרָא   אָנָּה יְיָ מַלְּטָה נַפְשִׁי: חַנּוּן יְיָ
וְצַדִּיק, וֵאלֹהֵינוּ מְרַחֵם: שֹׁמֵר פְּתָאיִם יְיָ, דַּלּוֹתִי וְלִי
יְהוֹשִׁיעַ: שׁוּבִי נַפְשִׁי לִמְנוּחָיְכִי, כִּי יְיָ גָּמַל עָלָיְכִי: כִּי חִלַּצְתָּ
נַפְשִׁי מִמָּוֶת, אֶת עֵינִי מִן דִּמְעָה, אֶת רַגְלִי מִדֶּחִי: אֶתְהַלֵּךְ

123

[God!] Pour out Your anger upon the nations that do not recognize You, and upon the kingdoms that do not call Your Name. For they have devoured Yaakov and destroyed his dwelling (Psalms 79:6-7). **Pour Your wrath upon them and let Your burning fury overtake them** (Psalms 69:25). Pursue them with anger and destroy them from beneath the heavens of God (Lamentations 3:66).

The door is closed and the following paragraphs from the Hallel (Psalms 115-118) are recited.

Not to us, God, not to us, but to Your Name give glory; for the sake of Your kindness and Your truth! Why should the nations say, 'Where, now, is their God?' Our God is in heaven, whatever He desires, He does! Their idols are of silver and gold, the work of human hands. They have a mouth but cannot speak; they have eyes but cannot see. They have ears but cannot hear; they have a nose but cannot smell. Their hands, do not feel; feet, they cannot walk; no sound comes from their throat! Those that make them should be like them, anyone that trusts in them. [But] Israel! Trust in God! He is their help and shield. House of Aharon! Trust in God! He is their help and shield. Those that fear God! Trust in God! He is their help and shield.

God will remember us, He will bless; He will bless the House of Israel, He will bless the House of Aharon. He will bless those that fear God, those small and great. May God add to you, to you and your children. You are blessed by God, the Maker of heaven and earth. The heaven is the heaven of God, but the earth He has given to man. The dead cannot praise God, nor those that go down in silence. But we will praise God, from now and forever, Hallelu-Yah!

I love God, for He hears my voice and my prayer. He has listened to me, therefore I will call to Him all my life. The ropes of death encircled me, the confines of the grave took hold of me, trouble and sorrow I found. [But] I called the Name of God: 'O, God, save my soul!' God is kind and righteous, God is full of compassion. God guards the fools; I was brought low, but He saved me. Return my soul to your rest; for God was good to you. You [God] delivered my soul from death, my eyes from tears, my feet from stumbling. I will walk before God in the land of the

לִפְנֵי יְיָ, בְּאַרְצוֹת הַחַיִּים: הֶאֱמַנְתִּי כִּי אֲדַבֵּר, אֲנִי עָנִיתִי
מְאֹד: אֲנִי אָמַרְתִּי בְחָפְזִי, כָּל הָאָדָם כֹּזֵב:

מָה אָשִׁיב לַיהוָֹה, כָּל תַּגְמוּלוֹהִי עָלָי: כּוֹס יְשׁוּעוֹת אֶשָּׂא,
וּבְשֵׁם יְהוָֹה אֶקְרָא: נְדָרַי לַיהוָֹה אֲשַׁלֵּם, נֶגְדָה נָּא לְכָל עַמּוֹ:
יָקָר בְּעֵינֵי יְהוָֹה, הַמָּוְתָה לַחֲסִידָיו: אָנָּה יְהוָֹה כִּי אֲנִי עַבְדֶּךָ,
אֲנִי עַבְדְּךָ בֶּן אֲמָתֶךָ , פִּתַּחְתָּ לְמוֹסֵרָי: לְךָ אֶזְבַּח זֶבַח תּוֹדָה,
וּבְשֵׁם יְהוָֹה אֶקְרָא: נְדָרַי לַיהוָֹה אֲשַׁלֵּם, נֶגְדָה נָּא לְכָל עַמּוֹ:
בְּחַצְרוֹת בֵּית יְהוָֹה בְּתוֹכֵכִי יְרוּשָׁלָיִם, הַלְלוּיָהּ:

הַלְלוּ אֶת יְהוָֹה כָּל גּוֹיִם שַׁבְּחוּהוּ כָּל הָאֻמִּים: כִּי גָבַר עָלֵינוּ
חַסְדּוֹ וֶאֱמֶת יְהוָֹה לְעוֹלָם, הַלְלוּיָהּ:

כִּי לְעוֹלָם חַסְדּוֹ:	הוֹדוּ לַיהוָֹה כִּי טוֹב,
כִּי לְעוֹלָם חַסְדּוֹ:	יֹאמַר נָא יִשְׂרָאֵל,
כִּי לְעוֹלָם חַסְדּוֹ:	יֹאמְרוּ נָא בֵית אַהֲרֹן,
כִּי לְעוֹלָם חַסְדּוֹ:	יֹאמְרוּ נָא יִרְאֵי יְהוָֹה,

מִן הַמֵּצַר קָרָאתִי יָּהּ, עָנָנִי בַמֶּרְחָב יָהּ: יְיָ לִי לֹא אִירָא, מַה
יַּעֲשֶׂה לִי אָדָם: יְיָ לִי בְּעֹזְרָי, וַאֲנִי אֶרְאֶה בְשֹׂנְאָי: טוֹב לַחֲסוֹת
בַּייָ, מִבְּטֹחַ בָּאָדָם: טוֹב לַחֲסוֹת בַּייָ, מִבְּטֹחַ בִּנְדִיבִים: כָּל גּוֹיִם
סְבָבוּנִי, בְּשֵׁם יְיָ כִּי אֲמִילַם: סַבּוּנִי גַם סְבָבוּנִי, בְּשֵׁם יְיָ כִּי
אֲמִילַם: סַבּוּנִי כִדְבוֹרִים דֹּעֲכוּ כְּאֵשׁ קוֹצִים, בְּשֵׁם יְיָ כִּי אֲמִילַם:
דָּחֹה דְחִיתַנִי לִנְפֹּל, וַייָ עֲזָרָנִי: עָזִּי וְזִמְרָת יָהּ, וַיְהִי לִי לִישׁוּעָה:
קוֹל רִנָּה וִישׁוּעָה בְּאָהֳלֵי צַדִּיקִים, יְמִין יְיָ עֹשָׂה חָיִל: יְמִין יְיָ
רוֹמֵמָה, יְמִין יְיָ עֹשָׂה חָיִל: לֹא אָמוּת כִּי אֶחְיֶה, וַאֲסַפֵּר מַעֲשֵׂי
יָהּ: יַסֹּר יִסְּרַנִּי יָּהּ, וְלַמָּוֶת לֹא נְתָנָנִי: פִּתְחוּ לִי שַׁעֲרֵי צֶדֶק, אָבֹא
בָם אוֹדֶה יָהּ: זֶה הַשַּׁעַר לַייָ, צַדִּיקִים יָבֹאוּ בוֹ:

living. I had much faith, therefore I spoke, though I deeply suffered — when I said in my panic, 'All men are liars!'

How can I repay God for all His kindness to me? I will lift up the cup of salvation, and call the Name of God. My vows to God I will fulfill, in the presence of His people. Precious in the eyes of God, is the death of His saints. Please, God, I am Your servant; I am Your servant, son of Your maid; You have unlocked my chains. I will sacrifice to You thanksgiving offerings, and in the Name of God I will call. My vows to God I will fulfill, in the presence of His people; in the courtyards of God's Holy Temple, in your midst, Jerusalem, Hallelu-Yah!

Praise God, all the nations; praise Him, all peoples. For His kindness overwhelmed us, and God's truth is eternal. Hallelu-Yah!

The following is said responsively:

Give thanks to God, He is good;	His kindness is forever!
Let Israel say:	His kindness is forever!
Let the House of Aharon say:	His kindness is forever!
Let those who fear God say:	His kindness is forever!

In distress, I called to God; He answered me extensively. God is with me, I will have no fear, what can man do to me? God is with me to help me, therefore, I can face my enemy. It is better to rely on God, than to trust in man. It is better to rely on God, than to trust in on princes. All nations surround me, in God's Name I [can] destroy them. They surround me, they encircle me, in God's Name I [can] destroy them. They surround me like swarming bees, they will burn out like fire [consuming] thorns; with God's Name I [can] destroy them. They pushed me that I might fall, but God assisted me. God is my strength and song, He is my salvation. The sound of rejoicing and salvation is in the tents of the righteous: God's right hand prevails. God's right hand is raised triumphantly, God's right hand prevails. I shall not die, [but] I shall live and relate the acts of God. God made me suffer, but He did not let me die. Open for me the gates of righteousness, I will enter them and thank God. This is the gate of God; the righteous will enter through it.

אוֹדְךָ כִּי עֲנִיתָנִי, וַתְּהִי לִי לִישׁוּעָה: אודך

אֶבֶן מָאֲסוּ הַבּוֹנִים, הָיְתָה לְרֹאשׁ פִּנָּה: אבן

מֵאֵת יְיָ הָיְתָה זֹּאת, הִיא נִפְלָאת בְּעֵינֵינוּ: מאת

זֶה הַיּוֹם עָשָׂה יְיָ, נָגִילָה וְנִשְׂמְחָה בוֹ: זה

אָנָּא יְהֹוָה הוֹשִׁיעָה נָא:　　אָנָּא יְהֹוָה הוֹשִׁיעָה נָא:

אָנָּא יְהֹוָה הַצְלִיחָה נָא:　　אָנָּא יְהֹוָה הַצְלִיחָה נָא:

בָּרוּךְ הַבָּא בְּשֵׁם יְהֹוָה בֵּרַכְנוּכֶם מִבֵּית יְהֹוָה: ברוך

אֵל יְיָ וַיָּאֶר לָנוּ, אִסְרוּ חַג בַּעֲבֹתִים, עַד קַרְנוֹת הַמִּזְבֵּחַ: אל

אֵלִי אַתָּה וְאוֹדֶךָּ, אֱלֹהַי אֲרוֹמְמֶךָּ: אלי

הוֹדוּ לַיהֹוָה כִּי טוֹב, כִּי לְעוֹלָם חַסְדּוֹ: הודו

יְהַלְלוּךָ יְיָ אֱלֹהֵינוּ כָּל מַעֲשֶׂיךָ, וַחֲסִידֶיךָ צַדִּיקִים עוֹשֵׂי רְצוֹנֶךָ, וְכָל עַמְּךָ בֵּית יִשְׂרָאֵל, כֻּלָּם בְּרִנָּה יוֹדוּ וִיבָרְכוּ, וִישַׁבְּחוּ וִיפָאֲרוּ, וִירוֹמְמוּ וְיַעֲרִיצוּ וְיַקְדִּישׁוּ וְיַמְלִיכוּ אֶת שִׁמְךָ מַלְכֵּנוּ, תָּמִיד, כִּי לְךָ טוֹב לְהוֹדוֹת, וּלְשִׁמְךָ נָאֶה לְזַמֵּר, כִּי מֵעוֹלָם וְעַד עוֹלָם אַתָּה אֵל:

כִּי לְעוֹלָם חַסְדּוֹ: כי	הוֹדוּ לַיְיָ כִּי טוֹב
כִּי לְעוֹלָם חַסְדּוֹ: כי	הוֹדוּ לֵאלֹהֵי הָאֱלֹהִים
כִּי לְעוֹלָם חַסְדּוֹ: כי	הוֹדוּ לַאֲדֹנֵי הָאֲדֹנִים
כִּי לְעוֹלָם חַסְדּוֹ: כי	לְעֹשֵׂה נִפְלָאוֹת גְּדֹלוֹת לְבַדּוֹ
כִּי לְעוֹלָם חַסְדּוֹ: כי	לְעֹשֵׂה הַשָּׁמַיִם בִּתְבוּנָה
כִּי לְעוֹלָם חַסְדּוֹ: כי	לְרוֹקַע הָאָרֶץ עַל הַמָּיִם
כִּי לְעוֹלָם חַסְדּוֹ: כי	לְעֹשֵׂה אוֹרִים גְּדֹלִים
כִּי לְעוֹלָם חַסְדּוֹ: כי	אֶת הַשֶּׁמֶשׁ לְמֶמְשֶׁלֶת בַּיּוֹם
כִּי לְעוֹלָם חַסְדּוֹ: כי	אֶת הַיָּרֵחַ וְכוֹכָבִים לְמֶמְשְׁלוֹת בַּלָּיְלָה
כִּי לְעוֹלָם חַסְדּוֹ: כי	לְמַכֵּה מִצְרַיִם בִּבְכוֹרֵיהֶם
כִּי לְעוֹלָם חַסְדּוֹ: כי	וַיּוֹצֵא יִשְׂרָאֵל מִתּוֹכָם

I thank You, for You answered me and were my salvation. repeat
The stone despised by the builders has become the cornerstone. repeat
This is from God; it is wonderful in our eyes. repeat
This day, God has made, we will rejoice and be glad in Him. repeat

God, please save us! God, please save us!

God, please let us prosper! God, please let us prosper!

Welcome to the one who comes in the Name of God; we bless you from the House of God. repeat

The Almighty is God and He gives us light; bind the festival [offering] with cords on the corners of the altar. repeat

You are my God and I will thank You; [You are] my God and I will exalt You. repeat

Give thanks to God, He is good; His kindness is forever. repeat

All Your works shall praise You, God, together with Your saints, the righteous, who do Your will, and Your people, Israel. With song will they thank, bless, praise, glorify, exalt, revere, laud, sanctify, and crown Your Name, our King, always. To You it is good to give thanks, and to Your Name it is proper to sing praises, for from the beginning of time to eternity, You are God.

(Psalm 136)

Give thanks to God, He is good;	His kindness is forever.
Give thanks to the God of gods;	His kindness is forever.
Give thanks to the Master of masters;	His kindness is forever.
Who alone does great wonders;	His kindness is forever.
Who makes the heaven with understanding;	His kindness is forever.
Who spreads the earth over the waters;	His kindness is forever.
Who makes great lights;	His kindness is forever.
The sun rule by day;	His kindness is forever.
The moon and the stars to rule by night;	His kindness is forever.
Who struck the Egyptians through their firstborn;	His kindness is forever.
Who removed Israel from their midst;	His kindness is forever.

	בְּיָד חֲזָקָה וּבִזְרוֹעַ נְטוּיָה
כִּי לְעוֹלָם חַסְדּוֹ:	לְגֹזֵר יַם סוּף לִגְזָרִים
כִּי לְעוֹלָם חַסְדּוֹ:	וְהֶעֱבִיר יִשְׂרָאֵל בְּתוֹכוֹ
כִּי לְעוֹלָם חַסְדּוֹ:	וְנִעֵר פַּרְעֹה וְחֵילוֹ בְיַם סוּף
כִּי לְעוֹלָם חַסְדּוֹ:	לְמוֹלִיךְ עַמּוֹ בַּמִּדְבָּר
כִּי לְעוֹלָם חַסְדּוֹ:	לְמַכֵּה מְלָכִים גְּדֹלִים
כִּי לְעוֹלָם חַסְדּוֹ:	וַיַּהֲרֹג מְלָכִים אַדִּירִים
כִּי לְעוֹלָם חַסְדּוֹ:	לְסִיחוֹן מֶלֶךְ הָאֱמֹרִי
כִּי לְעוֹלָם חַסְדּוֹ:	וּלְעוֹג מֶלֶךְ הַבָּשָׁן
כִּי לְעוֹלָם חַסְדּוֹ:	וְנָתַן אַרְצָם לְנַחֲלָה
כִּי לְעוֹלָם חַסְדּוֹ:	נַחֲלָה לְיִשְׂרָאֵל עַבְדּוֹ
כִּי לְעוֹלָם חַסְדּוֹ:	שֶׁבְּשִׁפְלֵנוּ זָכַר לָנוּ
כִּי לְעוֹלָם חַסְדּוֹ:	וַיִּפְרְקֵנוּ מִצָּרֵינוּ
כִּי לְעוֹלָם חַסְדּוֹ:	נֹתֵן לֶחֶם לְכָל בָּשָׂר
כִּי לְעוֹלָם חַסְדּוֹ:	הוֹדוּ לְאֵל הַשָּׁמָיִם

נִשְׁמַת כָּל חַי תְּבָרֵךְ אֶת שִׁמְךָ יְהֹוָה אֱלֹהֵינוּ וְרוּחַ כָּל בָּשָׂר תְּפָאֵר וּתְרוֹמֵם זִכְרְךָ מַלְכֵּנוּ תָּמִיד: מִן הָעוֹלָם וְעַד הָעוֹלָם אַתָּה אֵל וּמִבַּלְעָדֶיךָ אֵין לָנוּ מֶלֶךְ גּוֹאֵל וּמוֹשִׁיעַ: פּוֹדֶה וּמַצִּיל וּמְפַרְנֵס וְעוֹנֶה וּמְרַחֵם בְּכָל עֵת צָרָה וְצוּקָה אֵין לָנוּ מֶלֶךְ עוֹזֵר וְסוֹמֵךְ אֶלָּא אָתָּה:

אֱלֹהֵי הָרִאשׁוֹנִים וְהָאַחֲרוֹנִים, אֱלוֹהַּ כָּל בְּרִיּוֹת, אֲדוֹן כָּל תּוֹלָדוֹת, הַמְהֻלָּל בְּרֹב הַתִּשְׁבָּחוֹת, הַמְנַהֵג עוֹלָמוֹ בְּחֶסֶד, וּבְרִיּוֹתָיו בְּרַחֲמִים: וַיְיָ עֵר, הִנֵּה לֹא יָנוּם וְלֹא יִישָׁן:

הַמְּעוֹרֵר יְשֵׁנִים, וְהַמֵּקִיץ נִרְדָּמִים, וְהַמֵּשִׂיחַ אִלְּמִים, וְהַמַּתִּיר אֲסוּרִים, וְהַסּוֹמֵךְ נוֹפְלִים, וְהַזּוֹקֵף כְּפוּפִים, וְהַמְפַעֲנֵחַ נֶעְלָמִים, לְךָ לְבַדְּךָ אֲנַחְנוּ מוֹדִים. וְאִלּוּ פִינוּ מָלֵא שִׁירָה כַּיָּם, וּלְשׁוֹנֵנוּ רִנָּה כַּהֲמוֹן גַּלָּיו, וְשִׂפְתוֹתֵינוּ שֶׁבַח כְּמֶרְחֲבֵי רָקִיעַ, וְעֵינֵינוּ מְאִירוֹת

With a strong hand and outstretched arm;	His kindness is forever.
Who divided the Red Sea into lanes;	His kindness is forever.
Who brought Israel through;	His kindness is forever.
Who cast Pharaoh and his army into the Red Sea;	His kindness is forever.
Who led His people through the desert;	His kindness is forever.
Who smote great kings;	His kindness is forever.
Who slew mighty kings;	His kindness is forever.
Sichon, the king of the Emorites;	His kindness is forever.
And Og, the king of Bashan;	His kindness is forever.
Who gave their land as heritage;	His kindness is forever.
Heritage to Israel His servant;	His kindness is forever.
Who remembered us in our lowliness;	His kindness is forever.
And redeemed us from our enemies;	His kindness is forever.
He gives food to all flesh;	His kindness is forever.
Thank God of heaven;	His kindness is forever.

The remainder of the Seder Night Hallel is from the Shabbat and Festival Morning Liturgy

The soul of all living beings shall bless Your Name, God. The spirit of all flesh shall always praise and glorify Your fame, our King, forever. From all eternity You are God, and except for You we have no king, redeemer or helper. He Who rescues, and redeems, sustains and has compassion, in every time of trouble and distress, we have no King but You.

You are God of the first and of the last, God of all living creatures, Master of all peoples, Who is glorified in a multitude of praises, Who guides His world with kindness and His creatures with compassion. God does not slumber nor sleep;

He rouses the sleeping and awakens those who slumber; [He] makes the dumb speak, frees the captives, supports the fallen raises the bent and reveals the hidden. To You alone we give thanks.

Were our mouths full with song as the sea, our tongues full with joy as the many waves, our lips full with praise as broad as the heavens, our eyes as bright as the sun and the moon, our hands outspread as the eagles

כַּשֶּׁמֶשׁ וְכַיָּרֵחַ, וְיָדֵינוּ פְרוּשׂוֹת כְּנִשְׁרֵי שָׁמָיִם, וְרַגְלֵינוּ קַלּוֹת
כָּאַיָּלוֹת: אֵין אֲנַחְנוּ מַסְפִּיקִים לְהוֹדוֹת לְךָ יְיָ אֱלֹהֵינוּ וֵאלֹהֵי
אֲבוֹתֵינוּ וּלְבָרֵךְ אֶת שְׁמֶךָ מַלְכֵּנוּ, עַל אַחַת מֵאֶלֶף אֶלֶף אַלְפֵי
אֲלָפִים, וְרִבֵּי רְבָבוֹת פְּעָמִים, הַטּוֹבוֹת, נִסִּים וְנִפְלָאוֹת, שֶׁעָשִׂיתָ עִם
אֲבוֹתֵינוּ וְעִמָּנוּ:

מִמִּצְרַיִם גְּאַלְתָּנוּ יְיָ אֱלֹהֵינוּ וּמִבֵּית עֲבָדִים פְּדִיתָנוּ, בְּרָעָב זַנְתָּנוּ,
וּבְשָׂבָע כִּלְכַּלְתָּנוּ, מֵחֶרֶב הִצַּלְתָּנוּ, וּמִדֶּבֶר מִלַּטְתָּנוּ, וּמֵחֳלָיִם רָעִים,
וְרַבִּים, וְנֶאֱמָנִים, דִּלִּיתָנוּ: עַד הֵנָּה עֲזָרוּנוּ רַחֲמֶיךָ, וְלֹא עֲזָבוּנוּ
חֲסָדֶיךָ, וְאַל תִּטְּשֵׁנוּ יְיָ אֱלֹהֵינוּ לָנֶצַח:

עַל כֵּן אֵבָרִים שֶׁפִּלַּגְתָּ בָּנוּ, וְרוּחַ וּנְשָׁמָה שֶׁנָּפַחְתָּ בְּאַפֵּינוּ, וְלָשׁוֹן
אֲשֶׁר שַׂמְתָּ בְּפִינוּ, הֵן הֵם יוֹדוּ, וִיבָרְכוּ, וִישַׁבְּחוּ, וִיפָאֲרוּ, וִישׁוֹרְרוּ,
וִירוֹמְמוּ, וְיַעֲרִיצוּ, וְיַקְדִּישׁוּ, וְיַמְלִיכוּ אֶת שִׁמְךָ מַלְכֵּנוּ תָּמִיד, כִּי כָל
פֶּה לְךָ יוֹדֶה, וְכָל לָשׁוֹן לְךָ תִשָּׁבַע, וְכָל עַיִן לְךָ תְצַפֶּה, וְכָל בֶּרֶךְ לְךָ
תִכְרַע, וְכָל קוֹמָה לְפָנֶיךָ תִשְׁתַּחֲוֶה: וְכָל הַלְּבָבוֹת יִירָאוּךָ, וְכָל קֶרֶב
וּכְלָיוֹת יְזַמְּרוּ לִשְׁמֶךָ, כַּדָּבָר שֶׁכָּתוּב: "כָּל עַצְמוֹתַי תֹּאמַרְנָה יְיָ מִי
כָמוֹךָ: מַצִּיל עָנִי מֵחָזָק מִמֶּנּוּ, וְעָנִי וְאֶבְיוֹן מִגֹּזְלוֹ": שַׁוְעַת עֲנִיִּים
אַתָּה תִשְׁמַע, צַעֲקַת הַדַּל תַּקְשִׁיב וְתוֹשִׁיעַ:

מִי יִדְמֶה לָּךְ, וּמִי יִשְׁוֶה לָּךְ, וּמִי יַעֲרָךְ לָךְ. הָאֵל, הַגָּדוֹל, הַגִּבּוֹר
וְהַנּוֹרָא, אֵל עֶלְיוֹן, קֹנֵה שָׁמַיִם וָאָרֶץ: נְהַלֶּלְךָ וּנְשַׁבֵּחֲךָ וּנְפָאֶרְךָ
וּנְבָרֵךְ אֶת שֵׁם קָדְשֶׁךָ. כָּאָמוּר: "לְדָוִד בָּרְכִי נַפְשִׁי אֶת יְיָ, וְכָל קְרָבַי
אֶת שֵׁם קָדְשׁוֹ:

הָאֵל בְּתַעֲצֻמוֹת עֻזֶּךָ, הַגָּדוֹל בִּכְבוֹד שְׁמֶךָ, הַגִּבּוֹר לָנֶצַח
וְהַנּוֹרָא בְּנוֹרְאוֹתֶיךָ: הַמֶּלֶךְ, הַיּוֹשֵׁב, עַל כִּסֵּא רָם וְנִשָּׂא:

שׁוֹכֵן עַד מָרוֹם וְקָדוֹשׁ שְׁמוֹ. וְכָתוּב: "רַנְּנוּ צַדִּיקִים בַּיְיָ, לַיְשָׁרִים
נָאוָה תְהִלָּה":

וּבְשִׂפְתֵי צַדִּיקִים תִּתְבָּרַךְ:	בְּפִי יְשָׁרִים תִּתְרוֹמָם:
וּבְקֶרֶב קְדוֹשִׁים תִּתְקַדָּשׁ:	וּבִלְשׁוֹן חֲסִידִים תִּתְהַלָּל:

of the sky and our feet swift as deer — we could never sufficiently thank You, God, God of our fathers, or bless Your Name, for even one of the countless thousands upon thousands of good deeds, miracles and wonders which You did for our fathers and for us.

You delivered us from Egypt, God, and redeemed us from slavery. In hunger, You fed us; in plenty, You provided for us. From the sword, You spared us; from the plague, You let us escape; and from severe and grievous diseases, You preserved us. Until now Your compassion has helped us, Your kindness has not left us; please do not abandon us, God, forever.

Therefore, the limbs You gave us, the spirit and soul which You breathed into our nostrils, and the tongue which You placed in our mouth — all shall thank and bless, praise and glorify, exalt, revere, sanctify and crown Your Name, our King. Every mouth shall offer to You thanks, every tongue shall promise loyalty, every eye shall look toward you, every knee shall bend, all who stand shall bow, before You; all hearts shall fear You; and man's innards and thoughts shall sing praises to Your Name, as is written: 'All my bones shall say: "God, who is like You?" You help the poor from those stronger than he, the poor and needy from the one who would rob him' (Psalms 35:10). The call of the poor You listen to, the supplication of the impoverished You hearken to, and do help them.

Who is like You? Who is equal to You? Who can be compared to You? God Who is great, mighty, and awesome; God Who is most high, to Whom heaven and earth belong. We shall adore, praise and glorify You and bless Your holy Name, as it is written: 'Of David: My soul shall bless God, and my whole inner being shall bless His holy Name' (Psalms 103:1).

The Almighty! Mighty in Your strength; Great in the honor of Your Name; Powerful forever and awesome in Your deeds! The King Who sits upon a high and lofty throne!

He Who dwells forever, exalted and holy is His Name. It is written: 'Rejoice you righteous in God; for the just, praise is good to Him' (Psalms 33:1). In the mouths of the just, You shall be exalted; by the lips of the righteous, You shall be blessed; by the tongue of the pious, You shall be sanctified; and among the holy, You shall be praised.

וּבְמַקְהֲלוֹת רִבְבוֹת עַמְּךָ בֵּית יִשְׂרָאֵל בְּרִנָּה יִתְפָּאַר שִׁמְךָ מַלְכֵּנוּ
בְּכָל דּוֹר וָדוֹר. שֶׁכֵּן חוֹבַת כָּל הַיְצוּרִים, לְפָנֶיךָ יְהוָֹה אֱלֹהֵינוּ
וֵאלֹהֵי אֲבוֹתֵינוּ לְהוֹדוֹת לְהַלֵּל לְשַׁבֵּחַ לְפָאֵר לְרוֹמֵם לְהַדֵּר
וּלְנַצֵּחַ לְבָרֵךְ לְעַלֵּה וּלְקַלֵּס עַל כָּל דִּבְרֵי שִׁירוֹת וְתִשְׁבְּחוֹת דָּוִד
בֶּן יִשַׁי עַבְדְּךָ מְשִׁיחֶךָ.

וּבְכֵן יִשְׁתַּבַּח שִׁמְךָ לָעַד מַלְכֵּנוּ הָאֵל הַמֶּלֶךְ הַגָּדוֹל וְהַקָּדוֹשׁ
בַּשָּׁמַיִם וּבָאָרֶץ. כִּי לְךָ נָאֶה יְיָ אֱלֹהֵינוּ וֵאלֹהֵי אֲבוֹתֵינוּ. שִׁיר
וּשְׁבָחָה הַלֵּל וְזִמְרָה עֹז וּמֶמְשָׁלָה נֶצַח גְּדֻלָּה וּגְבוּרָה תְּהִלָּה
וְתִפְאֶרֶת קְדֻשָּׁה וּמַלְכוּת. בְּרָכוֹת וְהוֹדָאוֹת לְשִׁמְךָ הַגָּדוֹל
וְהַקָּדוֹשׁ וּמֵעוֹלָם וְעַד עוֹלָם אַתָּה אֵל: בָּרוּךְ אַתָּה יְהוָֹה אֵל מֶלֶךְ
גָּדוֹל וּמְהֻלָּל בַּתִּשְׁבָּחוֹת אֵל הַהוֹדָאוֹת אֲדוֹן הַנִּפְלָאוֹת בּוֹרֵא כָּל
הַנְּשָׁמוֹת רִבּוֹן כָּל הַמַּעֲשִׂים הַבּוֹחֵר בְּשִׁירֵי זִמְרָה מֶלֶךְ יָחִיד חֵי
הָעוֹלָמִים:

קודם שמברך על כוס רביעי יאמר זה:

הִנְנִי מוּכָן וּמְזֻמָּן לְקַיֵּם מִצְוַת כּוֹס רְבִיעִי מֵאַרְבַּע כּוֹסוֹת, לְשֵׁם יְחוּד קוּדְשָׁא בְּרִיךְ הוּא
וּשְׁכִינְתֵּיהּ עַל יְדֵי הַהוּא טָמִיר וְנֶעְלָם בְּשֵׁם כָּל יִשְׂרָאֵל: וִיהִי נֹעַם יְיָ אֱלֹהֵינוּ עָלֵינוּ
וּמַעֲשֵׂה יָדֵינוּ כּוֹנְנָה עָלֵינוּ וּמַעֲשֵׂה יָדֵינוּ כּוֹנְנֵהוּ.

בָּרוּךְ אַתָּה יְהוָֹה אֱלֹהֵינוּ מֶלֶךְ הָעוֹלָם בּוֹרֵא פְּרִי הַגָּפֶן:

ושותה בהסיבת שמאל, ואחר כך אומרים ברכה אחרונה:

בָּרוּךְ אַתָּה יְהוָֹה אֱלֹהֵינוּ מֶלֶךְ הָעוֹלָם עַל הַגֶּפֶן וְעַל פְּרִי הַגֶּפֶן וְעַל
תְּנוּבַת הַשָּׂדֶה וְעַל אֶרֶץ חֶמְדָּה טוֹבָה וּרְחָבָה שֶׁרָצִיתָ וְהִנְחַלְתָּ לַאֲבוֹתֵינוּ
לֶאֱכֹל מִפִּרְיָהּ וְלִשְׂבּוֹעַ מִטּוּבָהּ. רַחֵם נָא יְהוָֹה אֱלֹהֵינוּ עַל יִשְׂרָאֵל עַמֶּךָ
וְעַל יְרוּשָׁלַיִם עִירֶךָ וְעַל צִיּוֹן מִשְׁכַּן כְּבוֹדֶךָ וְעַל מִזְבְּחֶךָ וְעַל הֵיכָלֶךָ.
וּבְנֵה יְרוּשָׁלַיִם עִיר הַקֹּדֶשׁ בִּמְהֵרָה בְיָמֵינוּ וְהַעֲלֵנוּ לְתוֹכָהּ וְשַׂמְּחֵנוּ
בְּבִנְיָנָהּ וְנֹאכַל מִפִּרְיָהּ וְנִשְׂבַּע מִטּוּבָהּ וּנְבָרֶכְךָ עָלֶיהָ בִּקְדֻשָּׁה וּבְטָהֳרָה,
(בשבת וּרְצֵה וְהַחֲלִיצֵנוּ בְּיוֹם הַשַּׁבָּת הַזֶּה) וְשַׂמְּחֵנוּ בְּיוֹם חַג הַמַּצּוֹת הַזֶּה, כִּי
אַתָּה יְהוָֹה טוֹב וּמֵטִיב לַכֹּל וְנוֹדֶה לְּךָ עַל הָאָרֶץ וְעַל פְּרִי הַגָּפֶן: בָּרוּךְ
אַתָּה יְיָ עַל הָאָרֶץ וְעַל פְּרִי הַגָּפֶן:

133

And in the congregations of the myriads of Your people Israel, with joy, Your Name, our King, shall be glorified in all generations. For this is the duty of all creatures: before You, our God, God of our fathers, to thank, praise, honor, glorify, exalt, adore, show gratitude, bless, raise high, and sing praises — even more than all the songs and praises of David the son of Yishai, Your chosen servant.

Therefore, may Your Name be praised forever, our King, God, Who is great and holy in the heavens and on earth. To You, God, God of our fathers, are song and praise, honor and hymns, strength and power, victory, greatness and might, praise and glory, holiness and sovereignty; blessings and thanksgiving to Your great and holy Name, from this world and in the World to Come — You are God. Blessed are You, God, King, great and praised in glory, God of thanksgiving, Master of wonders, Who creates all the souls, [Who is] Master of all works, Who chooses songs of praise — King, One [God], Life of all worlds.

The blessing over the fourth and last cup is recited.

I am ready and prepared to perform the mitzvah of drinking the fourth cup of wine.

Blessed are You, God, King of the universe, Who creates the fruit of the vine.

One then drinks this entire cup while reclining on the left side.

After drinking the fourth cup, the following blessing is recited:

Blessed are You, God, King of the universe, for the vine, the fruit of the vine, and for the produce of the field; for the desireable, good and spacious land that You desired and gave our forefathers as a heritage, to eat of its fruit and to be satisfied with its good. Have mercy, we beg You, God, on Israel Your people; on Jerusalem, Your city; on Zion, home of Your glory; on Your altar, and Your Temple. Rebuild Jerusalem, the city of holiness, speedily in our days; bring us into it; make us happy with its rebuilding; let us eat from its fruit and be satisfied with its good; and we will bless You upon it in holiness and purity. (On Shabbat: Be pleased and strengthen us on this Shabbat.) Give us happiness on this Festival of Matzot; for You, God, are good, and do good to all, and we thank You for the land and for the fruit of the vine. Blessed are You, God, for the Land and for the fruit of the vine.

נרצה

אם עשה כסדר הזה יהיה רצוי לפני האל וכן יהי רצון. וכל המקיים מצות פסח
כהלכתו, לעד עומדת צדקתו ומגן ה' בעזרתו, אמן:

חֲסַל סִדּוּר פֶּסַח כְּהִלְכָתוֹ, כְּכָל מִשְׁפָּטוֹ וְחֻקָּתוֹ.
כַּאֲשֶׁר זָכִינוּ לְסַדֵּר אוֹתוֹ, כֵּן נִזְכֶּה לַעֲשׂוֹתוֹ.
זָךְ שׁוֹכֵן מְעוֹנָה, קוֹמֵם קְהַל עֲדַת מִי מָנָה.
בְּקָרוֹב נַהֵל נִטְעֵי כַנָּה, פְּדוּיִם לְצִיּוֹן בְּרִנָּה:

ג"פ לְשָׁנָה הַבָּאָה בִּירוּשָׁלָיִם

בליל ראשון אומרים "ויהי בחצי הלילה"
בליל שני אומרים "ואמרתם זבח פסח"

We have finished the Seder. (Halakhically, the Hallel is the conclusion of the
Seder. The custom of singing hymns is mentioned, though, as far back as the
Rokeach who lived in central Europe in the 12th-13th centuries C.E.)

But *have* we finished? Can man ever begin to do *anything* for the Infinite
Creator? Or can only *want* to?

God desires the heart (*Sanhedrin* 106b; *Zohar* II:162b). We desire God. We *want* to
serve Him, but we *know* that our actions are inadequate.

We have concluded the active portion of the Seder. All the Kadesh, U'rechatz,
etc. observances denote some act. All but the last one, that is. Nirtzah is passive.
No action. All we can do is stand before God with our hands raised.

We have long anticipated this night, we have extensively prepared for it. We
have done our human best.

Yehi Ratzon: May *You*, God, accept the longing of our hearts. And may next
year's Seder be even better (cf. *Oneg Shabbat*, p. 184).

NIRTZAH

If all was performed in the correct manner, then one is favored by God and this merit will last forever.

The Seder is completed in accordance with its laws,
With all its statutes and symbols;
Just as we merited to arrange it,
So may we merit to fulfil it.
Pure One, Who dwells on high,
Raise up Your countless congregation;
Soon, may You guide the plantings of Your vineyard,
Redeemed, to Zion, in joyous song.

(thrice)

NEXT YEAR IN JERUSALEM

On the first night recite "It was at Midnight."
On the second night recite "And say The Pesach Feast!"

נרצה — **FINISHING WITHOUT BEGINNING**
After drinking the fourth cup of wine and then thanking God for the fruit of the vine, we offer the Nirtzah Prayer of great yearning and longing: *Chasal Sidur Pesach*. Immediately following this, we proclaim: "L'Shanah habaah b'Yerushalayim — Next year in Jerusalem!" We remind ourselves and affirm that no matter where we find ourselves, no matter how much we've prospered individually and as a people — we must never forget that we are still in exile: the Mashiach has not yet come! And though this night was one of Exodus and Redemption, the like of which has never again been seen in the annals of mankind, even so, the Pesach Redemption was just a preview of the Final Redemption. We therefore conclude the Haggadah with this prayer/declaration: **"Next Year in Jerusalem!"** (*Nachat HaShulchan*).

וּבְכֵן וַיְהִי בַּחֲצִי הַלַּיְלָה:

בַּלַּיְלָה. אָז רוֹב נִסִּים הִפְלֵאתָ

הַלַּיְלָה. בְּרֹאשׁ אַשְׁמֹרֶת זֶה

לַיְלָה. גֵּר צֶדֶק נִצַּחְתּוֹ כְּנֶחֱלַק לוֹ

וַיְהִי בַּחֲצִי הַלַּיְלָה:

הַלַּיְלָה. דַּנְתָּ מֶלֶךְ גְּרָר בַּחֲלוֹם

לַיְלָה. הִפְחַדְתָּ אֲרַמִּי בְּאֶמֶשׁ

לַיְלָה. וַיָּשַׂר יִשְׂרָאֵל לְמַלְאָךְ וַיּוּכַל לוֹ

וַיְהִי בַּחֲצִי הַלַּיְלָה:

הַלַּיְלָה. זֶרַע בְּכוֹרֵי פַתְרוֹס מָחַצְתָּ בַּחֲצִי

בַּלַּיְלָה. חֵילָם לֹא מָצְאוּ בְּקוּמָם

לַיְלָה. טִיסַת נְגִיד חֲרוֹשֶׁת סִלִּיתָ בְּכוֹכְבֵי

וַיְהִי בַּחֲצִי הַלַּיְלָה:

בַּלַּיְלָה. יָעַץ מְחָרֵף לְנוֹפֵף אִוּוּי הוֹבַשְׁתָּ פְגָרָיו

לַיְלָה. כָּרַע בֵּל וּמַצָּבוֹ בְּאִישׁוֹן

לַיְלָה. לְאִישׁ חֲמוּדוֹת נִגְלָה רָז חֲזוֹת

וַיְהִי בַּחֲצִי הַלַּיְלָה:

Yaakov was returning to his father's home, when he was challenged by Esav's guardian angel. Yaakov was victorious that night (Genesis 32).

The Egyptian first-born died at midnight. They were left helpless, unable to protect themselves or prevent the Jews from departing (Exodus 12).

It was night when God caused the Kanaanite armies under Sisera's command to be defeated by the Jewish soldiers during the reign of Devorah the Prophetess (Judges 4,5).

The Assyrian army besieged Jerusalem and Sennacherib, their leader, claimed that God was powerless to stop him. On Pesach night he was repaid for this blasphemy: God smote Sennacherib's massive armies and he was forced to flee with but five surviving soldiers (one of whom was Nevukhadnezzar) (II Kings 19).

By showing that Bel was capable of speech, the mighty Nevukhadnezzar sought to give credence to his claim that his god surpassed all others. Actually, Nevukhadnezzar accomplished this by placing the captured *tzitz*, the High Priest's head-plate with the Ineffable Name on it, into the idol's mouth. Daniel realized

It was at Midnight.

Many miracles You performed at night,
At the beginning of the watch of this very night,
The righteous convert (Avraham) triumphed when the night was divided for him,

It was at Midnight.

You judged the king of G'rar (Avimelekh) during a dream at night,
You frightened the Aramean (Lavan) in the dark of night,
Israel (Yaakov) fought with an angel and overcame him by night,

It was at Midnight.

The first-born of Egypt You smote at midnight,
They did not find strength upon arising at night,
The army of Charoshet (Sisera), You swept away with the stars of the night,

It was at Midnight.

The blasphemous (Sennacherib) planned to rise against Your desired [Jerusalem] but You dried his [army's] corpse[s] at night,
Bel (Nevukhadnezzar's idol) with its pedestal was overturned in the darkness of night,
To the beloved (Daniel) was revealed the visions of night,

It was at Midnight.

The Seder celebration closes with a number of poems, which are customarily sung. With these hymns we extol God for the numerous miracles He performed for the Jewish people throughout the ages.

It Was At Midnight — On the first night of Pesach we begin with this ancient hymn which was composed by Yannai, an accomplished poet of the Holy Land. As the opening verses indicate, *It Was At Midnight* records the many miracles which occurred at midnight — the very hour of the Exodus. The poem has twenty-two stanzas, arranged alphabetically as well as chronologically. (Sources have been included, should the reader wish to study the references in greater depth.)

The "righteous convert" is a reference to Avraham, considered the first convert to Judaism. The poet refers to the night Avraham took up arms against the Four Kings, who had taken his nephew, Lot, into captivity (Genesis 14).

Avimelekh, the king of G'rar, took Sarah into his home. God appeared to him at night and warned him against harming Sarah. He was to return her to Avraham immediately (Genesis 20).

When Lavan went chasing after Yaakov, God appeared to him at night; warning him against harming Yaakov (Genesis 31).

138

מִשְׁתַּכֵּר בִּכְלֵי קֹדֶשׁ נֶהֱרַג בּוֹ   בַּלַּיְלָה.

נוֹשַׁע מִבּוֹר אֲרָיוֹת פּוֹתֵר בְּעֲתוּתֵי   לַיְלָה.

שִׂנְאָה נָטַר אֲגָגִי וְכָתַב סְפָרִים   בַּלַּיְלָה.

וַיְהִי בַּחֲצִי הַלַּיְלָה:

עוֹרַרְתָּ נִצְחֲךָ עָלָיו בְּנֶדֶד שְׁנַת   לַיְלָה.

פּוּרָה תִדְרוֹךְ לְשׁוֹמֵר מַה   מִלַּיְלָה.

צָרַח כַּשּׁוֹמֵר וְשָׂח אָתָא בֹקֶר וְגַם   לַיְלָה.

וַיְהִי בַּחֲצִי הַלַּיְלָה:

קָרֵב יוֹם אֲשֶׁר הוּא לֹא יוֹם וְלֹא   לַיְלָה.

רָם הוֹדַע כִּי לְךָ הַיּוֹם אַף לְךָ   הַלַּיְלָה.

שׁוֹמְרִים הַפְקֵד לְעִירְךָ כָּל הַיּוֹם וְכָל   הַלַּיְלָה.

תָּאִיר כְּאוֹר יוֹם חֶשְׁכַּת   לַיְלָה.

וַיְהִי בַּחֲצִי הַלַּיְלָה:

וּבְכֵן וַאֲמַרְתֶּם זֶבַח פֶּסַח:

אֹמֶץ גְּבוּרוֹתֶיךָ הִפְלֵאתָ   בַּפֶּסַח.

בְּרֹאשׁ כָּל מוֹעֲדוֹת נִשֵּׂאתָ   פֶּסַח.

גִּלִּיתָ לְאֶזְרָחִי חֲצוֹת לֵיל   פֶּסַח.

וַאֲמַרְתֶּם זֶבַח פֶּסַח:

Achashveirosh's sleep was withheld from him on the night that Haman arrived. It was the king's insomnia which eventually led to the salvation of the Jews and the wicked Haman's downfall (Esther 6).

...The remaining stanzas relate to the Future Redemption and are based on the prophesies of Isaiah and Zekhariah.

And Say: "The Pesach Feast!" — On the night of the second Seder we open this section of the hymns with a poem by the eminent Rabbi Elazar HaKalir. *And Say: "The Pesach Feast"* focuses on the miracles and incidents that occurred during Pesach itself. It's twenty-two stanzas also follow an alphabetical and chronological order.

The prophesy of the future midnight-exodus from Egypt was revealed to Avraham during Pesach, at the Covenant of the Halves (Genesis 15).

He (Belshatzar) who drank from the Temple's vessels was killed at night,
He (Daniel) who was rescued from the lions' den, who revealed the dreams of
the night,
The Aggagite (Haman) nursed hatred, and wrote decrees at night

It was at Midnight.

You subdued him when You disturbed his (Achashveirosh) sleep at night,
You will crush evil (Edom) to help those who ask the night-watchman, 'How
goes the night?'
He will cry out like a watchman, and say 'Morning comes and also night'

It was at Midnight.

Near is the Day (of the Mashiach) that is neither day nor night,
Most High! make known that that day is Yours and so is the night,
Appoint guards for Your city, all the day and all the night,
Light up as day, the darkness of the night,

It was at Midnight.

On the second Seder night recite the following:

And say: The Pesach Feast!

You displayed Your mighty powers on Pesach,
First of all festivals You elevated the Pesach,
To Ezrachi (Avraham) You revealed the coming midnight of Pesach,

And say: The Pesach Feast!

this, and when he was granted permission to "kiss" the statue, he removed the
tzitz. In the night, Bel fell from its pedestal and shattered into pieces (Daniel 3; *Shir
HaShirim Rabbah* 7:9).

It was night, when Nevukhadnezzar was suddenly awoken by a terrifying dream,
the details of which escaped him. He summoned all his advisors, none of whom
were capable of revealing another man's dream. Daniel, however, not only revealed
the dream but interpreted it correctly. For this amazing feat he was elevated above
all other ministers in Nevukhadnezzar's kingdom (Daniel 2).

Belshatzar dared to make use of the vessels from the Holy Temple. That same
night he saw the fiery handwriting on the wall. Though he could not interpret its
meaning, he was certain it was meant for him. He called for Daniel to decipher the
handwriting. And, just as Daniel indicated, Belshatzar was killed by his enemies
that very night (Daniel 5).

This refers to Daniel. He was delivered from the lions' den (Daniel 6).

Haman the Aggagite's hatred for us was so great, he went to Achashveirosh in the
middle of the night, seeking permission to hang Mordekhai and annihilate all the
Jews (Esther 5).

140

בְּפֶסַח.	דְּלָתָיו דָּפַקְתָּ כְּחֹם הַיּוֹם
בְּפֶסַח.	הִסְעִיד נוֹצְצִים עֻגוֹת מַצּוֹת
פֶּסַח.	וְאֶל הַבָּקָר רָץ זֵכֶר לְשׁוֹר עֵרֶךְ

וַאֲמַרְתֶּם זֶבַח פֶּסַח:

בְּפֶסַח.	זֹעֲמוּ סְדוֹמִים וְלֹהֲטוּ בָּאֵשׁ
פֶּסַח.	חֻלַּץ לוֹט מֵהֶם וּמַצּוֹת אָפָה בְּקֵץ
בְּפֶסַח.	טִאטֵאתָ אַדְמַת מוֹף וְנוֹף בְּעָבְרְךָ

וַאֲמַרְתֶּם זֶבַח פֶּסַח:

פֶּסַח.	יָהּ רֹאשׁ כָּל אוֹן מָחַצְתָּ בְּלֵיל שִׁמּוּר
פֶּסַח.	כַּבִּיר עַל בֵּן בְּכוֹר פָּסַחְתָּ בְּדַם
	לְבִלְתִּי תֵּת מַשְׁחִית לָבֹא בִּפְתָחַי בַּפֶּסַח.

וַאֲמַרְתֶּם זֶבַח פֶּסַח:

פֶּסַח.	מְסֻגֶּרֶת סֻגְּרָה בְּעִתּוֹתֵי
פֶּסַח.	נִשְׁמְדָה מִדְיָן בִּצְלִיל שְׂעוֹרֵי עֹמֶר
פֶּסַח.	שׂוֹרְפוּ מִשְׁמַנֵּי פּוּל וְלוּד בִּיקַד יְקוֹד

וַאֲמַרְתֶּם זֶבַח פֶּסַח:

פֶּסַח.	עוֹד הַיּוֹם בְּנֹב לַעֲמֹד עַד גָּעָה עוֹנַת
בְּפֶסַח.	פַּס יָד כָּתְבָה לְקַעֲקֵעַ צוּל
בְּפֶסַח.	צָפֹה הַצָּפִית עָרוֹךְ הַשֻּׁלְחָן

וַאֲמַרְתֶּם זֶבַח פֶּסַח:

Pul refers to Sennacherib, the king of Assyria (II Kings 15). The Ludim were warriors, perhaps Egyptians (Genesis 10) or Africans (Isaiah 66), who were apparently part of his mighty armies. They, too, were conquered on Pesach.

Nov is a place near Jerusalem from where Sennacherib sighted the Holy City and from where he intended to direct his attack against it (Isaiah 10). As mentioned in the previous poem, it was the Seder night when God utterly destroyed Sennacherib's armies (Isaiah 37).

This is the handwriting on the wall which Belshatzar saw, and which only Daniel could interpret. It foretold of the destruction of Zul, which is Babylon (Daniel 5).

141

You knocked at his (Avraham) door in the day's heat on Pesach,
He fed the angels with matzah-cakes on Pesach,
He ran to the herd in memory of the ox of Pesach,

And say: The Pesach Feast!

The Sodomites angered [God] and were destroyed by fire on Pesach,
Lot was saved and he baked matzot on Pesach,
You swept clean the soil of Egypt when You passed over on Pesach,

And say: The Pesach Feast!

You smote the firstborn on the night of Pesach,
Mighty One! You passed over the firstborn (the Jews) because of the blood of Pesach,
Not to let the destroying angel enter my door on Pesach,

And say: The Pesach Feast!

The walled city (Jericho) was besieged on Pesach,
Midian was destroyed (by Gideon) with the barley offering from the Omer on Pesach,
Pul and Lud were consumed in a great fire on Pesach,

And say: The Pesach Feast!

The day of Nov (Sennacherib) stood waiting for Pesach,
The Hand wrote on the wall (for Belshatzar), making a shadow on Pesach,
The watch was prepared, the table spread on Pesach,

And say: The Pesach Feast!

The three angels who visited Avraham after he underwent circumcision arrived on Pesach. Despite his weak condition, He fed them Matzot and veal in honor of the holiday. Such was the great measure of Avraham's hospitality (Genesis 18).

That same day, these angels went on to S'dom to overturn the city because of the wickedness of its inhabitants (Genesis 19).

Lot had learned hospitality from Avraham. When the angels arrived in S'dom, he invited them into his home and served them Matzot. Though they destroyed the city, these angels enabled Lot to flee for his life (Genesis 19).

Mof and Nof refer to Egypt (Hoshea 9; Isaiah 19). The next four verses refer to God's "sweeping clean" of Egypt on the night of Pesach; slaying their first-born, while, at the same time, protecting the first-born of the Jews (Exodus 12).

It was Pesach when Joshua and the Israelites laid siege to Jericho (Joshua 6).

And it was again Pesach when Gideon later took up battle against the Midianite nation which had been oppressing the Jews (Judges 7).

קָהָל כִּנְּסָה הֲדַסָּה צוֹם לְשַׁלֵּשׁ   בַּפֶּסַח.

רֹאשׁ מִבֵּית רָשָׁע מָחַצְתָּ בְּעֵץ חֲמִשִּׁים   בַּפֶּסַח.

שְׁתֵּי אֵלֶּה רֶגַע תָּבִיא לְעוּצִית   בַּפֶּסַח.

תָּעֹז יָדְךָ תָּרוּם יְמִינְךָ כְּלֵיל הִתְקַדֶּשׁ חַג   פֶּסַח.

וַאֲמַרְתֶּם זֶבַח פֶּסַח:

כִּי לוֹ נָאֶה. כִּי לוֹ יָאֶה:

אַדִּיר בִּמְלוּכָה. בָּחוּר כַּהֲלָכָה. גְּדוּדָיו יֹאמְרוּ לוֹ:

לְךָ וּלְךָ. לְךָ כִּי לְךָ. לְךָ אַף לְךָ. לְךָ יְהֹוָה הַמַּמְלָכָה.
כִּי לוֹ נָאֶה. כִּי לוֹ יָאֶה:

דָּגוּל בִּמְלוּכָה. הָדוּר כַּהֲלָכָה. וָתִיקָיו יֹאמְרוּ לוֹ: לְךָ וכו':

זַכַּאי בִּמְלוּכָה. חָסִין כַּהֲלָכָה. טַפְסְרָיו יֹאמְרוּ לוֹ: לְךָ וכו':

יָחִיד בִּמְלוּכָה. כַּבִּיר כַּהֲלָכָה. לִמּוּדָיו יֹאמְרוּ לוֹ: לְךָ וכו':

מוֹשֵׁל בִּמְלוּכָה. נוֹרָא כַּהֲלָכָה. סְבִיבָיו יֹאמְרוּ לוֹ: לְךָ וכו':

עָנִיו בִּמְלוּכָה. פּוֹדֶה כַּהֲלָכָה. צַדִּיקָיו יֹאמְרוּ לוֹ: לְךָ וכו':

קָדוֹשׁ בִּמְלוּכָה. רַחוּם כַּהֲלָכָה. שִׁנְאַנָּיו יֹאמְרוּ לוֹ: לְךָ וכו':

of Sennacherib's armies on the night of Pesach (Isaiah 30:29, Rashi):
May we merit seeing the Final Redemption, when, with the rebuilding of the Holy
Temple, we will partake of the Pesach sacrifice and recite the Hallel; speedily, and
in our time. Amen!

To Him Praise is Due — Malkhut, the Kingdom of Holiness, is constructed through
song (*Likutey Moharan* I, 3). Now that we have fulfilled all the Mitzvot of the night, we
are able to *sing* His praise through different songs; each of which, either manifestly
or recondidately, has the Kingdom of God as its theme (*Likutey Halakhot, Apatrupus* 3).
We begin with *To Him Praise is Due,* an anonymous, alphabetically arranged song
which had already made its appearance in the Haggadah in medieval times.

Hadassah (Esther) gathered a congregation for a three-day fast on Pesach,
The head of the evil house (Haman) was hung on a fifty-cubit gallows on Pesach,
Punishments will be visited upon the wicked kingdom (Utz) on Pesach,

May Your hand be strong, Your right arm raised, as on the night when You sanctified the Festival of Pesach,

And say: The Pesach Feast!

To Him praise is due! To Him praise is fitting!

Mighty in His kingdom, Chosen by right, His armies say to Him:

(chorus:) To You and only to You; to You, because it is Yours; to You, only Yours; Yours, God, is the kingdom. To Him praise is due! To Him praise is fitting!

Famous in His kingdom, glorious by right, His good ones say to Him: (chorus:)

Pure in His kingdom, powerful by right, His servants say to Him: (chorus:)

Alone in His kingdom, strong by right, His learned say to Him: (chorus:)

Ruling in His kingdom, awesome by right, His surrounding [hosts] say to Him: (chorus:)

Modest in His kingdom, redeemer by right, His righteous say to Him: (chorus:)

Before she would enter Achashveirosh's chambers, Esther requested that the Jews gather for three days of prayer and fasting (Esther 4). This took place on Pesach (*Megillah* 15a).

Haman was hung on the second day of Pesach (*Ibid.*).

Utz is a reference to Edom (Lamentations 4), this fourth and final exile in which we now find ourselves. For all the terrible suffering which Edom has inflicted upon us, we ask that he be punished with twice that which God inflicted upon the Egyptians on the night of Pesach.

And we conclude with a prayer. We ask God to "make His Hand strong" and to "lift up His Arm" — "as on *the night* You sanctified the festival," a reference to the Hallel recital on the night of the Exodus and to the destruction

תַּקִּיף בִּמְלוּכָה. תּוֹמֵךְ כַּהֲלָכָה. תְּמִימָיו יאמְרוּ לוֹ:

לְךָ וּלְךָ. לְךָ כִּי לְךָ. לְךָ אַף לְךָ. לְךָ יְהוָה הַמַּמְלָכָה. כִּי לוֹ נָאֶה. כִּי לוֹ יָאֶה:

אַדִּיר הוּא יִבְנֶה בֵיתוֹ בְּקָרוֹב: בִּמְהֵרָה בִּמְהֵרָה בְּיָמֵינוּ בְּקָרוֹב. אֵל בְּנֵה אֵל בְּנֵה. בְּנֵה בֵיתְךָ בְּקָרוֹב:

בָּחוּר הוּא. גָּדוֹל הוּא. דָּגוּל הוּא. יִבְנֶה בֵיתוֹ בְּקָרוֹב. במהרה:

הָדוּר הוּא. וָתִיק הוּא. זַכַּאי הוּא. חָסִיד הוּא. יִבְנֶה בֵיתוֹ בְּקָרוֹב. במהרה:

טָהוֹר הוּא. יָחִיד הוּא. כַּבִּיר הוּא. לָמוּד הוּא. מֶלֶךְ הוּא. נוֹרָא הוּא. סַגִּיב הוּא. עִזּוּז הוּא. פּוֹדֶה הוּא. צַדִּיק הוּא. יִבְנֶה בֵיתוֹ בְּקָרוֹב. במהרה:

קָדוֹשׁ הוּא. רַחוּם הוּא. שַׁדַּי הוּא. תַּקִּיף הוּא. יִבְנֶה בֵיתוֹ בְּקָרוֹב. בִּמְהֵרָה בִּמְהֵרָה בְּיָמֵינוּ בְּקָרוֹב. אֵל בְּנֵה. אֵל בְּנֵה. בְּנֵה בֵיתְךָ בְּקָרוֹב:

ספירת העומר

בליל שני של פסח מתחילין לספור ספירת העומר. בחוץ לארץ, כשיש שני ימים טובים, יש סופרין בתחילת הלילה, אבל לפי מנהגי האר״י ז״ל יש לספור ליד הסדר לפני ״אחד מי יודע״. ספירת העומר תמצא להלן.

אֶחָד מִי יוֹדֵעַ. אֶחָד אֲנִי יוֹדֵעַ: אֶחָד אֱלֹהֵינוּ שֶׁבַּשָּׁמַיִם וּבָאָרֶץ:

שְׁנַיִם מִי יוֹדֵעַ. שְׁנַיִם אֲנִי יוֹדֵעַ: שְׁנֵי לֻחוֹת הַבְּרִית. אֶחָד אֱלֹהֵינוּ שֶׁבַּשָּׁמַיִם וּבָאָרֶץ:

This time-honored song contains thirteen questions. The numerical value of the Hebrew word for one, *echad*, is thirteen. All thirteen questions add up to this single revelation: There is only the *One* God, the *One* King; Ruler of heaven and earth. Let us truly and totally accept upon ourselves the authority of His Kingdom.

Who Knows One?" asks thirteen questions... and gives ninety-one answers. *Ninety-one is also the numerical value obtained by uniting two Holy Names:*

Holy in His kingdom, merciful by right, His angels say to Him: (chorus:)

Powerful in His kingdom, supporter by right, His perfect ones say to Him: (chorus:)

Mighty is He, Mighty is He

(chorus:) He will rebuild His Temple soon, speedily, speedily, in our days, soon. God, rebuild, God, rebuild, rebuild Your Temple soon.

Chosen is He, Great is He, Famous is He (chorus:)

Brilliant is He, Faithful is He, Faultless is He, Meritorious is He (chorus:)

Pure is He, Alone is He, Sturdy is He, Learned is He, Royal is He, Awesome is He, Highest is He, Strong is He, Redeemer is He, Righteous is He (chorus:)

Holy is He, Merciful is He, Almighty is He, Powerful is He (chorus:)

COUNTING OF THE OMER

On the 16th day of Nissan, the second evening of Pesach, one begins to Count the Omer. Outside the Holy Land this takes place on the night of the Second Seder. Some begin counting in the synagogue at the conclusion of the Evening Service, but, according to the ARI, one should count at the Seder, prior to 'Who Knows One.' The Omer can be found below after the Haggadah.

Who knows one? I know one: One is our God, in heaven and on earth. Who knows two? I know two: two are the Tablets; One is our God, in heaven and on earth.

Mighty is He — The composer of this song also employs an alphabetical progression, this time to, as it were, extol God's virtues; while the chorus expresses our heartfelt desire for the long awaited rebuilding of the Holy Temple. Reb Noson points out that we sing this song at the end of the Haggadah, when it is already midnight, if not later. He explains that it corresponds to Tikkun Chatzot, the Midnight Lament, in which we bemoan the destruction of the Temple. In *Mighty is He* we ask, in a holiday spirit, that God Himself build the Temple — speedily, and in our time! (Oral Tradition).

Who Knows One — The first question is "Who knows one?" Having performed the Seder service and devotions, we acknowledge the wisdom which has descended upon us this night. We should now know that there is a One and Only God.

שְׁלֹשָׁה מִי יוֹדֵעַ. שְׁלֹשָׁה אֲנִי יוֹדֵעַ: שְׁלֹשָׁה אָבוֹת. שְׁנֵי לֻחוֹת הַבְּרִית.
אֶחָד אֱלֹהֵינוּ שֶׁבַּשָּׁמַיִם וּבָאָרֶץ:

אַרְבַּע מִי יוֹדֵעַ. אַרְבַּע אֲנִי יוֹדֵעַ: אַרְבַּע אִמָּהוֹת. שְׁלֹשָׁה אָבוֹת. שְׁנֵי
לֻחוֹת הַבְּרִית. אֶחָד אֱלֹהֵינוּ שֶׁבַּשָּׁמַיִם וּבָאָרֶץ:

חֲמִשָּׁה מִי יוֹדֵעַ. חֲמִשָּׁה אֲנִי יוֹדֵעַ: חֲמִשָּׁה חֻמְשֵׁי תוֹרָה. אַרְבַּע
אִמָּהוֹת. שְׁלֹשָׁה אָבוֹת. שְׁנֵי לֻחוֹת הַבְּרִית. אֶחָד אֱלֹהֵינוּ שֶׁבַּשָּׁמַיִם
וּבָאָרֶץ:

שִׁשָּׁה מִי יוֹדֵעַ. שִׁשָּׁה אֲנִי יוֹדֵעַ: שִׁשָּׁה סִדְרֵי מִשְׁנָה. חֲמִשָּׁה חֻמְשֵׁי
תוֹרָה. אַרְבַּע אִמָּהוֹת. שְׁלֹשָׁה אָבוֹת. שְׁנֵי לֻחוֹת הַבְּרִית. אֶחָד אֱלֹהֵינוּ
שֶׁבַּשָּׁמַיִם וּבָאָרֶץ:

שִׁבְעָה מִי יוֹדֵעַ. שִׁבְעָה אֲנִי יוֹדֵעַ: שִׁבְעָה יְמֵי שַׁבַּתָּא. שִׁשָּׁה סִדְרֵי
מִשְׁנָה. חֲמִשָּׁה חֻמְשֵׁי תוֹרָה. אַרְבַּע אִמָּהוֹת. שְׁלֹשָׁה אָבוֹת. שְׁנֵי לֻחוֹת
הַבְּרִית. אֶחָד אֱלֹהֵינוּ שֶׁבַּשָּׁמַיִם וּבָאָרֶץ:

שְׁמוֹנָה מִי יוֹדֵעַ. שְׁמוֹנָה אֲנִי יוֹדֵעַ: שְׁמוֹנָה יְמֵי מִילָה. שִׁבְעָה יְמֵי
שַׁבַּתָּא. שִׁשָּׁה סִדְרֵי מִשְׁנָה. חֲמִשָּׁה חֻמְשֵׁי תוֹרָה. אַרְבַּע אִמָּהוֹת.
שְׁלֹשָׁה אָבוֹת. שְׁנֵי לֻחוֹת הַבְּרִית. אֶחָד אֱלֹהֵינוּ שֶׁבַּשָּׁמַיִם וּבָאָרֶץ:

תִּשְׁעָה מִי יוֹדֵעַ. תִּשְׁעָה אֲנִי יוֹדֵעַ: תִּשְׁעָה יַרְחֵי לֵידָה. שְׁמוֹנָה יְמֵי
מִילָה. שִׁבְעָה יְמֵי שַׁבַּתָּא. שִׁשָּׁה סִדְרֵי מִשְׁנָה. חֲמִשָּׁה חֻמְשֵׁי תוֹרָה.
אַרְבַּע אִמָּהוֹת. שְׁלֹשָׁה אָבוֹת. שְׁנֵי לֻחוֹת הַבְּרִית. אֶחָד אֱלֹהֵינוּ
שֶׁבַּשָּׁמַיִם וּבָאָרֶץ:

עֲשָׂרָה מִי יוֹדֵעַ. עֲשָׂרָה אֲנִי יוֹדֵעַ: עֲשָׂרָה דִבְּרַיָּא. תִּשְׁעָה יַרְחֵי לֵידָה.
שְׁמוֹנָה יְמֵי מִילָה. שִׁבְעָה יְמֵי שַׁבַּתָּא. שִׁשָּׁה סִדְרֵי מִשְׁנָה. חֲמִשָּׁה
חֻמְשֵׁי תוֹרָה. אַרְבַּע אִמָּהוֹת. שְׁלֹשָׁה אָבוֹת. שְׁנֵי לֻחוֹת הַבְּרִית. אֶחָד
אֱלֹהֵינוּ שֶׁבַּשָּׁמַיִם וּבָאָרֶץ:

Who knows three? I know three: three are the Patriarchs; two are the Tablets; One is our God, in heaven and on earth.

Who knows four? I know four: four are the Matriarchs; three are the Patriarchs; two are the Tablets; One is our God, in heaven and on earth.

Who knows five? I know five: five are the Books of Torah; four are the Matriarchs; three are the Patriarchs; two are the Tablets; One is our God, in heaven and on earth.

Who knows six? I know six: six are the Orders of Mishnah; five are the Books of Torah; four are the Matriarchs; three are the Patriarchs; two are the Tablets; One is our God, in heaven and on earth.

Who knows seven? I know seven: seven are the days of the week; six are the Orders of Mishnah; five are the Books of Torah; four are the Matriarchs; three are the Patriarchs; two are the Tablets; One is our God, in heaven and on earth.

Who knows eight? I know eight: eight are the days until circumcision; seven are the days of the week; six are the Orders of Mishnah; five are the Books of Torah; four are the Matriarchs; three are the Patriarchs; two are the Tablets; One is our God, in heaven and on earth.

Who knows nine? I know nine: nine are the months of pregnancy; eight are the days until circumcision; seven are the days of the week; six are the Orders of Mishnah; five are the Books of Torah; four are the Matriarchs; three are the Patriarchs; two are the Tablets; One is our God, in heaven and on earth.

Who knows ten? I know ten: ten are the Ten Commandments; nine are the months of pregnancy; eight are the days until circumcision; seven are the days of the week; six are the Orders of Mishnah; five are the Books of Torah; four are the Matriarchs; three are the Patriarchs; two are the Tablets; One is our God, in heaven and on earth.

YHVH (26), the Ineffable Name of God, with ADoNoY (65), the Name indicating kingship and sovereignty. Whatever we know, whatever we do, whatever we talk about, we should always recognize that God is King. Let us joyfully accept upon ourselves the absolute sovereignty of His Kingdom (Nachat HaShulchan).

אֶחָד עָשָׂר מִי יוֹדֵעַ. אֶחָד עָשָׂר אֲנִי יוֹדֵעַ: אַחַד עָשָׂר כּוֹכְבַיָּא. עֲשָׂרָה
דִבְּרַיָּא. תִּשְׁעָה יַרְחֵי לֵידָה. שְׁמוֹנָה יְמֵי מִילָה. שִׁבְעָה יְמֵי שַׁבַּתָּא.
שִׁשָּׁה סִדְרֵי מִשְׁנָה. חֲמִשָּׁה חֻמְשֵׁי תוֹרָה. אַרְבַּע אִמָּהוֹת. שְׁלֹשָׁה אָבוֹת.
שְׁנֵי לֻחוֹת הַבְּרִית. אֶחָד אֱלֹהֵינוּ שֶׁבַּשָּׁמַיִם וּבָאָרֶץ:

שְׁנֵים עָשָׂר מִי יוֹדֵעַ. שְׁנֵים עָשָׂר אֲנִי יוֹדֵעַ: שְׁנֵים עָשָׂר שִׁבְטַיָּא. אַחַד
עָשָׂר כּוֹכְבַיָּא. עֲשָׂרָה דִבְּרַיָּא. תִּשְׁעָה יַרְחֵי לֵידָה. שְׁמוֹנָה יְמֵי מִילָה.
שִׁבְעָה יְמֵי שַׁבַּתָּא. שִׁשָּׁה סִדְרֵי מִשְׁנָה. חֲמִשָּׁה חֻמְשֵׁי תוֹרָה. אַרְבַּע
אִמָּהוֹת. שְׁלֹשָׁה אָבוֹת. שְׁנֵי לֻחוֹת הַבְּרִית. אֶחָד אֱלֹהֵינוּ שֶׁבַּשָּׁמַיִם
וּבָאָרֶץ:

שְׁלֹשָׁה עָשָׂר מִי יוֹדֵעַ. שְׁלֹשָׁה עָשָׂר אֲנִי יוֹדֵעַ: שְׁלֹשָׁה עָשָׂר מִדַּיָּא.
שְׁנֵים עָשָׂר שִׁבְטַיָּא. אַחַד עָשָׂר כּוֹכְבַיָּא. עֲשָׂרָה דִבְּרַיָּא. תִּשְׁעָה יַרְחֵי
לֵידָה. שְׁמוֹנָה יְמֵי מִילָה. שִׁבְעָה יְמֵי שַׁבַּתָּא. שִׁשָּׁה סִדְרֵי מִשְׁנָה.
חֲמִשָּׁה חֻמְשֵׁי תוֹרָה. אַרְבַּע אִמָּהוֹת. שְׁלֹשָׁה אָבוֹת. שְׁנֵי לֻחוֹת הַבְּרִית.
אֶחָד אֱלֹהֵינוּ שֶׁבַּשָּׁמַיִם וּבָאָרֶץ:

חַד גַּדְיָא. חַד גַּדְיָא. דְּזַבִּין אַבָּא בִּתְרֵי זוּזֵי. חַד גַּדְיָא חַד
גַּדְיָא:

וְאָתָא שׁוּנְרָא וְאָכְלָה לְגַדְיָא, דְּזַבִּין אַבָּא בִּתְרֵי זוּזֵי. חַד
גַּדְיָא חַד גַּדְיָא:

וְאָתָא כַלְבָּא וְנָשַׁךְ לְשׁוּנְרָא. דְּאָכְלָה לְגַדְיָא. דְּזַבִּין אַבָּא
בִּתְרֵי זוּזֵי. חַד גַּדְיָא חַד גַּדְיָא:

intervened and meddled where they should not have. And this is why revenge
was exacted against them as well. (This principle only applies after the assault
has been committed. If, however, one witnesses an assault against another person
or property, he is obliged to intervene to prevent it from happening; *Choshen
Mishpat 388, 425*). The *Chad Gadya* lesson is this: Although it may appear that
their actions were proper in meting out justice, who can presume to substitute
personal justice for what should rightfully be the Justice of God? Who can claim
to really understand and carry out true justice?

Who knows eleven? I know eleven: eleven are the stars [in Yosef's dream]; ten are the Ten Commandments; nine are the months of pregnancy; eight are the days until circumcision; seven are the days of the week; six are the Orders of Mishnah; five are the Books of Torah; four are the Matriarchs; three are the Patriarchs; two are the Tablets; One is our God, in heaven and on earth.

Who knows twelve? I know twelve: twelve are the Tribes; eleven are the stars; ten are the Ten Commandments; nine are the months of pregnancy; eight are the days until circumcision; seven are the days of the week; six are the Orders of Mishnah; five are the Books of Torah; four are the Matriarchs; three are the Patriarchs; two are the Tablets; One is our God, in heaven and on earth.

Who knows thirteen? I know thirteen: thirteen are the Attributes of Mercy; twelve are the Tribes; eleven are the stars; ten are the Ten Commandments; nine are the months of pregnancy; eight are the days until circumcision; seven are the days of the week; six are the Orders of Mishnah; five are the Books of Torah; four are the Matriarchs; three are the Patriarchs; two are the Tablets; One is our God, in heaven and on earth.

One kid, one kid, that father bought for two zuzim, one kid, one kid.

Along came a cat and ate the kid, that father bought for two zuzim, one kid, one kid.

Along came a dog and bit the cat, that ate the kid, that father bought for two zuzim, one kid, one kid.

Chad Gadya, One Kid — Though incorporated into the Haggadah as far back as the Middle Ages, the *Chad Gadya* song at the conclusion of the Pesach Seder may seem a bit out of place. It appears to be an allegorical portrayal of the injustice found in this world; by no means one of the more obvious themes of the evening's lessons. Why close this night of Exodus, Redemption and Higher Awareness with a comment on social reality?

Let's look at what happened here. Without provocation or prodding, the cat ate the kid. Surely the cat deserves to be punished. So along comes the dog to make sure that justice is done. How does he do this? He bites the cat. Everything seems fine and fair. But then we see that the dog is punished by the stick. Why? Didn't the dog do the right thing in avenging the kid?

The answer is that he did not. Why? because no one asked the dog to get involved. This applies equally to the stick, the fire, the water, and all those who

וְאָתָא חוּטְרָא וְהִכָּה לְכַלְבָּא דְּנָשַׁךְ לְשׁוּנְרָא. דְּאָכְלָה
לְגַדְיָא. דְּזַבִּין אַבָּא בִּתְרֵי זוּזֵי. חַד גַּדְיָא חַד גַּדְיָא:
וְאָתָא נוּרָא וְשָׂרַף לְחוּטְרָא דְּהִכָּה לְכַלְבָּא דְּנָשַׁךְ לְשׁוּנְרָא.
דְּאָכְלָה לְגַדְיָא. דְּזַבִּין אַבָּא בִּתְרֵי זוּזֵי. חַד גַּדְיָא חַד
גַּדְיָא:

Chad Gadya — On another level, this song relates to the ongoing struggle for control of this world: the battle between the Kingdom of Holiness and the Kingdom of Evil. Yaakov's sons (the cat) were jealous of their brother Yosef (the kid) and sold him into slavery. Because of this, they were exiled to Egypt (the dog), the Kingdom of Evil. Moshe's staff (the stick), from the Kingdom of Holiness, was used to strike the Egyptians. But then the Jews made the Golden Calf (fire), causing the Kingdom of Holiness to be subdued again. However, when they received the Torah (water), the Kingdom of Holiness was once more elevated [the Calf was made before Moshe descended from Mount Sinai with the Tablets].

Yet the matter did not end there. This battle between Holiness and Evil has gone on and on; from day to day, year to year, generation to generation, millennia to millennia. Esav (the ox) and his descendants [Rome] dominate us in our present exile. The Kingdom of Evil rules, always attempting to "devour" the Torah and those who remain faithful to it. And the measure of Esav's success can always be measured by the degree of Torah neglect which prevails at any one time. It is this neglect, in fact, which *is* the bitterness of exile. Eventually, Mashiach ben Yosef (the slaughterer) will subdue Esav. However, the Angel of Death will come and kill this Mashiach [as our Sages teach (*Sukkah* 52a): Mashiach the son of Yosef will die]. In the end, though, God Himself will mete out the ultimate, true justice. He will slaughter the Angel of Death and rectify the world completely. May this happen speedily, in our time. Amen! (*Nachat HaShulchan*).

Chad Gadya — Of the allegorical figures in the *Chad Gadya,* the fire, the ox and the Angel of Death can be seen as alluding to the Four Exiles into which the Jewish people were cast. Seen in this light, the stick represents the Kingdom of Judah; as in, "A stick shall come from the house of Yishai" (Isaiah 11:1).

The fire which burnt the stick alludes to the first exile, to Nevukhadnezzar and the Babylonian empire. It was then that our Holy Temple was destroyed by fire and Nevukhadnezzar threw Chananya, Mishael and Azariah into a flaming furnace. The second exile of the Jews directly followed the first one, as the Babylonians were superseded by the Persians and Medians who are also represented in the *Chad Gadya* by fire. During these exiles, however, the Jews were saved by the water which extinguished the fire. The water is indicative of the Torah, which

Along came a stick and beat the dog, that bit the cat, that ate the kid, that father bought for two zuzim, one kid, one kid.

Along came a fire and burned the stick, that beat the dog, that bit the cat, that ate the kid, that father bought for two zuzim, one kid, one kid.

In short, *Chad Gadya* teaches us that justice must be left to God. When Hillel saw a skull floating on the water, he remarked, "Because you drowned others, you yourself were drowned" (*Avot* 2:6). The ARI explains that this skull belonged to Pharaoh. He was guilty of having drowned the Jewish children in the Nile (*Sha'ar Ma'amarei Razal*). But, as Hillel goes on to say, "...and the end will be that those who drowned you will themselves be drowned." Thus, a person responsible for the drowning of another shall himself be drowned. Even so, this does not give anyone the right to freely execute justice on his own. While it is true that the guilty party is deserving of death, the enactment of judgment belongs to God. It is not for us to take matters into our own hands.

Both from a personal and a general perspective, the message is as obvious as it is difficult to fulfill: We are not truly capable of defining absolute truth because we see everything from *our own* viewpoint. For this reason, in our daily lives we must be very careful in our personal judgments. Rebbe Nachman teaches that we must judge each person favorably, focusing only on his good points (*Likutey Moharan* I, 282). True, he may have committed a crime or a sin — neither of which should be judged as anything else but what it really is; however, the person himself — he should be judged favorably. Do we really know the motivation or compelling force which brought him to this? And even if we do, does that provide us with the wisdom — the right — to exact judgment and justice on our own? (see *Azamra!*).

This is true from a broader, more general perspective as well. There are many things which have happened to us in our past, in the history of our people, in the annals of mankind, for which we have no satisfactory explanation; misfortune and suffering which we can neither justify nor understand as proper judgement. *Chad Gadya* tells us that we should never question God's judgment and His enactment of justice. Though we are incapable of seeing how or why, we must accept and even truly believe that God is always right.

And this is why we sing *Chad Gadya* on the Seder Night. The events related to Pesach — the redemption from slavery and the Exodus from Egypt — were God's enactment of *His* Justice in the world. It was His Hand, not ours, which punished the Egyptians. Even so, the revelation of Divine Justice was only partial. The Pesach Redemption was only a beginning, a taste, of the Perfect Judgement. The history of the Jewish people, and the life of every Jew individually, is proof that our perception of justice is is as yet incomplete. And we are again in exile. But, in the end, God will show us that His Justice does reign in the world: He will slaughter the Angel of Death. He will bring the Mashiach. And then, only then, will we be capable of understanding the rightness of everything which has happened from the very beginning of time (*Likutey Halakhot, Rosh Chodesh* 6).

וְאָתָא מַיָא וְכָבָה לְנוּרָא דְּשָׂרַף לְחוּטְרָא דְּהִכָּה לְכַלְבָּא
דְּנָשַׁךְ לְשׁוּנְרָא. דְּאָכְלָה לְגַדְיָא. דְּזַבִּין אַבָּא בִּתְרֵי זוּזֵי.
חַד גַּדְיָא חַד גַּדְיָא:

וְאָתָא תוֹרָא וְשָׁתָה לְמַיָא דְּכָבָה לְנוּרָא דְּשָׂרַף לְחוּטְרָא
דְּהִכָּה לְכַלְבָּא דְּנָשַׁךְ לְשׁוּנְרָא. דְּאָכְלָה לְגַדְיָא. דְּזַבִּין אַבָּא
בִּתְרֵי זוּזֵי. חַד גַּדְיָא חַד גַּדְיָא:

וְאָתָא הַשׁוֹחֵט וְשָׁחַט לְתוֹרָא דְּשָׁתָה לְמַיָא דְּכָבָה לְנוּרָא
דְּשָׂרַף לְחוּטְרָא דְּהִכָּה לְכַלְבָּא דְּנָשַׁךְ לְשׁוּנְרָא. דְּאָכְלָה
לְגַדְיָא. דְּזַבִּין אַבָּא בִּתְרֵי זוּזֵי. חַד גַּדְיָא חַד גַּדְיָא:

וְאָתָא מַלְאַךְ הַמָּוֶת. וְשָׁחַט לְשׁוֹחֵט. דְּשָׁחַט לְתוֹרָא
דְּשָׁתָה לְמַיָא דְּכָבָה לְנוּרָא דְּשָׂרַף לְחוּטְרָא דְּהִכָּה לְכַלְבָּא
דְּנָשַׁךְ לְשׁוּנְרָא. דְּאָכְלָה לְגַדְיָא. דְּזַבִּין אַבָּא בִּתְרֵי זוּזֵי.
חַד גַּדְיָא חַד גַּדְיָא:

וְאָתָא הַקָּדוֹשׁ בָּרוּךְ הוּא וְשָׁחַט לְמַלְאַךְ הַמָּוֶת. דְּשָׁחַט
לְשׁוֹחֵט. דְּשָׁחַט לְתוֹרָא דְּשָׁתָה לְמַיָא דְּכָבָה לְנוּרָא דְּשָׂרַף
לְחוּטְרָא דְּהִכָּה לְכַלְבָּא דְּנָשַׁךְ לְשׁוּנְרָא. דְּאָכְלָה לְגַדְיָא.
דְּזַבִּין אַבָּא בִּתְרֵי זוּזֵי. חַד גַּדְיָא חַד גַּדְיָא:

the Angel of Death is described as Tehom, the abyss. Throughout his rule, Edom
has mercilessly murdered millions of Jews; beginning with the destruction of
the Second Temple, until this very day. Indeed, this last exile does seem to be
an abyss and an unending deep. Still, *Chad Gadya* teaches us that hope is eternal.
The time will come when God will slaughter the Angel of Esav, Edom, the
Angel of Death, as well as all those nations which rose up against us. Amen.
Selah! (*Nachat HaShulchan*).

Along came water and extinguished the fire, that burned the stick, that beat the dog, that bit the cat, that ate the kid, that father bought for two zuzim, one kid, one kid.

Along came an ox and drank the water, that extinguished the fire, that burned the stick, that beat the dog, that bit the cat, that ate the kid, that father bought for two zuzim, one kid, one kid.

Along came a slaughterer and slaughtered the ox, that drank the water, that extinguished the fire, that burned the stick, that beat the dog, that bit the cat, that ate the kid, that father bought for two zuzim, one kid, one kid.

Along came the Angel of Death and killed the slaughterer, who slaughtered the ox, that drank the water, that extinguished the fire, that burned the stick, that beat the dog, that bit the cat, that ate the kid, that father bought for two zuzim, one kid, one kid.

Then the Holy One, blessed is He, came and slew the Angel of Death, who killed the slaughterer, who slaughtered the ox, that drank the water, that extinguished the fire, that burned the stick, that beat the dog, that bit the cat, that ate the kid, that father bought for two zuzim, one kid, one kid.

remained with them due to the efforts of the Tzaddikim exiled to Babylon during Yekhonya's reign (*Gittin* 88a). Later, under Persian domination, it was one of these Tzaddikim, Mordekhai, who saved the Jews from Haman's evil designs (*Ibid.*). Eventually, the Scribe and great Torah Scholar, Ezra — a man whose greatness was likened to that of Moshe Rabeinu himself — brought the exiled Jews back to the Holy Land (*Sanhedrin* 21b).

But then the ox came and "drank up" the water. This alludes to Alexander the Great of Macedonia and the Greek exile. Of Alexander the Great it is said that "His voice roared like a bull" (*Sefer Yosifun*); as he subdued the Jewish kingdom. Under the Greeks, the Jews were prevented from studying Torah — from "drinking of the water." A decree of conversion was issued: "Write on the horns of an *ox* that you have no portion in the God of you fathers!" (*Bereshit Rabbah* 44:20). The slaughterer then came and slaughtered the ox. Our Sages teach that "A goring ox is fit only for the [slaughterer's] knife" (*Bava Kama* 55b). The Hashmonaim — the slaughterers — confronted the Greeks in battle and were victorious.

And then the Angel of Death came and slaughtered the slaughterer. This angel is Edom [Rome], the progenitor of our current and final exile. Quite appropriately,

ואחר כך יאמר שיר השירים במתון ובנעימה. חייב אדם לעסוק בהלכות פסח
וביציאת מצרים ולספר בנסים ונפלאות שעשה הקדוש ברוך הוא לאבותינו עד
שתחטפנו שינה.

collection of Holy Songs that are sung to praise and thank God for all the miracles
He performed for our benefit. And, this being the case, what greater song is there
than Shir HaShirim itself? It can endow us with all the powers of the ten different
types of song that derive from the four different letters of God's Name; enabling
us to be finely attuned to the Future Song that will be sung in Heaven by the
angels when the true redemption of the Jewish people finally comes (*Likutey Halakhot,
Apatrupus* 3; *Nachat HaShulchan*).

155

Many recite the Song of Songs after the Haggadah. One should then continue to occupy himself with the Story of the Exodus (selections of which appear on the following pages) until sleep overtakes him.

Song of Songs — With the conclusion of the Seder, many have a custom to recite the Shir HaShirim, Song of Songs. Much of the imagery of this "most holy of songs" is based upon the story of the Jewish bondage in Egypt, their Exodus, and the Revelation at Mount Sinai. There are also allusions to the great miracles which will occur with the arrival of Mashiach and the Final Redemption. In discussing this custom, Reb Noson takes particular notice of the power of song that is revealed on this night of Pesach. He sees the Haggadah itself as a

קידוש ליום טוב

לשבת:

וְשָׁמְרוּ בְנֵי יִשְׂרָאֵל אֶת הַשַּׁבָּת, לַעֲשׂוֹת אֶת הַשַּׁבָּת, לְדֹרֹתָם, בְּרִית עוֹלָם. בֵּינִי וּבֵין בְּנֵי יִשְׂרָאֵל, אוֹת הִיא לְעוֹלָם, כִּי שֵׁשֶׁת יָמִים עָשָׂה ה' אֶת הַשָּׁמַיִם וְאֶת הָאָרֶץ, וּבַיּוֹם הַשְּׁבִיעִי שָׁבַת וַיִּנָּפַשׁ:

זָכוֹר אֶת יוֹם הַשַּׁבָּת לְקַדְּשׁוֹ. שֵׁשֶׁת יָמִים תַּעֲבֹד וְעָשִׂיתָ כָּל מְלַאכְתֶּךָ. וְיוֹם הַשְּׁבִיעִי שַׁבָּת לַה' אֱלֹהֶיךָ, לֹא תַעֲשֶׂה כָל מְלָאכָה אַתָּה, וּבִנְךָ, וּבִתֶּךָ, עַבְדְּךָ, וַאֲמָתְךָ, וּבְהֶמְתֶּךָ, וְגֵרְךָ אֲשֶׁר בִּשְׁעָרֶיךָ. כִּי שֵׁשֶׁת יָמִים עָשָׂה ה' אֶת הַשָּׁמַיִם וְאֶת הָאָרֶץ, אֶת הַיָּם וְאֶת כָּל אֲשֶׁר בָּם, וַיָּנַח בַּיּוֹם הַשְּׁבִיעִי,

עַל כֵּן בֵּרַךְ ה' אֶת יוֹם הַשַּׁבָּת וַיְקַדְּשֵׁהוּ:

אֵלֶּה מוֹעֲדֵי ה' מִקְרָאֵי קֹדֶשׁ אֲשֶׁר תִּקְרְאוּ אֹתָם בְּמוֹעֲדָם:
וַיְדַבֵּר מֹשֶׁה אֶת מֹעֲדֵי ה' אֶל בְּנֵי יִשְׂרָאֵל:

סַבְרִי מָרָנָן וְרַבָּנָן וְרַבּוֹתַי:

בָּרוּךְ אַתָּה יְהֹוָה אֱלֹהֵינוּ מֶלֶךְ הָעוֹלָם בּוֹרֵא פְּרִי הַגָּפֶן:

YOM TOV MORNING KIDDUSH

On Shabbat (The Festival or the Intermediate Shabbat) first recite the following:

The Children of Israel shall keep the Shabbat, to observe the Shabbat throughout all their generations. It is a perpetual covenant between Myself and the Children of Israel; for in six days did I, God, create the heavens and the earth, and on the Seventh Day, I abstained and rested (Exodus 31:16-17).

Remember to sanctify the Shabbat day. Six days you may work and complete all your labor; but on the Seventh Day, it is Shabbat to the Lord your God, you shall not do any work: not you, not your son, your daughter, your servant, your maid, your livestock, nor the stranger in your midst; for in six days did God make the heavens and the earth, the seas and all that are in them, and on the Seventh Day He rested.

Therefore did God hallow the Seventh Day and sanctify it (Exodus 20:8-11).

On Yom Tov begin here:

These are the Festivals of God, holy gatherings, that you shall proclaim them in their seasons (Leviticus 23:4).

And Moshe proclaimed the Festivals of God to the Children of Israel (Leviticus 23:44).

Attention my masters:

Blessed are You, God, King of the universe, Who creates the fruit of the vine.

קידוש במקום סעודה — **SPARKING THE PHYSICAL**

The Jewish soul is very noble. It is eternal. A spark of the Divine. In everything a Jew does, it thirsts only for God.

The repository of that soul is earthly. It is transient. Distant from God. It has its needs; it craves for them to be met.

When we prepare for a meal, the poles of our existence, the conflicting natures which govern the different aspects of our being, come to the fore. In the process, we are confronted by the physical element of our humanness. Let us then make Kiddush; flaming the spark within us. Let us yearn for God. He is so close, even in the remoteness of our physicality (*Likutey Halakhot, Netilat Yadaim* 6:20).

סדר ספירת העומר

לְשֵׁם יִחוּד קוּדְשָׁא בְּרִיךְ הוּא וּשְׁכִינְתֵּיהּ, בִּדְחִילוּ וּרְחִימוּ לְיַחֵד שֵׁם י"ה ב־
ו"ה בְּיִחוּדָא שְׁלִים בְּשֵׁם כָּל יִשְׂרָאֵל. הִנְנִי מוּכָן וּמְזֻמָּן לְקַיֵּם מִצְוַת (עֲשֵׂה
שֶׁל) סְפִירַת הָעוֹמֶר כְּמוֹ שֶׁכָּתוּב בַּתּוֹרָה: "וּסְפַרְתֶּם לָכֶם מִמָּחֳרַת הַשַּׁבָּת
מִיּוֹם הֲבִיאֲכֶם אֶת עוֹמֶר הַתְּנוּפָה שֶׁבַע שַׁבָּתוֹת תְּמִימֹת תִּהְיֶינָה. עַד
מִמָּחֳרַת הַשַּׁבָּת הַשְּׁבִיעִית תִּסְפְּרוּ חֲמִשִּׁים יוֹם וְהִקְרַבְתֶּם מִנְחָה חֲדָשָׁה
לַה': וִיהִי נֹעַם יְיָ אֱלֹהֵינוּ עָלֵינוּ, וּמַעֲשֵׂה יָדֵינוּ כּוֹנְנָה עָלֵינוּ, וּמַעֲשֵׂה יָדֵינוּ
כּוֹנְנֵהוּ:

בָּרוּךְ אַתָּה יְהֹוָה אֱלֹהֵינוּ מֶלֶךְ הָעוֹלָם אֲשֶׁר קִדְּשָׁנוּ בְּמִצְוֹתָיו וְצִוָּנוּ עַל סְפִירַת הָעוֹמֶר:

הַיּוֹם יוֹם אֶחָד לָעוֹמֶר: חסד שבחסד

הַיּוֹם שְׁנֵי יָמִים לָעוֹמֶר: (2	גבורה שבחסד
הַיּוֹם שְׁלֹשָׁה יָמִים לָעוֹמֶר: (3	תפארת שבחסד
הַיּוֹם אַרְבָּעָה יָמִים לָעוֹמֶר: (4	נצח שבחסד
הַיּוֹם חֲמִשָּׁה יָמִים לָעוֹמֶר: (5	הוד שבחסד
הַיּוֹם שִׁשָּׁה יָמִים לָעוֹמֶר: (6	יסוד שבחסד
הַיּוֹם שִׁבְעָה יָמִים שֶׁהֵם שָׁבוּעַ אֶחָד לָעוֹמֶר: (7	מלכות שבחסד
הַיּוֹם שְׁמוֹנָה יָמִים שֶׁהֵם שָׁבוּעַ אֶחָד וְיוֹם אֶחָד לָעוֹמֶר: (8	חסד שבגבורה
הַיּוֹם תִּשְׁעָה יָמִים שֶׁהֵם שָׁבוּעַ אֶחָד וּשְׁנֵי יָמִים לָעוֹמֶר: (9	גבורה שבגבורה
הַיּוֹם עֲשָׂרָה יָמִים שֶׁהֵם שָׁבוּעַ אֶחָד וּשְׁלֹשָׁה יָמִים לָעוֹמֶר: (10	תפארת שבגבורה
הַיּוֹם אַחַד עָשָׂר יוֹם שֶׁהֵם שָׁבוּעַ אֶחָד וְאַרְבָּעָה יָמִים לָעוֹמֶר: (11	נצח שבגבורה
הַיּוֹם שְׁנֵים עָשָׂר יוֹם שֶׁהֵם שָׁבוּעַ אֶחָד וַחֲמִשָּׁה יָמִים לָעוֹמֶר: (12	הוד שבגבורה
הַיּוֹם שְׁלֹשָׁה עָשָׂר יוֹם שֶׁהֵם שָׁבוּעַ אֶחָד וְשִׁשָּׁה יָמִים לָעוֹמֶר: (13	יסוד שבגבורה
הַיּוֹם אַרְבָּעָה עָשָׂר יוֹם שֶׁהֵם שְׁנֵי שָׁבוּעוֹת לָעוֹמֶר: (14	מלכות שבגבורה
הַיּוֹם חֲמִשָּׁה עָשָׂר יוֹם שֶׁהֵם שְׁנֵי שָׁבוּעוֹת וְיוֹם אֶחָד לָעוֹמֶר: (15	חסד שבתפארת
הַיּוֹם שִׁשָּׁה עָשָׂר יוֹם שֶׁהֵם שְׁנֵי שָׁבוּעוֹת וּשְׁנֵי יָמִים לָעוֹמֶר: (16	גבורה שבתפארת
הַיּוֹם שִׁבְעָה עָשָׂר יוֹם שֶׁהֵם שְׁנֵי שָׁבוּעוֹת וּשְׁלֹשָׁה יָמִים לָעוֹמֶר: (17	תפארת שבתפארת
הַיּוֹם שְׁמוֹנָה עָשָׂר יוֹם שֶׁהֵם שְׁנֵי שָׁבוּעוֹת וְאַרְבָּעָה יָמִים לָעוֹמֶר: (18	נצח שבתפארת
הַיּוֹם תִּשְׁעָה עָשָׂר יוֹם שֶׁהֵם שְׁנֵי שָׁבוּעוֹת וַחֲמִשָּׁה יָמִים לָעוֹמֶר: (19	הוד שבתפארת
הַיּוֹם עֶשְׂרִים יוֹם שֶׁהֵם שְׁנֵי שָׁבוּעוֹת וְשִׁשָּׁה יָמִים לָעוֹמֶר: (20	יסוד שבתפארת

SEFIRAT HA'OMER

Prior to Counting the Omer the following is said:

I am ready and prepared to perform the mitzvah of Counting the Omer, as it is written in the Torah: 'You shall count for yourselves from the day after the [festival] rest, from the day you bring [before Me] the Omer Sacrifice, seven full weeks shall they be. Until the day after these seven full weeks [Shavuot] shall you count fifty days, and then shall you bring a New Offering to Me' (Leviticus 23:15-16). 'May God's pleasantness rest upon us and may the work of our hands be blessed; please God may our efforts prosper' (Psalms 90:17).

Blessed are You, God, King of the universe, Who has made us holy with His mitzvot, and commanded us to Count the Omer.

1) Today is one day of the Omer.

On each night substitute the correct number, then continue below.

2) Today is two days of the Omer.
3) Today is three days of the Omer.
4) Today is four days of the Omer.
5) Today is five days of the Omer.
6) Today is six days of the Omer.
7) Today is seven days, which are one week of the Omer.
8) Today is eight days, which are one week and one day of the Omer.
9) Today is nine days, which are one week and two days of the Omer.
10) Today is ten days, which are one week and three days of the Omer.
11) Today is eleven days, which are one week and four days of the Omer.
12) Today is twelve days, which are one week and five days of the Omer.
13) Today is thirteen days, which are one week and six days of the Omer.
14) Today is fourteen days, which are two weeks of the Omer.
15) Today is fifteen days, which are two weeks and one day of the Omer.
16) Today is sixteen days, which are two weeks and two days of the Omer.
17) Today is seventeen days, which are two weeks and three days of the Omer.
18) Today is eighteen days, which are two weeks and four days of the Omer.
19) Today is nineteen days, which are two weeks and five days of the Omer.
20) Today is twenty days, which are two weeks and six days of the Omer.

מלכות שבתפארת

(21) הַיּוֹם אֶחָד וְעֶשְׂרִים יוֹם שֶׁהֵם שְׁלֹשָׁה שָׁבוּעוֹת לָעוֹמֶר:

חסד שבנצח

(22) הַיּוֹם שְׁנַיִם וְעֶשְׂרִים יוֹם שֶׁהֵם שְׁלֹשָׁה שָׁבוּעוֹת וְיוֹם אֶחָד לָעוֹמֶר:

גבורה שבנצח

(23) הַיּוֹם שְׁלֹשָׁה וְעֶשְׂרִים יוֹם שֶׁהֵם שְׁלֹשָׁה שָׁבוּעוֹת וּשְׁנֵי יָמִים לָעוֹמֶר:

תפארת שבנצח

(24) הַיּוֹם אַרְבָּעָה וְעֶשְׂרִים יוֹם שֶׁהֵם שְׁלֹשָׁה שָׁבוּעוֹת וּשְׁלֹשָׁה יָמִים לָעוֹמֶר:

נצח שבנצח

(25) הַיּוֹם חֲמִשָּׁה וְעֶשְׂרִים יוֹם שֶׁהֵם שְׁלֹשָׁה שָׁבוּעוֹת וְאַרְבָּעָה יָמִים לָעוֹמֶר:

הוד שבנצח

(26) הַיּוֹם שִׁשָּׁה וְעֶשְׂרִים יוֹם שֶׁהֵם שְׁלֹשָׁה שָׁבוּעוֹת וַחֲמִשָּׁה יָמִים לָעוֹמֶר:

יסוד שבנצח

(27) הַיּוֹם שִׁבְעָה וְעֶשְׂרִים יוֹם שֶׁהֵם שְׁלֹשָׁה שָׁבוּעוֹת וְשִׁשָּׁה יָמִים לָעוֹמֶר:

מלכות שבנצח

(28) הַיּוֹם שְׁמוֹנָה וְעֶשְׂרִים יוֹם שֶׁהֵם אַרְבָּעָה שָׁבוּעוֹת לָעוֹמֶר:

חסד שבהוד

(29) הַיּוֹם תִּשְׁעָה וְעֶשְׂרִים יוֹם שֶׁהֵם אַרְבָּעָה שָׁבוּעוֹת וְיוֹם אֶחָד לָעוֹמֶר:

גבורה שבהוד

(30) הַיּוֹם שְׁלֹשִׁים יוֹם שֶׁהֵם אַרְבָּעָה שָׁבוּעוֹת וּשְׁנֵי יָמִים לָעוֹמֶר:

תפארת שבהוד

(31) הַיּוֹם אֶחָד וּשְׁלֹשִׁים יוֹם שֶׁהֵם אַרְבָּעָה שָׁבוּעוֹת וּשְׁלֹשָׁה יָמִים לָעוֹמֶר:

נצח שבהוד

(32) הַיּוֹם שְׁנַיִם וּשְׁלֹשִׁים יוֹם שֶׁהֵם אַרְבָּעָה שָׁבוּעוֹת וְאַרְבָּעָה יָמִים לָעוֹמֶר:

הוד שבהוד

(33) הַיּוֹם שְׁלֹשָׁה וּשְׁלֹשִׁים יוֹם שֶׁהֵם אַרְבָּעָה שָׁבוּעוֹת וַחֲמִשָּׁה יָמִים לָעוֹמֶר:

יסוד שבהוד

(34) הַיּוֹם אַרְבָּעָה וּשְׁלֹשִׁים יוֹם שֶׁהֵם אַרְבָּעָה שָׁבוּעוֹת וְשִׁשָּׁה יָמִים לָעוֹמֶר:

מלכות שבהוד

(35) הַיּוֹם חֲמִשָּׁה וּשְׁלֹשִׁים יוֹם שֶׁהֵם חֲמִשָּׁה שָׁבוּעוֹת לָעוֹמֶר:

חסד שביסוד

(36) הַיּוֹם שִׁשָּׁה וּשְׁלֹשִׁים יוֹם שֶׁהֵם חֲמִשָּׁה שָׁבוּעוֹת וְיוֹם אֶחָד לָעוֹמֶר:

גבורה שביסוד

(37) הַיּוֹם שִׁבְעָה וּשְׁלֹשִׁים יוֹם שֶׁהֵם חֲמִשָּׁה שָׁבוּעוֹת וּשְׁנֵי יָמִים לָעוֹמֶר:

תפארת שביסוד

(38) הַיּוֹם שְׁמוֹנָה וּשְׁלֹשִׁים יוֹם שֶׁהֵם חֲמִשָּׁה שָׁבוּעוֹת וּשְׁלֹשָׁה יָמִים לָעוֹמֶר:

נצח שביסוד

(39) הַיּוֹם תִּשְׁעָה וּשְׁלֹשִׁים יוֹם שֶׁהֵם חֲמִשָּׁה שָׁבוּעוֹת וְאַרְבָּעָה יָמִים לָעוֹמֶר:

הוד שביסוד

(40) הַיּוֹם אַרְבָּעִים יוֹם שֶׁהֵם חֲמִשָּׁה שָׁבוּעוֹת וַחֲמִשָּׁה יָמִים לָעוֹמֶר:

יסוד שביסוד

(41) הַיּוֹם אֶחָד וְאַרְבָּעִים יוֹם שֶׁהֵם חֲמִשָּׁה שָׁבוּעוֹת וְשִׁשָּׁה יָמִים לָעוֹמֶר:

מלכות שביסוד

(42) הַיּוֹם שְׁנַיִם וְאַרְבָּעִים יוֹם שֶׁהֵם שִׁשָּׁה שָׁבוּעוֹת לָעוֹמֶר:

חסד שבמלכות

(43) הַיּוֹם שְׁלֹשָׁה וְאַרְבָּעִים יוֹם שֶׁהֵם שִׁשָּׁה שָׁבוּעוֹת וְיוֹם אֶחָד לָעוֹמֶר:

גבורה שבמלכות

(44) הַיּוֹם אַרְבָּעָה וְאַרְבָּעִים יוֹם שֶׁהֵם שִׁשָּׁה שָׁבוּעוֹת וּשְׁנֵי יָמִים לָעוֹמֶר:

תפארת שבמלכות

(45) הַיּוֹם חֲמִשָּׁה וְאַרְבָּעִים יוֹם שֶׁהֵם שִׁשָּׁה שָׁבוּעוֹת וּשְׁלֹשָׁה יָמִים לָעוֹמֶר:

נצח שבמלכות

(46) הַיּוֹם שִׁשָּׁה וְאַרְבָּעִים יוֹם שֶׁהֵם שִׁשָּׁה שָׁבוּעוֹת וְאַרְבָּעָה יָמִים לָעוֹמֶר:

הוד שבמלכות

(47) הַיּוֹם שִׁבְעָה וְאַרְבָּעִים יוֹם שֶׁהֵם שִׁשָּׁה שָׁבוּעוֹת וַחֲמִשָּׁה יָמִים לָעוֹמֶר:

יסוד שבמלכות

(48) הַיּוֹם שְׁמוֹנָה וְאַרְבָּעִים יוֹם שֶׁהֵם שִׁשָּׁה שָׁבוּעוֹת וְשִׁשָּׁה יָמִים לָעוֹמֶר:

מלכות שבמלכות

(49) הַיּוֹם תִּשְׁעָה וְאַרְבָּעִים יוֹם שֶׁהֵם שִׁבְעָה שָׁבוּעוֹת שָׁבוּעוֹת לָעוֹמֶר:

הָרַחֲמָן הוּא יַחֲזִיר לָנוּ עֲבוֹדַת בֵּית הַמִּקְדָּשׁ לִמְקוֹמָהּ בִּמְהֵרָה בְיָמֵינוּ אָמֵן סֶלָה:

לַמְנַצֵּחַ בִּנְגִינוֹת מִזְמוֹר שִׁיר: אֱלֹהִים יְחָנֵּנוּ וִיבָרְכֵנוּ, יָאֵר פָּנָיו אִתָּנוּ סֶלָה: לָדַעַת בָּאָרֶץ דַּרְכֶּךָ, בְּכָל גּוֹיִם יְשׁוּעָתֶךָ: יוֹדוּךָ עַמִּים אֱלֹהִים, יוֹדוּךָ עַמִּים כֻּלָּם: יִשְׂמְחוּ וִירַנְּנוּ לְאֻמִּים, כִּי תִשְׁפֹּט עַמִּים מִישׁוֹר, וּלְאֻמִּים בָּאָרֶץ תַּנְחֵם סֶלָה: יוֹדוּךָ עַמִּים אֱלֹהִים, יוֹדוּךָ עַמִּים כֻּלָּם: אֶרֶץ נָתְנָה יְבוּלָהּ, יְבָרְכֵנוּ אֱלֹהִים אֱלֹהֵינוּ: יְבָרְכֵנוּ אֱלֹהִים, וְיִירְאוּ אוֹתוֹ כָּל אַפְסֵי אָרֶץ:

161

21) Today is twenty-one days, which are three weeks of the Omer.

22) Today is twenty-two days, which are three weeks and one day of the Omer.

23) Today is twenty-three days, which are three weeks and two days of the Omer.

24) Today is twenty-four days, which are three weeks and three days of the Omer.

25) Today is twenty-five days, which are three weeks and four days of the Omer.

26) Today is twenty-six days, which are three weeks and five days of the Omer.

27) Today is twenty-seven days, which are three weeks and six days of the Omer.

28) Today is twenty-eight days, which are four weeks of the Omer.

29) Today is twenty-nine days, which are four weeks and one day of the Omer.

30) Today is thirty days, which are four weeks and two days of the Omer.

31) Today is thirty-one days, which are four weeks and three days of the Omer.

32) Today is thirty-two days, which are four weeks and four days of the Omer.

33) Today is thirty-three days, which are four weeks and five days of the Omer.

34) Today is thirty-four days, which are four weeks and six days of the Omer.

35) Today is thirty-five days, which are five weeks of the Omer.

36) Today is thirty-six days, which are five weeks and one day of the Omer.

37) Today is thirty-seven days, which are five weeks and two days of the Omer.

38) Today is thirty-eight days, which are five weeks and three days of the Omer.

39) Today is thirty-nine days, which are five weeks and four days of the Omer.

40) Today is forty days, which are five weeks and five days of the Omer.

41) Today is forty-one days, which are five weeks and six days of the Omer.

42) Today is forty-two days, which are six weeks of the Omer.

43) Today is forty-three days, which are six weeks and one day of the Omer.

44) Today is forty-four days, which are six weeks and two days of the Omer.

45) Today is forty-five days, which are six weeks and three days of the Omer.

46) Today is forty-six days, which are six weeks and four days of the Omer.

47) Today is forty-seven days, which are six weeks and five days of the Omer.

48) Today is forty-eight days, which are six weeks and six days of the Omer.

49) Today is forty-nine days, which are seven weeks of the Omer.

Continue here:

May the All Merciful return to us the service in the Holy Temple, speedily in our days, Amen. Selah!

To the musician, a psalm with song. God! grace us and bless us, shine Your Countenance upon us, Selah. To make known on the earth Your ways; amongst all the nations Your salvation. The nations will praise You, God; all the nations will thank You. Let the nations be happy and sing joyously, for You will judge all peoples with equity; and govern them upon the earth. The nations will praise You, God; all the nations will thank You. The earth has given forth its fruits; bless us God, our God! God will bless us; and all those that are distant [from Him] shall fear Him (Psalms 67).

אָנָּא בְּכֹחַ גְּדֻלַּת יְמִינְךָ תַּתִּיר צְרוּרָה: אב"ג ית"ץ

קַבֵּל רִנַּת עַמְּךָ שַׂגְּבֵנוּ טַהֲרֵנוּ נוֹרָא: קר"ע שט"ן

נָא גִבּוֹר דּוֹרְשֵׁי יִחוּדְךָ כְּבָבַת שָׁמְרֵם: נג"ד יכ"ש

בָּרְכֵם טַהֲרֵם רַחֲמֵם צִדְקָתְךָ תָּמִיד גָּמְלֵם: בט"ר צת"ג

חֲסִין קָדוֹשׁ בְּרוֹב טוּבְךָ נַהֵל עֲדָתֶךָ:   חק"ב טנ"ע

יָחִיד גֵּאֶה לְעַמְּךָ פְּנֵה זוֹכְרֵי קְדֻשָּׁתֶךָ:   יג"ל פז"ק

שַׁוְעָתֵנוּ קַבֵּל וּשְׁמַע צַעֲקָתֵנוּ יוֹדֵעַ תַּעֲלוּמוֹת: שק"ו צי"ת

בָּרוּךְ שֵׁם כְּבוֹד מַלְכוּתוֹ לְעוֹלָם וָעֶד:

רִבּוֹנוֹ שֶׁל עוֹלָם. אַתָּה צִוִּיתָנוּ עַל יְדֵי מֹשֶׁה עַבְדֶּךָ לִסְפּוֹר סְפִירַת הָעוֹמֶר כְּדֵי לְטַהֲרֵנוּ מִקְּלִפּוֹתֵינוּ וּמִטֻּמְאוֹתֵינוּ כְּמוֹ שֶׁכָּתַבְתָּ בְּתוֹרָתֶךָ: "וּסְפַרְתֶּם לָכֶם מִמָּחֳרַת הַשַּׁבָּת מִיּוֹם הֲבִיאֲכֶם אֶת עוֹמֶר הַתְּנוּפָה שֶׁבַע שַׁבָּתוֹת תְּמִימֹת תִּהְיֶינָה: עַד מִמָּחֳרַת הַשַּׁבָּת הַשְּׁבִיעִית תִּסְפְּרוּ חֲמִשִּׁים יוֹם", כְּדֵי שֶׁיִּטַּהֲרוּ נַפְשׁוֹת עַמְּךָ יִשְׂרָאֵל מִזֻּהֲמָתָם. וּבְכֵן, יְהִי רָצוֹן מִלְּפָנֶיךָ ה' אֱלֹהֵינוּ וֵאלֹהֵי אֲבוֹתֵינוּ, שֶׁבִּזְכוּת סְפִירַת הָעוֹמֶר שֶׁסָּפַרְתִּי הַיּוֹם, יְתֻקַּן מַה שֶּׁפָּגַמְתִּי בִּסְפִירָה (פלונית השייך לאותו הלילה), וְאֶטָּהֵר וְאֶתְקַדֵּשׁ בִּקְדֻשָּׁה שֶׁל מַעְלָה. וְעַל יְדֵי זֶה יֻשְׁפַּע שֶׁפַע רַב בְּכָל הָעוֹלָמוֹת וּלְתַקֵּן אֶת נַפְשׁוֹתֵינוּ וְרוּחוֹתֵינוּ וְנִשְׁמוֹתֵינוּ מִכָּל סִיג וּפְגָם, וּלְטַהֲרֵנוּ וּלְקַדְּשֵׁנוּ בִּקְדֻשָּׁתְךָ הָעֶלְיוֹנָה, אָמֵן סֶלָה:

Please, with the mighty strength of Your Right Hand, unbind the restrained.
Accept the prayers of Your People, elevate and purify us, Awesome One.
Please, Mighty One, those who seek Your Oneness, watch them as the pupil of the eye.
Bless them, purify them, pity them, always grant them Your righteousness.
Strong and Holy One, with Your great goodness, lead Your flock.
[The] One Who is exalted, turn to Your nation, those who remember Your holiness.
Accept our supplications; hearken to our cries; [He] Who knows the hidden.
Blessed is the Glorious Name of His Kingdom, forever and ever.

Master of the universe! through Moshe Your servant You commanded us to Count the Omer, in order to purify us from our *kelipot* and our impurities; as You wrote in Your Torah: 'You shall count for yourselves from the day after the [festival] rest, from the day you bring [before Me] the Omer Sacrifice, seven full weeks shall they be. Until the day after these seven full weeks [Shavuot] shall you count fifty days,' so that the souls of Your Nation, the Jews, shall be purified from their defilement. Therefore, let it be Your will, God, our Lord, and God of our fathers, that in the merit of the Counting of the Omer that I counted today, Rectification should be attained in the Sefirah that applies to this day. I should [be worthy to] become pure and holy with holiness from Above. Through this, let there be great abundance in all the Worlds, and let there be Rectifications for our souls — the *nefesh, ruach* and *neshamah* — from all impurities and blemishes: to purify and sanctify us, in Your exalted Holiness, Amen. Selah!

REFLECTIONS

A person is required to recall any miracle that may have happened to him and his family. This should be commemorated with a festive meal and with the giving of charity (Chayey Adam, Hilkhot Megillah *41*).

Rabbi Avraham Danzig, author of the *Chayey Adam* and other Halakhic works, writes: My family celebrates the miracle that occurred to us on the 16th of Kislev, 5564 (December 1,1803), when there was an explosion in the courtyard where we lived. Our house, which caved in on us, was totally demolished. My wife, my children and I all suffered serious injury. The almost total destruction of our neighborhood was so great that thirty-one people were killed. We commemorate the loss of the dead; and celebrate our miraculous salvation (*Ibid.*).

Some people have the custom of commemorating a personal salvation at a specific time of the year, rejoicing in God and thanking Him for helping them rebuild their lives after a devastating tragedy. Others reminisce their good fortunes and salvations on Pesach Eve, when the family is gathered to rejoice in the Exodus from Egypt and from all exiles.

These pages have been set aside for you to record your own personal joyous moments, special occasions and anniversaries, as well as personal triumphs over hardship and tragedy. May God bless us all with the ability to turn these empty pages into a "HAGGADAH," filled with multiple entries of joy and happiness; holidays and festivals; true *nachat* and *simchot*; and our own reporting of the Coming of Mashiach and the Redemption of all Israel, speedily in our time, Amen!

* * *

days, so too, Teshuvah, repentance, comes after the hard work needed to purify oneself. Thus, for us to be able to complete our Teshuvah, we must do Teshuvah upon Teshuvah. Between Pesach and Shavuot we are given seven weeks. Six weeks correspond to the six workdays and the seventh to complete Teshuvah. Only then can we truly attain Torah (*Likutey Halakhot, Sefirah* 1).

*

The Egyptian exile was brought about by Adam's sin. By eating from the Tree of Knowledge, he confused his knowledge. This caused everything to descend into this world in a confused, unclear form. Our Sages taught that Matzah corresponds to the Manna. When the Jews left Egypt, the Matzah they took along tasted to them like Manna (*Kiddushin* 38a). One of the miracles of the Manna was that it was absorbed in the body, producing no waste at all. This teaches us that the Matzah we eat is a "pure" food, free of any "additives" that might confuse one's knowledge. Similarly, the *Zohar* (II, 183b) teaches that Matzah is known as a healing food, one that brings a person to clear faith and knowledge.

After the Splitting of the Red Sea, on the last day of Pesach, the Jews were given permission to eat Chametz. They were allowed to do this even though Chametz is filled with "additives" that can confuse one's knowledge. But now, the Children of Israel had attained complete faith in their Tzaddikim, their Sages. It is written, "The Jews believed in God and His servant Moshe" (Exodus 14:31). The *Mekhilta* teaches that "whoever believes in God it is as if he believes in the Faithful Shepherd (Moshe). And, whoever believes in the Faithful Shepherd it is as if he believes in God." Complete faith in our Sages is comparable to complete faith in God. By recognizing and accepting the Tzaddikim, the righteous men whose knowledge of God is clear, we can rectify everything. However, time is needed. We need the full seven weeks for purifying ourselves and coming to the level which can finally be attained on Shavuot.

Shavuot itself is synonymous with the great knowledge and understanding that is achieved through Torah. By receiving the Torah and studying it, we know how to act and how to conduct ourselves in our daily lives. A person must see every day as a chance for him to renew his belief in God, the Torah and in the Tzaddikim. This will enable him to properly serve God. For "Torah was given only to those who ate Manna" (*Mekhilta* 17). By eating Manna, pure food — purifying our minds and accepting the guidance of our Tzaddikim — we can attain true knowledge and understanding of God. This is the great value of the holiday of Shavuot (*Likutey Halakhot, Pikadon* 5).

*

Revelation of Torah primarily comes through the Mitzvah of charity. It is written, "You shall celebrate the holiday of Shavuot... a free offering of your hand that you will give..." (Deuteronomy 16:10). The verse teaches that in proportion to our *giving,* so will we *feel* the holiday. Thus, to truly feel and celebrate Shavuot we must give as much charity as we can (*Likutey Halakhot, Kiddushin* 3).

* * *

Rebbe Nachman was accustomed to remaining awake both days and nights of Shavuot. In 5567 (1807), the year his wife passed away, the Rebbe spent the holiday away from home, in Zaslov. With him were Reb Noson and Reb Naftali, the Rebbe's major disciples, who also stayed up both nights. On the night following Shavuot the three of them were together in the Rebbe's room. When Rebbe Nachman left for a moment, the two chassidim fell down exhausted. It was the first time in two days that they had a chance to rest. Suddenly, the Rebbe walked in and, seeing them laying there, said, "Why are you sleeping away your years?!" Reb Noson and Reb Naftali immediately got up as if they hadn't been tired at all (Siach Sarfei Kodesh, 1-171).

*

A person must purify himself at the onset of each festival (Rosh HaShanah 16b). The Talmud tells us that the reason for this is so that when one comes to Jerusalem he can enter the Holy Temple. The Shulchan Arukh implies that this need for purification applies even today when we are without the Temple (Chayey Adam 79:1; Tosefot Chaim, Ibid.). In a sense, this purification is particularly applicable to the festival of Shavuot, the Giving of the Torah. The Jews journeying in the wilderness were only able to receive the Torah after they immersed in water (Kritut 10a). We, too, should see to immerse ourselves in a Mikvah before Shavuot, and thus purify ourselves to receive the Torah.

After remaining awake throughout the night, it is customary to immerse in a Mikvah just before dawn. This Mikvah, this purity, is drawn from the highest Source, from the very beginning of Creation. Actually, at Creation, the Lower Waters were one with the Upper Waters. Soon afterwards they were separated. Yet, even now, the Lower Waters of the Mikvah on Shavuot night draw from those Upper Waters, which are symbolic of great kindness and mercy. Shavuot itself, also corresponds to this great kindness. When God revealed Himself to the Jews at Mount Sinai, He appeared to them as elderly and sagacious, filled with compassion and lovingkindness (Mekhilta 20). Thus, the Giving of the Torah itself represents kindness and compassion. A person should therefore make every effort to immerse in the Mikvah on Shavuot morning (Likutey Moharan I, 56).

*

Rebbe Nachman taught that even when we repent, which of us can say that he has become so pure that his repentance was complete? Because we can't, we have to repent again and again. And each time we do so, we realize that our previous conception of God's Greatness was inferior and of little worth when compared to what we now know. This is Teshuvah, a returning to God; and Teshuvah upon Teshuvah (Likutey Moharan I, 6).

There are Sheva Shabbatot, seven weeks, from Pesach to Shavuot (Leviticus 23:15). SHaBbaTot corresponds to TeSHuVah. Just as Shabbat comes after six work

light, but they were unable to maintain it. Why? because there was no love and harmony between them. They lacked the bonds which would have given them the "strength" to absorb the Torah's great light and have it be a blessing. As a result, they died. And their deaths took place precisely during the Sefirah period, when we should be trying to rectify ourselves so as to receive the Torah.

Rabbi Shimon bar Yochai and his group of disciples were very different than Rabbi Akiva's students. Their relationship was a rectification. And through the "strength" which their bonds of love created, Rabbi Shimon was able to bring down a great light. This was the revelation of the *Zohar,* the basic source of the Kabbalah as it is known to us today. Not only were his students able to receive the brilliant light of their teachers Torah insights without it harming them, but Rabbi Shimon's revelations of God's Greatness were such incredible rectifications that, even today, no matter where a person has fallen spiritually, he can always come back to God. This is why Eliyahu the Prophet told Rabbi Shimon that his teachings — the *Zohar* — will lead the Jews out of exile (*Likutey Halakhot, Minchah* 7).

* * *

SIVAN AND SHAVUOT

The Children of Israel arrived at Mount Sinai on Rosh Chodesh Sivan. They camped at the foot of the hill as one: united in their common purpose and goal. From this we see that if *we* are to receive the Torah, there must be unity. Now, there are many levels to this unity. On an personal level, we should not be divided in heart or mind in our decision to serve God. To receive the Torah, we need to accept full belief in God and strive to attain this true unity within ourselves. On another level, to receive the Torah we must have unity with and within our families. Each of us should be in harmony with his or her spouse and children, so that the family operates as a unit and not as individuals. This doesn't imply negating individuality, but each of us should see that uniqueness within the broader scope of a working whole. A person should also strive for peace and harmony with his neighbors and friends. By doing so, he will be able to receive the Torah (*Likutey Halakhot, Sefirah* 1).

*

It is customary to remain awake the entire night of Shavuot, to recite the Tikkun Leyl Shavuot and study Torah. The reason for this is that on the night before they were given the Torah at Mount Sinai, the Children of Israel went to sleep. Moshe had to awaken them and hurry them to the foot of the mountain. Today, we remain awake to rectify that sleep. It symbolizes the need for us to not sleep away our days and nights. We must rectify time by making use of every moment. For *our* receiving of the Torah is in direct proportion to the effort we expend in obtaining it.

This is the explanation of the verse, "The Tzaddik is lost... because of the evil that approaches...." The Tzaddik's entire being is devoted to destroying and combating evil. However, his ability to do this is limited by his physical body. Therefore, God removes this Tzaddik from the world prior to the evil's coming. This is so that the Tzaddik's body will no longer restrict his efforts to help the Jews. In heaven, he is free to mitigate the harsh decree. And this is the true reason for the great celebration on Lag B'Omer. On the 33rd Day of the Omer many, many years ago, Rabbi Shimon bar Yochai's powers to bring help and salvation to all of Israel increased manifold (*Likutey Halakhot, Hekhsher Keilim* 4).

*

On the 33rd day of the Omer Counting we celebrate the holiday called LaG B'Omer. The Talmud relates that Rabbi Akiva had 24,000 students, all of whom were very great rabbis. Rabbi Akiva himself was one of the greatest rabbis in the Talmud. Yet, during this period of just 33 days, all these 24,000 students died because they did not act respectfully to one another. When they died, the world was left desolate until Rabbi Akiva came and taught Torah to five new students: Rabbi Meir, Rabbi Shimon bar Yochai, Rabbi Yosi, Rabbi Nechemya and Rabbi Yehudah. These great Tzaddikim were later responsible for restoring the entire Torah. They are the rabbis of the Mishnah (*Yebamot* 63a).

Reb Noson explains that during the Days of the Omer, we work to purify ourselves in order to receive the Torah. The Torah was originally received because the Jews came to Mount Sinai as one unit, with one heart (*Rashi,* Exodus 18:1). The students of Rabbi Akiva did not have this fellowship and unity, and they died during this Sefirah period. They were followed Rabbi Shimon bar Yochai and his disciples, a very closely knit group. The great love and unity displayed between Rabbi Shimon bar Yochai and his students, for which we find references throughout the *Zohar,* brought rectification to the 24,000.

The greatness of Lag B'Omer is that it represents the conclusion of the period of mourning. Through the spiritual strength and power of Rabbi Shimon bar Yochai, and through the unity and peace between all Jews, it is possible to rectify even the greatest losses and tragedies that befall the Jewish People (*Likutey Halakhot, Rosh Chodesh* 6).

*

Original Torah insights provide great spiritual light for the world. But this light, which emanates from the Ein Sof (the Infinite One), can only be drawn down and brought into this world through contraction and limitation. Otherwise, it is far too overwhelming for man to appreciate. He just doesn't have the spiritual "strength." One way to get that "strength" is by joining together with other Jews. This in itself is a form of self-contraction for the sake of the larger group. Through this we can understand why the 24,000 students of Rabbi Akiva died. Each of these students was very outstanding in his own right, and received many Torah insights from his most illustrious teacher. These Torah insights brought them great spiritual

Rabbi Shimon said, "I have the power to correct the entire world; I can exempt the whole world from Judgment" (*Sukkah* 45b).

Rabbi Shimon was leaving the cave where he and his son Rabbi Elazar had been in hiding from the Romans for thirteen years. They were talking about the righteousness which exists in the world when Rabbi Shimon said, "It is enough that you and I are in the world." Another time he said, "I myself have sufficient merit for the entire world" (*Shabbat* 33b; *Sukkah* 45b).

Rabbi Shimon bar Yochai was the Foundation of the world, the True Tzaddik.

These teachings only reveal a small degree of Rabbi Shimon's greatness and give only a partial glimpse the true benefit he brought to the world. This being the case, Reb Noson asks the following question: On the 33rd day of the Omer Counting we *celebrate* the passing of the True Tzaddik, Rabbi Shimon bar Yochai. This in itself is a great wonder, an obvious contradiction. How can we celebrate and enjoy Lag B'Omer, when it is recalls the day when such great good and benefit was taken from the world? What kind of celebration is this? On the contrary, we should rend our garments, as for the destruction of the Temple; as our Sages taught, "The passing of a Tzaddik is more severe than the Temple's destruction!"

To answer this, Reb Noson quotes the verse, "The Tzaddik is lost; yet nobody bothers to note what has happened. People of kindness are taken away; yet no one understands. It is because of the evil that approaches, that the Tzaddik is lost" (Isaiah 57:1). Our Sages teach that the very great Tzaddikim pass away prior to the onset of terrible evil in the world. For them, this is a blessing; so that they should not have to witness the great suffering which Heaven has decreed, so that their eyes should not have to see all the multitude of troubles that is about to befall the Jewish People (*Sanhedrin* 113b).

Reb Noson then goes on to explain that the powers of the "Tzaddikim are greater after their passing than when they were alive" (*Berakhot* 18a). If we examine the Tzaddik's main purpose in life, we see that all his efforts are devoted to rectify the Jews and bring about goodness, both physical and spiritual. Through the Tzaddik comes an abundance of wealth and livelihood, an abundance of Torah and repentance. However, as long as the Tzaddik's soul is housed in a body, he is restricted. This is because the body, by definition, is a physical limitation. The Tzaddik is therefore prevented from rising to the greatest heights, and even the abundance which he does bring is governed by this restriction. His influence can only go so far, until such time that his souls is divested of its bodily enclosure.

And this is why there is cause for celebration on LaG B'Omer. True, it is the day that Rabbi Shimon bar Yochai passed away from this world. But, Rabbi Shimon is in heaven; Rabbi Shimon is spiritual. If, during his lifetime he had sufficient merit to keep the world in existence, how much more so now that he is no longer restricted by the physical? His powers can presently reach such incomprehensible heights and levels that the abundance and benefit he can now bring to the world far surpasses whatever had been possible when he was alive.

call all Jews Tzaddikim. By elevating the Jewish People, they are able to guarantee them a portion in the World to Come (*Likutey Halakhot, Nezikin* 4).

* * *

PESACH SHEYNEE — THE SECOND PESACH

God told the Jews to prepare for the Pesach festival. There were Jews who were impure and were not ready in time. They came to Moshe and asked, 'How can we still partake of the Pesach, when it was too late for us to purify ourselves?' Moshe asked God and He replied, 'They can have a second chance. Let them celebrate the holiday of Pesach Sheynee, one month later, on the fourteenth day of the month of Iyar' (Numbers 9).

"How great these impure people must have been! They were able to initiate the revelation of a new law of Torah" (*Rashi, ad. loc.*).

Reb Noson explains that this came about specifically because of their great desire to partake of the Mitzvah. These people were impure. It was their own negligence that brought them to be distanced from the rest of the Jews on Pesach and thus not being able to participate in the Paschal lamb. Still, they never gave up hope. They came before the Tzaddik, Moshe, pleading, "We are impure, we know we're impure, but we do not want to fail to be included in the sacrifice to God."

Similarly, continues Reb Noson, every Jew should come to the Tzaddik and say, "I'm impure. I know I'm impure. Still, why should I be held back? Why should I not come close to God, to learn Torah, to pray, to repent? Is it because I am so distant that there is no hope for me whatsoever? God can always help, even those who are very distant from Him." A person must know that if he always turns to God and constantly searches for the True Tzaddik who can show him the right path, he will definitely come to true repentance (*Likutey Halakhot, Birkhat HaPeirot* 5:15, *G'viat Chov M'Yetomim* 3).

* * *

LAG B'OMER: IN PRAISE OF RABBI SHIMON BAR YOCHAI

Rabbi Shimon bar Yochai alone was given permission to reveal the great mysteries contained in the Hidden Teachings (cf. *Zohar* III:124b).

Prior to Rabbi Akiva's passing, this great teacher of the Jewish People summoned his two beloved disciples, Rabbi Shimon and Rabbi Meir. They asked Rabbi Akiva which of them would be replacing him. Rabbi Akiva said, "Rabbi Meir shall take over the position as head of the Yeshiva." Then, turning to Rabbi Shimon he said, "It is sufficient that your Creator and I know the level your greatness" (*Yerushalmi, Sanhedrin* 2).

of the Red Sea demonstrated how this arrogance could be completely broken. Moshe turned the seabed into dry land. Earth is associated with the concept of modesty. Great rushing water, with its powerful waves — sure of its strength and unchallenged power — is everything that a person views as the epitomy of greatness. Yet, within a short period of time, God destroyed the water's arrogance by changing it into dry earth. Thus, the song that Moshe and the Jews sang when the Red Sea split was one of praise to God, for He is great and rules over all those who are arrogant and haughty (*Likutey Halakhot, Orlah* 4).

*

When the Jews left Egypt and came close to God, they received great wealth. This is because wealth is rooted in the same source of holiness as the soul. However, there is one bad trait through which it is possible for a person to lose all his wealth. This trait is anger. When the opposing forces see that a person is about to receive wealth and blessings, they try to bring him to anger. CHeMaH, anger, creates a breach in his CHoMaH, his protective wall, which is also his wealth (see *Likutey Moharan* I, 68).

It is forbidden to eat Chametz on Pesach, for Chametz is the concept of anger. Chametz rises. Like arrogance and anger, it is blown up. Likewise, we must avoid exaggeration in our lifestyles. The way we live should also not be arrogant and blown up. When the Red Sea split, the waters stood like a wall (chomah) for the Jews. Afterwards, the Jews were able to withstand any anger (chemah) and were permitted to have Chametz. This is why, after the Seventh Day of Pesach, Chametz is permitted (*Likutey Halakhot, Harsha'ah* 4).

* * *

PIRKEY AVOT — ETHICS OF THE FATHERS

During the summer months it is customary to recite Pirkey Avot, Ethics of the Fathers (*Orach Chaim* 292:2). There are six chapters, one chapter per Shabbat afternoon, which we study until Rosh HaShanah. This practice begins during the Days of the Omer, right after Pesach. Pirkey Avot contains moral teachings from our Tanaim and conceptually is the receiving of rebuke from the True Tzaddikim. Through these lessons a person can achieve great understanding and wisdom on how to serve God properly. Such service brings the kindness of God to be revealed and allows the glory of His Kingship to be elevated.

Introducing Pirkey Avot, we recite the Mishnah, "All Jews have a portion in the World to Come" (*Sanhedrin* 90a). This is to teach us that the rebuke of the great Tzaddikim is not intended to turn people away, or distance them from serving God; but, rather, to bring people closer to Him. The Tzaddikim are always seeking the good points that exist in every single Jew. They are the Tzaddikim and yet they

corresponds to the concept of eating which is rectified on the holiday of Sukkot. Rebbe Nachman explains that a lust for food indicates a blemish of honor and is synonymous with embarrassing others (*Likutey Moharan* I, 67). "Respect for others brings respect and honor upon oneself. Disrespect for others, dishonors oneself" (Avot 4:1). Now, the primary Mitzvah of Sukkot is *eating* in the Sukkah. This rectifies the lust for food. The conclusion of Sukkot is called Simchat Torah. This is the day when everybody is called up to the Torah. "Honor of Torah, is true honor" (Avot 6:3). Thus, the first and last days of the festival rectify honor, i.e., the lust for food.

On Pesach and Sukkot we have Intermediate Days because each of these festivals encompasses two concepts: idolatry (lack of faith) and a lust for money rectified on Pesach; lack of honor and respect and a lust for food rectified on Sukkot. In both cases, time is required between the first and last days of the Yom Tov in order to fully implement a correction of these qualities.

Shavuot, however, has no Intermediate Days because the lust for women and desecrating the Covenant are one and the same. They are comparable to the one day of the festival. Thus, the holiday of Shavuot has the power to simultaneously nullify the lust and help a person attain the levels of purity synonymous with guarding the Covenant (*Likutey Halakhot, Chol HaMoed* 5).

* * *

SHEVI'I SHEL PESACH: THE SPLITTING OF THE RED SEA

Rebbe Nachman taught:

> Even if a person should fall to the lowest level, he must never assume that he is beyond hope. Our forefathers found themselves in similar circumstances on the shores of the Red Sea. Before them, the sea; behind them, the Egyptians; wild animals and wilderness on either side. In the worst of possible situations they did not give up hope. They cried out to God and were heard. Similarly, no matter how far one is from God, there is still hope. Atik is the highest, most lofty spiritual level in existence (*Etz Chaim, Sha'ar Atik*). It is from there that assistance comes to a person, even if he is to be found in the lowest levels. Thus, the miracle of the Splitting of the Red Sea can be summed up this way: even though all seems lost, there is still hope for a redemption (*Likutey Moharan* I, 21).

Reb Noson teaches that a further concept tied in with the Splitting of the Red Sea is the breaking of haughtiness. Pharaoh said "Who is God that I should listen to Him!" During the entire episode, Moshe Rabeinu tried to convince Pharaoh that God rules the world and that He could destroy Pharaoh completely. However, the Egyptian ruler had declared himself a deity. Thus Pharaoh, like most people in a position of power, is characterized by arrogance and haughtiness. The Splitting

And this is exactly what took place during our Exodus from Egypt. Pharaoh allowed the Jews to leave. This was the first day of the holiday, a time for celebration. But, immediately afterwards Pharaoh regretted his decision. He pursued the Jews in order to enslave them once again. Thus, the Jews were forced to once more "battle" against him. This all took place on the Intermediate Days of Pesach. Then, on the last day of Pesach, Pharaoh and the Egyptian army were entirely subdued with the Splitting of the Red Sea. Again it was time for celebration.

The same came be said of Sukkot, which begins and concludes with Yom Tov and has a period of Intermediate Days in between. However, a question arises when we come to the festival of Shavuot. Why does this holiday not have any Intermediate Days? The answer is that the primary rectification of anything in this world is only through the power of Torah. Torah reveals the Greatness of God and gives us the strength with which to do battle against the Other Side. It offers advice and sets the conditions by which we overcome the Other Side. Shavuot was when we received the Torah, when we were given this power. The subjugation of the Other Side, of the opposing forces, is thoroughly completed without the need for Intermediate Days and a Yom Tov afterwards (*Likutey Halakhot, Chol Hamoed* 4).

*

One of the main purposes of the Three Festivals is to rectify the cardinal lusts: money (Pesach); women (Shavuot); food (Sukkot). This can be accomplished through prayer. However, there are three types of sins that undermine the power of prayer: ridiculing others, loss of faith, and blemishing the Covenant. Control in subduing these sins causes the Jews to be redeemed from exile (*Likutey Moharan* II, 1).

The connection between the three cardinal lusts and the festivals is as follows. Prayer, our direct relationship with God, is undermined by a loss of faith. This is directly related to idolatry, which corresponds to the *worshipping* or lusting for money. This lust and the idolatry implied therein are corrected on Pesach. The Children of Israel departed from Egypt on the first day of Pesach. When they left, they took with them the treasures of Egypt. The Jews were all wealthy, just as God had promised Avraham. Even so, in His eyes the fulfillment of that promise was not complete. On the final day of Pesach, the seventh day of the Exodus, God split the Sea and drowned the entire Egyptian army. The booty which the Jews took then far outweighed what they had taken earlier. They were now incredibly wealthy. Yet, despite their great wealth, God provided for all their material needs in the wilderness. The message was clear: They were being told to put their trust in God, not money. What then was the purpose of the great wealth which they had been given? The answer is that the wealth of Egypt was to be elevated by being offered as a donation for the building of the Mishkan, the Tabernacle, in the desert. The destruction of the Egyptians is therefore synonymous with the destruction of idolatry and the elimination of the lust for money.

A second sin which undermines the power of prayer is ridiculing others. This

devour holiness. However, the True Tzaddikim of the generation can attach Desire to its Source — the highest levels of holiness — and are able to nullify and destroy these philosophers. Charity also has this power. Giving charity is so great that it enables people to hear the Call of Holiness and brings people to repentance (*Likutey Moharan* II, 4).

Reb Noson shows how all of the concepts in Rebbe Nachman's lesson are, in fact, related to the concepts of Yom Tov and Chol HaMoed. On the festival, the Will of God is revealed on a level which precludes the need for work. In this sense, it resembles Shabbat. However, unlike Shabbat whose holiness is intrinsic, Yom Tov is a Call of Holiness dependent upon the Sages. They are the ones who determine the New Moon and thus govern the arrival of the festivals which are figured according to the days of the month (*Rosh HaShanah* 24a). Therefore, it is from the Sages, the Tzaddikim of the generation, that the holiness of Yom Tov is drawn. And it is also drawn from charity. We are commanded to give charity on the holidays; so that a person provides not only for his family, but for needy neighbors, widows, orphans, etc. Such charity, in fact, reveals the Will of God.

Now, Yom Tov is followed by the Intermediate Days which, in turn, are followed by Yom Tov. Actually, Chol HaMoed is also called Yom Tov, despite the leniency which is applied to the prohibition against work on these Intermediate Days. This is because primarily, the type of work permitted is limited to that which avoids incurring a loss. What is a loss? It alludes to those sparks of holiness which have become lost to the Other Side, to the realm of the impurity. However, even that which is "lost" will always try to come back, especially when there is a call to return. Thus, in response to the Yom Tov Call of Holiness these sparks desire to return and be included in God's Will. They are given that opportunity on the Intermediate Days. And this is why certain work is permitted on Chol HaMoed: so as to raise up these sparks and thereby undo the loss of holiness. However, when holiness increases, the Other Side wishes to do the same. Perhaps *this time* it will succeed against holiness, especially now that — on the Intermediate Days — holiness has descended out of Yom Tov into the workdays in search of those sparks which fell. This is the reason we have a second day of Yom Tov immediately after Chol HaMoed. Through it we can draw from the higher level of Yom Tov holiness and preserve the fallen sparks which have been elevated from the Other Side (*Likutey Halakhot, Chol HaMoed* 3).

*

Each of the festivals, and not Pesach alone, commemorates the Exodus from Egypt. On the first days of the holiday, we celebrate with joy and happiness, prayer and Torah study. Work has no place in our celebration of the Yom Tov. However, on the Intermediate Days, when certain work is permitted, there is strength — though not in abundance — to subdue the forces which oppose holiness. However, this subjugation of impurity is short-lived. The opposing forces return almost immediately, resuming the battle as before. Therefore, we turn to the final days of the holidays, when we again celebrate as we did on the first days — with joy and abstention from work.

CHOL HAMOED — THE INTERMEDIATE DAYS OF THE FESTIVAL

Rebbe Nachman taught:

> Every nation's characteristics are embedded in its tongue, its language. A holy tongue brings to holiness, the opposite brings the reverse. Thus, by speaking a Holy Tongue one can purify himself. Conversely, there are foreign tongues which bring a person to impurity. Between these two is the language of Aramaic; a combination of the holy and the unholy, which bridges the gap between them (*Likutey Moharan* I, 19).

On Yom Tov, the festival, all work is forbidden. The holidays were given for us to enjoy and to use as a time of introspection and contemplation. On the Intermediate Days, however, some types of work are permitted and others forbidden. Although Chol HaMoed, these *festive weekdays,* have similar laws to the holiday, they are not actually "holy days" in and of themselves. Thus, whatever work needs to be done for Yom Tov can be carried out on these Intermediate Days. Additionally, if by not working on Chol HaMoed a person would incur a loss, then whatever work is required to prevent the loss is also permitted. The finer points of what is permitted or forbidden has been decided by our Sages.

Reb Noson compares the concept of the Intermediate Days to the concept of the Aramaic language. Just as Aramaic stands between two tongues, the holy and the unholy, so Chol HaMoed stands between the holiness of a day where one is completely free from his work load and the lack of holiness which predominates on the weekdays when one must work.

The way we begin any festival is by celebrating a Yom Tov (a Good Day), a holy day free of work and toil. This indicates that our initial action must be to bring everything into total holiness. However, often times we exceed our level and must descend to a level of holiness closer to our true attainments. Even so, we should not fall into the realm of total physicality, a level of weekday. Until we can truly attain the holiness of the "Holydays" on all our days, we must find a middle-ground. This is Chol HaMoed, the *Intermediate* Days. They remind us that we can, with proper effort, ascend back into the realm of holiness (*Likutey Halakhot, Chol HaMoed* 1).

*

Rebbe Nachman taught:

> The holidays reveal the Will and Desire of God. The three festivals are known as Mikra'ey Kodesh, the Call of Holiness. They call out to everyone to recognize the Greatness of God. Through this recognition, abundance comes to the world so that a person will not have to do any type of work whatsoever. All aspects of his life will be a clear expression of the Desire and Will of God. Nothing will be concealed as an "Act of Nature." In contrast to the Call of Holiness, there is a Call of Impurity — the philosophers who believe in the power of nature. They try to

a great desire to repent. It is almost as if we are being called by a voice we cannot locate, or guided by an invisible hand. Later, the light of this guiding force disappears and we must continue our quest for God under our own inspiration.

The reason this happens is not always understood by most people, though it is essential that it should be. The truth is that by seemingly pushing a person away from God, one is actually drawing him closer to Him. Think about it. Didn't the Egyptians let the Children of Israel leave? Didn't they allow them to go into the wilderness to serve God? The Jews must have understood that they were getting closer to Him. But then they saw the Egyptians running after them. The Jews were left wondering if the Almighty was really with them. Were they really getting closer? It was then that they were told to turn their eyes Heavenward and pray. The very same thing happens to each of us. The only way we can achieve our personal redemption is by raising our eyes to God and praying to Him for help. Even when we feel distant rather than close, we must always bear in mind that God is very close to us and He is really trying to bring us closer. Indeed, God's kindness is such that it will even bring closer those who are very, very distant from Him.

Nevertheless, from the Sefirah we learn that the process cannot be hurried. When we look forward to something, we want it to happen immediately. Most of the time, especially if the thing we look forward to is something meaningful, it just can't happen right away. The issue cannot be forced at all. We find ourselves with no choice but to wait. Well, the same is true in achieving closeness to God and receiving His Torah. We must wait to achieve it; wait to receive it. Just as the Jews in the wilderness had to wait until Shavuot. And though on Pesach they received a tremendous light and wanted to serve God properly, they still could not reach their goal until the 50th day. It is the same for us. However, if we persist in our desire to achieve this level, eventually we will acquire this great light of Shavuot (*Likutey Halakhot, Shiluach HaKen* 5).

* * *

QUEEN ESTHER'S MEAL

The second day of Pesach was the day that Esther prepared a feast for Achashveirosh and Haman (Esther 5; *Megillah* 15b). On the second day of Pesach it is customary to add an extra dish to the meal in commemoration of the feast, as this was the beginning of Haman's downfall (*Orach Chaim* 490:2, *Mishnah Berurah*).

Interestingly, Rebbe Nachman taught that originally, all beginnings emanated from the holiday of Pesach, which was the beginning of Jewish nationhood. Now, however, all beginnings emanate from Purim (*Likutey Moharan* II, 74). This points to the direct link between Purim and Pesach. The miracle of Purim came about through the extra feast that was held by Esther on the Pesach holiday.

* * *

before God, he can be likened to an animal without the power of speech. As a result of the embarrassment he feels for having gone against God's Will and transgressed, he cannot lift up his head or raise his voice. Thus, a major step in repentance and returning to God is remaining silent as we hear and feel ourselves being embarrassed. Teshuvah means that we no longer rush to counter the insult with rationalizations, excuses, or just plain arrogance. By truly accepting that everything is from God, then even when we know that the person ridiculing or chastising us is no better than we are, we say nothing. We understand that he is no more than God's messenger, and we remain silent and embarrassed before the One who sent him.

This is the significance of the elevation, the Tenuphah, of the Omer. TeNUPhaH can be read TeNU-PeH — give mouth! This implies that a person who counts the Sefirat Ha'Omer, thereby rectifying his speech, raises himself from the level of animal to that of man. He becomes a complete person.

Seven weeks later, on Shavuot, the sacrifice which was brought consisted of wheat. Unlike the lowliness of barley, wheat is a "human" grain. Yet, wheat also carries an aspect of being silent, for there are, in fact, two levels of silence. The first level, the animal level, is someone who is so embarrassed by his sins that he can't speak. He finds himself speechless because he recognizes his guilt. But then he repents. He acquires speech, as in, "Take with you *words* and return to God" (Hoshea 14:3). And through his returning and coming closer to God, he can achieve the second level of silence: the Gate to Wisdom (Avot 3:17). This higher silence corresponds to the Divine Emanation, the Sephirah, of Keter; itself an aspect of Shavuot.

On Shavuot, after 49 Days of Counting — after the 49 Gates of Repentance and Tehillim reciting — the higher level of silence is finally attained. Even so, it must be remembered that all this begins with PeSaCH — with Peh SaCH, a talking mouth. For the only path to these upper levels is through Tefillah, the true speech of calling out to God (*Likutey Halakhot, Simanei Behemah v'Chayah T'horah* 4).

*

When looking forward to a particular event or special occasion, it's only natural that we mark our calendars and count the days. It's the same thing when we anticipate receiving the Torah on Shavuot. We count the days. We look forward to its coming. Actually, this is the main intent of the Omer Counting. By realizing that every day counts, by taking the very most we can out of it, by making sure that every single minute matters, we can *receive* the Torah.

The Children of Israel first came close to God on Pesach, after the Redemption from Egypt. To remove them from Egypt, God instantaneously pulled them from 49th level of impurity into which they had fallen. But then they had to enter the 49 levels of holiness on their own, step by step. This can be compared to a child first learning to walk. As soon as he shows signs of realizing there is something better than crawling on all fours, we enforce and encourage his desire to develop. We hold his hand is held for the first step. But then we let go, so that he learns to walk by himself. It is no different in coming closer to God. We start off with

the essence of day is light — spiritual light. Each day, we have to try to attain this light. How? by extracting the good that is inherent in today, in every single day. The day, however, starts with night. It begins with darkness — the barriers that prevent us from reaching our goal. We have to always strengthen ourselves and make every possible attempt to break through the obstructions and obstacles surrounding us on that day. Only by discovering the good in every single day and utilizing the knowledge that God is in control of everything that happens — He is King — only then can we recognize and draw closer to Him.

Reb Noson teaches that the daily obstacles we encounter are in direct proportion to the spiritual levels and wisdom we seek to achieve. We should therefore not feel discouraged when we see our improvement in serving God suddenly countered by more difficulties. As long as we maintain our Mochin de'Gadlut, the forces opposing our advancement cannot affect us. For it is only when we descend to Mochin de'Katnut, to depression and despair, that we find it very difficult to stand up against these obstacles.

In fact, taking heart and strengthening ourselves each day is the one protection we have. Even when there are difficulties or obstacles, we have to realize that *today* is also part of our allotted time on earth. It, too, is a day during which we can and must accomplish whatever possible in coming closer to God. If we cannot pray or study Torah properly, then we should say Tehillim or perform other mitzvot — doing whatever we can. For "God wants the Jews to be rewarded; and therefore He gave them the Torah to study and many mitzvot to perform." In other words, we must never fool ourselves into thinking that since the day started wrong, *today* is a wasted day, God forbid! We must never allow ourselves to say that there is no point in trying to know God or returning to Him on this day; that we are better off waiting until tomorrow. Rather, we must realize that every day is important — every moment counts. And this is the lesson of Sefirat Ha'Omer, the 49 Days of Counting. It teaches us to make the best and the most of what we have, since *every day does count!* (*Likutey Halakhot, Pikadon* 4).

*

Sefirah is synonymous with purification. When we are ready to purify ourselves, we discover that it isn't a speedy process. Only through gradual progression will we attain our goal. And to be fully purified, we must wait until after the Sefirah, after we've counted again and again. In the meantime, we have to count one day at a time; slowly building up purity until we are able to overcome all the undesirable and impure aspects of our lives.

On the 16th day of Nissan, the Omer Sacrifice — a barley offering — was brought. Using barley, which serves as feed for animals, would seem to indicate the low nature of this offering. But, because animals lack the power of speech, this makes barley a most appropriate choice. This is because the Omer is brought to rectify and endow the power of speech, elevating from the lower level of animal to the more purified level of man. And this is its connection to the Sefirah. During the Sefirah we try to rectify ourselves. Quintessentially, Teshuvah is our accepting that everything which happens is from God. When one is embarrassed

SEFIRAH — THE OMER COUNTING

Rebbe Nachman taught:

> The 49 Days of Sefirat Ha'Omer correspond to the 49 Gates of Return. These 49 gates, in turn, correspond to the 49 letters which make up the names of the Twelve Tribes. Thus, each tribe has individual gates for each of its members, so that everyone can return to God through his *own* gate. And then there is the 50th, the highest gate: Shavuot. This gate is, as it were, the Teshuvah, the "return," of God.
>
> The way for a person to come to his individual gate is through the Tehillim. Thus, during the 49 Days of Sefirah, as well as on all days of repentance (the month of Elul, Rosh HaShanah), we should recite Psalms. This will bring us to our Gate of Repentance. And, by achieving this, we will merit purity and coming back to God.
>
> That these 49 Days are a most amenable time for reciting Psalms and repenting can be learned from the beginning of the Book of Exodus. The verse reads, "These are the names of the Children of Israel who went down to Egypt; each man and his wife, they came." In the Hebrew, the last letters of these words make up the words Tehillim and Teshuvah. The verses which follow then list the names of the Tribes (their 49 letters). They correspond to the 49 Days of Sefirah, corresponding to the 49 Gates of Teshuvah (*Likutey Moharan* II, 73).

The ARIzal, Rabbi Yitzchak Luria, explains that on the night of Pesach it was vital that the Jews be on a level of Mochin de'Gadlut, expanded consciousness. This was because they were so lacking in holiness and steeped in impurities, they would otherwise never have been able to leave Egypt. The Jews were therefore *given* Awareness, and not in the gradual, progressive manner in which expanded consciousness is normally acquired. Their levels of consciousness came to them in an inverted manner: Mochin de'Gadlut prior to Mochin de'Katnut, the level of constricted consciousness. However, the very next day, the day after the Exodus, they were back to "normal" — receiving the Katnut and having to progressively achieve the Gadlut.

It is possible for us to receive Mochin, this consciousness or wisdom, every single day. A person begins his day attempting to serve God and, as the day wears on, he himself progresses; reaching ever greater understanding in serving God. Every single day we must try to draw this wisdom upon us. It is the wisdom to recognize and understand God, to come close to Him, and to devote ourselves to serving Him.

Just as no two days of our lives are exactly the same, the wisdom of today is never the same as the wisdom of yesterday or tomorrow. Each day provides us with a different set of concepts and experiences which make up *that* day's wisdom; the wisdom we are to use in order to know and come closer to Him *today!* Now,

APPENDIX C
Until Shavuot

in Olam HaTohu, the World of Confusion, will be to get up, say Tikkun Chatzot and dance *Ashreinu*. Others will be punished by being forced to perform the same acts *they* did in this world" (*Siach Sarfei Kodesh* 1-786).

* * *

isru... ba'avotim — bind with cords. Reb Noson himself was once complaining to Rebbe Nachman about the hardships and opposition he was facing in his becoming a follower of the Rebbe. Rebbe Nachman said to him, "I trapped you in my sack." To which Reb Noson replied, "Bind me tightly, so that I can't escape!" (*Siach Sarfei Kodesh* 1-129).

* * *

sheb'shiflainu... — remembers us in our lowliness. When Reb Noson first came to the Rebbe, Rebbe Nachman gave him the *Shevachey Ha'ARI*, a compilation of stories about the ARI and his closest disciple, Rabbi Chaim Vital. Afterwards, the Rebbe asked him what in the book had impressed him the most. Reb Noson answered that he had been very moved by Rabbi Chaim Vital's humility and modesty. The Rebbe said that that was exactly what he wanted Reb Noson to see (*Aveneha Barzel*, p. 20 #16). Reb Noson himself was known for his exceptional modesty and humbleness (see *Tzaddik* #338).

* * *

chad gadya...Angel of Death. "It is quite an undertaking for the Angel of Death to take on the entire world. Actually, there are two in the world that have impossible jobs: the Evil One and the Angel of Death. Therefore," said Rebbe Nachman, "the Angel of Death has his assistants — doctors — to help him kill people physically; and the Evil One has his assistants — unqualified rabbis and leaders — to help him kill the people spiritually" (*Aveneha Barzel*, p. 43; #64).

* * *

chad gadya...God slew the Angel of Death. "God saw all that He did and it was *very good*..." (Genesis 1:31). "*Very good* refers to the Angel of Death" (*Breishit Rabbah* 9:5). Haughtiness is compared to idolatry, death. Every person has this haughtiness. It is manifested in his desire to rule, to exercise his own power (*Likutey Moharan* I, 10:3,4). But, in the end, "God will be King over all the world..." (Zekhariah 14:9), that is, He will reign supreme. Then, "Death will be destroyed forever, and God will wipe away the tears from man's face (Isaiah 25:8).

* * *

Nachman, God gave me the privilege of knowing Rebbe Nachman's closest disciple, Reb Noson. He taught me Rebbe Nachman's lessons and brought me to serve God.

"This is where I am now.

"And now, when I think about this, I cannot help but wonder. How — after being so distant from God all those years — how is it possible that I should merit such a great light? How could someone so undeserving come to know of Rebbe Nachman? I only understood this after I studied the Hallel. 'The stone despised by all the builders became the cornerstone.' This soul — the very same soul which had been discarded by all the great Tzaddikim — has now come to a Tzaddik who is *the cornerstone,* the foundation of the entire world. 'This has come from God; it is wonderful in our eyes.' It is truly wondrous how God deals with every single soul, making certain that it achieves its *tikkun.* The great Tzaddikim never give up trying to correct all the souls, because this is what God truly wants.

"I saw from all of this" Reb Pinchas Yehoshua concluded, "that no matter what happens to us, we must understand that there is salvation. We can always come back to God. And, this is why the next words we say in the Hallel are, 'This day, God has made, we will rejoice....' For *this day,* in our generation, God gave us such a great leader, Rebbe Nachman, who instilled in us the faith to always turn to God — no matter where we are. God will then redeem the Jewish People, and we will have nothing but great joy and happiness all the rest of our days, Amen!" (*Tovot Zikhronot,* pp. 151- 156).

* * *

nagilah v'nishmichah — rejoice and be glad. Someone asked Reb Noson how could he become happy when he had so many problems and difficulties. "Borrow it!" Reb Noson answered. [He wanted us to take it from the future salvations that God will send our way.] (*Siach Sarfei Kodesh* 1-736).

*

In Teplik, there was a Breslover chassid known as Feivel-Ashreinu. He used to wake up each midnight to recite the Tikkun Chatzot, the Midnight Lament. Then, because of the great happiness which he felt from having performed the mitzvah, he would dance joyously as he sung the words *Ashreinu, mah tov chelkeinu* (How fortunate we are, how good is our portion) over and over again. Eventually, people started calling him Feivel-Ashreinu.

Whenever Reb Noson would visit the town of Teplik, Reb Feivel would joyously come out to greet him. Once, Reb Feivel failed to appear. When Reb Noson asked about him, the people wanted to know which Feivel he was referring to. "Oh! You must mean Feivel-Ashreinu!" they finally said in jest. "He passed away." Reb Noson understood what it was that prompted them to ridicule him, and he took them to task for it. "I'll tell you this," Reb Noson said, "Reb Feivel's 'punishment'

righteous leaders were powerless to include me in the buildings of holiness which they built."

I looked at Reb Motele Shochet and he looked back at me. Neither of us could believe what we were hearing. We stood there transfixed as Reb Pinchas Yehoshua went on. "When building a building," he said, "a mason gathers all the stones that he needs for the first level of the building and begins by cutting and chipping away at the corners. He forms the stones so that each one fits properly into place. When he's finished the first level, he again gathers the stones he needs and shapes them so that he can then erect the second level. And so it goes, level after level. At each level, the mason must make sure that all the stones he uses for the building are suitably formed. Many times we see that builders come across certain odd-shaped stones which they try to use, only to find them too awkward to be made into a proper fit. In the end, they have no choice but to discard them.

"The same is true in spirituality. The great Tzaddikim try to build — by attempting to rectify the Jewish souls. The Torah calls these souls stones. The Tzaddikim work hard at this. Each stone they came across, every soul they encounter, they do their very best to fit it into the building of holiness they try to erect."

Reb Pinchas Yehoshua interrupted his words with a long, deep sigh. Then, with an even greater intensity, he began again. "When it was my soul's turn to play it's part in the building, I came before this great Tanna. He attempted to correct me, but found that he could not. He worked very hard to 'shape me,' trying all different angles. But, no matter what he tried, it didn't work. As soon as as he corrected me on one side, I was found to be crooked on another side. Whichever way he turned my soul, it was still impossible for him to find me a place in his "building." Seeing that it was futile, this Tanna just left me alone. There was absolutely nothing he could do. The exact same thing happened the second time my soul descended into this world. And so it was with every subsequent reincarnation. All the Tzaddikim tried to rectify me, but their efforts failed. I was left alone through all those generation, thrown away like an odd-shaped stone; to be thrown and kicked about forever.

"Yet, God, whose kindness is forever, wants all the Jews to be rectified, no matter what they've done. He saw my difficulties and sent me back to this world, again. But this time, in my current reincarnation, I found something completely new — a tzaddik with a "building" power which I had never seen before, in any of my previous incarnations. This was Rebbe Nachman of Breslov! All the Upper Worlds tremble in fear of his greatness and his holiness. Rebbe Nachman believed that a person can always come close to God, no matter how distant he was. In a strong voice he called out from the depths of his heart, 'NEVER GIVE UP! NEVER DESPAIR!' This Rebbe Nachman described himself as 'a river which can cleanse all stains.' From Creation, until today, there was never a Tzaddik who spoke such words and with such strength and such power. And, in addition to hearing about Rebbe

even moasu... — the stone despised... This has come from God. Reb Pinchas Yehoshua was the son of Reb Isaac the scribe, a very close disciple of Reb Noson. He was extremely poor, yet well-known for his piety and great devotions. Once, a very poor person, who had no children, was about to pass away. He called for Reb Pinchas Yehoshua and asked him to recite the Kaddish. In return, he would leave his *tefillin* to Reb Pinchas Yehoshua for his son. Reb Pinchas Yehoshua agreed. A few weeks later, an extremely wealthy person, also childless, was about to pass away. He also wanted Reb Pinchas Yehoshua to recite the Kaddish for him. The wealthy man was willing to leave Reb Pinchas Yehoshua enough money to support him for many years. But Reb Pinchas refused. "I am already reciting Kaddish for someone else" he told him. Reb Pinchas Yehoshua was afraid the poor person for whom he had already begun saying Kaddish might object, as his request was first.

One day, Reb Pinchas Yehoshua made the pilgrimage to Rebbe Nachman's gravesite in Uman, together with Reb Avraham Sternhartz and Reb Motele Shochet, both of whom were very close to him. The three of them prayed there for many hours.

Reb Avraham Sternhartz writes:

> As we turned to leave Rebbe Nachman's gravesite, Reb Pinchas Yehoshua began to tremble with great trepidation. "My friends," he said, "I looked at myself and I saw that I have been reincarnated time and again into this world." He then began detailing the various generations in which he lived. He said that he had been alive in the time of a certain Tanna, and then in the generation of a particular Tzaddik... As he spoke, Reb Pinchas Yehoshua weighed his every word; their tremendous truth being clear. We believed him because we knew of his greatness and his incredible devotion to God. He even told us how many times his soul had already come back to this world. [Translator's note: this took place in about 1885.]
>
> Reb Pinchas Yehoshua found it was very difficult to understand why he — of all the people that were in the world when his soul was first incarnated — why he alone should have to endure this. The Tanna rectified other souls, why not his? Why did he have to suffer so many incarnations. Reb Pinchas Yehoshua began saying to himself, "How come my soul was left without its rectification? How come I was left in the depths, in the abyss of my sins, so that I had to come down again? Perhaps I'll be rectified the second time around?" Then he told us that came back in the generation of a different Tzaddik. This Tzaddik worked to rectify the Jewish souls and bring them back to their source. But again his soul was left without its *tikkun,* and he had to return again and again and again. "I tried as hard as I could to understand why this was happening," Reb Pinchas Yehoshua continued. "Finally, I realized that I, alone, was responsible for my fate. I, myself, my difficult nature and improper deeds, were what made it impossible for anyone to ever provide me with a *tikkun.* Have I not learned in the Talmud that 'the Tzaddikim are builders.' Then it must have been my fault that these

kol rinah — the sound of rejoicing. Reb Noson said to his follower, Reb Aharon Nissan, "If you would always be happy, you wouldn't see Gehennom" (*Kokhavey Or,* p. 78 #28).

*

Reb Noson wrote to Reb Ozer: I heard that you are very, very religious. Yet, from Rebbe Nachman I heard that "the main thing is joy... and religion too!" Reb Noson once said to Reb Moshe Breslover, "I will give you a [way to achieve] repentance: Dance every day!" (*Aveneha Barzel,* p. 62 #28,29).

* * *

lo omus kee echyeh — I shall not die, I shall live. Once, while sitting at the table with his followers, Rebbe Nachman remarked, "A man can be so foolish. The Angel of Death is right behind him and he can still be thinking of his foolishness." One particular follower, Reb Chaim Saras of Breslov, took the Rebbe's words very much to heart. Remaining behind after the others had gone, he approached the Rebbe. "When you said what you said about the Angel of Death, I know you meant me." Reb Chaim Saras pleaded with the Rebbe to pray for him to live. The Rebbe said, "My son is very ill. I am going to Medzeboz, to the gravesite of my grandfather, the Baal Shem Tov, to plead for his life. Come with me and I will pray for you as well." Reb Chaim Saras agreed to accompany the Rebbe on the trip. In Medzeboz, Rebbe Nachman spent an exceptionally long time praying to God at the Baal Shem Tov's grave. As they were leaving, the Rebbe said to Reb Chaim Saras, "For you I succeeded; for myself, I did not!" Reb Chaim lived at least another forty years (*Kokhavey Or,* p. 60 #43).

*

Once, near Zlatipolia, a very charitable woman was near death. One of her beneficiaries was a follower of Rebbe Nachman. He went to the Rebbe, asking him to pray on her behalf, as there were many, many people who were being helped through her goodness and kindness. The Rebbe told him to quickly bring an assortment of coins, which he did. After looking at and weighing many coins, Rebbe Nachman chose one. He then told his follower he could return home, the woman would recover.

After she'd recovered, the woman told the following story: "I found myself before the Heavenly Court which was then in the process of debating my fate. The judgment went against me. Suddenly, a young man [she described Rebbe Nachman whom she'd never met] came rushing in. He threw a coin onto the Scale of Justice. It was just enough to tip the balance in my favor. I was given life." More than anything else, what amazed the follower was that Rebbe Nachman knew the exact size coin needed to save the woman's life. He now understood why the Rebbe had been checking each coin for its size and weight (*Kokhavey Or,* p. 62 #44).

* * *

We slept overnight on the road and only continued on once morning had come. The progress was slow and I realized there was no way I was going to make it to Nemirov for Shabbat, let alone Breslov. I felt very disheartened, as my desire to see the Rebbe and to be with him for Shavuot had grown even stronger because of the effort it took to bring me this far. As we approached the next village, Marachve [some thirty miles from Nemirov], it occurred to me that perhaps I should hire my own horses. But I realized that the money which I had borrowed for the journey would not be sufficient to do this. I was dismayed. Even if I had the money, Marachve was a small village and the likelihood of finding a coach with four horses which could bring me to Breslov in time for Shabbat was almost non-existent. I didn't know what to do?

"On the bridge at the entrance to the village, I lifted my eyes and heart to God: 'Master of the Universe! Send me a wagon with four horses so that I may get to Breslov in time for Shabbat!'

"After we entered the village, the wagon driver stopped to get feed for his horses. While making his purchase, the driver heard of a merchant who was just about to leave for Breslov. The merchant had a wagon with four horses and he agreed to take me with him. It was an obvious manifestation of Divine Providence. Can there be any doubt that the Almighty listens to all the prayers of those who wish to draw close to Him and gives strength to all those who seek Him (*Yemey Moharnat*, pp. 18-19; see *Until the Mashiach*, chapter 19; *Tzaddik*, pp. 61-75).

* * *

...mebtoach b'adam — **better to rely on God than on man.** One of Reb Noson's followers had a small business. This man very much wanted to devote all his time and energy to studying Torah, and was ready to give up his business. He would rely on others for his income. He presented his plan to Reb Noson and was surprised that it did not meet with his approval. "Right now, your heart is burning with a desire and yearning for Torah. You are willing to accept the hardships of such a lifestyle. But what will happen when this fire cools off? What will you eat then? I suggest that before you go to your work each day, you set aside certain hours for Torah study. I also advise you to keep Torah books in your store, so that you can study whenever you have a quiet moment. If you keep to these hours on a steady basis and still feel a burning desire for Torah, then close your store an additional hour a day and use that extra time for Torah study. If you gradually increase your commitment to Torah and pray to God that He provide you with the freedom to learn full-time, then eventually you will succeed in overcoming all obstacles and be able to devote all your energy to Torah study. And if you cannot maintain the schedule, then at least you will have a livelihood (*Aveneha Barzel*, p. 49 #2).

* * *

Reb Noson said that a person must always beg and plead with God to lead him on the path of *His* truth. With our own truth we can deceive ourselves. But God's truth, is the *real* truth, the eternal truth (*Siach Sarfei Kodesh* 1-502).

* * *

min hameitzar... — in distress, I called out; He answered me. In the spring of 1807, Rebbe Nachman was in Zaslov, where his wife was seeking medical help for tuberculosis. Shavuot was approaching and it was customary for the Rebbe's followers to be with him for the holiday. And though, this year he was far away from his home in Breslov, his disciples made every effort to join him in Zaslov.

A half-a-year before this, Reb Noson and his family had moved to Mohelov, where his father-in-law, Rabbi Dovid Zvi, was head of the district's rabbinical court. With Shavuot not far away, Reb Noson started thinking about the journey to Zaslov. He knew that the obstacles to such an undertaking were numerous. Firstly, his wife and children were still weak due to an illness from which they had only recently recovered. Reb Noson understood that this in itself would make his father-in-law, who was in any case well known for his opposition to Chassidut and to Reb Noson's relationship to the Rebbe, absolutely opposed to his leaving home at this time. Aside from this, the long trip to Zaslov would cost more money than than he now had. And, as if these obstacles weren't enough, Reb Noson knew that Rebbe Nachman had sent word that he definitely did not want his followers to undertake the arduous journey.

Despite all this, Reb Noson could not bring himself to accept being away from the Rebbe for the holiday. A few months earlier, the Rebbe himself had been seriously ill and had even sent a letter asking them to pray for him. Reb Noson felt it important that, especially now, Rebbe Nachman's chassidim be at his side. After an exchange of letters, it was agreed that they would make the journey.

Reb Noson set out from Mohelov towards his hometown of Nemirov, from where he intended to make his way to nearby Breslov. There he hoped to join up with the group of followers which would be leaving for Zaslov on Sunday. As it was a Thursday afternoon, he realized that he would have to reach Breslov in time for Shabbat. This would be the only way to catch the last coach that could get him to Zaslov in time for Shavuot. Reb Noson writes:

> The time was short and I wanted the wagon driver to hurry. I was very anxious that we move as quickly as possible. It was already too late when I realized that the large wagon I had hired was only being drawn by two horses. Such a wagon requires four, and at the very least three horses, to pull it at any speed. When I questioned the driver about this told me that on his way to Mohelov one horse had taken sick. But, we would soon be arriving at the place where he'd left it, and hopefully it would now be fit enough to help us get to Nemirov more quickly. When we reached the horses location, we were greeted with the "good news" that the horse died. Worse yet, more time was lost as the driver had to dispose of his dead horse.

59

kol haadam kozev! — all men are liars! Rebbe Nachman said, "People are mistaken when they claim that a Tzaddik cannot commit an *avlah,* a false or wrong deed. And, if he commits such an act, they say he's no longer a Tzaddik. But I say the Tzaddik remains a Tzaddik and what was done wrong, remains wrong" (*Siach Sarfei Kodesh* 1-46).

* * *

nedaray ashalem — my vows I will fulfill. The Rebbe once told Reb Noson that when he was young, he made many vows. Reb Noson asked, "But the Codes say that one should not make vows?" (*Yorah Deah* 203). "That was said for *shleimzalnikers* like you!" the Rebbe answered (*Aveneha Barzel,* p. 25 #15).

* * *

yakar b'einei HaShem — precious in God's eyes. Reb Noson had a follower, Reb Shaul, whose devotions were carried out with great fervor. He studied Torah day and night, and prayed intensely. Whenever students in the study hall encountered difficult questions they could not solve, they would ask Reb Shaul. He would go into a private room, pray to God to "reveal before my eyes the wonders of Your Torah" (Psalms 119:18), and then answer the students. With all of this, Reb Noson still told Reb Shaul that he did not have *nachat* from his devotions and dedication to God. But, were Reb Shaul to fall from his devotions and though he fell, remain strong in his will to serve God until he could raise himself again — that would be precious in God's eyes, and then Reb Noson would feel complete trust in him. Reb Shaul died young. The verse (Genesis 5:24), "He is no longer, for God took him" was applied to him. As Rashi explains, from the verse we see that Chanokh, though a Tzaddik, would have sinned had he remained alive. Therefore, God took him from the world when he was yet young (*Sichot V'Sipurim,* p. 146 #57).

* * *

emet...l'olam — truth is eternal. Reb Ber of Tcherin was a very wealthy businessman. Once, he agreed in principle to enter into a deal with another person. Soon afterwards, Reb Ber received information indicating that this deal was not financially sound and he would incur a huge monetary loss. Without hesitating, Reb Ber went to the rabbi of his town and informed him that he intended to take part in this deal. He revealed this to the rabbi so that he would not be tempted to cancel the deal, even though no contract had been signed and there hadn't even been a verbal agreement on the exact details of their deal (*Aveneha Barzel,* p. 45 #70).

*

Rebbe Nachman said, "A person should be careful not to let his smallness — his modesty, overshadow his greatness — his good qualities" In other words, a person will sometimes allow himself the "luxury" of thinking he is insignificant and accordingly makes no attempt to grow spiritually (*Siach Sarfei Kodesh* 1-34).

* * *

lo hameisim — the dead cannot. Reb Chaikel asked the Rebbe to show him the soul of a dead person. The Rebbe agreed to do so and soon afterwards enabled Reb Chaikel to see the soul of the town baker, who had just passed away. The baker's soul was pleading with Rebbe Nachman, saying, "I always supplied your followers with bread and *challah* for their Melavah Malkah. Now I ask you to bring about a *tikkun,* a rectification, for my soul." "Because you contributed to my followers, I will work to help you" (*Kokhavey Or,* p. 56 #34).

* * *

yishmah... tachanunai — hears...my prayer. Reb Yitzchak of Tulchin, Reb Noson's son, would frequently discuss his difficulties in spiritual development with his father. He once expressed his frustrations, saying that his devotions had weakened and he could not meditate properly. Reb Noson told his son that King David's greatness manifested itself in precisely just such a predicament. Many times King David himself would want to pray, but could not find the words to speak to God. But he knew that one should never despair. Instead of giving up, he would groan and cry out to God that his mouth was closed and that he could not find the appropriate words to pray. *This* became his prayer. God would then accept his entreaties, and provide King David with the inspiration to find the right words with which to pour out his heart. Indeed, God wants us to pray to Him that we should be capable of praying properly (*Aveneha Barzel,* p. 70 #53).

* * *

nafshi mimavet — delivered my soul from death. Reb Shimon's son was deathly ill and it was a very worried father who came to the Rebbe asking him to pray for the child's recovery. Rebbe Nachman, however, did not respond. Forlorn and without hope, Reb Shimon returned home. His wife understood the implication of the Rebbe's refusing to answer. Yet, instead of despairing, she sat at the infant's crib the entire night, praying for her child. The following morning, when Rebbe Nachman saw Reb Shimon, he ran towards him with great joy, saying, "Look at the great power of prayer! Last night the decree was sealed. The infant's death was imminent. And now, not only has the decree been nullified, but Heaven has granted him long life as well!" (*Aveneha Barzel,* p. 39 #60). [Translator's note: this child lived to be nearly 100 years old.]

* * *

Rebbe Nachman once told of a famous "rebbe" who would pray in his private room [adjacent to the synagogue]. Hearing sounds outside his door and thinking it to be his chassidim trying to catch a glimpse of their master's devotions, the "rebbe" prayed with great fervor and enthusiasm. Later, he discovered that the sounds had been caused by a cat scratching at the door. "For nine years he prayed to a cat! God save us!" (*Aveneha Barzel*, p. 25 #13).

*

On a different occasion, one of Rebbe Nachman's followers came to him complaining that he had no means of earning his livelihood. He was now thinking that perhaps he should take a rabbinical position and serve as a community leader, as the famous rabbis of his time did. The Rebbe, however, did not approve. "You'll become so involved with impressing people and maintaining your status that you won't even be able to recite Birkhat Hamazon, the Grace after Meals, with proper intentions!" (Oral Tradition).

* * *

haktanim im hagedolim — the small and great. The following question was put to Reb Noson: Seeing that Mashiach hasn't yet come despite all the efforts of all the very great Tzaddikim in all the previous generations, how will he come in these few remaining and much weaker generations. Reb Noson told a parable to explain this paradox:

> There was once a city that was very well fortified. It was enclosed by a thick stone wall, thought to be impenetrable. A wise king decided to conquer this fortified city. After inspecting the fortifications, he sent his mightiest soldiers to bring down the wall and attack the city. These soldiers fell. He next sent a second wave of less mighty soldiers, and then a third wave, and so on. Before long, his entire army had been depleted and the wall had not come down. But the king did not give up. Once again he circled the city, inspecting its walls. "How can you expect to capture this city if all your mighty soldiers are gone?" he was asked. The wise king smiled. "If you look closely, you will see that though the soldiers could not breach the wall, they did succeed in cracking it. It is no longer strong and impenetrable. Now, with even the weak and wounded I can bring down the wall." The king then sent his few remaining and weakest soldiers into battle and conquered the city.

Reb Noson explained that though they did not succeed in bringing the Mashiach, all the great Tzaddikim of the previous generation did succeed in cracking the wall of obstacles which stand in the way. Now, though we are weak and haven't the strength or the power, if we would but make a concerted effort, we *could* bring the wall down and bring the Mashiach (*Ma'asiot U'Meshalim*, p. 36-37).

*

It was to be the last morning of Reb Nosson's life and a number of his close followers had already gathered to be with him during these final hours. After putting on his *talis* and *tefillin,* and praying with all his energy, Reb Noson sat down to his daily study of Halakhah and completed his review of the *Shakh* [a gloss on the major codification of Jewish law, the *Shulchan Arukh*]. Then, after reciting the daily portion of Psalms, he asked to be brought *kol tuv.* No one understood what Reb Noson wanted, until he explained that he was asking for a *Tanakh* [the complete Bible]. "That is *kol tuv!*" he said (*Likutey Halakhot, Orach Chaim* III end in letter).

* * *

brakhah... she'achalnu — send a blessing... we have eaten. Once, Rebbe Nachman, Reb Noson and Reb Naftali came to an inn where they were served a meal which included cheese. Rebbe Nachman and Reb Naftali had both contracted tuberculosis and eating dairy would aggravate their condition. Reb Noson was too embarrassed to eat the cheese by himself. "Don't worry," he said to Reb Naftali, "you can eat it. It won't harm you." Reb Naftali turned to Reb Noson, *"You're* telling me [that it won't harm me] to eat it? If the *Rebbe* tells me to eat, then I'll eat!" Rebbe Nachman heard this and told Reb Naftali to eat the cheese together with Reb Noson, which he did. On the way home, Reb Naftali coughed. "You see!" Rebbe Nachman said to him, "your cough has completely changed. I thought your illness was so severe that you would pass away before me. Now I see that you're going to get better" (*Kokhavey Or,* p. 51 #24). [Translator's note: Rebbe Nachman passed away in 1810; Reb Noson in 1844; Reb Naftali in 1860.]

* * *

...zakanti — ...have now grown old. Reb Noson was once talking about how quickly time passes us by. "At first, there isn't *yet* anyone to talk to. Then there isn't *any longer* anyone to talk to!" (*Siach Sarfei Kodesh* 1-510).

* * *

kee l'shimkha — not to us, but to Your Name. The followers of the Baal Shem Tov were in a very good mood. They had just finished praying with great fervor and elation. But now, much to their surprise, the Baal Shem Tov looked very disturbed. In an uncharacteristically stern tone he said to them, "You prayed with such fervor, the Evil One succeeded in bringing you all to arrogance. I had a most difficult time sweetening the Heavenly decrees against you which resulted from your haughtiness." Reb Noson told this story to show just how vital it is for us to avoid haughtiness. He then went on to emphasize the need for our constantly praying to be able to remove all traces of arrogance and haughtiness from ourselves (*Kokhavey Or,* p. 72 #10).

Shulchan Orekh — The Meal. Rebbe Nachman's daughter Adil lived in Breslov and the Rebbe would eat in her house on the last day of Pesach. Each year, Adil would serve her father two *kneidlach,* matzah balls, with his soup. One time, the Rebbe said to her, "In reward for these two *kneidlach* you will be blessed with two children." After this, Adil always regretted not having honored her distinguished guest with more *kneidlach (Aveneha Barzel,* p. 33 #43).

* * *

Barekh - Reciting Grace. The Breslover Chassidim had once gathered for a festive occasion. As was the custom, the men had their meal in one room, the women in the other. Seeing that it was taking a very long time, the women asked Adil, the Rebbe's daughter, if perhaps the men had already recited Grace and gone. "When my father's followers recite the Birkhat HaMazon, you *hear* it!" Soon afterwards, the women could clearly hear Grace being recited with great fervor (*Aveneha Barzel,* p. 34 #35).

* * *

matnat basar v'dam — dependent upon the gifts of men. In Lemberg (Lvov), there lived a very hospitable man who always had many guests. When Rebbe Nachman was in Lemberg (in 1808), he visited him. The Rebbe later said that he envied this person. The man sat at the head of his table, as a prominent rabbi would. However, whereas a rabbi receives money from others, this person distributed money to all those who came to him (*Aveneha Barzel,* p. 26 #18).

* * *

mekol tuv — all manner of good. Reb Noson was once in Uman. Moshe Landau (see *Until the Mashiach,* p. 75), who had just returned from a business trip and hadn't yet gone home, heard that Reb Noson was in town and ran to greet him. In the course of their conversation, Reb Noson began talking about the vanities of this world and how one is better off using his energy for seeking God. Landau questioned his wisdom, saying that he had just returned from Berdichov laden with many goods and presents of great value. "I have with me *kol tuv,* and you want to tell me its worthless?" Reb Noson said to him, "A husband can bring his wife the most exquisite ring as a gift — if she is unhappy with it, death might be preferable to the argument which is likely to erupt!" Landau went home. As it happened, he had brought back a gold ring for his wife. But she was so displeased with it, that it led to a fight. Landau went running back to Reb Noson. "Oy! Did you get it right!" (*Sipurim Niflaim,* p. 9).

*

Reb Noson retorted that it was better to pray slowly. Praying quickly, a person can rush through the entire prayer with foreign thoughts. But, by praying slowly, there was always a chance that he might properly concentrate in at least a few parts of the prayer (*Aveneha Barzel*, p. 61 #25).

* * *

Matzah. Rebbe Nachman would eat only Sh'murah Matzah, "guarded Matzah." Once, the Rebbe picked up a piece of Matzah and said, "Guarding the Covenant is Sh'murah Matzah!" (*Siach Sarfei Kodesh* 1-37).

*

Another time, the Rebbe took hold of a piece of Matzah and said, "Holding Matzah in one's hand is like holding God[liness] in one's hand" (*Ibid.,* 1-51).

*

Rebbe Nachman said that a person whose custom it is to eat *gebruchts,* matzah which came in contact with water, should continue to do so. However, if one has not been eating *gebruchts* on Pesach, then he should not change his custom (*Siach Sarfei Kodesh* 1-69; see *Orach Chaim,* 461:4 for discussion on these customs).

* * *

Korekh — A Sandwich. Once, on an Intermediate Day of Pesach, a young man came to Reb Avraham Sternhartz to speak to him about Rebbe Nachman's teachings. Since the young man had only recently become interested in Breslover Chassidut, Reb Avraham spoke with him at length. At the end of the conversation, Reb Avraham looked at the chassid and saw how sad and troubled the young man appeared. The young man sensed this and began to relate all the difficulties and opposition he was encountering since becoming a Breslover chassid.

Reb Avraham said to him, "Nu! Today is Pesach, the time of our redemption," and started speaking to him about the greatness of Pesach, the Exodus and the true meaning of freedom. He gave him much advice and encouragement to help him through these trying times. At the end of the conversation, Reb Avraham said to him, "PeSaCH has the same numerical value as [Rebbe] NaCHMaN (148). How can we connect Rebbe Nachman and the concepts of Pesach? The Haggadah teaches us: This is what Hillel did! He took the Pesach, Matzah and Maror, and ate everything together."

He advised this young man to accept Hillel's teaching. We can partake of the Pesach — the True Tzaddik — only by experiencing bitterness and difficulty! Then we can fully appreciate these teachings. "Now," Reb Avraham said, "go home and have a very joyous Pesach!" (Oral Tradition).

* * *

v'nomar...shirah chadashah — sing before Him... a new song. Reb Noson was with Reb Nachman of Tulchin at a *sholem zochor,* a welcoming of a newborn boy, in Lipovec. Reb Noson asked the cantor of the town to honor the gathering with a song, as was the custom. This *chazan,* an opponent of Breslover Chassidim, refused. Reb Noson then asked Reb Nachman to sing, which he did. Reb Noson later remarked that he hadn't been aware that Reb Nachman could sing. Actually, Reb Nachman did not at all have a good voice. It was only after Reb Noson told him to sing, that his voice acquired its pleasing and sweet quality. Reb Nachman of Tulchin later became *chazan* of the Breslov synagogue in Uman. Reb Abba of Tcherin said, "If the only thing gained from being in Uman on Rosh HaShanah is hearing Reb Nachman Tulchiner pray, this alone would make the journey worth it" (*Sichot V'Sipurim* p. 137 #48).

*

Right before moving to Breslov, Rebbe Nachman expressed his desire for Reb Chaikel, who served as the Rebbe's *chazan,* to abandon his businesses activities and devote himself to being a cantor; from which he could also earn his livelihood. The Rebbe told him, "If you move to with me to Breslov, you will become unique in your field [*chazanut*], the way I am in mine" (*Siach Sarfei Kodesh* 1-222).

* * *

me'mizrach shemesh — the rising of the sun. One Shavuot, the Rebbe sat down with his followers in the late afternoon, shortly before sunset. Stopping only to pray the Evening Service, they spent the entire night discussing Torah at the table. When the sun rose the next morning, the Rebbe remarked, "The sun should wonder. It left people at the table and returned to find them still there" (*Aveneha Barzel,* p. 35 #49).

* * *

m'keeme mei'afar dal — raises the poor out of the dust. After Reb Noson printed his *Likutey Tefilot* (the Collected Prayers), his followers said to him that he should be known as the Master of Prayer. [This is a reference to the the main character of the 12th story in *Rabbi Nachman's Stories,* entitled "The Master of Prayer."] Reb Noson replied, "The Master of Prayer is Rebbe Nachman. If I am considered as one of the King's men, I am the Bard. I can even find merit in a person who transgressed the entire Torah 800 times!" (*Siach Sarfei Kodesh* 1-591).

* * *

ki tanus — that you turn back and run. Someone suggested to Reb Noson that perhaps it was better to pray quickly, and in so doing, avoid foreign thoughts.

seepeyk tzorkheinu — provided for our needs. It was very close to Pesach and Reb Noson still had no money with which to purchase his family's needs for the holiday. On the morning of the last market day before Pesach, Reb Noson was about to leave for the morning prayers when his wife stopped him. In no uncertain terms she gave him to "understand" the severity of their situation. Or as Reb Noson himself described it, "She taught me a chapter in depression this morning." Even so, Reb Noson reassured himself and prayed with his usual devotion.

After the prayers, Reb Nachman of Tulchin noticed a complete change in Reb Noson's countenance. The expression on his mentor's face had entirely changed to one of hope and joy, as if all his prayers were answered. Later that day, some of Reb Noson's followers were among the people arriving in Breslov for the market day. They brought with them a considerable sum of money which they gave Reb Noson for Pesach. It was enough to cover all his expenses.

Reb Nachman of Tulchin later said, "There was a noticeable change on Reb Noson's face after he prayed. But, I did not see any change after he received the money." Such was the power of Reb Noson's faith: He was so certain that his prayers would be answered, it was as if he already had the money in his pocket (*Aveneha Barzel*, p. 75 #64).

* * *

natan lanu et haTorah — given us the Torah. Reb Noson said that the Torah — the study of the laws of Torah — God gave us through Moshe Rabeinu. But the Torah — the ways and means to actually feel and fulfill Torah — God gave us through Rebbe Nachman's teachings (*Kokhavey Or*, p. 69 #5). Reb Noson also said that Rebbe Nachman's way brought together the virtuous qualities of both the Chassidim and the Mitnagdim. The Chassidim of his day were very steeped in prayer, but were not deeply involved with Torah study. The Mitnagdim, on the other hand, were entirely given over to Torah study, but not devoted to prayer. Rebbe Nachman placed emphasis on both Torah and prayer [on each individually, and on the inter-connection between the two] (*Aveneha Barzel*, p. 52 #10). Thus, when someone asked the Rebbe, "How does one become a truly religious Jew?" Rebbe Nachman answered, "Only by prayer, and study, and prayer!" (*Rabbi Nachman's Wisdom* 287; *Siach Sarfei Kodesh* 1-220).

* * *

Beit HaBechirah — the Holy Temple. Someone once asked Reb Noson whether it was better to be a small person attached to a Tzaddik, or a great person by one's self? Reb Noson replied that the answer to this can be deduced from the Tabernacle. Any person, great or small, who wanted to donate something to the House of God, if he brought it to Moshe, it was accepted. If, however, he decided to donate something to the Tabernacle without bringing it to Moshe, it had no value (*Aveneha Barzel*, p. 74 #62).

* * *

began discussing various deep philosophical conundrums. Reb Noson became very excited. Shaking as he spoke, Reb Noson cried out, "How can you talk to me about God's existence? I tell you, I *saw* God!" (*Kokhavey Or,* p. 79 #32).

* * *

mateh — this staff. Reb Chaikel was once explaining to Rebbe Nachman that with the proper knowledge, it is possible to pick up a snake without being bitten. Rebbe Nachman threw his handkerchief to the ground where it turned into a snake. Then he said to Reb Chaikel, "Pick it up!" which he did. "Don't hold it in your hand because I've told you to, hold it because of your knowledge!" Reb Chaikel declined (*Aveneha Barzel,* p. #73).

* * *

va'ya'ar... va'ya'aminu — when Israel saw... they believed. Reb Nachman of Tulchin once told Reb Noson that he regretted not having been born when Rebbe Nachman was still alive. He would have very much wanted to see him. "Who then saw the Rebbe?" asked Reb Noson. "Do you think Yosef Paronek [the boatman who ferried people across the river] saw him? *Seeing* Rebbe Nachman is to understand his teachings and engrave them upon your heart!" (*Siach Sarfei Kodesh* 1-735).

* * *

vaya'aminu — they believed. Reb Noson said, "Mashiach will have more difficulty with the chassidim [to convince them of who he is], than he will with the atheists. He will perform one miracle and the atheists will believe in him. But the chassidim...." (*Siach Sarfei Kodesh* 1-525).

* * *

kama ma'alot tovot — so many favors. Reb Meir of Teplik was visiting Reb Noson. Asked about a certain person living in Teplik, Reb Meir replied very matter-of-factly, as if to say that the man wasn't much to talk about. Reb Noson said to him, "If you want look at things negatively and with an unfavorable eye you'll find fault with everyone in the whole world. Think of the people living in Teplik. Start with the person living at the edge of town. If you look at him carefully, you'll certainly find some shortcomings. Now go from house to house until you get to *your* house. Are you the only good Jew in the whole town?" "Me? I'm also not very righteous," Reb Meir quickly replied. "If you're not, then who is?" asked Reb Noson. "But, if you'd look at the world favorably," he continued, "you'd find good in even the worst person; and then certainly in everyone else" (*Kokhavey Or,* p. 75 #18).

* * *

Rebbe Nachman taught that we should meditate in the fields at night (*Likutey Moharan* I, 52). When Calev went to Hebron to pray at the graves of the Patriarchs, he was in considerable danger of being caught by the inhabitants of the land. He went anyway, because a person under pressure and in desperate need of something, doesn't take the dangers into account. He knows only that he must act (*Zohar* III:158b). Reb Noson taught that the same is true in serving God, especially in our practicing *hitbodedut,* meditation in the fields. We should feel the pressure we are under — from the Evil Inclination — and not make an accounting of all the so called dangers involved in serving God (*Kokhavey Or,* p. 71 #9).

*

On another occasion, when discussing this lesson and the practice of going into the fields at night, Reb Noson told of the time the Haidemacks [a band of Cossaks] fell upon a town and forced its inhabitants to flee. Among those running away was a man known to be afraid of literally everything. While fleeing, this man found himself alone in the town's cemetery. Having no choice, he spent the entire night there. The next day, when the inhabitants returned to the town, they asked him, "How were you able to stay alone in the cemetery?" "I was too afraid to be afraid!" he replied (*Siach Sarfei Kodesh* 1-555).

* * *

va'yotzi'einu — brought us out. One of the six questions put to a person by the Heavenly Court is: Did you hope for the Redemption (*Shabbat* 31a). Reb Nachman of Tulchin said that this refers not only to the redemption of the Jewish people in its entirety, but also to the personal redemption for each individual. "Did you hope for God's salvation to bring you out of your troubles? Or, did you lose hope and give up?" (*Aveneha Barzel,* p. 80).

* * *

geeluy Shekhinah — revelation of the Divine Presence. Reb Noson would recite the Haggadah with great fervor and emotion. Often, the members of his family were too afraid to look at him during the Seder. So great was the awe and fear visible upon Reb Noson's face. His grandson, Reb Avraham Sternhartz, related that the Seder night was a very trying time for Reb Noson's family. They were never sure that he would make it through the Seder without fainting. Once, while reciting these words, "The revelation of the Divine Presence!" he became so filled with emotion and a yearning for God that he actually did faint (*Oral Tradition*).

*

Reb Noson was once talking to Hirsh Ber, one of the *maskilim,* a secular Jew, with whom Rebbe Nachman had dealings (see *Until The Mashiach,* p. 75). Hirsh Ber

Reb Noson and his wife also had difficulties having children. When he mentioned this to Rebbe Nachman, the Rebbe told him that he would have to "pay" for children. The Rebbe then said, "For this that I made you my follower and thus closer to God, *I* will have to pay you, as it is my merit. But, for you to be blessed with children — *you* must bring a *pidyon,* a redemption." Reb Noson said that he, in any case, intended to bring the Rebbe a gift of fine chairs. Reb Noson had six chairs made for the Rebbe and he eventually had six children, five sons and a daughter *(Aveneha Barzel,* p. 26 #19). Reb Noson later said that had he known he was going to have as many children as the amount of chairs, he would have ordered a dozen *(Siach Sarfei Kodesh* 1-231).

* * *

zu hadchak — the pressure. Another of the Rebbe's followers, Reb Chaikel, had a relative who was extremely poor. Once, while traveling with Rebbe Nachman, Reb Chaikel instructed the wagon driver to stop at this relative's house. Once inside, Reb Chaikel pointed out the man's poverty and asked the Rebbe to give him a blessing for wealth. The Rebbe said to Reb Chaikel, "I have no blessings for him. If you want him to have a blessing, you give it." After making certain that he'd heard correctly and obtaining the Rebbe's assurances that he wouldn't mind his "presumptuousness," Reb Chaikel emptied a pitcher of water across the floor. Then he spread the water in all directions, saying, "Abundance to the east, abundance to the west, to the north and the south." Then, Rebbe Nachman and Reb Chaikel left.

Shortly afterwards, a group of merchants came to this man's home asking to purchase food and drink. Replying that he had none, they gave him the sufficient money to make these purchases for them. From then on, whenever these merchants came to the area, they would lodge at his house and they eventually commissioned him to sell their wares for them. Before long, the man prospered and became very wealthy.

Whenever he came to Breslov, this man had always made certain to visit the Rebbe. But now, the more he prospered, the more engrossed he became in his business dealings. He no longer had the time to visit the Rebbe. Once, while rushing around Breslov on business, he passed by the Rebbe's house. Rebbe Nachman saw him and called him in. Looking directly at him, the Rebbe said, "Did you glance at the sky today?" The man replied that he hadn't. Calling him to the window, the Rebbe said, "Tell me, what do you see?" "I see wagons and horses and people scurrying about," he replied. "Believe me," Rebbe Nachman said to him, "Fifty years from now there will be other market days. There will be other horses, other wagons, different people. What is here today will no longer be. I ask you, what pressure are you under? What's making you so busy that you don't even have time to look at Heaven?" *(Kokhavey Or,* p. 41 #5).

*

When Reb Noson became a follower of Rebbe Nachman, he would spend an occasional Shabbat in Breslov. On Friday night, after everyone had gone to sleep, he would descend to the bank of the Bug River, and spend the night crying out to God. He would say, "God! There is a fire burning in Breslov. Enflame my heart with that fire!" (Siach Sarfei Kodesh 1-689).

* * *

va'yeianchu — the children of Israel moaned. Reb Noson once stopped at an inn together with a friend. While eating, a small bone became lodged in Reb Noson's throat. Opening his mouth wide, as though he were choking, the bone became unstuck. "Did you see," said Reb Noson to his friend, "when the bone was stuck I opened my mouth and looked upward? There is nothing else we can do but to look to Heaven for all our needs, even when we cannot speak, but only moan" (Kokhavey Or, p. 71 #8).

* * *

preeshut derekh eretz — separation of husband and wife. Reb Noson said, "If I had wanted to include in my works advice for married couples, I would have had to double my writings" (Siach Sarfei Kodesh 1-740). [Translator's note: Reb Noson's magnum opus, the Likutey Halakhot, is an eight volume (approx. 2,000 pages) work filled with practical advice on how to overcome the difficulties we encounter in this world and how to recognize God in all aspects of life.]

* * *

amaleinu, eilu ha'banim — our burden, these are the children. Reb Noson said, "Ask anyone who ever lived, 'For what or whom are you working so hard?' and he'll tell you, 'for my children.' In that case, after all this time, our children should be perfect. Why else would it be worth sacrificing our entire lives? I fear," he concluded, "that I am still waiting to see this perfect child" (Oral Tradition).

*

Rebbe Nachman's daughter, Adil, was childless for many years. She had suffered a series of miscarriages and had had a number of her children die in infancy. After one such occasion, Rebbe Nachman went to console his daughter. Sitting between her husband, Reb Yoske, and Adil, the Rebbe said, "Believe me, the world will yet envy you for your offspring." Turning to Reb Yoske the Rebbe said, "You will live to see children"; then facing Adil he added, "and grandchildren." Reb Yoske passed away young. However Adil, the eldest of Rebbe Nachman's children, did live to see her grandchildren (Aveneha Barzel, p. 22 #7).

*

va'yiven...lePharaoh — they built for Pharaoh. People work their whole lives. But, toward what end? What are they hoping to build with their efforts. Reb Noson remarked, "Whoever doesn't think about what awaits him when his time comes, of such a person I have nothing to say. He is no better than an animal. However, for the person who thinks of his end, of what will happen when he reaches his Judgment Day — it is for him that I wrote my work [*Likutey Halakhot*]. Such a person will certainly find that life presents many obstacles to his spiritual development, and this book will strengthen and help him along the way" (*Kokhavey Or*, p. 74 #13).

* * *

b'pharekh — slave labor. Reb Nachman of Tulchin labored tirelessly to erect Reb Noson's *sukkah*. That evening, while sitting in the *sukkah*, Reb Nachman remarked, "There is a different feeling of joy and satisfaction when sitting in a *sukkah* which one has worked very hard to build." Reb Noson replied, "You have not yet tried this. Spend an entire day crying out to God: 'Master of the Universe! Let me taste the true taste of *sukkah!*' Then see what feelings a person can experience in the *sukkah*" (*Aveneha Barzel*, p. 52 #12).

*

The Rebbe once said, "Why do you work so hard when nothing will remain? Labor less so that something will remain!" [As one labors for the material things of this world, his time is taken up. But he must eventually leave it all behind. By working less for the physical, a person can have time for that which does remain with him — his spiritual accomplishments] (*Siach Sarfei Kodesh* 1- 263).

* * *

vanitz'ak — and we cried out. Reb Noson very much wanted people to cry out to God, using his *Likutey Tefilot* to get us started. "Now that the prayers [the *Likutey Tefilot*] have come out in the world, people will have to give an account for each day they failed to recite them" (*Kokhavey Or*, p. 77 #24). Reb Noson also said, "People ask if there is *ruach hakodesh*, divine inspiration, in these prayers. They are even higher than *ruach hakodesh*, for they emanate from the 50th level!" (*Ibid.*, #25).

*

Once, Reb Noson attended the funeral of a person he hardly knew. "A person always has to cry before God," he explained. "When the situation presents itself, we should take the opportunity to pray" (*Siach Sarfei Kodesh* 1-635).

*

Mashiach will come. Therefore, it is not right to build a permanent home outside the Holy Land." [Purchasing an already built home seems not to be included in the Rebbe's objection.] Only few of the Rebbe's followers were capable of fulfilling this (*Siach Sarfei Kodesh* 1-35).

* * *

m'tzuyanim — Jews were distinctive. Reb Noson said, "No matter what I hear from a Jew's lips — even things that are not in accordance with our faith — I know that deep in his heart, he will always be a Jew" (*Kokhavey Or*, p. 79 #35).

* * *

paru... va'timaley — fruitful... the land was filled with them. The Rebbe said that each couple should have as many children as they can. "No matter how they will turn out!" This is because when Mashiach comes, he will rectify everybody in the world, from the time of Creation and for all time (*Aveneha Barzel*, p. 21 #4). This ties in with the Talmudic teaching that Mashiach will only come once all the souls that were created have been born into this world (*Nidah* 13b). Thus, each additional child, irregardless of what type a person he will be or what hardships he may have to encounter in life, hastens the coming of the Mashiach.

*

Another time the Rebbe said, "Even Mashiach's parents won't be so *ay, ay, ay...*" As if to say, even they won't be such outstanding people (*Siach Sarfei Kodesh* 1-83).

* * *

tikrenah milchamah — beset by war. Once, a man came crying to Rebbe Nachman that his daughter, an only child, had disappeared. The man had searched everywhere and was now beside himself. "The young woman is in the home of the village priest," Rebbe Nachman told him. "Quickly, hire a coach and send two men to get her. When they come to the priest's home, your daughter will be standing outside. She will readily go with them." The man followed the Rebbe's instructions, and sure enough the man's daughter returned home. When the priest realized that the young woman whom he'd convinced to convert had been spirited away from him, he incited the gentiles to take up arms against the Jews. "Go outside with clubs and sticks in your hands, and stand up to them," said the Rebbe. When the gentiles saw the Jews coming out to face them in battle, they retreated. The Rebbe later arranged a marriage for this young woman and she was blessed with sons who were rabbis and distinguished figures in their communities (*Kokhavey Or*, p. 52 #26).

* * *

you, Shmuel, take the soup!" No one understood what the Rebbe meant. After they returned home, Reb Abba passed away. His son, Reb Shmuel, became very wealthy (*Aveneha Barzel*, p. 48 #76).

*

The Rebbe instructed Reb Ber of Tcherin to give not ten, but twenty percent of his earnings to the poor. Reb Ber fulfilled this during his lifetime. Shortly before he passed away, he said, "With my twenty percent I am not afraid of what awaits me in the Heavenly court! I'll come through okay" (*Kokhavey Or*, p. 24 #19).

* * *

tzei u'lmad — go and learn. Reb Noson related, "When I first began studying Torah, I found it very difficult. I entered the study hall intending to devote all my energy into the studies. But as I began, I inevitably encountered numerous diversions. No matter how determined I was, each day brought a new diversion and a different distraction, one which I had not anticipated and was helpless to avoid. I was at my wit's end, at the point of giving up. But then I came to Rebbe Nachman. The Rebbe told me that 'A little is also good!' Hearing this changed my attitude totally. If I could not study as much as I desired, I was satisfied with whatever I did manage to accomplish. This way, I countered my difficulty in studying by grabbing in a little bit here, a little bit there, until I developed into a serious student."

[Translator's note: From this, one can understand Reb Noson's great modesty and humbleness. He was 22 when he became a follower of Rebbe Nachman. Nine years earlier, at the age of 13, he was married to the daughter of Rabbi Dovid Zvi Orbach, a prominent Torah scholar and head of the Kaminetz-Podolsk Rabbinical Court. Rabbi Dovid Zvi recognized Reb Noson's virtues, particularly his achievements in Torah, and therefore chose him as his son-in-law, saying, "I see he has a strong shoulder" — a reference to a strong commitment to Torah study (*Siach Sarfei Kodesh* 1-615). Furthermore, by the time he came in contact with the Rebbe, Reb Noson was very well versed in all of the Talmud, the Codes, etc. There is even a tradition that he had already mastered the "seven wisdoms" (mathematics, rhetoric, astronomy, etc.; see *Tzaddik* #69, 313, 333, 338). One only has to look at Reb Noson's writings to see the length and breadth of his knowledge, and to know that in his comment about serious studying, Reb Noson was referring to a level of such intensity and concentration that is almost never achieved by even the most studious of scholars.]

* * *

lagur ba'aretz — to live in this land temporarily. Rebbe Nachman was insistent that a Jew not build his own home in the Diaspora. "A Jew must always hope that

Yaakov u'vanav — Yaakov and sons went down to Egypt. Reb Nachman of Tulchin, the most devoted of Reb Noson's followers, became very annoyed whenever he heard someone complaining against Heaven. People should realize that everything comes from God, and that judgments from Heaven are true Judgments. One should never complain that His ways are unjust, God forbid (*Sichot V'Sipurim,* p. 114 #23). [Though it pre-dated them, we see that the Patriarchs knew about the Heavenly decree of exile which their descendants would suffer, and they accepted it as God's Will.] When Reb Noson's enemies succeeded in getting the authorities to banish him from Breslov (1835-1839), he saw it as Heaven's decree and refused to allow his supporters to say or do anything that could harm his enemies (*Ibid.,* #24).

In the early part of 1835, a ruthless and unrelenting campaign was begun against Reb Noson, to prevent him from spreading Rebbe Nachman's teachings. His enemies informed the government that he was operating an illegal printing press in his home. Until an official case could be presented, the authorities installed a tannery in Reb Noson's home. When the eve of Pesach arrived and the time to search for Chametz had come, Reb Noson was allowed only one room for himself. The other rooms of his home were occupied by gentiles, none of whom were about to remove their bread and grain products for his sake.

But, when Reb Noson recited the blessing for the removal of Chametz, he said it with such feeling and fervor that the gentile workers were deeply impressed by his righteousness. They promised they would do everything possible to enable Reb Noson to keep Pesach properly. By the next morning, these gentiles were gone from the house.

That night, at the Seder, Reb Noson was his usual, awe-inspiring self. He recited the Haggadah and fulfilled the other mitzvot of the night with great devotion and concentration. Once the festive meal had begun, the family began discussing Reb Noson's enemies and the suffering they were inflicting upon him. Reb Noson became upset by this talk. "On a holy and precious night as this, how can you talk of such matters. And besides, these people you are talking about are our brothers! We should look to see how we can help and rectify them, not talk against or even about them!" (*Yemey HaTalaot,* p. 172- 173).

* * *

bir'khush gadol — with great wealth. Rebbe Nachman made it clear that he wanted his followers to be by him for Rosh HaShanah. In 1809, two of his followers, Reb Abba and his son, Reb Shmuel, were delayed by heavy rains and could not find a wagon driver willing to take them to Breslov in time for the holiday. Reb Abba was carrying a beautiful silver goblet which he intended to present to the Rebbe. Now, there seemed to be no alternative but to sell the goblet and use the money to induce a driver to make the difficult trip.

When Reb Abba arrived in Breslov, the Rebbe said to him, "In *this* world, there is no suitable reward for the sacrifice which you made on my behalf. And

Nachman responded, "On Rosh Chodesh, one goes to mikvah before praying" (*Aveneha Barzel,* p. 22 #6).

* * *

me'tchilah... la'avodato — former times... to serve Him. Someone came to Reb Noson, gave him some money for a *pidyon,* a redemption, and asked him to pray for him. Before Reb Noson could even ask the person what he wanted him to pray for, the man started walking away. Reb Noson said to him, "Do you remember the last time you were in trouble and came to me for help? You promised God you would serve Him. God helped you, but you forgot your promise. Then it happened again and again and.... Now you are coming again for help and want me to pray for you once more. Am I your employee that you can ask me to do this for you time and again? These troubles come from Above so that *you* should turn to God and serve Him!" (*Siach Sarfei Kodesh* 1-700).

* * *

va'ekach et Avraham — and I took Avraham and led him. [Avraham was chosen because God knew that Avraham would raise his children to serve Him and teach them to be righteous people; Genesis 18:19.] Our forefather Avraham would tell his followers that one day, God would give the Land over to his seed. Reb Noson said to his followers, "I say to you that when Mashiach comes there will be Yeshivot established to study Rebbe Nachman's teachings!" (*Aveneha Barzel,* p. 89).

* * *

mei'eyver hanahar — from beyond the Euphrates. In the wee hours of the morning of Shabbat Chanukah, 1844, two weeks before Reb Noson passed away, word had gotten out that the building which housed the *mikvah* had caved in making it impossible to immerse. At daybreak, it was learned that the *mikvah* was still intact and only a distant part of the building had been destroyed. Reb Noson, who was quite ill at the time, began speaking about the importance of *mikvah.* When Ezra brought the Jewish people back across the Euphrates River to the Holy Land during the Persian exile, he found that many of his brethren had intermarried. Ezra was appalled and outraged. The communal leaders came to him saying, "But is there no *mikvah,* no hope?" (Ezra 10:2). Reb Noson pointed out that the word *mikvah* has two meanings: it refers to the ritual bath and it means hope. Whoever sins, no matter how terrible his transgression, there is still great hope — so great is *mikvah,* it can bring him spiritual cleanliness (*Kokhavey Or,* p. 80 #37).

* * *

awake during the wee hours of the morning could tell when it was three a.m. by Reb Ber's arrival at the synagogue (*Kokhavey Or,* p. 25 #21).

* * *

z'man kriat Sh'ma — reading the morning Sh'ma. When asked by Reb Meir of Teplik how people in Germany [the *maskilim*] could shave their beards and *peyot* with a razor, a daily transgression of five Torah prohibitions, Reb Noson remarked, "And how can they [the 'religious' people in Russia] daily miss out reading the morning Sh'ma in its correct time?" (*Kokhavey Or,* p. 75 #17).

* * *

ad shedarsha — until Ben Zoma explained it. Reb Simchah once asked Reb Noson whether the novel insights and teachings which a later Tzaddik finds in a Talmudic passage were known to the Tanna, the early sage who authored the original passage. Reb Noson's answer was that they were not known. But, because the Tanna was a truly righteous person, his statement was enveloped with such holiness and *ruach hakodesh,* divine inspiration, that it emanated directly from God Himself. It therefore embodied all the future insights and teachings which various Tzaddikim would find in it (*Kokhavey Or,* p. 70 #7).

* * *

chakham... rasha — wise one... wicked one. The Breslover Chassidim in Heisin suffered unrelenting opposition from the rabbi of their town. When the situation became unbearable, the chassidim brought their plight to the Rebbe. Rebbe Nachman told one of their number, Reb Reuven Yosef, to "sit at the door of the rabbi's house. Whenever this rabbi issues a ruling, tell those who asked the questions to return to the rabbi and inform him that you disagree with his decision! That the law is actually just the opposite of what he ruled! Do not even bother to check the law in the Codes. Just rely on me." Reb Reuven Yosef was himself very learned and well respected. When he did as the Rebbe had told him, the people of Heisin began to doubt their rabbi's rulings. The scholars of the town did their own checking, and found that in each case their rabbi's ruling was indeed wrong. This rabbi was forced to relinquish his position and leave town in shame (*Kokhavey Or,* p. 50 #19; *Siach Sarfei Kodesh* 1-128).

* * *

Rosh Chodesh. One Rosh Chodesh morning, as the quorum began the Hodu prayer, Rebbe Nachman walked over to Reb Naftali and said to him, "Naftali, *mikvah?!*" Reb Naftali answered that he intended to immerse after praying. Rebbe

Rebbe's gravesite on the eve of Rosh HaShanah and then join in the *kibutz*, the gathering for the Rosh HaShanah prayers. Each succeeding year saw an increase in the number of those who made the journey to Uman. However, not having a synagogue of their own, it became more and more difficult to find a suitable place for the growing ranks of Breslover Chassidim to pray. Reb Noson realized that if a synagogue were not built to house the Rosh HaShanah gathering, the large crowd would inevitably start to dwindle. With each passing year, the difficulties were becoming harder to bear.

In 1830, Reb Noson started collecting funds to build a Breslover synagogue in Uman. He began in the town of Ladizin, which had a large contingent of Breslover Chassidim. His plan was received with great enthusiasm. One chassid who was particularly excited was Reb Menachem Mendel, a poverty stricken schoolteacher. Hearing Reb Noson describe the project, Reb Menachem Mendel ran home to get his entire savings, a total of *two rubles*. At first, Reb Noson did not want to accept his contribution. He knew the full extent of the poverty by which Reb Menachem Mendel was afflicted, and did not think it right to take his last penny, his bread money. Reb Menachem Mendel would not hear of it. He begged and pleaded with Reb Noson to accept his gift. How could he be denied this opportunity to take part in such a great mitzvah! Reb Noson pondered this last point. Which would be the greater pity? To deny him the mitzvah or the money? Reb Menachem Mendel was the first contributor towards the Breslov synagogue in Uman (*Sichot V'Sipurim*, pp. 140-143).

Upon completing the building in 1834, Reb Noson said, "We have to ask ourselves, how was the synagogue built? Was it with the money of the wealthy or the desires of those afflicted by poverty? It would be correct to say that it was the desires of the poor which built it!" (*Reb Eliyahu Chaim Rosen*). [Translator's note: The building, which was renewed by Reb Sender Terhovitza in 1865-66, is still standing today.]

* * *

v'eelu lo hotzee — had not brought out our fathers. Rebbe Nachman said, "Where would we be today if our forefathers had not been brought out of Egypt? We would be *tzugainers*, nomads" (*Siach Sarfei Kodesh* 1-7).

* * *

hegee'ah z'man — the time has arrived. Reb Ber of Tcherin very much wanted to rise at midnight to recite *Chatzot,* the Midnight Lament. But he found it impossible to wake up. When nothing else worked, he hired a man to wake him and stand over him until he got dressed. However, Reb Ber would get headaches from lack of sleep. Finally, Rebbe Nachman told him that his *Chatzot* was at three in the morning, thus giving him a few more hours of unbroken sleep. "Sleep and eat, just watch your time," the Rebbe told him. After this, those chassidim

Reb Noson managed to catch a glimpse of Rebbe Nachman sitting at the Seder. He was so impressed by what he saw, that he never forgot it. It was, in fact, the only time Reb Noson got to see the Rebbe at the Seder, as Rebbe Nachman's custom was to spend the Seder night alone with his family (*Aveneha Barzel*, p. 16 #13). Reb Noson also did not have his followers join him for the Pesach Seder (*Siach Sarfei Kodesh* 1- 791).

* * *

Kadesh — Reciting Kiddush. Once, Rabbi Nochum of Tchernoble spent Shabbat with Rabbi Dovid Zvi Orbach, Reb Noson's father-in-law. After they'd returned from synagogue, Rabbi Dovid Zvi said to his distinguished guest, "I would offer you Kiddush, but my wife has not yet returned from synagogue." Rabbi Nochum remarked, "The Baal Shem Tov taught that in Mashiach's time all the women's sections in the synagogues will be closed down." After telling this story, Reb Noson commented, "But Rebbe Nachman taught us otherwise. The Rebbe taught that a woman's prayers are very, very important in God's eyes" (*Siach Sarfei Kodesh* 1-663).

* * *

Yachatz — Breaking the Matzah. Reb Noson once said, "Nothing can help a person break his unwanted desires except prayer. The reason for this is quite simple. Normally, a person who breaks his desires, is left with two desires; just as when one breaks anything and is left with two pieces." But with prayer, a person is able to free himself of all undesirable desires (*Siach Sarfei Kodesh* 1-511).

* * *

Yachatz-Magid — Breaking-Telling. A man once came complaining to Reb Noson that he had to repeat his prayers over and over again. The man explained that he felt obliged to do this because it was very difficult for him to recite the words with the proper intentions. Reb Noson said, "Is this the only way for you to serve God? With these particular words? If these words come out broken, [*Yachatz,*] then go on to some other devotion — such as the Psalms, or another prayer..." [*Magid*] (*Aveneha Barzel*, p. 90).

* * *

ha lachma anya — the bread of affliction. Rosh HaShanah is, without a doubt, the most important day in the Breslov calendar. Years after Rebbe Nachman's passing, his chassidim continue to gather in Uman for the holiday. In 1811, the first year following the Rebbe's passing, there were sixty followers who came to pray at the

We present here a collection of stories and anecdotes about Rebbe Nachman, his closest chassid, Reb Noson, and other Breslover Chassidim. The theme of each story is generally connected to some aspect of Pesach and the Seder night, and more specifically to the excerpt from the Haggadah text with which the story has been prefaced.

Preparing for the holidays. It happened that the Rebbe and Reb Noson were once invited to the *sukkah* of a simple Jew. When Reb Noson questioned the validity of the *sukkah*, Rebbe Nachman remarked, "A Jew works very hard to build his *sukkah*, and you seek to invalidate it based on stringencies found in the Codes?!" (*Aveneha Barzel*, p. 25 #17).

*

When Rebbe Nachman was young, he himself sought to fulfill the strictest opinions found in the Codes. On one occasion, he even considered moving to another city, where the water supply could be better guarded during the holiday. Such was the seriousness with which the Rebbe took the prohibition against Chametz on Pesach (see *Orach Chaim* 467:13). However, as he grew older, he came to realize that stringencies in keeping the Codes was actually superfluous. The Rebbe said, "If only we were able to perform the mitzvot with simple sincerity. 'The Torah was not given to ministering angels' (*Berakhot* 25b). A person should choose one mitzvah and observe it strictly, with all its fine points; all the other mitzvot should be kept without any stringencies whatsoever" (*Rabbi Nachman's Wisdom* #235).

*

Reb Noson once remarked, "Sometimes, because a person tries excessively hard to perform a mitzvah in the very best way possible, he ends up not performing the mitzvah at all" (*Siach Sarfei Kodesh* 1-571).

* * *

The Seder. In the spring of 1803, the Rebbe married off his daughter Sarah in the city of Medvedevka. Reb Noson, who lived in Nemirov, made the journey to be with the Rebbe for Purim and Pesach (see *Until the Mashiach* pp. 94-98). On the Seder night, Reb Noson prayed the Evening Prayer with great fervor, finishing long after everyone else. Because Rebbe Nachman's followers prayed in his house, the Rebbe, who prayed in the adjoining room, was able to hear Reb Noson recite the blessing for Hallel [it being the Chassidic custom to recite the Hallel with its blessing following the Evening Prayer on the first night of the holiday.] Rebbe Nachman said, "Lucky are the parents of such a son." As he was leaving,

APPENDIX B
Pesach Anecdotes

The Jews also had a stone which followed them from one encampment to the next. This stone miraculously provided them with fresh water in the desert. Whenever the Jewish People camped, the head of each tribe would take his staff and draw a line in the ground running from the stone to the area of his tribe. The water would then flow from the stone, reaching every Jew as he needed it. In addition to this, grass and trees grew around the stone to sustain all the livestock.

And then there was the Seven Clouds of Glory which stayed with the Children of Israel during the forty years the Jews spent in the wilderness. These miraculous Clouds not only kept them completely hidden from sight, but also provided them with many additional benefits. The Clouds functioned as their guide, pointing out their designated route and straightening the road upon which they journeyed. They never had to climb a mountain or descend a valley. In addition, the Clouds provided the Jews with protection from the harsh elements of the desert and from attack by their enemies. Though they went out to battle against Amalek, the Emorites, Midianites, Sichon and Og, not one Jewish soldier died in battle.

These Clouds entirely surrounded the Jews, so that when they traveled, the Clouds actually carried them: "I carried you as on the wings of eagles." Furthermore, each day the Clouds would clean and press the garments of the Jews, obviating the need to expend energy on caring for their clothing which remained in perfect condition throughout their sojourn in the desert. As for their children's clothing, as a child grew, his clothes grew with him.

With the erection of the Tabernacle (after the Torah was given), which was as wondrous and incredibly beautiful as the Creation itself, the Jews were provided with yet another miracle: a daily revelation of the Divine Presence.

The Jews traveled on until they reached Mount Sinai. They camped there, at the foot of the mountain. The Revelation they were about to witness was certainly one of the greatest miracles of all time. Yet, the Haggadah tells us: "If God had led us to Mount Sinai, but not given us the Torah, *Dayeinu!*" The question is obvious. Was it not the purpose of the Exodus so that the Jews might receive the Torah. Of what value would it be to arrive at Mount Sinai, if the Torah were not given? *Rashi* explains that when the Jews camped at the foot of the mountain, they camped as "one man with one heart" (*Rashi,* Exodus 19:2). The commentaries add, "Reaching the foot of the mountain would itself have been enough, if only to attain such unity!" For the Jews to have achieved such a level of unity and togetherness, this alone made it worth bringing them to Mount Sinai!

Nevertheless, the most significant miracle was the Revelation at Mount Sinai. There, God appeared to the Children of Israel and gave them the Torah. The world and everything in it was created for this moment of the Revelation; so that all could receive His word and know that God brought about the Jewish Exodus from Egypt. The Revelation at Mount Sinai and Giving of the Torah is the single most important reason why the holiday of Pesach, and specifically the Seder Night, is celebrated.

34

king of Ninveh. When Yonah was sent to prophesy in Ninveh that unless the people repented they would be destroyed (Jonah 3), it was Pharaoh's first-hand experience of God's power which encouraged the people to return from their evil ways.

Originally, the sea had swallowed up all the Egyptians and their horses. This made the Jews anxious and afraid. "Just as we came out of the sea on this side, perhaps the Egyptians will emerge in another area. How can we be certain that they are dead?" God then caused the sea to spit out the Egyptian bodies and all their horses. Anticipating victory, the Egyptians had adorned themselves and their horses with whatever remaining gold and precious stones they could find. This booty, which was far in excess of what the Jews had taken with them from Egypt, now lay on the shore. Though Moshe now wanted the Children of Israel to move forward, on to the Holy Land, with such huge fortunes tempting them he had a very difficult time getting the Jews to move on from the Red Sea (much like today).

*

After witnessing all the wondrous miracles which had been performed on their behalf, the Children of Israel began to sing in praise of God. They also looked to the future, praying that they be worthy of receiving the Torah, entering the Holy Land and building the Holy Temple. The verse tells us that "they believed in God and His servant, Moshe." The *Mekhilta* comments: "If they believed in God, what was this belief they had in Moshe? From this we are to understand that whenever a person has faith in the true Tzaddik, it is as if he believes in the Creator of the World." The reverse of this is also true. One cannot attain true belief in God unless he has faith in the true Tzaddikim, for they are His messengers — bringing His word into this world.

Nor did God's miracles end with the Splitting of the Red Sea. Manna descended every day for the forty years the Jews were in the desert, with each family being provided with a daily portion according to its size. In early morning, dew would descend and upon it the Manna. Then another layer of dew would descend on top of the Manna to protect it. When the Jews would rise, the miraculous Manna was already waiting for them. If, however, they delayed taking their daily allotment until after three hours of the day, the Manna would be absorbed by the dew and flow away from the camp. Eventually, this mixture of Manna and dew make its way to some distant area where the wild animals would drink it. Any person who then caught one of these animals and ate it would taste the special taste of the Manna and praise God and His nation, the Jews.

On Shabbat the Manna would not descend. Rather, a double allotment would descend on Friday, for both days. In addition, the Manna came to each person according to his deeds. If he were righteous, the Manna would descend right next to his tent. If not, he would have to go out to get it. Furthermore, every person could taste in the Manna any taste he wanted. It would be warm or cold, depending on his particular preference at that time! The Manna was also completely absorbed by the bodies of those who ate it, producing no waste matter at all.

Jew emerged on the far side, the last Egyptian set foot on the seabed. To remind the Egyptians of what they had done to the Jews, God turned the seabed into deep mud and thick clay, causing the Egyptian horses and chariots to become stuck in the mire. Then the Clouds of Glory and the Pillar of Fire began heating the clay. As the chariots started burning, havoc and confusion overwhelmed the Egyptian camp. Without warning, the walls of water which the sea had formed fell back into place, swallowing the entire Egyptian army in one fell swoop.

This trapping of the Egyptians in the bowels of the sea sparked off an argument in heaven. The protecting angel of Egypt pleaded on their behalf before God. "Have the Egyptians destroyed and killed all the Jews? True, they burdened them with slave labor, but the Children of Israel left Egypt alive and with full pay!" the angel protested. "Let us sit in judgment on this matter," God answered, as He convened the Heavenly Tribunal. First the Almighty stated His case: "Was it not Yosef who saved Egypt from famine? And how did the Egyptians show their gratitude? They enslaved Yosef's descendants. Then they issued harsh decrees against the Jews. I instructed Moshe to return to Egypt and redeem the Jews. What was Pharaoh's response? He proclaimed even harsher edicts against them. Finally, I Myself redeemed them. Now the Egyptians are chasing after the Children of Israel to either kill them or enslave them once again. I ask you, upon whom should I have compassion?!" Though it was now Egypt's protecting angel's turn to speak, he had nothing with which to counter God's argument. The angel could only ask for compassion. "You are a God of mercy. I beseech You to take pity on my children!" At that moment, the defending angel of the Jews, Michael, descended to Egypt and took the body of a Jewish child which had been embedded in the bricks. He presented this exhibit before the Heavenly Court, saying, "Upon whom shall God have mercy? Upon these wicked Egyptians who used the bodies of innocent children for bricks?" With this, the death-sentence against the Egyptians was sealed.

The vengeance with which the sea walls came down upon the Egyptians caused the axles of their chariots to snap. The Egyptians were violently tossed back and forth, and all their bones were broken. But God kept their souls intact. He wanted them to feel every ounce of pain and suffering. He wanted to give them a taste of what the Jews had experienced in Egypt. Many Egyptians were thrown from their chariots, causing them to be trampled by their fellow soldiers and their horses. Those at the rear of the Egyptian troops tried to return to the shore. Yet, even if they succeeded in getting onto dry land, the water rose onto the shore and swallowed them up. God also kept the riders glued to their horses, hurling them about in the water like food in a boiling pot.

And, just as the Egyptians who chased after the Jews were punished, so were the Egyptians who remained in Egypt. They were killed by fire and other equally horrible forms of death. God made it so that each Egyptian was forced to watch the suffering of his fellow countryman. This forced them to finally recognize that they were being punished by the Hand of God and not through sorcery or natural disasters. Pharaoh was the only Egyptian allowed to survive this ordeal. The Midrash teaches that he lived for nearly another thousand years and became the

32

God performed numerous miracles for the Jews when they crossed the Red Sea. These included:

1) The actual splitting of the sea.

2) The seabed instantaneously turned into a dry land, so that the Jews could cross unhindered.

3) The seabed upon which the Jews walked was made level. In those areas where the seabed had been deep, the water froze into marble-like stone, so that the Jews did not have to walk on an incline.

4) The walls of water separating the paths of the twelve tribes were transparent and the Jews were able to see that everyone had crossed over safely. Also, the waters of the sea formed a dome over their heads.

5) Sweet waters flowed from the walls, so that the Jews were able to drink it. The water which was not drunk remained suspended in mid-air.

6) All types of fruit-bearing-trees sprouted from the seabed, so that those who desired could enjoy eating fruit. Vegetation grew to feed the livestock accompanying the Jews.

7) An aroma from the Garden of Eden accompanied the Jews through the sea.

8) The entire crossing by a few million people lasted only a few hours.

9) The Jews merited seeing the Divine Presence. Among the Jews were those whose mothers had abandoned them following birth, leaving them in the fields because of the decrees of the Egyptians. They now actually recognized the Divine Presence and exclaimed, "This is my God and I will praise Him!" — recognizing God from when they were infants. This revelation of God at the Red Sea was so great that our Sages taught: "A maid-servant saw more at the Red Sea than the prophet Yechezkel [saw in his Vision of the Chariot]."

10) The angel Gavriel moved about through the water of the Red Sea, carrying a warning for each of its four directions. "Take care of the Jews on their left side, for they will wear Tefillin on their left hand. Take care on their right side, for they will receive Torah from God's right hand. Take care in front, for that is where they will be circumcised. Take care to the rear, for the rear knot of their Tefillin will be on the back of their necks."

*

The Children of Israel completed their crossing of the Red Sea at dawn. The Egyptians presumed that if the Jews could cross over the Red Sea, so could they. Chasing after the Jews, they entered the sea, which was still parted. Just as the last

the angel argued that the Jews were not worthy of being saved. On the contrary, he insisted that this was the appropriate time for them to be punished. "They deserve to die!" he demanded. Because of this, the Jews were actually in very grave danger at that time.

God said to Moshe, "My children are in danger, yet you stand here in prayer? Now is not a time to pray!... Raise your staff and extend your hand over the Red Sea and I will cause the sea to split." The *Zohar* adds that the judgments and accusations against the Jews were so severe, that God had to call upon a level of mercy which emanates from the very highest of levels in the Supernal Worlds, from Atik, where there are no judgments whatsoever. Only mercy extended from this level was capable of nullifying the decrees then threatening the Jews.

*

It was now the night of the seventh day of the Exodus, the 21st day of Nissan and the Seventh Day of Pesach. God instructed Moshe, "Tell the Jews to start moving. Raise your staff and extend your hand over the Red Sea and I will cause the sea to split... Egypt will then know that I am God." The Cloud of Glory which had been in front of the Jewish camp moved behind it, serving as a buffer between their camp and that of the Egyptians. The Pillar of Fire illuminated the Jewish camp all night, while the Cloud of Glory spread total darkness over the Egyptians. All night long the Egyptians shot arrows and threw spears at the Jews, but the Clouds of Glory absorbed them and not one Jew was harmed. In fact, according to some opinions, these weapons were turned back and, together with the "suspended" hail which had been held over from the plague, rained down upon the hapless Egyptians.

Moshe did as God had told him. He extended the staff in his hand over the Red Sea, but the sea refused to split. The sea exclaimed, "I was created before you were, and I will not split before man!" Moshe argued that he was coming in God's Name. Still the sea refused to obey. Meanwhile, with Pharaoh and the Egyptians closing in on them, the Jews were growing more and more anxious. They turned to Moshe, who assured them that they would be descending into the sea and crossing over. Even as Moshe raised his staff over the sea, and the Egyptians were coming ever nearer, the sea still would not part. To make matters worse, the Jews then caught sight of the mud and clay at the seashore. This brought back horrible memories of their bondage in Egypt. "In Egypt we were swamped and buried in mud. Here too?!" they exclaimed. It was a test of faith on the very highest level. Nachshon, the son of Aminadav, from the Tribe of Yehudah, believed in Moshe Rabeinu and jumped into the seething sea. Still the sea remained adamant. The water rose to his nose, threatening to engulf him entirely.

Then, at that moment, God Himself appeared over the sea. Instantaneously it parted into twelve paths, one for each tribe. When the Red Sea split, so did *all* oceans, rivers, and lakes; every body of water in the world parted, even water in drinking glasses. This served to inform the entire world of the miracle which God had wrought.

the Pillar of Fire when darkness fell. In a sense, the Cloud and the Pillar were God Himself, cloaking Himself in these garments in order to protect His beloved nation.

On the sixth day after the Exodus, the Jews were camped near Baal Tzefon. This was the name of the most cherished of the Egyptian deities, and it was here, at the site of this huge idol, that the Egyptians had buried the great treasures which were brought to them during the years of famine. The Jews knew of this hiding place and now helped themselves to the booty, worth many times more than what they had taken with them out of Egypt. The *Megaleh Amukot* mentions that each Jew left Egypt with no less than ninety mules laden with gold, silver and precious stones. Korach had three hundred mules just to carry the keys to his treasures! Naturally, when the Egyptians saw the Jews gathering in these treasures as well, it angered them even more.

By now, Pharaoh and the Egyptian army were nearly upon the Children of Israel. The Jews found themselves surrounded on all four sides. In front of them was the Red Sea. On one side was a desert, in which God caused illusory wild beasts to appear. On the other side was Pi HaChirot, an impassable range of two very tall, straight cliffs with a valley in between. From behind, the Egyptians were coming after them in full force and fury.

The Jews panicked. They came to Moshe pleading, "Weren't there sufficient graves in Egypt? Why did you have to bring us here to die in the desert?" They divided into four groups. Some Jews said, "Let us drown in the sea rather than return to Egypt." Others said, "Let us return to Egypt, perhaps our former masters will have pity on us." Some argued, "Let us go into the desert a face the wild beasts." While others argued, "Let us stand and do battle." But Moshe said, "Don't be afraid. God will protect us from the Egyptians and you will never see them again. Let us pray to God for salvation." The Jews realized that this was the correct choice and they began to pray. Moshe also stood in prayer before God.

As Pharaoh was chasing after the Jews, drawing nearer and nearer, he began having second thoughts. Egypt had just been stricken by ten disastrous plagues and he himself had suffered both personal and financial losses. On the other hand, Pharaoh told himself that the Jews were confused by their newly found freedom and he trusted that Baal Tzefon would protect him. But again he faltered, thinking that perhaps it would be better to accept his losses and not risk any further setbacks. It was concerning this that God had told Moshe, "I will harden his heart and he will chase after you. This way, I will perform greater miracles and elevate My Glory, so that all will know there *is* a God!"

Our Sages tell us that each nation on earth has a protecting angel in heaven who presents that nations requests and defends it against its enemies. This angel also acts as a heavenly attorney, prosecuting any nation which it feels is likely to bring harm upon its nation. While the Jews were in Egypt, the protecting angel of the Egyptians constantly argued against the Children of Israel, accusing them of being idolators and therefore no better than the Egyptians themselves. Unfortunately, this was true; they had worshipped idols in Egypt. Now, with their lives being threatened,

29

want the Jews to think that a similar fate awaited them. Once the three days were over, Pharaoh's guards demanded that the Jews return to Egypt. Naturally, the Jews refused. They then set upon and killed most of these Egyptian guards. Those who survived fled back to Egypt. Meanwhile, the Egyptians were having second thoughts about having freed the Jews from bondage. "Who will tend our fields and crops? Who will do our work?" they asked each other. When the guards came back to Pharaoh and informed him that the Jews were not intending to return, this fueled the long-standing hatred and enmity the Egyptians felt for their former slaves. Immediately, they all called for Pharaoh and his army to give chase and bring the escaping Jews back to Egypt.

The way the Jews were wandering about in a circular route led Pharaoh to believe that the idol Baal Tzefon had confused them and caused them to become trapped in the wilderness. This convinced Pharaoh that he could chase after the Jews and force them to return to Egypt. Pharaoh rallied his troops, saying, "I will not act as a king. A king takes choice pick of the spoils of war. I, however, am now prepared to equally share the booty with all of you!" Not waiting for his servants, Pharaoh himself harnessed his royal chariot and led his army into the desert. The Egyptians ran after the Children of Israel, and on the sixth day following the Exodus, they spotted the Jewish encampment near the Red Sea.

The following well-known Talmudic teaching, quoting Rabbi Shimon bar Yochai, provides us with a most important and enduring lesson even, or especially, for today: From where did the Egyptians get the horses they rode on and harnessed to their chariots so that they could now chase after the Jews? Were not all their animals killed either in the Plagues of Pestilence or Hail? These horses could not have been horses belonging to the Jews, because they took all their animals with them when they left. There weren't any horses in Egypt; certainly not enough for the six hundred chariots of the choice warriors, the thousands of chariots used by the remainder of the chariot corps and the more than a million soldiers who rode after the Jews! The answer is that these horses had remained alive because they belonged to those Egyptians who feared God. They believed Moshe's warning and had kept their livestock indoors during the plagues. These were the Egyptians who feared God! Yet, now, after having seen God's chosen ones go free, they are chasing after the Jews with a vengeance. "From here we learn," said Rabbi Shimon, "the best of the Mitzri'yim, kill! The best of snakes, crush its head!" There are those who can *never* be trusted to truly befriend the Jewish People.

*

When the Children of Israel left Egypt, God provided them with the Seven Clouds of Glory. All those who had faith in God were enveloped by these Clouds. However, those whose faith was lacking were not granted this protection. It was these Jews who lacked faith that were seen by the enemy, such as Amalek, and were chased after and attacked. In addition, God provided a Pillar of Fire to illuminate the Jewish camp at night. The Clouds would appear in the morning and

The Jews hurriedly gathered their belongings and packed for the journey. Because they were rushed and could not wait for the dough of their bread to fully rise, they baked Matzah, flat breads. With packs on their backs and all the great riches they had gathered, the Children of Israel left Egypt. However, they only had a very limited supply of food, just enough for thirty days. Yet the Jews had complete faith in God, and they were confident that the Almighty would supply them with food and drink even in the wilderness.

*

The Exodus took place on the 15th day of Nissan, in the 2,448th year of Creation. Joyously, the Jews left Egypt after "sojourning" there for 210 years; 86 of which saw them suffering indescribable torture and affliction. This was a truly great miracle: 600,000 men and myriads more women and children leaving their former masters openly in the full light of day, without anyone muttering a word of protest. This was an especially painful experience for the Egyptians. On the one hand, they were still occupied with burying whatever remained of their dead after the dogs and rats had decimated their bodies; on the other, they looked on helplessly as their former slaves went free.

The Midrash offers the following parable to depict Pharaoh's situation: A king ordered his servant to buy him fish. The servant went and bought a rotten, foul-smelling fish. The king was incensed and said, "You have three choices. You can either eat it, receive 100 lashes, or pay for it." The servant chose to eat the fish, as this seemed to be the least of the three evils. But, after just one taste, he agreed to take the 100 lashes. Finally, after receiving almost half of the lashes, he agreed to pay for the fish. Pharaoh was asked to free the Jews. He refused, but in the end Pharaoh realized that: 1) The Jews were anyway set free. 2) He had suffered ten catastrophic plagues. 3) He himself contributed to the great wealth which the Jews took with them as they departed.

*

The Splitting of the Red Sea

Moshe's original request of Pharaoh was that the Jews be given permission to leave Egypt for three days so that they might serve God. Now, despite all the suffering he and the Egyptians had experienced, Pharaoh thought it would suffice to merely grant the Children of Israel freedom from enslavement. He never intended to allow them to leave permanently. To make certain that the Jews would return to Egypt after the third day, he had guards and policemen accompany them into the wilderness.

For three days Moshe took the Jews on a circular route: not straight into the desert, but southward, towards the Red Sea and near the idol of Baal Tzefon. One of the reasons was so that the Jews should not come across the remains of those from the Tribe of Efraim who left prematurely from Egypt. Moshe did not

morning," he told the Egyptian ruler. Pharaoh pleaded, telling Moshe that he was also a firstborn and therefore feared for his life. Moshe assured Pharaoh that he would be spared, for God wanted him to witness even greater miracles in the future.

*

It was not only Pharaoh who sought to send the Jews out in a hurry. All the Egyptians gathered around Goshen, pleading with the Jews to leave. The Jews responded that they could not even leave their homes until morning. At daybreak, the morning of the Exodus, the Egyptians again tried to pressure the Children of Israel to leave. The Jews asked them for remuneration, saying, "Lend us some of your garments, your gold and silver objects...." At first, the Egyptians denied having anything of value. "But we saw it in your house... in such-and-such a room," the Jews insisted. Realizing that the Jews could have earlier taken whatever they wanted without anyone stopping them, the Egyptians relented and gave them everything of value. In this way, the Jews became extremely wealthy and God's promise to Avraham, that He would provide the Jews with great wealth when He redeemed them, was fulfilled. Even Pharaoh himself presented the Jews with many presents and livestock.

While the Jews were occupied with gathering as much wealth as they could, Moshe went looking for Yosef's coffin. Before they died, each of Yaakov's sons had made their children promise that when they left Egypt, they would take their fathers' bones back with them to the Holy Land. As he had been the Regent of Egypt, Yosef knew that Pharaoh and the Egyptians would want to keep his body there, because they worshipped him for having saved Egypt from famine. He made his brothers and descendants swear an oath that they would take his body with them. Now that the time of the Exodus had arrived, Moshe went searching for Yosef's coffin.

Some commentaries maintain that Yosef was buried in the Tomb of the Pharaohs. Moshe went there and called out, "Yosef, the time of Redemption has come!" One coffin moved and Moshe took it with him. Others suggest that Pharaoh was aware of the oath which Yosef had secured and realized that if the coffin could not be found, the Jews would never leave Egypt. He therefore had Yosef's coffin sunk in the Nile. When the time came, Moshe took a gold plate upon which he inscribed the Ineffable Name and the words "Aley Shor" (Rise, O ox), a reference to Yosef. Moshe then placed this plate in the Nile and the coffin rose to the surface.

Yet a third commentary maintains that Serach, Asher's daughter, showed Moshe the burial place in the Nile. Moshe cried out, "Yosef, the time of Redemption has come. If you rise now, we will take you with us. Otherwise, we are free of our oath." The coffin then surfaced. Our Sages tell us that it was Serach who, more than two hundred years earlier, had informed Yaakov that Yosef was still alive. Because of this, Yaakov gave her a blessing that she would live forever. Thus, Serach was still alive when Yosef died. She witnessed his burial, and was still alive to show Moshe where the coffin lay buried.

converted into something else. All the other plagues involved outside influences, but did not entail altering Creation by changing one substance into something else.

*

The Exodus

Horrified by the death and destruction which now surrounded him on every side, Pharaoh finally accepted that there was no longer any hope of keeping the Children of Israel in bondage. Angry at those who had counseled him to keep the Jews enslaved, he gave an order for them to be killed. This was actually the third type of killing which took place that night. The Egyptian firstborn had killed their parents, the plague had taken the lives of all the firstborn sons, and now Pharaoh had his top advisors and generals put to death. Regarding Pharaoh's behavior, our Sages tell us that this is the way of the wicked: at first they refuse to believe. When shown beyond any shadow of a doubt that they are wrong, they seek excuses. And finally, when faced with destruction, they blame others, and never themselves, for the suffering and misfortune they have wrought.

Pharaoh began calling for Moshe Rabeinu. He was ready to allow him to take the Jews out of Egypt. Pharaoh's palace was half way across Egypt from the land of Goshen. Yet, because of his great fear, Pharaoh screamed so loudly for Moshe that his voice could be heard in Goshen. When Moshe did not come, Pharaoh went running through the streets of Egypt looking for him. Eventually, he reached Goshen, calling for Moshe all the while. However, Pharaoh had no way of knowing where Moshe was. As God had commanded, all the Jews remained in their homes until morning. He therefore had no choice but to knock on every door in Goshen. But, whomever he asked either refused to answer or misled him as to Moshe's whereabouts.

Wherever Pharaoh went that night, he found his fellow Egyptians crying and bemoaning their fate; while the Jews at whose door he knocked were reciting the Hallel in joyous expectation of the upcoming Exodus. The night was dark for Pharaoh. But for the Jews, who had a great light shining upon them, the night was as radiant as the brightest day. Pharaoh's daughter, Batyah, was eating together with Moshe and his family. "Why do the Egyptians have to suffer this ghastly punishment?" she asked him. "Did not my family save you and raise you?" "Yes," Moshe answered, "and this is why you personally did not suffer whenever a plague came. As for Pharaoh, I asked him to release the Jews and then I warned him before each plague. Yet, each time I did this, he made mockery of God and refused to take heed. This is his punishment!"

Pharaoh, who had previously ordered Moshe never to come before him again, now feverishly sought out Moshe. Finally, he found him. "Hurry, leave quickly! Now!" Pharaoh demanded. "Are we thieves that we must leave in the middle of the night?" Moshe asked. "God commanded us not to leave our homes until

the righteous and the wicked. Therefore, God Himself, not an angel, smote the firstborn. However, being a Kohein (a priest), He was, as it were, proscribed from defiling Himself with the dead. This is why He sent the Angel of Death to complete the task. Furthermore, an angel or seraph, cannot distinguish between a firstborn child and other children. Only God can do this, and He did!

There are certain objects worshipped by men, such as the sun, which a human messenger is incapable of destroying. It was therefore necessary for God Himself to intervene, not through any messenger, in order to counter the idolatrous beliefs of the Egyptians. Thus, with the conclusion of the final plague, the only form of idolatry left for the Egyptians to believe in was the worship of Baal Tzefon. God allowed the Egyptians to continue putting their trust in this deity so as to lure them to the Red Sea, where they suffered their final defeat. Therefore God said, "I, and no one else; not even Baal Tzefon, for this idol shall also be destroyed."

*

The Haggadah calls our attention to various items and plagues prior to actually mentioning the Ten Plagues. These are: Pestilence, the Sword, the Revelation of the Divine Presence, Moshe's Staff and Blood.

Pestilence is singled out because it appeared together with each of the other plagues. This is intended to show that the phrase, "A strong hand," which the Haggadah tells us is what God used to bring the Plague of Pestilence, actually applies to all the Ten Plagues.

The Sword denotes the tenth plague, during which the Egyptian firstborn sons slew their parents. It also refers to the Angel of Death, who killed the Egyptian firstborn with his sword.

The Revelation of the Divine Presence is mentioned because God promised Yaakov that He Himself would appear in Egypt to free his descendants from bondage. This revelation took place when He slew the firstborn. Though the land of Egypt was filled with impurity and idolatry, and was therefore unfit for such a revelation, God Himself appeared there to redeem His nation.

Moshe's Staff is mentioned because the name of each of the Ten Plagues was inscribed on his staff. This staff was created on the evening of the Sixth Day of Creation. Adam, who took possession of it, passed it on to Chanokh, who gave it to Noach. He gave the staff to Avraham, and it was then passed on from father to son, from Yitzchak to Yaakov and then to Yosef. After Yosef's house was ransacked by Pharaoh's servants, the staff remained in Pharaoh's palace until his advisor, Yitro, took it with him when he fled to Midian. There, it came into the Moshe Rabeinu's possession, in whose hands it was empowered by the Angel Metat.

Blood is used as a generic term to refer to all the Ten Plagues. Actually, the Plague of Blood was the only one in which a physical entity, water, was miraculously

24

the Jews not to venture out of their homes on the night of the 15th of Nissan, when the Plague of Slaying of the Firstborn was to take place.

This tenth plague was visited upon the Egyptians because they had willfully killed Jewish children by drowning them in the river, using them as bricks, and slaughtering them for Pharaoh's blood-baths, etc. Exactly at midnight, God Himself passed through the land of Egypt, smiting all the firstborn of Egypt. Anyone or anything that was considered a firstborn was afflicted. Thus, Pharaoh's eldest son, who was to be his heir, was struck dead. So, too, were all the firstborn of his advisors and generals, and even the firstborn of the captives and imprisoned. Though these captives and imprisoned had not directly taken part in the enslavement of the Jews, they were also struck dead. This was because at one point, when the Egyptians themselves thought they might set the Jews free, they offered these prisoners who were all facing death the opportunity to replace the Jews as slaves. But they chose to remain in captivity rather than have the Jews set free.

When Moshe announced this final plague, the Egyptian firstborn sons took his warning seriously. They begged their parents to take heed and protect them. But the parents, who were afraid of Pharaoh, did nothing. This angered many of the firstborn, who rose up against their parents and killed them. Even those firstborn sons whose parents did heed Moshe Rabeinu's warning and placed them in Jewish homes were also slain. Not even an illegitimate firstborn son, whose illegitimacy had been a secret prior to this plague, managed to escape with his life. Many of the Egyptian women were promiscuous and had had relations with other men. A woman could thus have five "firstborns" in her home. All these firstborn, whether from their father or mother, were also struck down. If there was no firstborn son, then the eldest in the house died. Pregnant women carrying a child destined to be a firstborn, miscarried. The Egyptian firstborn living in other countries, even the firstborn of other nations present in Egypt, also died that night. When morning came, in all of Egypt not one household could be found which had escaped the Angel of Death.

Even the firstborn of the livestock were smitten. This was intended to prove to the Egyptians that their firstborn animals, to whom they attributed special abilities, had no power against God. To compound their anguish, the Egyptians were incapable of preventing the flesh and bones of their dead from being devoured by packs of dogs and rats, right in the open. Even though God struck the firstborn at midnight, they suffered death throes until morning, when the Jews, who had been commanded to remain in their homes throughout the night, were able to witness the expiry of their enemies. Thus we are told that God struck the firstborn at midnight, which He did; whereas, it was the Angel of Death who came and took their souls in the morning.

*

God said, "I, not an angel; I, not a seraph; I, not a messenger; I, and no one else." When an angel is given permission to destroy, it cannot differentiate between

a Jew stood alongside an Egyptian, he had light and the Egyptian had nothing but darkness. This is how it will be during the Final Redemption, as well.

Avraham had been given God's promise that his descendants would depart from bondage with great wealth. Yet, to this point, with the Exodus so close at hand, the Jews still had not amassed any riches. This was because God had chosen the Plague of Darkness as the time to initiate the steps which would fulfill His promise. The Jews, who were all able to see, now entered the darkened Egyptian homes undisturbed. There they would walk about freely, making note of all the gold, silver and precious stones, all the expensive garments and utensils that the Egyptians possessed. Even so, the Jews took nothing; they merely observed. Later on, during the actual Exodus, the Jews demanded remuneration from those who had enslaved them. When an Egyptian denied having anything of value, the Jew would then say, "But I saw such- and-such an object in such-and-such a closet in such-and-such a room..." The Egyptian was forced to admit to the truth and provide his former Jewish slave with the object he had requested. This way, the Jews were able to amass huge fortunes, having been privy to the full extent of the Egyptians' wealth. Nevertheless, Pharaoh continued to deny the Jews their freedom.

*

SLAYING OF THE FIRSTBORN. Prior to the Plague of Darkness, when Moshe warned Pharaoh of the coming plague, Pharaoh became enraged and ordered that Moshe never again appear before him. At that time, Moshe also warned of the tenth and final plague, the Slaying of the Firstborn. Pharaoh, himself a firstborn, was frightened. He chased Moshe from his palace. As he was leaving, Moshe said to Pharaoh, "What you say is correct. I will not come to you anymore. The next time, it will be you who will come to me!"

On the 10th of Nissan, which was a Shabbat, the Jews were commanded to take a lamb and keep it for the 14th day of Nissan. Then they were told to slaughter the lamb as a sacrifice to God and to place its blood on the outer doorpost of their homes. This served as a sign that there were Jews living in the house, Jews who steadfastly maintained their belief against all odds, that God was about to redeem them from their bitter exile. This was the Paschal Lamb. That the Jews were able to do this was in itself a miracle; for the Egyptians also worshipped the sheep (the zodiac sign of the month of Nissan), yet now, the Jews were free to do with the Egyptian deity as they pleased.

On the morning of the 14th of Nissan, the Jews reinstituted the mitzvah of circumcision. Another miracle occurred: Moshe Rabeinu somehow had sufficient time and strength to circumcise all of the 600,000 Jews who were to take part in the Exodus. (One of the laws regarding the Paschal Lamb requires that those who partake of it must be circumcised.) As mentioned earlier, as the time for the Exodus drew near, the Jews found themselves without mitzvot. The merit of these two mitzvot, circumcision and the Paschal Lamb, both performed on the same day, was to be their spiritual "passport" for leaving Egypt. God also commanded

additional explanation suggests that, as was the case with those which preceded it, this plague was meant to punish the Egyptians for their cruel subjugation of the Children of Israel. Because the Egyptians had compelled the Jews to labor for very long hours, even in darkness, they were now made to suffer the Plague of Darkness.

Furthermore, our Sages tell us that in Egypt there were many Jews who lacked faith in God. They did not believe that the Almighty would redeem them as He had promised the Patriarchs. Because of their lack of faith, these Jews were not worthy of being redeemed, and they were condemned to die in Egypt. God brought the Plague of Darkness upon Egypt so that the Egyptians would not see these myriads of Jews dying and later vaunt the fact that the Jews had also suffered during the Ten Plagues. All the Jews who died then were buried during the six days of darkness.

Unlike the earlier plagues, each of which went on for a whole week, the Plague of Darkness lasted for only six days. The remaining seventh day was held over until the Splitting of the Red Sea, when at the same time that the Jews had light, the Egyptians experienced darkness. Others are of the opinion that the seventh day of darkness occurred on the night of the tenth plague, the Slaying of the Firstborn. A further difference between this plague and those which preceded it was that the other plagues began promptly at daybreak, whereas darkness only descended once the sun had fully risen. God did this so that the Egyptians would not be able to claim that it was nothing more than an extension of the night.

The Plague of Darkness was also unique in that it came in two separate parts. More than just an absence of light in which shapes are sometimes discernible, the darkness of the first three days was a very thick darkness in which it was impossible to distinguish anything at all. The stars did not shine, and it was as if all of Egypt had been covered by a dense, dark cloud. Even so, the Egyptians were able to move about in the darkness. During the second three days, however, the darkness took on an actual, physical existence. The Egyptians were enveloped by this darkness so that whoever had been sitting could not stand up and whoever had been standing could not sit down. They were held stiff in their positions for three consecutive days.

Part of the miracle was that the Egyptians remained alive during these last three days of the plague. The darkness was so encompassing, it filled their mouths and noses, making it impossible for them to breathe. Yet, God wanted the Egyptians to have a taste of what was in store for them at the Red Sea, when they would be kept alive under the water so that they could suffer the torment of being tossed about by the sea. Some commentaries maintain that this darkness was the darkness of Gehennom. When one sins, he believes no one sees him. His punishment is that he is prevented from seeing anyone else.

As opposed to the Egyptians, the Jews had nothing but light for the duration of the six days. The light shone brightly for the Jews, even during the night, and they were then able to appreciate the great magnitude of the miracle being wrought for their benefit. Wherever the Jews went they had this light with them. Even when

21

"suspended" hail came down during Yehoshua's battle for Givon (Joshua 10:11). The remainder will come down during the battle of Gog and Magog (Ezekiel 38:22), when the miracles of the Final Redemption will be far greater than the miracles of the Exodus. Once the plague of hail was stopped, Pharaoh's heart was again hardened and he refused to release the Jews.

*

LOCUSTS. This plague was an additional punishment for the Egyptians having forced the Jews to plant for them, thereby keeping the Jewish men in the fields and preventing them from procreating. The locusts swarmed all over the land of Egypt and decimated whatever crops had not already been destroyed by the hail.

Although the Egyptians generally viewed an attack by locusts on their crops as a natural occurrence, the Plague of Locusts was unlike anything they'd ever seen. These locusts came as one unit, totally blackening the skies over the entire land of Egypt. At one fell swoop they descended upon and consumed all the existing crops. Then, rather than moving on to other sites of vegetation, the locusts moved to the city center, entering Pharaoh's palace and the homes of his advisors. From there they spread out to the outlying towns and villages, infesting the homes of all the Egyptians. The locusts were very powerful. Their sting, like that of the hornet, had the strength to blind and kill its victim. No matter where they went, the Egyptians were unable to find rest or respite from the attack.

Though the locusts were in abundance, they were not permitted outside the land of Egypt. This proved to be a blessing for the peoples of neighboring countries who had border disputes with the Egyptians. It was now obvious that the areas which remained free of the locusts' attack belonged to the bordering country. (The same was true of the plague of Frogs.) Some Egyptians tried to flee Egypt and take their crops to the neighboring lands, but the locusts formed a wall at the border, preventing anyone from crossing.

In Goshen, the locusts did not disturb the Jews or their crops. Yet, unlike the Plague of Hail, if an Egyptian had crops in a Jewish field in Goshen, the locusts did consume it. If a Jew had bought a tree from an Egyptian for its wood, the roots were eaten but the tree remained. If an Egyptian had bought a tree from a Jew for its wood, the tree was eaten but the roots remained.

Despite everything, the Egyptians hoped to have some gain from this plague. Storing the locusts in barrels, they preserved them in salt, intending to eat them as a delicacy. However, when the plague ended, God gave life to all these locusts and they were carried away by a strong east wind. Pharaoh's heart was again hardened and once more he declined to release the Jews.

*

DARKNESS. Aside from worshipping the Nile, the Egyptians also worshipped the sun-god. To crush their belief in the power of their idol, God made obvious the sun's limited powers by having darkness descend upon the land of Egypt. An

20

Pharaoh himself suffered greatly from this plague. His entire body was covered with these boils. He may have even been ready to free the Jews right then and there. But it was too late. Of his own volition Pharaoh had hardened his heart after each of the first five plagues. He had refused to heed Moshe's warnings to release the Jews. Now, it was no longer up to him. His free choice was now taken from him. God said, "Evil one! Since you did not soften your heart to My requests, I will now harden your heart and make you suffer My full revenge for your despicable acts!"

*

HAIL. Aside from the regular labor which the Egyptians forced on the Jews, they also made them plant and care for their gardens and orchards. This, too, was in order to keep the Jews away from their own homes. In addition, they would beat the Jews without mercy, causing them to scream bitterly for their lives. Tit for tat, God sent the Plague of Hail upon the Egyptians. The hail destroyed whatever crops and orchards the Jews had planted for their masters. It also descended with ferocious fury, stoning, beating and killing whoever remained outdoors during the plague. The accompanying thunder was symbolic of the screams of the Jews. The ferocity of the hail, which comprised both fire and ice, was a reminder of the punishment of Gehennom which consists of both fire and ice.

God had Moshe Rabeinu advise the Egyptians that those who did fear the Almighty should bring all their livestock indoors; where they, too, were told to remain for the duration of the plague. Part of God's intention in issuing this warning was so that the Egyptians would later have the horses with which to chase after the Jews following the Exodus.

The hail consisted of huge balls of very sharp pieces of transparent ice. Inside the ice there was fire. God created a harmony between these opposing elements so that the fire did not evaporate the water and the water did not extinguish the fire. This combination of forces descended with such a fury, that the ice would slice through a tree as though it were paper, while the fire would leap forth and consume whatever stood in its path. Many crops were destroyed. Those that were left were spared intentionally, so that the locusts, which followed the hail, would also have something to destroy.

The balls of hail fell so close to one another that if any livestock stood out in the open, it was immediately surrounded by the ice and freeze instantaneously. If an Egyptian slaughtered the animal and tried to remove its meat for food, birds would come and take the flesh away. Once again Goshen remained totally unaffected. And, even if an animal belonging to a Jew was standing next to an Egyptian's animal, the hail would kill the Egyptian's animal, but the Jew's animal would survive intact. It was even free to move about and graze while the hail was descending!

Pharaoh pleaded with Moshe to have the thunder and hail cease. Moshe prayed, and the Plague of Hail came to an end. Any hail which had been descending at the time Moshe's prayers were answered remained where it was. Part of this

PESTILENCE. In order to keep the Jews away from their homes and thereby prevent them from having more children, their Egyptian masters forced them to tend their flocks in the desert. To further subjugate and demoralize their Jewish slaves, the Egyptians would put a harness on the Jew and have him pull the plough in place of an ox. They also connived to cheat the Jews of their own flocks. The Egyptians knew that the Jews hardly had enough time to meet their daily work quotas, let alone to properly care for their flocks, and they used this as an excuse to take their animals from them.

For this, God repaid the Egyptians with the Plague of Pestilence. There are those who maintain that pestilence actually appeared with each of the plagues. Wherever the Egyptians had their flocks, they were afflicted and died. Also, unlike the other plagues, the pestilence struck all the cattle and flocks in one second! Whether on their own land or in Goshen with the Jewish herds, the Egyptian flocks were smitten. Yet, once again, the possessions of the Jews were totally unaffected. If a Jew had his entire flock or even a single animal with an Egyptian, it remained untouched by the plague. To prove to the Egyptians that the Children of Israel would be saved, even the sickly cattle or sheep belonging to the Jews were free of the pestilence. God said, "Let a deadly pestilence and plague set upon those who would wipe out an entire nation, a nation that would gladly give up its life for My sake." Though instantaneous, the plague lasted a week. Thus, if an Egyptian attempted to replenish his livestock, his newly acquired animals were also stricken. But Pharaoh again hardened his heart and did not release the Jews from bondage.

*

BOILS. God commanded Moshe and Aharon to fill both their hands with ashes. Moshe then put his two handfuls in one hand, added Aharon's handfuls to his, and threw these ashes up to the heavens. This in itself was a great miracle. Not only did the palm of Moshe's hand hold four handfuls, but he was also able to take ashes, which are very light, and throw them up so high. These ashes then spread out over the entire land of Egypt and its provinces, turning into boils on the Egyptians' bodies.

The Plague of Boils was brought upon the Egyptians because they would force the Jews to boil foods which had already been boiled and cool off that which had already been cooled. Now, having been afflicted by this plague, the Egyptians could touch neither. The boils which God fashioned consisted of blood and pus on the inside and very dry leprosy on the outer skin. The Egyptians were covered from head to toe with these very painful boils. And, if the suffering was not enough, their appearance brought them tremendous denigration and insults from any non-Egyptian who saw them. Furthermore, our Sages tell us that even though the Egyptians themselves were healed after the seven day period of the plague, the Egyptian sorcerers never completely recovered. This was to make it clear that their powers had been diminished and that they could never return to their former status.

the lice continued to be imbedded on their faces and between their eyes. Even washing their bodies had no effect on the lice.

The Hand of God was clearly revealed in this plague. During the first two plagues, the Egyptian magicians partially duplicated Moshe's acts. They too were able to turn water into blood and they brought frogs. As a result, they were convinced that Moshe was nothing more than a sorcerer, albeit greater than they; for the afflictions which came through Moshe were much more severe than anything the Egyptian sorcerers could reproduce. However, when it came to the Plague of Lice, the sorcerers were incapable of duplicating Moshe's actions. This was because lice are minute, and sorcery has no power over anything that small. "It is a finger of God!" the magicians were forced to admit. But they would only admit to a finger. As with the other plagues, Goshen was untouched and the Jews were not affected by the lice. Even so, Pharaoh again hardened his heart and did not heed Moshe Rabeinu's warnings.

*

WILD ANIMALS. This plague was brought upon the Egyptians because they would send the Jews into the forests to bring back wild animals for sport and hunting. God said to the Egyptians, "I will now bring you the animals directly to your home. I will make it so that you no longer have any need for hunting!" The Hebrew word for this plague is Arov, a mixture. The Plague of Wild Animals comprised all sorts of wild beasts: lions, leopards, wolves, bears, apes, snakes, scorpions, insects, frogs and any other animal or beast that was either very annoying or deadly. Even birds of prey were among the attacking animals. This itself was a miracle. Usually, each animal remains with its own kind, never mixing with other species. Birds, in particular, will not hunt together with animals. Yet in the Plague of Wild Animals, all the species acted in unison to fulfill God's command.

With the advent of this plague, the Egyptians began to shutter their doors and windows. But the animals would break through the roofs and open the doors from the inside, allowing the rest of the beasts to enter and wreak havoc and destruction in the Egyptians' homes. God also caused dense forests to appear in the Egyptian cities so that the animals would feel comfortable in their environment. Our Sages tell us that Egyptian parents would send their children for a walk with one of their servants. When the servant would return home without the children, the parents would cry, "Where are our children?" "I'll tell you," the servant would answer. "The lion took one, the wolf a second, the bear a third, and so on."

Goshen was unaffected by the Plague of Wild Animals. The Jews were also able to roam about Egypt freely, as the beasts would not harm them. This time Pharaoh called Moshe and asked him to remove the plague, promising to release the Jews as soon as the animals were gone. However, after the plague ended Pharaoh again hardened his heart and refused to keep his promise or heed Moshe Rabeinu's admonitions.

*

frogs. The Egyptians had mocked the Jews, forcing them to collect vermin and insects for the Egyptians to play with. In return, God sent the frogs to "play" with the Egyptians. The frogs would enter their bodies and croak from their innards.

The Plague of Frogs began with Moshe extending his staff and the appearance of one huge frog. This frog then called for many more frogs to join him. God made the frogs amoebae-like, so that when an Egyptian tried to kill a frog by striking it, the frog would split and multiply. As a result, there were frogs everywhere. They entered the beds, the clothing and the ovens of the Egyptian People. There was no possibility of hiding from them. Even walls of marble split open for the frogs to enter and fulfill God's command.

With the Egyptians' ovens invaded by frogs, all the cooked foods they ate were mixed with frogs. The Egyptians had not even allowed the Jewish slaves enough time to break from their work in order to eat. Because of this, the Jews had no choice but to eat their meals while mixing the mortar, and the filth and dust which covered their food disgusted them. In return for this, the Egyptians now found all their food disgusting, as everything they ate was layered with frogs. And, once swallowed, the frogs were resurrected in the bellies of the Egyptian oppressors, causing them unbearable discomfort. Just as the Jews had suffered under their yoke without a minute of rest, so too, the Egyptians were not given a moment's peace during the Plague of Frogs.

God concluded the plague not by having the frogs disappear, but by having them die instantly. This meant that the frogs died where they were, in the clothes, the food and the stomachs of the Egyptians. It was therefore very difficult to remove the carcasses, and the terrible stench which filled Egypt proved insufferable. The only place which remained totally unaffected by the frogs was the Land of Goshen, where the Jews resided.

Ten times the word frogs appears in the verses relating to this plague. Our Sages tell us that from this we can learn that the Plague of Frogs was as severe as all the ten plagues together. Nevertheless, Pharaoh still did not heed the warning; he only became more obstinate, and hardened his heart all the more.

*

LICE. In addition to the building which the Jews were made to do, they were also forced to do housework for their Egyptian masters. They were constantly being given chores such as sweeping and cleaning the Egyptian homes, gardens, streets and fields. And, even though they were filthy from this work, the Egyptians never allowed them to wash and clean their bodies. Measure for measure, God sent the Plague of Lice upon the Egyptians, infesting their earth and their bodies. In fact, the earth itself turned into lice. These earth-lice were two cubits (about 2 feet or 50 cm) above the earth and a cubit into it. Now, when the Egyptians themselves tried to sweep their houses, there was nothing to sweep except lice. The lice also infested their bodies, causing them to itch intolerably. For relief, the Egyptians began scraping themselves against walls and tearing at their skin. Yet terrible plagues would be visited upon Egypt, the first being the Plague of Blood. God was about to turn the entire Egyptian water supply into blood.

Pharaoh, however, refused to heed Moshe's admonition. Every morning, for three consecutive weeks, Moshe repeated his warning, yet Pharaoh paid no attention. Then, without any further notice, the plague struck. Every drop of water suddenly turned into blood. Whether in the rivers, reservoirs, wells, storage or drinking vessels, all the water became blood. Even the Egyptians' spittle turned to blood. The water in the dough turned to blood. New wells dug by the Egyptians produced only blood. The Nile river entered Egypt as water, turned to blood, and after crossing the Egyptian border turned back into water. And, whereas the Egyptians thirsted for water, the Jews were totally unaffected by the plague. The people of Egypt could not help but see the Hand of God in this.

A number of opinions have been offered to explain why God saw fit to send a plague on the Egyptian water supply. Firstly, the Egyptians worshipped the Nile, which was their only source of water and a symbol of their power. Other reasons given are that God wanted to punish Pharaoh's water, either because he slaughtered three hundred Jewish children daily to wash in their blood, or because he issued a decree to drown all newborn Jewish males. Yet another explanation is that the Egyptians knew that the Jewish women kept the laws of family purity. Hoping to curtail the growth of the Jewish population, the Egyptians refused to allow the women to perform the ritual immersion in water, thereby preventing them from having relations with their husbands.

According to some opinions, as soon as this plague began, the Jews ceased working. The Egyptians could no longer control them and the slavery stopped. (Others say that only the cruelest forms of servitude stopped now, but the enslavement of the Jews only came to an end with the Plague of Pestilence). However, the time had not come for the Jews to leave Egypt, and they had not, as yet, been given the great riches promised them by God. This wealth only began to materialize during the Plague of Blood. Though the Egyptians could find no water in all of Egypt, the Children of Israel had plenty of water. When an Egyptian observed a Jew drinking water, he would take it away. But it would do him no good. As soon as the Egyptian took the water, it turned into blood. When he handed the blood to the Jew, it turned back into water. If the Egyptian would then command the Jew to drink from the glass together with him, the Jew drank water and the Egyptian drank blood. The only way the Egyptian's water would remain water was if he had purchased it from a Jew. This way, the Jews began to collect the wages due to them for all the years of labor they had been forced to perform. The Plague of Blood, as well as all the other plagues, lasted for one week, after which, Pharaoh hardened his heart and refused to release the Jews.

*

FROGS. Again Moshe warned Pharaoh that a plague was about to descend upon Egypt. Pharaoh did not listen and the land of Egypt was invaded by an army of

tall and straight, and very majestic in their appearance. Pharaoh sent his trained lions to attack Moshe and Aharon, but Moshe tamed the beasts before they could carry out their master's bidding. This impressed Pharaoh and he asked them the purpose of their mission. Moshe Rabeinu declared that he had come in God's Name, requesting Pharaoh to release the Jews from bondage. At the time, Pharaoh was the most powerful ruler in the world, and Egypt the strongest land. It was so fortified, no slave had ever succeeded in escaping from there.

When Moshe, in God's Name, requested that the Jews be given their freedom, Pharaoh laughed at him. Pharaoh considered himself to be a deity and boasted that he had never heard of the Jewish God. Angrily, he chased Moshe and Aharon from his palace, declaring that he would never release the Jews from his control. It was at this time that he issued his fourth decree: using Jewish children as bricks and requiring the Jews to seek their own supplies.

Moshe was angered by Pharaoh's rejection and complained to God over his having been sent on a futile mission. His appearance before Pharaoh had only succeeded in making things worse for his brethren. God's response was that Moshe would now see the miracles and wonders He was about to perform. The Egyptians would not only set the Jews free, they would chase them into freedom.

*

The Ten Plagues

God instructed Moshe to return to Pharaoh and repeat His request for the release of the Jews. This time, God gave Moshe a miracle to perform. This was to be his sign that he was the Almighty's messenger. When Moshe appeared before Pharaoh, he threw down his staff and it became a serpent. When the Egyptian magicians did likewise with their staffs, Moshe's serpent swallowed up the other serpents. The Egyptian magicians scoffed at this, claiming that if he were indeed a true messenger, his staff would swallow their staffs. Moshe turned his serpent back into a staff and it swallowed the Egyptians' staffs. Even though they were impressed by Moshe's powers, the magicians attributed it to sorcery. The Midrash teaches that Moshe's staff was actually the Ministering Angel, MeTaT, who is known as MaTeh, a staff. Despite the miracle he had witnessed, Pharaoh refused to release the Jews, and Moshe departed.

*

BLOOD. Pharaoh wanted the Egyptians to believe that he was a deity and offered as proof the fact that no one had ever known him to relieve himself of human waste. Early each morning Pharaoh would go down to the Nile, where he would relieve himself without anyone seeing. At God's instruction, Moshe went to meet Pharaoh at the Nile, to expose Pharaoh's secret and warn him of the severe punishment which would befall him if he continued to deny the Jews their freedom. Ten

The Egyptians had expected that all their decrees would weaken the Jews physically and morally and deprive them of any hope for the future. When these enactments proved unproductive, the Egyptians appointed Jewish guards who were made responsible for meeting the quotas. These guards were ordered to whip those Jewish slaves who failed to produce according to Pharaoh's wishes. This was intended to further demoralize the Jews by having them participate in their own destruction, much as the Nazi's appointed Jewish *kapos* to do much of their own dirty work. But, the Jewish guards in Egypt refused to whip their brethren and were themselves severely beaten when the quotas were not met. For this, they were later rewarded, becoming the Elders and leaders of the fledgling nation. However, when they complained to Pharaoh about the beatings, he decreed that an additional burden be placed upon the Jews. Without diminishing from their daily quotas, the Jewish slaves were now required seek straw and other supplies for making the mortar, which the authorities would no longer provide. As a result of this decree, the Jews and their Jewish guards had no way of avoiding the daily beatings which the Egyptians inflicted upon them.

During this period some descendants of the tribe of Efraim calculated that the 400 years of exile were over and forced their way out of Egypt. Their mistake was calculating the decree of exile from the Brit bein HaBitarim and not 30 years later from the birth of Yitzchak. Their escape was premature and they were all killed on their way to Kanaan by the Philistines.

*

Moshe, meanwhile, was tending to Yitro's flocks in Midian. One day, he led them to Mount Sinai, where he saw the Burning Bush. Though the bush was on fire, it was not being consumed. This was meant as a sign, telling Moshe that though the Jews were suffering, they would not be destroyed. The Holy One then appeared to him and commanded him to go down to Egypt and redeem the Jews. God told Moshe that His promise to Avraham that "your descendants will suffer exile and oppression for 400 years" had already been fulfilled, and that now the time had come to fulfill the second part of this promise: "I will bring judgment against the nation that enslaves them, and they will then leave with great wealth." God also told him that after the Exodus, He would give the Torah on this mountain, Mount Sinai.

Moshe deemed himself unworthy of such a mission and sought to avoid being sent. God told him that the reason Pharaoh's servants had been struck blind, deaf and dumb, thereby keeping Moshe from harm, was so that he could carry out this present mission. Moshe Rabeinu then complied with God's command and descended to Egypt. He gathered the Elders of the Jews and informed them of the coming Exodus. The Jews expressed their belief in God and were filled with gratitude for His promise to put an end to their enslavement and bondage.

Moshe, together with his elder brother Aharon, then went directly to Pharaoh's palace; a place where no Jew was permitted to go. Entering the great hall where Pharaoh sat on his throne, the ruler of Egypt gazed at them in awe. They were

The Torah tells us that when Moshe was a young man, he went out among the Jews. Seeing their suffering, and the hardships which the Egyptians inflicted upon them, Moshe tried to lessen their burden. He advised Pharaoh that working all seven days of the week was too much and that the "slaves" would produce more efficiently if they were allowed to rest. Pharaoh agreed to permit the Jews to take off on Shabbat. In addition, Moshe was able to arrange for an equitable distribution of the work, so that the strong and able-bodied were given the heavier loads while the weaker were given smaller loads.

Once, while walking, he spotted an Egyptian mercilessly beating a Jew. Moshe pronounced the Ineffable Name and the Egyptian died. Moshe then hid the body in the sand. Though he did not know it, his act was witnessed by two evil Jews, Datan and Aviram. The following day Moshe found these two Jews fighting, with one ready to strike the other. He rebuked them. In retaliation, they went to Pharaoh and testified that Moshe had killed the Egyptian. Moshe was sentenced to death by beheading. But, when Moshe's neck was struck by the executioner's sword, it became as hard as stone. God then sent an angel in the likeness of Moshe to replace him in captivity. This allowed Moshe to flee, after which the angel itself disappeared. When Pharaoh asked about Moshe whereabouts, his servants were stricken blind, deaf and dumb, so that no one could give him an answer. Moshe meanwhile fled to Ethiopia where he remained for many years. Afterwards, he moved to Midian. There he married, Tzipporah, the daughter of Yitro, the sheik of Midian.

*

Salvation

While Moshe was in Midian, Pharaoh was stricken with leprosy and his physicians told him to bathe daily in the blood of the Jewish children. Pharaoh ordered the slaughtering of a hundred and fifty children each morning and another hundred and fifty each night so that he could immerse his body in their blood. Mortified by this extreme cruelty, the Jews finally began sighing and screaming for God to save them. Others teach that Pharaoh died and when all of Egypt, including the slaves, attended the funeral, the Jews had a small respite from their work. Seeing the Jews following the coffin and crying, the Egyptians thought they were bemoaning the loss of Pharaoh. Actually, the Jews had at long last found themselves with an opportunity to cry out to God. And this was the beginning of their salvation.

According to the opinion that there was now a new Pharaoh on the throne in Egypt, this crying out to God was brought on by a further decree which had been issued against the Jews. To dispel any notion that he would be more lenient than his predecessor, the new Pharaoh ordered that any Jew who failed to produce his work quota would have his children implanted as stones in the walls which the Jews were erecting.

12

Adar, 2368). This enabled Yocheved to keep her baby's birth a secret, and she was able to hide Moshe for a full three months. At his birth, Amram and Yocheved knew that their son was destined for greatness. The entire house was filled with radiant light.

*

On the 6th of Sivan, when Moshe was three months old, Yocheved put him in a basket made of reeds and placed him in the water. Pharaoh's astrologers immediately informed him that the destined leader of the Jews had been thrown into the Nile, and the decree to drown the babies was voided. This prompted Amram to question the validity of his daughter's prophecy, and so Miriam went to the river to see what fate awaited her brother Moshe.

Now, Pharaoh's daughter had decided to convert to Judaism. On the same day that Moshe was placed in the water, she had gone down to the river to immerse, as in a Mikvah, in order to purify herself from her pagan beliefs. When she saw the basket, Pharaoh's daughter wanted to retrieve it. Her maidservants attempted to block her way, but the angel Gavriel descended and moved them aside. Though the basket was a distance of 60 cubits (a cubit is about one-and-a-half feet) from where she was standing, another miracle occurred and her hand extended to the basket. When she opened it, she saw the boy and understood him to be a Jewish child. Immediately she decided that she would take the baby home in order to save him. Because she had shown compassion and was ready to take her father's future adversary into her home as her son, God called Pharaoh's daughter Bat-YaH — "My Daughter" — and promised her that she would never experience the taste of death.

When Batyah's attempts to nurse the crying Moshe failed, she had others try, but without success. God had said, "The mouth that will one day speak with the Divine Presence should suckle only pure milk." Miriam, who had been watching all this, offered to bring a wet-nurse from the Jews. This suggestion pleased Pharaoh's daughter and Miriam brought Yocheved, the baby's own mother, to nurse him. Moshe was kept by his mother for twenty-four months, after which she brought him to Pharaoh's palace, where he was brought up.

Thus, Pharaoh himself, the arch-enemy of the Jews, helped raise Moshe Rabeinu, the hope and salvation of the Jewish People. It is worth noting that similar situations have developed more than once in Jewish history and continues to occur even today. Though we have numerous enemies, many times they themselves unwittingly provide us with the means for our salvation. Furthermore, this will also be the case in the future. As mentioned earlier, Esav and Yishmael rejected Avraham's Covenant and refused to participate in the suffering implied therein. In so doing, the burden fell solely upon Yaakov. However, because he paid the debt and accepted the Covenant, Yaakov alone will receive the reward, a reward which will be provided by none other than Esav and Yishmael themselves!

*

Pharaoh's enactment of forced hard labor and sleeping in the fields, this additional harsh decree against the Jews also failed to inhibit the growth of the Jewish People.

Seeing that he could not rely on the midwives to assist him in preventing the birth of the Jewish leader, Pharaoh took another approach. His advisors had also told him that the leader destined to redeem the Jews would meet his fate "through water." (Moshe, in fact, was denied permission to enter the Holy Land because he "struck" the rock to produce water, rather than speaking to it.) Pharaoh's third cruel decree was to have all the Jewish male children drowned in the river, a fate similar to the one suffered by these same souls in the Generation of the Flood (*Sha'ar HaPesukim, Shemot*). A total of 600,000 infants were thrown into the Nile. On the day that Moshe was born, Pharaoh's astrologers informed him that the redeemer of the Jews had come into the world. Having no indication as to whether this was a Jew or an Egyptian, he decreed that even the newborn Egyptian infants be drowned. The Midrash tells us that all of the 600,000 Jewish infants thrown into the Nile were saved in Moshe's merit (*Likutey Halakhot, Birkhat HaShachar* 5:62).

As for the newborn Jewish females, their fate was not to be the same as the males. Though Pharaoh wanted males drowned, he insisted that the newborn females be allowed to live. His intention was to either to sell them to other nations or keep them as slaves for the Egyptians.

*

When Pharaoh issued his decree for the Jewish infants to be killed, Amram, then the leader of the Jews, divorced his wife, Yocheved. Amram reasoned that it was senseless to bring children into the world only to see them killed soon after they were born. And, once their leader had done this, all the Jewish husbands followed his example and divorced their wives. Miriam, Amram's five year old daughter, rebuked her father. "Your decree is harsher than Pharaoh's!" she told him. "Whereas Pharaoh's decree only applies to the males, yours is against males and females! Pharaoh's decree only affects this world, your decree affects this world and the next! (Without being born into this world it is impossible to attain the World to Come; once born, however, even if one is killed or dies prematurely, it is possible to achieve the next world.) Pharaoh issues a decree, and perhaps it will be carried out, perhaps not; however, as a Tzaddik, your decree must be fulfilled!"

Being the true leader that he was, Amram accepted his five-year-old daughter's rebuke and agreed to remarry Yocheved. But not only this. In order that his fellow Jews see and learn from his example, Amram arranged for the marriage to be announced publicly, and the wedding was conducted with great ceremony and pomp. Afterwards, all the other Jewish men remarried their wives as well. Miriam, who was a prophetess, foresaw that now that her parents were back together, they would have a son who was destined to free the Jews from their bondage.

From the day Amram and Yocheved remarried, the Egyptians began counting the months, waiting for a child to be born so that they could kill him. However, Moshe was born on the first day of the seventh month of Yocheved's pregnancy (7

to endure great suffering. Bilaam alone agreed to advise Pharaoh, suggesting that the Jewish midwives be made to kill the newborn infants. For this advice, Bilaam was rewarded by Pharaoh. Divine Retribution saw to it that he was later killed by the Jews themselves.

Pharaoh's star-gazers had told him that a male child would be born to the Jews, a child who would one day lead them out of Egypt. In addition, Pharaoh presumed that the reason Esav had not succeeded in killing his brother Yaakov was because he waited until Yaakov was married and had offspring before making his attempt. Not wanting to make the same mistake with this future leader, Pharaoh's solution was to have all the Jewish males killed at birth.

The Midrash further relates that Esav ridiculed Cain for killing Hevel during Adam's lifetime. If Cain wanted the whole word for himself, he should have realized that Adam was still alive and could have other children? No, Esav was not going to make the same mistake. He would wait until Yitzchak's death and then kill his brother Yaakov. Later, it was Pharaoh's turn to scoff at Esav. Didn't Esav know that Yaakov could have children during Yitzchak's lifetime? There would be little gained by killing Yaakov if he had children to follow after him. Pharaoh thought himself smarter than this. He would kill all the Jewish males at birth. Generations after this, it was Pharaoh's turn to be thought a fool, by Haman. Didn't Pharaoh understand that even if one Jew were left alive, he could bring about the rebirth of the nation? Haman's plan was to destroy the entire Jewish nation! The Midrash concludes by teaching that, in the future, Gog and Magog will deride Haman. Was not Haman aware that the Jews have a Father in Heaven? He would never let them be destroyed. Gog and Magog will first do battle with God (i.e., make the Jews forget Torah and mitzvot and their closeness to God). This will enable them to destroy the Jews. But God's answer to this will be clear: "I have many messengers whom I can send into battle. But this battle against Gog and Magog I shall wage Myself. Their destruction shall be complete."

*

Pharaoh wasted no time in carrying out Bilaam's advice. He called for the Jewish midwives, Yocheved and her daughter Miriam, and ordered them to kill all males born to the Jewish women. But Yocheved and Miriam were truly God-fearing and they ignored his command. Not only did they assist the births, they also brought food and drink and did everything they could to help the mothers and infants. Lest the baby be born with a defect, Yocheved and Miriam would pray to God: "If this child is born with a defect, the Jews might say we caused it in order to please Pharaoh. Please, God, allow this infant to be completely healthy." God listened to their prayers and the babies were born without any defect. Then again, the Midrash tells us of an even greater miracle accomplished by the prayers of these midwives. If it happened that they delivered a still-born baby, Yocheved and Miriam would protest to God that the mothers might accuse them of abiding by Pharaoh's decree. As a result of the midwives' prayers and their self- sacrifice on behalf of the Jews, these infants were given life by God! As was the case with

the earth like a flower, and then accurately make his way to his own parents' home. Thus, even with all their evil intentions and harassment, the Egyptians could not destroy the Jews, who were compared to "the grass of the fields...."

*

Nevertheless, the bondage took a very severe toll on the Jews, especially on the spiritual life of the nation. The Haggadah says that the Children of Israel "were naked and bare" — they did not perform mitzvot in Egypt. Even the mitzvah of circumcision was forgotten. When the time for the redemption finally arrived, God gave the Jews two mitzvot to perform: the Paschal Lamb and circumcision, both of which involved blood. The mitzvah of the Paschal Lamb required sprinkling the animal's blood on the doorposts (a sign which protected the house from the Angel of Death) and the act of circumcision entails a loss of blood. In reward for these two "bloods," God said: "Live! because of the blood [of the Paschal Lamb]. Live! because of the blood [of circumcision]."

*

The *Zohar* teaches that the primary affliction of the exile was the inability of the Jews to have clarity of thought, clarity of Torah. Thus, the Torah tells us that "the Egyptians made their lives bitter with:
"avodah KaSHA (hard labor)" — this is KuSHyA, difficult questions;
"b'CHoMeR (clay)" — this is CHuMRe, difficult issues;
"u'viLBaiNim (bricks)" — this is LiBuN hilkhata, clarifying the laws;
"all works in the fields" — this refers to the Braiytot or unclassified laws;
"all of their labors" — referring to the Toseftot which are similar to the Braiytot;
"that they worked them b'PHaReKh (hard labor)" — this is PiRKHa, extremely difficult questions.
In this way, the Egyptians successfully prevented the Jews from prayer and Torah study, this being the major cause of Jewish suffering in all our exiles.

*

The Birth of Moshe Rabeinu

Before long, Pharaoh realized that he was incapable of stopping the Jews from growing in numbers, even by forcing the men to sleep in the fields. He sought counsel from his three chief advisors, Yitro, Iyov and Bilaam. He hoped they could suggest ways of eliminating the Jews completely. Yitro, who fled rather than plot against the Jews, was rewarded by God: he converted and generations later his descendants were members of the Sanhedrin. Iyov advised Pharaoh to enslave the Jews and take their possessions. For this suggestion he was later made

own land. Soon enough, the Children of Israel would become so numerous and powerful that they would take over and expel them from their land. Drastic measures had to be taken. Pharaoh took counsel with his advisors. It was decided to enslave the Jews. Degrading labor, poverty and harassment would keep them under control.

At first, the cunning Pharaoh spoke softly to the Jews, asking them to help him build the cities of Pisom and Ramses and offering them high wages for their labor. Pharaoh himself initiated the work. He mixed the mortar for building, while his Egyptian subjects assisted. To prove their own superior industriousness (a typically Jewish characteristic even today), the Jews readily joined in the building. The amount they produced surpassed that of their Egyptian counterparts. This is exactly what Pharaoh had anticipated. He then decreed that whatever each Jew had produced on that first day would be his daily quota. A further decree had the men doing household chores, while the women were forced to chop wood and do other work in the fields. This disproportionate distribution of workloads was designed to weaken their spirit and further sap their strength. Furthermore, despite Pharaoh's grandiose promises, the Jews received absolutely no pay for their hard labor. They were expected to find a way of supporting themselves.

Yet, even this did not satisfy Pharaoh. He appointed cruel guards who inflicted severe beatings and whippings upon the helpless Jews. In addition, the Jewish men were forced to sleep in the fields, as the Egyptians hoped that through attrition the Jewish population would diminish. The *Shney Luchot HaBrit* adds that the Egyptians knew that with prayer, the Jews could nullify the decrees against them. They therefore pushed the Jews mercilessly and with ever increasing cruelties and afflictions, so that the Children of Israel would be too frail and weak to pray.

Despite all this, God had promised Avraham that his seed would multiply as the "stars", and multiply they did! The Midrash adds that Pharaoh tried to outsmart God, telling the Egyptians to "stop the Jews from multiplying." But, God countered, "I said they would multiply and you say they should not! We will see whose word stands, yours or Mine!" Our Sages tell us that it was in the merit of the righteous women that the Jews deserved to be redeemed from Egypt. God miraculously caused the water which the women would draw from the wells to be half water and half fish. Cooking the fish and boiling the water, they brought food and drink to their husbands in the fields. While there, they comforted their weary husbands and aroused them to marital relations. And so, even with all of Pharaoh's machinations, the Jewish women bore more and more children.

When it came time to have their babies, these righteous Jewish women went out to the fields, and gave birth under the trees. God Himself administered the childbirth and sent angels to care for the infants. Before long, the Egyptians discovered that the Jewish women were giving birth in the fields and went out to kill the babies. Miraculously, the earth swallowed up these infants before they could be found. The Egyptians began plowing the earth, hoping to uncover them. God made certain that all their efforts were futile. For sustenance, each baby was given two stones which turned into fountains, one flowing with milk and the other with honey. When the child reached the age of three, he would sprout forth from

location for another reason. The sheep was the abomination of Egypt. By living in this province, the Jews were able to remain as far away from the Egyptians as possible.

...and even though they intended to stay only a short time, and were living separately from the Egyptians, the Jews eventually bought homes and settled there; making their sojourn a permanent one (*Targum Yonatan, VaYigash*). And this, unfortunately, has been an oft repeated mistake in the history of our People.

Nevertheless, the Haggadah tells us that while in Egypt, the Jews stood out. True, their temporary stay had turned into a permanent settling in, but they were always careful not to assimilate. And it was this which made them worthy of salvation. They never changed their Jewish names, their language (the Holy Tongue), or their Jewish apparel, which kept them distinctive and apart.

*

The Torah tells us that "Yaakov lived in Egypt for seventeen years." (He was 130 years old when he descended to Egypt and passed away at the age of 147 years.) Although he had arrived in Egypt with only 70 family members, Yaakov did not pass away until after he had seen 600,000 descendants. In those generations people were capable of procreating from the age of eight. With his offspring multiplying so quickly, every day saw Yaakov going to a brit or a kiddush, a wedding, bar-mitzvah or some other simchah. Thus, after all his years of suffering, at the hands of Lavan and Esav, with the tribulations of Dinah and the disappearance of Yosef, etc., he *lived* for seventeen years.

Actually, the Talmud and Midrash differ as to just how fast the Children of Israel multiplied. Some are of the opinion that there were six children in a womb at one time. Others maintain that twelve children were delivered with each birth. Still others say that the births were so miraculous that the Jewish women resembled Sheratzim (insects) and gave birth to seventy children at one time. A similar debate is found concerning the amount of people who died in Egypt during the Plague of Darkness. The verse reads, "And the Children of Israel went up *chamushim* from Egypt" (Exodus 13:18). *Rashi* sees in this word the word *chamesh* (five); thus, one out of every five Jews left Egypt. Since 600,000 ascended from Egypt, 2,400,000 died there. (Why they died is explained in the Plague of Darkness.) The *Yalkut* states that the word *chamushim* could mean one of out of five, one out of fifty, or one of five hundred. Rabbi N'horoi takes this even further. He suggests that not even one out of five hundred Jews left Egypt; as the Haggadah tells us, "You were abundant as the grass that grows in the fields."

*

Bondage and Slavery

As Yaakov's children multiplied, so did the envy and contempt which the Egyptians had for them. The Egyptians feared becoming a minority in their

Egypt which eventually caused the brothers to descend there and, ultimately, to the enslavement of the Jews. Thus, in a certain sense, Lavan's plan did in fact succeed. Had Yaakov first married Rachel as he intended, Yosef would have been the eldest of Yaakov's children. His receiving of their father's special attention would have then been acceptable to the brothers. But, the switching of Rachel with Leah delayed Yosef's birth, so that his inheritance of the birthright caused jealousy and brought about the Exile.

It had been Heaven's decree that Avraham's offspring, the Jews, be the ones to rectify Adam's sin. Accordingly, they would have, in any event, been obligated to experience the exile in Egypt. However, the sale of Yosef added the necessity for this exile to be under oppressive conditions and with great suffering, which would not have otherwise been included. The 210 years of exile and bondage correspond to the blemish in the Holy Name of God, EHYeH. This Name, which accompanies the Jews in exile, has the numerical value of 21. Each of the 10 brothers was held responsible for the sale of Yosef to Egypt and had to atone separately for this sin. Thus 10 times 21 totals the 210 years of the Exile (*Zohar Chadash, VaYeshev*).

*

Yaakov himself did not want to leave the Holy Land, he was forced to! If Yaakov had not gone willingly, he would have been brought to Egypt in chains. This was because the bondage in Egypt was a necessary part of the Covenant of Avraham, a debt which he and his offspring were obliged to pay. Esav and Yishmael, also Avraham's descendants, refused to acknowledge this debt and withdrew from the Covenant. This can be understood from the following parable: There was once a man who had two sons. The man was in debt. One of the sons ran away while the other served his father. When the man died and the creditor came demanding payment, the remaining son argued, "Do I have to pay the whole debt just because I served my father?" "You are right," the creditor answered. "Therefore, when your brother is caught, I will give him to you as a servant!" So too, in reward for Yaakov's assuming responsibility for the payment of this debt, the descendants of Esav and Yishmael will be subservient to Yaakov's children when Mashiach comes.

*

Yaakov's children only intended to go down into Egypt temporarily, for the duration of the famine. Even so, Yaakov was not willing to spend any amount of time, even a few short years, in a land which was completely void of holiness. Therefore, as he made his way to Egypt, Yaakov sent Yehudah on ahead. He wanted his son to establish Yeshivot for Torah study and thus prepare the land spiritually.

When they arrived, the Children of Israel settled in Goshen. Many years earlier, Pharaoh had given this land to Sarah (*Yalkut Reuveni, VaYigash*). It was a fertile land, ideal for grazing, and the Jews had many cattle and sheep. Goshen was a suitable

boy, her sister Rachel would have a lesser portion in the Twelve Tribes than the handmaids. The Yerushalmi (*Berakhot* 9) tells us that Rachel was actually carrying a girl and Leah another boy, but an angel came and switched the children around before they were born.

After Yaakov's eleventh son, Yosef, was born (Binyamin was born after Yaakov returned to the Holy Land), and a long fourteen years had passed, Yaakov asked Lavan's permission to return to his father's home. Lavan, not yet satiated by the prosperity Yaakov had brought him and not yet willing to forgo his deception, requested that he stay on, and Yaakov agreed to remain for an additional six years. Again, he dutifully watched Lavan's flocks and brought his father-in-law even greater prosperity. God then appeared to Yaakov and told him to leave Lavan's house. Yaakov quickly gathered his family and possessions and ran away. When Lavan learned that it was he who had been deceived, he gave chase and quickly caught up with Yaakov's slowly moving camp. Lavan intended to destroy Yaakov and his entire family. Only the angel Michael's raising his sword against Lavan stopped him from carrying out this final treachery.

Unable to carry out his desire to ensure the ultimate destruction of the "Jewish People," Lavan resigned himself to a peace pact with Yaakov. He would no longer seek to harm "his own family." Yet, even this was not to be. Yaakov's departure from Lavan's house also saw the departure of the blessing which had only resided there in the Tzaddik's merit. Lavan returned home to find that in his absence thieves had come and taken all his possessions. He was beside himself and sent a message to his nephew Esav, informing him of Yaakov's return to his father's home. Lavan accused Yaakov of having absconded with all his valuable possessions, and implied that Esav would soon suffer a similar fate. His own evil scheming having been defeated, Lavan hoped that he could at least rekindle the burning hatred which Esav felt for his younger brother.

Thus, the Haggadah makes a point of recalling Lavan's wickedness and his thwarted attempts at destroying the Jewish nation. The bitter taste of exile must still have been in Yaakov's memory as he prepared to return his family to a foreign land. Had God not assured Yaakov that He, too, would go to Egypt and that He would bring him back, it is inconceivable that Yaakov would have ever willingly done so.

*

The Descent into Egypt

As his sons grew, Yaakov taught them all the teachings he had received from his father. Yet, he favored one. Though Yosef was the second youngest of the brothers, he was his father's main disciple. Yaakov did not even attempt to hide his great love for Rachel's oldest son, honoring him with an ornamented robe of fine wool. This led to the brothers becoming jealous of Yosef, which, in turn, brought them to sell him into slavery. And it was Yosef's forced descent into

the "appreciative" father-in- law altered the contractual terms 100 times over, each time to his own advantage.

Lavan's attempts to deceive Yaakov were not merely for financial gain. They were aimed at something of much greater import: the undermining of the Jewish nation's spirituality at its inception. This is what Lavan hoped to achieve by denying Yaakov the opportunity to marry his wives in proper order. When this proved unsuccessful (not because his trickery failed, but because kabbalistically Yaakov had to marry Leah first and therefore Lavan actually helped him), he tried to cheat Yaakov out of his wages. Here again, Lavan intended more than just a gratifying victory over a son-in-law to whom he owed all his personal prosperity. No, Lavan was not going to be satisfied with anything less than seeing to it that the Jews would forever be poverty stricken and unable to expand their influence. This too failed.

When the Haggadah discusses the topic of exile, it makes reference to all the exiles, beginning with the very first one: Yaakov in the house of Lavan. Yaakov's personal exile is a prototype for all the Jewish exiles; his encounter with Lavan a prototype of all the different attempts by those who hoped to destroy the Jewish People down through the millennia.

*

The events surrounding the birth of the Twelve Tribes are also to be reckoned among the miracles of the Exodus. Our forefather Yitzchak had two sons. His brother-in-law, Lavan, had two daughters. Leah, the elder daughter, was destined to marry Esav, the elder son. However, word of Esav's wickedness had reached as far away as Aram Naharayim, and Leah constantly prayed that this not be her fate. Leah's prayers were answered. Though Lavan and even Yaakov presumed otherwise, it was actually her prayers and not her father's machinations which won her a place as a mother of the Jewish People.

After Yaakov married Leah and Rachel, Lavan's daughters from his wife; he married Bilhah and Zilpah, Lavan's daughters from his concubine. The Matriarchs knew that Yaakov would have twelve sons, twelve tribes; corresponding to the twelve permutations of the Tetragrammaton (YHVH). And here again, the power of Leah's prayers was to be seen. Though Yaakov's wives were four, Leah was blessed with being mother to half of his twelve sons.

*

All of the brothers (save Binyamin) were born during Yaakov's second seven-year period in Lavan's house, each following a seven month pregnancy. Leah gave birth to her first four sons: Reuven, Shimon, Levi and Yehudah; after which, Dan and Naftali were born to Bilhah, and Gad and Asher were born to Zilpah. Leah then gave birth to Yisakhar and Zevulun. Only then did Rachel give birth to Yosef. Dinah, Leah's daughter, was born at the same time as Yosef. In fact, during the pregnancy, Leah prayed for a girl. She knew that because she herself already had six boys and Bilhah and Zilpah had two each, were she to now have another

Also at the Brit bein HaBitarim, God promised Avraham that his descendants would leave Egypt with great wealth. This wealth was amassed during the seven years of famine. Yosef had warned the Egyptians to prepare for seven lean years. They stored food, but their supplies rotted away. They had no choice but to purchase everything from Pharaoh's storehouses, which Yosef controlled. Eventually, this depleted all the Egyptians' personal wealth, which filled Pharaoh's coffers in exchange for food. Then, when the Egyptians had also sold their land and no longer had any means to continue buying, they were forced to sell themselves to Pharaoh, for which Yosef gave them their daily sustenance. Also during the years of famine, people from all countries came to Egypt to buy food and grain. This, together with revenues from the heavily taxed Egyptian income, enabled Pharaoh to amass huge treasures. These treasures subsequently became the booty the Jews took with them when they left Egypt.

At the time the Egyptians were selling themselves to Pharaoh, Yosef used his position of authority to insist that they circumcise themselves. He knew that these Egyptians were the same souls which Adam had blemished, and saw this as *his* role in their rectification. Yosef the Tzaddik understood that through the Covenant he would be able to initiate the purification which had eluded them in both Babel and Sdom (*Sha'ar HaPesukim, Miketz*). And, it was their descendants, the offspring of these circumcised Egyptians, who formed the mixed-multitude that left Egypt together with the Jews during the Exodus (*Ibid., Shemot*).

*

Yaakov and Lavan; The Birth of the Twelve Tribes

Years before our forefather Yaakov led his descendants down to Egypt, he himself was given to taste the bitterness of exile when forced to leave the place of his birth and his parents' home. Seeking refuge from Esav, whose birthright and blessing he had rightfully pirated, Yaakov eventually made his way to the house of his uncle in Aram Naharayim (Mesopotamia, some 400 miles from the Holy Land). But his mother's brother, Lavan, only reluctantly allowed him in.

At the time of Yaakov's arrival, Lavan was so poor that he could not even afford to hire a shepherd. This is why we are told that his daughter, Rachel, tended the flocks. However, Yaakov's coming brought a blessing upon the entire city and Lavan's house in particular, from which Lavan became a very wealthy man. In order to gain permission to marry Rachel, Lavan's younger daughter, Yaakov offered to tend Lavan's flocks for seven years. On the wedding night, Lavan expressed his "gratitude" for all that Yaakov had done for him by putting Leah, his oldest daughter, in Rachel's place. In so doing, he knew that Yaakov would be willing to remain in Aram Naharayim for an additional seven years so that he might marry Rachel as he'd intended. After the fourteen years, Lavan contracted Yaakov for an additional period of labor, and during the next six years

2

Sdom, their wickedness prevented them from undoing the blemish. Ultimately, the city was overturned, reduced to clay and rubble.

After this, the rectification of Adam's sin began in earnest, in Egypt. These blemished souls reappeared as Egyptians who sold themselves to Pharaoh during the famine and as the Children of Israel born into slavery. In order to clear themselves of the blemish which began with Adam's wasting of seed, it was necessary for these souls to undergo the misery and suffering of bondage: toiling with the clay of the Flood and Sdom, laboring with the bricks and mortar of the Tower of Babel.

*

The decree of 400 years exile upon Adam's seed had already been made known to Avraham at the Brit bein HaBitarim, the Covenant of the Halves, during the 2,018th year of Creation, and 30 years prior to Yitzchak's birth. With this pact between God and Avraham, the first positive step was taken towards the rectification of these blemished souls.

Actually, all of Avraham's descendants were originally included in the decree of exile. Ishmael, however, left Avraham's home, leaving the decree to fall upon the offspring of Yitzchak. When Yaakov told his brother Esav that the decree could apply to either of them, Esav went away to Mount Seir, leaving Yaakov to bear the brunt of the exile.

The period of this Exile began with the birth of Yitzchak in 2,048. The calculation is as follows: Yitzchak was 60 when Yaakov was born in 2,108, and Yaakov was 130 when he came before Pharaoh (in 2,238). Hence, 190 years passed from Yitzchak's birth to the descent of the "Jewish People" into Egypt. Now, *Rashi* (Exodus 2:1) tells us that Yaakov's grand-daughter, Yocheved, was born when her grandfather brought the entire family to Egypt and that she was 130 years old when she gave birth to Moshe. We also know that Moshe was 80 when the Exodus took place (in 2,448). Thus, the 190 years before entering Egypt together with the 210 years in Egypt give a total of 400 years of exile.

*

Interestingly, Yaakov was 130 years old when he descended to Egypt. Yaakov embodied the soul of Adam, and for the first 130 years of his life he toiled ceaselessly to rectify Adam's 130 years of separation. Thus, Yaakov's descent to Egypt completed *his* contribution towards the rectification (*Sha'ar HaPesukim, VaYigash*). In a similar vein, Moshe was born to Yocheved only after she was 130- years-old. Moshe was the incarnation of Sheth, the son born to Adam after his abstention from Chavah for 130 years. Yocheved was the incarnation of Chavah. Just as the First Woman gave birth to Sheth at the age of 130, Yocheved was that same age when she gave birth to Moshe (*Ibid., Shemot*).

*

To have truly fulfilled the Mitzvah of reciting the Haggadah, it is necessary to reminisce the wonders and miracles of both the Bondage and the Exodus (Orach Chaim, 473, 481).

We present a selection of Talmudic and Midrashic teachings on the themes of the Seder night, beginning with the Decree of Exile and concluding with the Children of Israel journeying in the desert and the Revelation at Mount Sinai. These teachings have been selected from *Talmud, Midrash, Zohar, Sefer HaYashar* and *Yalkut.* Source references have not been given except where texts other than these have been used, as most of the material already appears in translation (e.g. *Rashi, Me'am Loez Torah Anthology, The Midrash Says, Artscroll,* etc.). It is worth noting that there are times when, at first glance, the opinions of the commentators seem to be incongruous, or even contradictory to one another. This, however, is not so. Our Sages addressed this very point when they said that *these and those are the words of the living God!* The Talmud asks: "Why did Esther invite Haman to her feast?" No fewer than thirteen different Tannaim and Amoraim offer reasons for Esther's actions. Indeed, when Reb Noson asked Eliyahu the Prophet which reason Esther herself actually had in mind, he replied, "Like all the Tannaim and all the Amoraim!" (*Megillah* 15b). The point is this: When each individual statement is understood according to the intended meaning of the one who said it and in the context of when it was said, we find nothing but agreement and harmony among the differing opinions.

The Decree of Exile

The ARI (*Sha'ar HaPesukim, Shemot*) teaches that the First Man's soul encompassed the souls of all mankind. Had he succeeded in heeding God's command, thus fulfilling his mission, Adam would have rectified all of Creation. But Adam ate from the Tree of Knowledge and was banished from the Garden of Eden. Feeling remorse for what he had done, he separated from his wife, Chavah. However, as the holy ARI tells us, he experienced nocturnal emissions and his wasting of seed caused many souls to be blemished. The first incarnation, for the rectification of these souls, occurred during the Generation of the Flood. But, instead of cleansing themselves of the blemish caused by Adam, they committed their own misdeeds and repeated Adam's sin; resulting in the loss of many more souls. Except for those in the ark with Noah, all humanity was wiped out — man was turned back into clay by the waters of the Flood. These blemished souls were reincarnated again, first as those who built of the Tower of Babel and later as the inhabitants of Sdom. In the generation of the Tower of Babel, they were not guilty of Adam's sin, but they rebelled against God. Their efforts in building the Tower with bricks and mortar, increased the power of evil. As the people of

APPENDIX A

The Story of the Exodus

Table of Contents

Section A: (other end of book)

Publisher's Preface 7

Foreward 9

Overview 11

The Haggadah 21

Searching for Chametz 22

Burning the Chametz 22

Eruv Tavshilin 24

Candle Lighting 24

The Seder Plate (preparing for the Seder) 24

Yom Tov Morning Kiddush 156

Sefirat Ha'Omer 158

Section B:

Appendix A: The Story of the Exodus 1

Appendix B: Pesach Anecdotes 39

Appendix C: Until Shavuot 69

Reflections 85

הגדה של פסח

THE BRESLOV HAGGADAH

The Traditional Pesach Haggadah

with commentary based on the teachings of
Rebbe Nachman of Breslov

compiled and adapted by
Rabbi Yehoshua Starret

including the Story of the Exodus, related anecdotes
and additional commentary on Pesach, the Omer and Shavuot
compiled and translated by
Chaim Kramer

Edited by
Moshe Mykoff

Published by
BRESLOV RESEARCH INSTITUTE
JERUSALEM/NEW YORK